GOLD DUST

GOLD DUST

Donald Dale Jackson

University of Nebraska Press
Lincoln and London

First Bison Book printing: August 1982

Most recent printing indicated by the first digit below:
1   2   3   4   5   6   7   8   9   10

Library of Congress Cataloging in Publication Data
Jackson, Donald Dale, 1935–
  Gold Dust.
    Reprint. Originally published: 1st ed. New York : Knopf, 1980.
    Bibliography: p.
    Includes index.
    1. California—Gold discoveries.
  · 2. Voyages to the Pacific coast.
    3. California—History—1846–1850.
    4. Frontier and pioneer life—California.
  · I. Title.
  [F865.J19   1982]   979.4'0   82–2719
                         AACR2
ISBN 0-8032-7555-2

Published by arrangement with Alfred A. Knopf, Inc.

For Darlene

*It was a wild, I may almost acknowledge a hare-brained adven-
ture, and yet it is over and past; a recollection of it is mingled
with many pleasant as well as unpleasant reflections. In looking
back there are no regrets, no wishes that it had not been under-
taken. With California, and all that is in it, I quit even.*

—WILLIAM M'COLLUM, M.D. (1850)

CONTENTS

Contents

MAPS

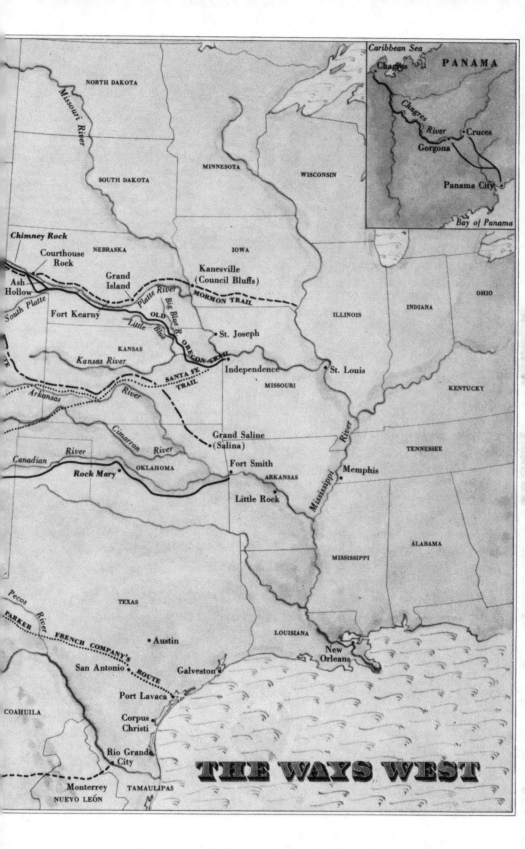

THE WAYS WEST

THE GOLD COUNTRY

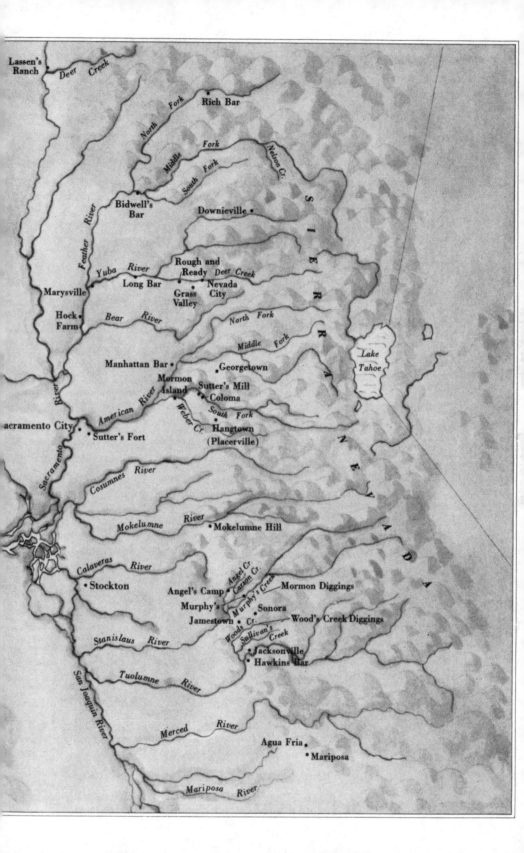

James W. Marshall, 1884

Enos Christman, 1851

Mary Conway,
aged 17

John Woodhouse Audubon

John A. Sutter

Bayard Taylor

Four anonymous gold-seekers

Moses Pearson Cogswell

Lucius Fairchild

A FEW OF THE FORTY-NINERS

William Perkins, 1845

Sam Brannan

J. Goldsborough Bruff,
self-portrait
in the Sierras, 1850

GOLD DUST

PROLOGUE

THE MORNING was fresh with the glow of mountain summer, and the Feather River at my feet trilled softly across the shiny boulders. The banks which had once echoed the raucous clatter of a thousand gold washers were dense with brush and silent. A battalion of pines, dry and brittle in the beginning heat, marched boldly up the cliff above me. I put my hand in the water and drew it out; the miners were right, it was cold.

Downstream the river curved around an ash-colored promontory and narrowed to a belt of foam no wider than a wagon road. A squirrel bounded across a fern-carpeted clearing and vanished, drawing the desultory attention of a hawk on a high branch. Wild flowers sprouted incongruously from shallow crevices in the riverside boulders. I found the shadowy traces of an old trail, now choked with brush and barren of tracks. I was alone with the river and the sky and the hills and my imagination. . . . Was it imagination, or was it some memory in the blood I sensed, some distant rattling in the subconscious? Surely this place looked to me as it did to them, still and grand and rich with promise. Could I feel what they felt? No, but I could see what they saw, I could walk where they walked and drink the foaming river as they did, and dream their dreams.

A thousand men, five thousand, had fled their homes and families to come to this place and dig for gold, risking health and even life for the treasure beneath these rocks. They had come in hope; they had built their canvas city and filled it with music and money; and then they had gone, disappeared, as stripped and spent as the ground they worked. Now the land was silent again. Bushes covered the trail and flowers blossomed in the paydirt. The rocks and the river remained, glazed with the amber light of morning.

The continent they had crossed, like the spirit that propelled them, is changed but changeless. Asphalt and steel now band long reaches of their routes, but there are detours and shortcuts that the bulldozers have ignored, stretches of sage-flecked plain and fiery desert that preserve the wild isolation the forty-niners beheld. I camped for three days a few years ago on the Black Rock Desert in northwestern Nevada, a gray and roadless waste that was transformed for a few giddy months in 1849 into a highway. I filled my jug with the boiling, alkali-tinged water from the spring that they used and peered from my unshaded tent at a bleak vista unbroken by signs of man, save only the skeleton of a forlorn and long-abandoned wagon. When they reached that spring they were suffering, all of them, and their only balm was a blessed ignorance of the further travail that awaited them. On the trail along the Platte they had buoyantly etched their initials into the sentinel rocks, but here they could only stare at the salt-encrusted earth and pray for strength.

It may be that the enduring fascination of the California gold rush lies in the fact that it was a leap of the imagination, a bold quest that summons some buried impulse in all of us. The land has always been the arena where Americans pursue their private visions of wealth and triumph, of freedom and adventure and home. The land offers liberty and demands that a man's skills and imagination be equal to it. Few forty-niners realized when they set out that California would be an anti-climax; the glory was in the going, in confronting the promise and challenge of each new day and overcoming its obstacles. The confidence, the strength, and the sense of freedom that they gained were infinitely more important—to them as individuals and to their collective character—than all the gold they won and lost.

The gold rush is a metaphor for our national youth. The Americans of 1849 were restless, adventurous, and eager to flex their developing muscles. The recent war with Mexico, the profusion of industrial and technological advances such as railroads, steamships, and the telegraph, the inexorable westward surge toward America's "manifest destiny"—all bespoke a nation on the march; wealth and power—greatness—lay just over the next ridge, just beyond the next stream. And the gold was accessible to any man lucky enough to find it and strong enough to dig it out. The California bounty was not restricted to the rich and privileged; this was confirmation of the democratic dream that enchanted Jacksonian America: the wealth was there for the taking, and every man (provided he was white and American) had an equal chance at it. They left home to the brave lyrics of their anthem: *"I'll scrape the mountains clean, my boys, I'll drain the rivers dry, A pocket full of rocks bring home, so brothers, don't you cry."*

The forty-niners were exuberant and generous and courageous and capable. They were also bigoted and narrow-minded and impatient and violent. Their faults and virtues were in many ways a reflection of their youth, and ours: they were impetuous, open to change, willing to take risks. The society they created shared those qualities.

MY INTENT in this book is to tell the story of the gold rush through the experiences, feelings, and thoughts of the people who participated in it. I want to convey what it was like to be on the trail and in the diggings, what the forty-niners felt and feared and dreamed, how they viewed themselves and their companions, and what they saw and heard and smelled. My goal is to put the reader inside the skins of those heroic, sad, and reckless men.

I think it is difficult to evoke a place without walking the ground and trying to gain some sense of it. I have liberated my imagination along forty-niner trails and beside the shimmering streams in the Sierra Nevada foothills. I was born in San Francisco, the city built by gold, and I grew up with the stories and myths and jingles—*"The miners came in '49, the whores in '51, And when they got together they produced the native son"*—that have endured as part of its heritage. I no longer live in California, but I shall always be a Californian.

Join me now in the drowsy Sacramento Valley in January 1848.

I

SUNRISE IN A BOTTLE

SUTTER'S FORT, 1848

THE COUNTRY was winter-lush and green. The rich bottomlands of the Sacramento Valley stretched dark and flat to the foothill fringes of live oaks on the eastern horizon. Beyond were the great granite towers of the Sierra Nevada, where narrow white streams rattled down the canyons like runaway wagons and grizzlies dozed in pine-bordered meadows. Verdant little valleys hid among the steep hills on the western slope, pockets of breathtaking beauty crowded with pines and redwoods and oaks and wild flowers, alive with deer and bird song and the rush of wild water. A man could get lost in this country and grow fat before he was found. It was a land so luxurious that it almost discouraged effort.

John Augustus Sutter had come here to fulfill his dream of an agrarian empire. He envisioned a self-sufficient domain of waving grain-fields, pastureland, vineyards and mills and tidy villages of workshops and stores. Sutter had coaxed the wary valley Indians into working for him; now they harvested his wheat and ate in long animal troughs in the courtyard of his adobe fort. Mexican vaqueros, so natural astride a horse that they seemed part of the animal, tended the vast herds bearing his swirly JAS brand. European-born vintners looked after his vineyards. A motley corps of Americans—deserters from merchant ships, drifters from Oregon, survivors of the hideous Donner expedition of 1846—bustled briskly about the fort's business.

At the end of 1847 Sutter was closing in on his goal. The recent war with Mexico had left him with unexpected spoils, a cadre of about 150 Mormons who had come to California as soldiers. En route to the new settlement at Salt Lake, these men had been halted by a messenger from Brigham Young telling them to remain in California through the winter: Zion was on short rations. Sutter was ecstatic. Many of the Mormons were skilled craftsmen: carpenters and tanners, wagonmakers and mechanics. Sutter could use them to build the flour mill and sawmill he had long coveted. Construction of the two mills began almost immediately, the flour mill at a site about five miles upstream from the fort and the sawmill in the wildly beautiful little Coloma Valley another forty-five miles up the American River.

Sutter's choice to supervise the erection of the sawmill was a strange, somber man named James Marshall, a New Jersey-born carpenter who had wandered down from Oregon two years earlier. Marshall was a self-contained loner who was regarded as somewhat "notional" or peculiar; he believed he could see visions of future events. No one doubted his skill with his hands or his craggy honesty.

Marshall and his nineteen-man detail built a frame for the sawmill and a crude dam to divert the river. By January they had installed the iron machinery and a flutter wheel. The work crew had also dug a 150-yard-long tailrace ditch to channel water from the river to the wheel.

Late on the clear, crisp afternoon of January 24 Marshall inspected the downstream end of the tailrace to check its depth. After a while he walked over to the men and remarked calmly that he believed he had found a gold mine.

The laborers, who were about to quit for the day, were unimpressed. "No such good luck," said one. It sounded like another of Marshall's odd notions. No one even bothered to look at the ditch where he had been poking around. Henry Bigler, a Mormon from Virginia, was the only one who thought the incident worth noting: "This day some kind of mettle was found in the tail race that looks like goald," he wrote in his diary.

In the morning, at Marshall's request, Bigler and another workman closed the gate at the upper end of the tailrace, packing dead leaves and dirt around the edges to make it watertight. The day was clear and cold. Marshall went alone to the place where he had seen what he thought was gold.

He carefully examined the granite bedrock on the floor of the ditch. He saw something shining beneath about six inches of water, reached down, and picked up a tiny piece of brass-colored metal. His heart was pounding. The piece was the shape of a pea and about half as large. He noticed several smaller flakes and gathered them up, then sat down on a rock. He had suspected there were minerals in this river; he had seen what looked like silver. This was too yellow to be silver but didn't seem bright enough for gold. The only other possibility he could think of was iron pyrite. He knew that pyrite was brittle while gold was malleable. He placed a piece of the metal on one rock and hammered it with another. It flattened but did not break.

Marshall put the pieces he had collected into the crown of his white slouch hat and walked back to the mill, his face aglow with excitement. The first man he came to was William Scott, at the carpenter's bench. "Boys, by God I believe I have found a gold mine," he exclaimed.

Scott glanced at the metal flakes in the hat. "I guess not," he said.

Marshall set the hat on a workbench. Azariah Smith pulled out a five-dollar gold piece and compared it with the flakes; the coin looked brighter and whiter—the result of its alloy, they guessed. James Brown stuck a piece in his mouth and tried to twist it, but it wouldn't give. Their skepticism was eroding.

Marshall led the now-eager little band to the lower end of the tailrace. Everyone peered at the bottom. One after another they spied tiny flecks of the glistening metal either resting on bedrock or lodged in seams and crevices. Bigler scraped a piece off a rock with his jackknife. Others pried it loose with their fingers. Marshall produced a small vial in which each deposited his finds. They were beginning to tingle with excitement.

They tried another test. Jennie Wimmer, the only woman in camp, dropped a piece of the metal into a kettle of soap she was boiling to see if lye would corrode it. The gold emerged with its luster undimmed. She later described the gold as resembling "a piece of spruce-gum just out of the mouth of a school-girl"—flat and full of toothmarklike indentations.

For the moment the gold was their secret. There were no other white men within twenty-five miles, and nothing to prevent Marshall and his crew from abandoning Sutter's mill and digging into the riverbanks with whatever tools were handy. But Marshall had signed an agreement with Sutter to build the mill (in exchange for half-ownership) and he intended to honor it. He promised the men that if they completed the job he would give them time to prospect later. Astonishingly, they agreed. "Every man went to work at his regular day labor," Bigler reported in his laconic style, "but gold was the talk."

Marshall may also have perceived that the sawmill was something he could cope with while gold was not. Building a sawmill suited him; it turned him loose in the wilderness with his skills and his tools. He had always been good at fixing things; in his youth, back in Lambertville, New Jersey, he had helped his father build wagons. At twenty-two he had headed west—first to Indiana, then Illinois, then a farm on the Missouri River, finally to Oregon. Marshall's was a sergeant's view of the world: he ran things, made them work, got the job done. Sutter sat at headquarters tent and plotted grand strategy.

There was a suggestion of sorrow about Marshall, as if he bore some mysterious burden of woe. He was thirty-seven but seemed older. He was always a little apart, always alone. The story was that he had twice proposed marriage and twice been spurned, once in New Jersey and again in Missouri.

The mill workers' golden secret remained in the mountains only two days; on the twenty-seventh Marshall galloped off for the fort to show the gold to Sutter. "I believe this is gold," Marshall reported cautiously, "but the people at the mill laughed at me and called me crazy."

Sutter suggested that they test the samples further. They dabbed at them with nitric acid and the metal held its color. Then they rounded up a handful of silver coins and balanced them on a set of scales with the gold. Lowering the scales into two bowls of water, they watched as the gold, with a higher specific gravity, sank to the bottom. They found an encyclopedia and read the article on gold; again the facts seemed to check. Sutter was satisfied and realized immediately what the discovery meant.

There were the two mills, both close to completion, both essential to his dream of dominion. The men building the gristmill would undoubtedly quit if they heard about the gold upstream. They must not be told. There were also the hundreds of employees at the fort, the whole varied and talented force that Sutter had recruited through a combination of charm, promises, and regular meals. How many could be trusted with this news? The best expedient was to trust no one, keep it secret, at least until the mills were finished. This would also give Sutter and Marshall a chance to establish their own claims. How to exploit their advantage would require more thought, but for now they would tell no one. Sutter would not even tell his journal, since others had access to it. Next to January 28 he wrote coyly, "Mr. Marshall arrived from the Mountains on very important business."

It was a business that could either inflate Sutter's empire or destroy it, and he knew it. He had connived and cajoled and struggled to create this barony in the valley. He had acquired creditors of a half-dozen different nationalities—Russian, Danish, Mexican, American—and was still in arrears to most of them. He had discreetly cultivated both the past and present rulers of California, the Mexicans who granted him land in 1839 and the Americans who now governed California as a conquered province.

Sutter had succeeded through a felicitous blend of politesse and vision. His style was aristocratic, even regal, full of grand flourishes of manner and speech. Despite his short and pudgy physique he was an imposing figure, always erect and well-dressed and clasping a cane. He was forty-four, with lively blue eyes, curly blond hair, and well-tended sidewhiskers. His courtly manner, abetted by his indeterminate accent, suggested minor European nobility, perhaps the venturesome second son of a Balkan count. But the truth was that Sutter had been scrambling all his life. He had left Switzerland not on a knight-errant's leisurely quest for adventure but on a bankrupt merchant's urgent flight from his creditors. Back in the Alpine village of Burgdorf were a wife and four children he had not seen in thirteen years. In America he invented a more romantic past for himself: he was Captain John A. Sutter, late of the Royal Swiss Guards of King Charles X of France. In time the fiction became so comfortable that he believed it himself.

Sutter had the ability to convert personal charm into tangible assets, but his most winsome quality was his generosity: his hospitality had already become frontier legend; any straggling pioneer could find food and shelter at the fort for as long as he needed it. Sutter saw himself as the benign master of the colony he had named New Helvetia, but like other feudal lords he could not always resist the temptations of power. His weaknesses were wine and well-formed Indian girls, whom he treated like concubines.

Even before gold was found, Sutter had viewed the year 1848 as radiant with potential. The American conquest of California would attract an influx of immigrants from Oregon and Missouri. They would need beef and milk from his herds, flour and lumber from his mills, leather from his tannery, manufactured goods from his store. He allowed himself to believe that he might even escape from debt. But the gold changed everything, altering Sutter's life as it transformed this land he loved. It was going to be a bonanza year, all right, but not in the way he had expected. And not for him.

MARSHALL returned immediately to the mill after meeting with Sutter. "Oh boys, by God it is the pure stuff," he told his crew. "I and the Old Cap went into a room and locked ourselves up and we were half a day trying it."

The dour Marshall was becoming practically giddy. The "Old Cap" would be there soon to see the gold for himself, he told them. Why not make it easier for him by sprinkling the dust where he would be sure to find it? Marshall reckoned that the old sport would be so thrilled that he would pass around his ever-present bottle of brandy.

Sutter, handsomely dressed as always, arrived with gifts of pocketknives for everyone. But before he could inspect the carefully salted ditch, the young son of mill hand Peter Wimmer raced ahead and gathered up all the easily visible specks of gold. When Sutter saw them he stabbed his cane into the ground and cried, "By Jo, it is rich," and handed the bottle around anyway.

Sutter and Marshall worked out a plan. First they would establish legal title to the gold by drawing up an agreement with the local Yalesumni Indians. Then they would mark off their own claims. The mill hands could work the claims in exchange for half of whatever gold they found. Sutter, whose cavalier way with business details had frequently hurt him, had learned the importance of putting his case on paper.

The chiefs were summoned. Sutter, who conveniently doubled as Indian agent for the region, presented them with a cleverly worded document which proposed a twenty-year lease of a triangular section of land covering about twelve square miles. The lease said nothing about gold. The key clause was buried about two-thirds of the way along, trailing references to timber cutting, road building, erection of the mill, and farming. It gave Sutter and Marshall the right to "open such Mines and work the Same as the aforsaid tract of land May Contain." In return for their various dispensations the Yalesumnis would receive $150 a year in tools and clothing. One by one the chiefs solemnly placed their **X** on the agreement. Sutter had two of his white workmen sign as witnesses.

The lease was meaningless without the approval of the military government of California, so on his return to the fort Sutter wrote to Governor Richard Mason, one of the politically prominent Masons of Virginia. Sutter's letter was as devious as his lease. Neglecting to mention the real reason for his request, he wrote airily that the agreement would protect the foothill Indians from the more aggressive mountain tribes and help American settlement as well. Charles Bennett, one of Marshall's crew from the mill, was dispatched to the capital at Monterey with the documents and a small pouch of gold dust.

Sutter had asked the mill workers to tell no one about the gold for six weeks, the time needed to finish the sawmill. But this was too glorious a secret; it was like trying to contain a sunrise in a bottle. The only way was to isolate everyone who shared it, lock them up in the Coloma Valley. But it was already too late for that.

Sutter himself was about to explode. He hinted broadly to his friends at the fort that something momentous had happened. Heinrich Lienhard, a Swiss who worked as his overseer, thought he was "acting queerly." Sutter held out less than a week before writing his friend Mariano Vallejo, who owned a large rancho in the rolling country around Sonoma, just north of San Francisco, that he had discovered a *"mina de oro"* that was *"extraordinariomente rica."*

At about this time, Sutter's emissary Bennett was confronting his first temptation, and succumbing. Halted at the little village of Benicia on the way down to San Francisco, he heard a group of men discussing a recent coal discovery. Unable to keep silent, he pulled out his bag of gold.

Meanwhile, back at the mill, teamster Jacob Wittmer heard about the gold from the Wimmer children when he delivered provisions from Sutter's fort. Jennie Wimmer not only confirmed it but gave him a few particles of evidence. When he returned to the fort in mid-February he used the gold to buy brandy at the store. Now the whole fort knew. The blacksmith heated one of Wittmer's kernels of gold and hammered it flat while a dozen men watched intently. "The silence was broken by a wild shout of joy," Lienhard wrote. They laughed and shouted and danced around the anvil like children.

The mill, the eye of the growing storm, was strangely quiet. The excitement had moved downstream with the snowmelt, and the tiny valley was left with its morning stillness, the lonely cry of coyotes, and the sound of hammering. Henry Bigler, the placid, methodical Mormon who had recorded the discovery in his journal, was the only man with gold fever.

Bigler was the first California prospector. Alone among the mill workers, he spent Sundays poking in the rocks with his knife. He told his cabin mates that he was hunting ducks and deer. Bigler weighed out his findings on wooden scales he had made; by Washington's birthday, when he arose to find the ground covered with snow, he had accumulated about $30, reckoning the gold at $16 an ounce.

Marshall gave the workers the day off because of the snow, and Bigler mushed off for a cluster of rocks across the river where he had found gold dust. This time he made a real strike. "I felt close in every crevice, and finally down near the water's edge, in the sand, I began to find it," he wrote. He stayed there all day, scooping out grain after grain with the point of his knife. The others at the cabin, growing suspicious about his hunting expeditions, demanded an explanation when he returned. In reply Bigler unrolled his knotted shirttail and took out his dust. He had an ounce and a half from his day's work. It was becoming difficult to concentrate on carpentry.

Charles Bennett, Sutter's gold-bearing messenger, stopped at a San Francisco hotel and began talking again. He showed the gold to at least two men. One of them, Isaac Humphrey, had mined gold in Georgia. Humphrey allowed that this California metal looked richer than what he had seen in Georgia. He was right.

Bennett reached Monterey on March 4. He presented the gold, along with Sutter's crafty lease and letter, to Governor Mason. Mason summoned his adjutant, a red-haired, twenty-eight-year-old lieutenant named William Tecumseh Sherman. Sherman, who had seen native gold before, bit into the largest piece, then flattened it with a hatchet. It was gold, he said. Mason thereupon dismissed Sutter's lease in a crisp letter which declared that the United States did not recognize the right of Indians to sell or lease land. Bennett stowed the letter in his saddlebag and headed back to New Helvetia with the bad news.

The taciturn Bigler was the next one to spill the secret. He mentioned the discovery in a letter to friends at the still unfinished flour mill near the fort, asking them to tell no one else. A week later three Mormons who had heard the news from Bigler's friends appeared at the sawmill. One promptly found a flake worth six dollars. This trip led to the discovery of a second major gold deposit on the South Fork of the American. Prospecting along the river on their way back to the flour mill, Sidney Willis and Wilford Hudson found gold dust on a large sandbar about midway between Coloma and the fort. A group of Mormons soon commenced serious digging at the site. When Bigler next saw them a month later, they were taking $250 worth of gold a day from the bar. By then it was known as Mormon Island.

Sutter watched morosely as the first cracks appeared in his well-ordered empire. Writing about it a few years afterward, he conveyed the impression that his workers had abandoned him immediately and en masse; in fact, their defection was gradual, a few at a time, continuing through the spring. The Mormon gristmill workers were the first to go; the tanners followed, leaving vats of half-cured leather behind; eventually even the Indians deserted. "Everybody left me from the Clerk to the Cook," he complained. "I began to harvest my wheat, while others was digging and washing Gold, but even the Indians could not be keeped longer at Work, they was impatient to run to the mines, and other Indians had informed them of the Gold and its value. . . ."

By the second week of March Sutter's secret had swept down from the Coloma Valley to the fort, clattered through the workshops and sheds of New Helvetia, and floated by launch to Benicia and the promising metropolis of San Francisco. A few of the land-rich Mexican dons knew about it—"As the water flows through Sutter's millrace," Mariano Vallejo remarked with characteristic grace, "may the gold flow into Sutter's purse." Mason and Sherman, the officers in charge of the military government at Monterey, kept silent—possibly because they regarded the gold as insignificant. On March 11 Marshall and his disciplined Mormon crew at last finished the sawmill as they had promised, and the men were free to prospect full-time. Their skepticism had capitulated to Henry Bigler's persistence.

The news was still traveling by word of mouth, but on the fifteenth it appeared in print for the first time. The story on the last page of the four-page San Francisco *Californian* was only one paragraph long and almost apologetically self-effacing: GOLD MINE FOUND, it read. "In the newly made raceway of the Saw Mill recently erected by Captain Sutter, on the American Fork, gold has been found in considerable quantities. One person brought thirty dollars worth to New Helvetia, gathered there in a short time. California, no doubt, is rich in mineral wealth; great chances here for scientific capitalists. Gold has been found in almost every part of the country." The last sentence was a whopper, but the rest was accurate if oddly tentative, as if the editor was reserving the right to disavow it later.

San Francisco remained unmoved. The 850 residents of the little city displayed no reaction whatever. Three days later the other San Francisco weekly paper, the *California Star*, carried a similarly low-key item, using more space to report a coal discovery that later proved false. San Franciscans had heard all this before; talk of gold and other minerals was in the air; it came and went like the fog. Some people thought that this might just be old Sutter trying to shore up his credit. They would wait for more evidence.

San Francisco on the eve of the gold rush was just beginning to stir after a long siesta. The Spanish days were done, their memory preserved in the presence of the Mission Dolores a few miles south of town and the stone presidio perched on the lip of the narrow, turbulent channel which John Frémont had named the Golden Gate. The city was built around a beautiful crescent-shaped cove on the bay. Ramshackle buildings crowded the waterfront along the embarcadero, the main business street. Dozens of tents roosted on the sand hills which meandered south and west amid low scrub and chaparral. The town huddled on the leeward side of the hills, which acted as a buffer against the cold wind which slammed off the ocean every afternoon, blowing away the morning fog and holding temperatures down. Late at night the fog hugged hills and bay alike and gave way only grudgingly to the little puffs of orange light from lanterns and candles.

In 1835, when Richard Henry Dana, Jr., visited the port during his two years before the mast, there had been only the mission, the fort, and a single board shanty occupied by an English trader. Ships like Dana's *Pilgrim* anchored in the deep water off the cove and traded for hides and tallow from the herds of wild cattle which roamed the interior foothills and valleys. By 1847, after two years of American occupation, the city had two hundred buildings, including a dozen mercantile houses, two hotels, and an already disproportionate number of saloons. There were two newspapers, the beginnings of regular Protestant churches, bowling alleys and billiard parlors, and two partially finished wharves jutting into the bay from the low shoreline cliffs. There was talk of a public school.

Like all seaports, San Francisco was a savory compound of strange colors and scents and people: cocoa-skinned "Kanakas" from Hawaii, then known as the Sandwich Islands; Mexicans in sombreros and flowing serapes; brisk, cool-eyed New England traders; sailors from four dozen different ports; there were even three Chinese from Canton, amiably referred to as "Celestials" and clearly the most exotic of a cosmopolitan cast.

San Franciscans looked to the sea for almost everything they needed. Food, lumber, tools, and other essentials came around Cape Horn from the States or down the coast from Oregon. Newspapers, often more than six months old, arrived by ship. Most of the residents had come by sea as well, including a contingent of more than two hundred Mormons in 1846. From the sandy hummock called Telegraph Hill a semaphore signaled the arrival of the eagerly awaited cargo vessels which gingerly probed the fog of the Golden Gate.

The most important man in San Francisco in March of 1848 was probably a black-haired, smooth-cheeked native of Maine named Sam Brannan. Brannan had all the instincts of the great nineteenth-century financial pirates. He was a natural leader, fearless, and the shrewdest businessman on the Pacific Coast. Still a year short of thirty, he was a Mormon convert and the leader of the substantial Mormon colony in the state. And he took his spiritual obligations seriously, at least for a while. In 1847 he rode the sketchily marked California Trail to the Green River east of Salt Lake to try to persuade Brigham Young that California and not Utah was the promised land. The failure of that mission may have permanently soured his relations with the Mormon eminence; Brannan continued to collect a tithe from California Mormons in the name of the church, but he neglected to forward the money to Salt Lake.

Brannan's tracks were everywhere. He built two flour mills in San Francisco. He established an agricultural colony in the San Joaquin Valley. He founded the *California Star*, cranking it out on a press he had brought from the East. He opened a commission house which sold imported goods, and later became a major dealer in Chinese merchandise. At one time he owned most of what later became Market Street in San Francisco, as well as about a fourth of downtown Sacramento. He also had the foresight to open a store at Sutter's fort, in partnership with a man named C. C. Smith.

No one was in a better position to capitalize on the discovery of gold than Sam Brannan, nor better equipped to do so. When Sutter's teamster Jacob Wittmer exchanged his pinch of gold for a bottle of brandy at the fort, the man who scooped it up was C. C. Smith. Smith asked Sutter to confirm that it was indeed gold, then immediately sent word to Brannan. Brannan may have been initially skeptical, as the first report in his newspaper suggested, or he may have been biding his time. He was a plunger, but like other gifted capitalists he was never reckless; Brannan would make his move when the time and the profits were right.

Another canny San Franciscan was already laying the foundation for one of the city's great fortunes. James Lick had sailed into town from Lima, Peru, only seventeen days before Marshall found gold. Lick brought with him an iron safe filled with $30,000 in gold doubloons, his savings from a twenty-five-year career as a piano maker in South America. Unlike Brannan, the short-tempered, fifty-two-year-old Lick had no private sources to inform him of the gold discovery. As a man who had seen several of the world's ports, however, he recognized the potential of San Francisco. He began buying city lots within weeks of his arrival, at first paying only $16 each. Through March and April, while the city idly awaited proof of the gold find, Lick was amassing lots at an average price of $22.50. He kept buying until September, when the price reached $3,000. By the fall of 1849, when San Francisco was aburst with new-made millionaires and the dullest merchant was merely wealthy, James Lick was the richest man in town. By that time he had been joined by an old neighbor from Peru, a chocolate maker named Domingo Ghirardelli.

Sam Brannan's first move came in late March. He prepared a special "booster" edition of his *California Star* for potential Californians in the Missouri and Mississippi valleys. The issue, dated April 1, included a long article on "The Prospects of California" by Victor Fourgeaud, a versatile San Francisco physician who coincidentally had just finished assaying some gold specimens for Sutter.

Fourgeaud waxed rhapsodic in the overripe style of the day: "California, like a good mother, promises to take the best care of all her worthy children." Wounds healed faster there, the doctor reported, fruits and vegetables grew wild, and the riches in the ground awaited only the tools to release them. And gold—yes, there was gold, though its first mention came a curious three-fourths of the way through the article: "We saw a few days ago, a beautiful specimen of gold from the mine newly discovered on the American Fork," Fourgeaud wrote. "From all accounts the mine is immensely rich. . . ." He predicted "a Peruvian harvest of the precious metals" as soon as mining men reached the state to "commence disimbouging her rich hidden treasures." A shorter, unsigned story in the same issue described the gold "vein" on the American River as twelve to eighteen feet thick, three feet below the surface, and at least seventeen miles long—a report based on enthusiasm rather than research.

Brannan printed two thousand copies of the paper and dispatched an express party to carry them overland to Missouri. Brannan himself accompanied the expressman on the journey's first leg to Sutter's fort, stopping there long enough to learn the latest, then hurried back to the city.

The booster edition reached St. Joseph, Missouri, around the end of July, too late in the season for travelers to start west. Copies were sent on to St. Louis. In both St. Joseph and St. Louis the local newspapers politely reprinted excerpts of Fourgeaud's California propaganda. But both papers missed one of the greatest scoops in American journalistic history: they ignored the mentions of gold. First the caution in the San Francisco press and now this; journalists, forever skeptical of their neighbors' dreams of glory, had plainly underreacted to James Marshall's discovery. In the months to come they would make up for it and then some.

THE TRANQUIL California of early 1848 was an improbable stage for the great drama that was about to unfold. This province of velvet valleys, adobe villages, and glistening mountain streams had slumbered in blessed isolation for generations. Nature had strewn its gifts so lavishly in California—wild fruits and vegetables, broad grasslands, fish-filled streams, and mountains rich with game—that labor (any labor, much less the groaning toil of gold digging) seemed superfluous. Vast herds of horses and cattle grazed the gentle lowlands near the coast; brilliantly colored wild flowers brushed the riverbanks and canyons; the sea lapped lazily at shining beaches and breached the coastal cliffs in placid coves. And now the gold, gold in the foothill rivers—nature's ultimate blessing, perhaps, or perhaps one gift too many, a visitation that would foul this Eden forever.

California had only begun to come into focus as a part of America. A prize of the recently concluded war with Mexico, the region known as Alta California ("Upper California," as distinct from Baja California or "Lower California") had passed the war placidly as occupied territory. Yankee soldiers and settlers had elevated the population to some fourteen thousand, in addition to the uncounted Indians, though only about two thousand of the total were Americans; the rest were Mexicans, either refugees from the tumultuous land to the south or California-born and thus called Californios. To most Americans this was still a strange and little-known land, penetrated only by explorers, a few hardy pioneers, and an occasional trader, and so distant as to be more rumor than fact, beyond the reach of their consciousness.

In the years preceding the war, the Spanish-speaking Californians had enjoyed a life-style as generous and carefree as man has ever devised. The settlements that grew up around the eighteenth-century Spanish missions and presidios had evolved into trading ports for California's only

marketable commodities—tallow and the hides that sailors called California banknotes, both produced by the great cattle herds that roamed
the unfenced valleys. The Californios had neither banks nor industries
nor lawyers, and needed none. The men spent their days on horseback,
cultivating an unparalleled grace and skill in the saddle. Richard Henry
Dana, Jr., was startled to see that the vaquero disdained stirrups in
mounting, preferring to "spring into the saddle" from behind and "go
off on the full run." A man would catch a horse in the morning, saddle
him and ride him for the day, and turn him loose at night, then rope
another the next day.

A Californio prided himself on his graciousness and hospitality. "If
he has a farm and I have none he will divide with me," an American
wrote. They loved to sing, to play the guitar and dance at fandangos,
dressed in bloused pants and embroidered waistcoats. The women wore
sleeveless silk gowns of bright colors and sashes around the waist. Dana
was enchanted by the leisurely elegance of their speech. "They sometimes
appeared to me to be a people on whom a curse had fallen," he wrote,
"and stripped them of everything but their pride, their manners, and their
voices."

The Californios lived primarily in the sun-washed towns either on or
near the coast—San Jose, Santa Barbara, Los Angeles, San Diego, Monterey—or on great land-grant ranches in the neighboring valleys. They
built their adobe houses around a central courtyard and roofed them in
red tile. The landed dons staffed their ranches with Indian servants, as
the Franciscan monks before them had subjugated the coastal Indians and
used them as serfs. The small but growing English-speaking colony was
divided between the port cities and a number of ranches scattered through
the central valley. In the prewar years a foreigner had to ingratiate himself with the Mexican authorities in order to acquire land. Ex-sailor John
Gilroy and others had done so by marrying *señoritas* and promising to
raise their children as Catholics. John Sutter had relied on letters of
introduction and native charm.

The country between the long central valley and the great granite
peaks of the Sierras, an enchanting district of tumbling streams and oak-
shaded canyons, pine groves and gravel bars and fields of amber oats—
the gold country—was inhabited by no one but shy foothill Indians. Here
the great rivers flowing down from the Sierra fastness bore names from
three different cultures—Indian names like Tuolumne and Mokelumne,
Spanish names like Calaveras and Mariposa, and American names like

Bear and Feather and—don't tread on me—the American River itself. Here lay a single vein of gold 120 miles long, from Coloma in the north to Mariposa in the south, which the Mexicans would call *la veta madre* and the Americans the Mother Lode. Elk moved through this country and coyote, bear and deer and cougar; trout glided beneath the foaming surface of the rivers.

Lying primarily at elevations between two thousand and five thousand feet, the gold country varied from perpendicular canyons in the north to undulating hills in the south. The land to the south, along the tributaries of the San Joaquin River, was softer and drier than the northern diggings. The pines and cliff-hugging chaparral of the colder country gave way to scrub oaks and sun-bleached oatfields. The northern rivers—Yuba, Feather, American—were faster and bolder. Flat bars of gold-bearing gravel bulged into the rivers from beneath boulder-lined banks. The placers in the south were more likely to be located in what the miners came to call "dry diggings"—shallow ravines and gulleys, sometimes no wider than a trench, which ran full in the rainy winters but turned dry in the arid summers. It was a wild and gloriously varied country, full of secret canyons and sudden vistas of breathtaking grandeur.

The great heaving of the earth's crust that had sent the Sierras thrusting toward the sky was responsible for the veins of gold and other metals in these hills. The ore was deposited when masses of underground magma were brought to the surface along with the granite folds that formed the peaks. The gold had lain in long narrow veins, originally fissures in the rock, through the unfathomable reaches of geologic time. Rain and snow eroded the mountains every winter, eventually slashing chunks from the great towers of rock and breaking boulders into pebbles, pebbles into flakes, flakes into dust. Season after season the dirt and gravel rolled off the cliffs and into the rivers, bringing along tiny particles of gold. Heavier than most of the debris around it, the river-borne gold fell into crevices, lodged against boulders, and settled into the deepest holes in the riverbeds. The Spanish word *placer* referred to gold in its loose or eroded state as opposed to vein or hardrock gold. The California foothill region, in the year 1848, was perhaps the greatest trove of undiscovered placer gold in history.

"In the hands of an enterprising people," Dana wrote of California in 1840, "what a country this might be." It would be indeed, with gold or without it; the gold rush would surely accelerate the settlement of California, but nature and the tide of American history had already made such settlement inevitable. The fact that James Marshall's discovery occurred at the precise historical moment when California became part of America is the kind of barely credible coincidence that would generate a conspiracy theory in this cynical age. But so it did, and moreover it happened at a time when Americans were ready and eager for just such a spin of fortune's wheel. Dana wondered whether it was possible to remain enterprising in such a sun-gentled land. He thought not, but the gold rush proved him wrong.

FOR JAMES MARSHALL, the first wave of euphoria was already past; his habitual wariness and moodiness were back. The problem was nattering, undependable humanity: Governor Mason had rejected their Indian lease; the blabbermouths had spread the word to everybody and his brother-in-law; the flour mill workers had quit to prospect at Mormon Island. Then came storms and high water, overflowing the little dam at the sawmill and halting the production of boards a few days after it began.

On a brief trip to the fort in early April Marshall met a man who he thought might change his luck: Isaac Humphrey, the onetime Georgia gold miner whom Charles Bennett had encountered in San Francisco. Humphrey was probably the only person in the city who needed no further convincing; he had held the evidence in his hands. Humphrey accompanied Marshall back to the sawmill. Together with Sutter they formed a partnership—Sutter as usual would contribute the provisions, Marshall would select likely sites, and Humphrey would supply the knowhow. For a few days Marshall's spirits soared once more, but the plan fell through. Like a few hundred thousand later prospectors, they picked the wrong spots. The partnership dissolved.

Henry Bigler and his Mormon brothers were doing better. On the completion of the sawmill they had gone to the fort to collect their wages from Sutter, preparatory to leaving for Salt Lake City, but the little Swiss had deflected them with promises. They had finally agreed to wait until June before departing. Their families were in Utah and Brigham Young's settlement needed them, gold or no gold; it was their duty. In the meantime they would prospect.

The seven Mormons working at Mormon Island were using tightly woven Indian baskets to wash out their paydirt when Bigler visited them on April 12, the day they made $250. While Bigler continued on to the sawmill, two of the Mormon Island prospectors rode to C. C. Smith's store at the fort and deposited what Sutter described as a "good deal of gold." Storekeeper Smith promptly hustled up to the Mormon diggings to see for himself, then sent the news back to his partner, Brannan. Brannan, in his role as a Mormon elder, advised the miners that he would accept their tithes and turn them over to Brigham Young; he also asked for, and received, a share of their claim. Instinctively he saw a dozen routes to profit; he would, of course, have stores wherever the miners were, and sell them what they needed for whatever price he could get; the possibilities were infinite.

The editor of Brannan's *California Star*, nineteen-year-old Edward Kemble, now announced his intention to "ruralize among the rustics" for a few weeks. He traveled to the fort and on to the sawmill, with the ever gracious Sutter jouncing awkwardly beside him on his favorite mule. Marshall greeted them grumpily. When Kemble asked about the gold, Marshall and his men responded with gruff and evasive replies. The visitors' attempts at gold panning were fruitless—no salting for the Old Cap this time. Around the campfire that night they were joined by several Yalesumni Indians who came to see the white father Sutter. As one old chief began to speak, another Indian translated his words into Spanish. The gold was bad medicine, the chief said. Their ancestors had told them about it. The gold belonged to a demon who dwelled in a lake. The demon devoured all who sought the gold. The old chief said that one of his own tribe had been seized by the demon while hunting the elusive metal.

Kemble had suspected that the gold was a chimera. His visit to the mill confirmed his suspicions. He saw no one prospecting—though only a mile downstream Bigler and his friends were digging successfully. He saw, in fact, no sign of gold. Marshall gave him no reason to believe the rumors. It sounded like humbug to Kemble, and "HUMBUG" is what he wrote, in large letters, across the top of his notes. The story he printed when he returned home bore the same message but conveyed it more subtly: "Great country—fine climate," Kemble wrote. "Visit this Great Valley, we would advise all who have not yet done so. See it now. Full flowing streams, mighty timber, large crops, luxuriant clover, fragrant flowers, gold and silver. 'Great country this.' " It was a coy brushoff, but still a brushoff. (Thirty-seven years later Kemble could laugh at his mistake. Recalling his advice that Californians ignore the gold reports, he would write, "I sometimes think, fool though I was, I did the state some service.")

Bigler meanwhile was enjoying the final days of serenity at the Coloma mill, methodically extracting an average of an ounce a day and noting it all in his journal: on April 14 he made $11; on the fifteenth, $22; on the eighteenth, the day Kemble was writing "humbug" on his notes a mile away, he got $11; he collected $30 on the twenty-first and $25 on the twenty-second. Bigler was earning as much in a good day as a laborer in an eastern city made in a month; a dollar a day was a fair wage in 1848. Soldiers received as little as $7 per month, while congressmen were paid $8 a day. But an eastern dollar also covered more distance than its California counterpart: it would buy a day's meals in most places, with enough left over for a glass of beer. A book could be purchased for 25 cents.

On Sunday the twenty-third came the first wave of the deluge: "a lot of Gentiles came into our camp to look for gold," Bigler wrote, "but found none." The unlucky Gentiles probably came from the fort or the ranchos in the valley—all of Sutter's neighbors, scattered as they were, had heard the news by now. At least two of the new arrivals brought their families along. The city folks would not be far behind. Both San Francisco papers reported the Mormon Island finds in late April, even as Kemble ruralized. "We have seen several specimens," his own paper said, "to the amount of eight or ten ounces of pure, virgin gold."

The long pause, the period of hesitation and doubt, was almost over. Now it was only a matter of time and the velocity of the news. The man who started it all was already feeling crowded. Marshall found a likely spot about three miles upstream from the sawmill, where the gold was so plentiful that he picked up bean-sized nuggets with his fingers. Marshall was back at the mill by the end of April, when the high water subsided enough to permit the flutter wheel to turn and woodcutting to resume.

San Franciscans remained stubbornly dubious. There was no rush yet, no stampede for sudden wealth. Kemble's skepticism was widely shared, and it persisted even after a newspaper report on May 3 that seven diligent diggers (probably the seven at Mormon Island) had earned $1,600 in fifteen days. It was going to take prodding to rouse San Francisco, and the man with the prod was Sam Brannan.

Brannan went back to Sutter's fort on the fourth and the next day accompanied his partner Smith (whose interest he would soon buy out) to Mormon Island. He selected a site for a store, collected tithes from the Mormon miners, and moved on to Coloma, where he laid out another store location. Then he returned to the fort to talk to Sutter about a warehouse he wanted to erect at the Sacramento River landing—in the heart of what would soon become Sacramento City.

The fort was in a frenzy. Sutter's ex-employes were either off at the diggings, on their way there, or hastily loading wagons and pack horses. The place looked storm-struck. Tools lay where they had been abandoned by decamping artisans. Men just back from the mines displayed pouches of gold to the new arrivals. Others gathered in animated clusters and compared rumors.

"To all appearances," Heinrich Lienhard, Sutter's overseer, wrote, "men seemed to have gone insane. . . . Each man had to stop and ask himself, 'Am I mad? Is all this real? Is what I see with my own eyes actually gold, or is it merely my imagination? Is it a chimera? Am I delirious?'" Sutter nodded courteously at the strangers, conferred importantly with his friends, and fretted about his wheat crop.

On the same day that Brannan arrived at the fort a military courier in the far-off village of Los Angeles was saddling up for a journey to Washington. In his saddlebags were letters and a copy of the April 1 *California Star*—the first news of the gold discovery to be sent to the East Coast.

The courier was a small, unpretentious-looking man, stoop-shouldered and freckled, taciturn in the manner of mountain men. Nothing about him suggested celebrity, but in fact he was one of the most famous men of his time, already lionized as the greatest of the western scouts: Kit Carson. Traveling with only a few other men, he rode to Santa Fe and on to Missouri, continuing to the capital by steamboat and coach. It took him three months to reach Washington.

BRANNAN was finally ready, and so was San Francisco. New rumors arrived in the city almost daily through the first ten days of May. The esteemed Mormon elder had built as many conduits from the gold to his pockets as his calculating imagination could conceive of, and it was time to let it flow. On about May 12 he stepped ashore at San Francisco and held a quinine bottle full of gold in the air, waving his hat with his other hand. "Gold," he cried. "Gold! Gold from the American River." The gold was the tithes he had extracted from his spiritual wards.

Brannan was engulfed. Excited people crowded close to see the gold. The news buzzed along the embarcadero, up to the old Spanish plaza, and on to the shanties and tents in the sand hills. The city was like an explosive lacking only the spark of Brannan's gleaming nuggets to detonate. Here was proof positive that Sutter's gold was no humbug; it was real and unimaginably rich, richer than they dared to dream. How many ounces could a man find? How many streams slashed the mountains? How many stars filled the sky?

The male population of San Francisco on May 12, 1848, was approximately six hundred. On May 15 it was perhaps two hundred. Everyone else was on his way to the American River. On the fourteenth an armada of launches, packed to the gunwales with feverish, clamorous gold hunters, set sail on the five-day voyage to the fort—across San Francisco Bay, through narrow Carquinez Strait and the mosquito-clouded Sacramento Delta, then up the Sacramento River. People who couldn't get on a launch left by wagon, going down the peninsula and around the twenty-seven-mile-long southern arm of the blue-gray bay. The wagons backed up in a long line at Carquinez Strait, waiting for a raftlike ferry that could carry only two wagons and their horses at a time. At Benicia, the lone settlement between San Francisco and the fort, all but a few of the male inhabitants joined the hot-eyed throng. On their way upriver the caravan of launches passed a boat heading downstream with a large cargo of gold, most of it from Mormon Island.

John Sutter fixed May 19, 1848, as the day "the great rush from San Francisco arrived at the fort." Sutter's regiment of servants had dwindled to a single Indian boy "to make them roasted Ripps, etc. . . . All was in Confusion," he wrote afterwards, "all left their wives and families in San Francisco, and those which had none locked their doors, abandoned their houses, offered them for sale cheap. . . . Some of these men were just like crazy." Foreshadowing what would become a tide of desertion, thirty-four of the fifty soldiers at the San Francisco Presidio joined the gold seekers. Even the eccentric James Lick went along, clad in a long overcoat and a tall plug hat. Only the teenaged Kemble was left to huff ineffectually at the storm as it passed. The gold was "all sham," he wrote on May 20, "as superb a take-in as was ever got up to 'guzzle the gullible.' "

One of the first of the gullible to reach Coloma was a San Franciscan named John H. Bourne. Bourne watched entranced as a dozen bare-legged men, calf-deep in the river, swirled sand and gravel in their tin pans.

"Can you tell us where we can go and wash out gold too?" he asked.

"Anywhere along the fork," came the reply. "The sandbars and gravel are just lousy with gold. The only trick is to find the richest."

Bourne and his friends moved a short distance downstream to a narrow sandbar and dug down five feet into coarse gravel. Their first panfuls yielded a fourth of an ounce to the pan, a rate that would net them ten ounces or $160 a day. A few of the men, still unsatisfied, pushed farther downstream and found even richer gravel.

The mob swarming through the fort was transforming the adobe outpost into what Sutter called "a veritable Bazaar." The lone two-story building became a boardinghouse jammed with tenants. Traders and storekeepers took over the abandoned workrooms or set up shop in tents. Sutter's daily journal became a succession of hasty and redundant entries: "A small launch arrived with many passengers. . . . Continually people arriving from below. . . . More and more people coming bound for the Mountains." On May 25 the journal stopped; Sutter no longer had the time, or perhaps the heart, to keep a daily record.

The news was on the wing now: California merchants were writing their eastern suppliers; Kit Carson was halfway to Missouri with Brannan's booster edition; the golden gossip was moving steadily down the coast to the settlements at San Jose and Monterey, where it would precipitate more instant evacuations. And the people of San Francisco, recovered from their three-month paralysis, had capitulated totally: the city was desolate—stores closed, ships deserted, houses abandoned; the cries of the gulls echoed down the empty streets.

On May 29 the San Francisco *Californian* shut down with a bang: "The whole country," it said, "resounds with the sordid cry of '*gold!* Gold!! GOLD!!!*' while the field is left half planted, the house half built, and everything neglected but the manufacture of shovels and pickaxes." There were no readers left. The *Californian*'s story contained the first published mention of a phrase that would soon become the label for the swirling, glittering hysteria that engulfed them all: in "the rush for gold," the paper said, it was every man for himself.

Two weeks later the *Star* blinked out as well. "We have done," Kemble wrote. "Let our word of parting be, *Hasta luego*." At long last yielding to the inevitable, Kemble too slogged off for the mines.

II

THE GILDED SUMMER

MORMON BAR

FRENZY seized my soul: unbidden my legs performed some entirely new movements of polka steps. . . . Piles of gold rose before me at every step; castles of marble, dazzling the eye with their rich appliances; thousands of slaves bowing to my beck and call; myriads of fair virgins contending with each other for my love—were among the fancies of my fevered imagination. The Rothschilds, Girards, and Astors appeared to me but poor people."

The symptoms permitted no doubt; Sergeant James Carson of the U.S. Army, Monterey, California, was afflicted with gold fever. Carson's case had been brought on by the arrival from the hills of his friend Billy, carrying a bag of gold. Within an hour of his seizure the sergeant had obtained a furlough from his garrison and saddled up for Mormon Island, where he found forty or fifty men averaging eight ounces a day. Carson, like hundreds of others who were lucky enough to be in California in 1848, would be wealthy before the year was out.

The fever was spreading like a wind-borne epidemic. Vaqueros flew from ranch to ranch in the interior valleys with the news: *"Oro en el río Americano."* Horsemen trailed clouds of dust into the sleepy little Spanish villages with their adobe-and-tile bungalows and their crumbling missions. In town after town—Sonoma, San Jose, San Miguel, Santa Ines, Santa Barbara—people peered at the yellow metal and vamoosed for the foot-hills and mountain streams. The Pueblo de San Jose began to empty in the last week of May after several residents returned from the mines with their saddlebags full. The story is told that the keeper of the San Jose jail, Henry Bee, was so anxious to light out that he brought along his ten Indian prisoners, two of whom were charged with murder.

One of the most sophisticated of the 1848 Californians, a Yale gradu-ate named Walter Colton, was working down the coast in Monterey as a navy chaplain. A fifty-one-year-old New Englander, Colton had a varied background as a schoolteacher, clergyman, and journalist. As a Wash-ington editor he had won the admiration of President Andrew Jackson, who offered him a naval commission in 1830. In Monterey he had estab-lished the *Californian*, the state's first newspaper, and served as alcalde, the chief administrative and judicial officer in the town.

Colton had an agile mind and a flair for brightly colored writing. On May 29, the day that he learned of the gold discovery, he reported his neighbors' disbelief in his journal. "The sibyls were less skeptical," he added. "They said the moon had, for several nights, appeared not more than a cable's length from the earth; that a white raven had been seen playing with an infant; and that an owl had rung the church bells."

Colton sided with the sibyls, but he sent a messenger to the mines for corroboration. The townspeople, he wrote, "could not conceive that such a treasure could have lain there so long undiscovered. The idea seemed to convict them of stupidity." The courier's return erased any doubt: his pockets were full of gold. Monterey joined the rush—all but the women, the prisoners, and the deskbound alcalde himself. The Monterey-based men of Company F of the 3d Artillery fought an uneven battle with their consciences. One soldier illuminated his anguish in a letter home: "I hate to desert—I hate to soldier for six dollars a month—I am almost crazy." Most of them eventually deserted.

San Francisco was all but closed. Teamsters, seamen, mechanics, gamblers, bartenders, lawyers, and doctors were gone. So were the schoolteacher—Henry Bigler saw him at Coloma—and the constable. The collector of the port, U.S. Army Captain Joseph Folsom, wrote that he daily expected to find himself alone in the city. Cooks who had earned $2 a day only a month earlier were offered $20 and more to work for hastily formed groups of miners. Who wanted to waste time cooking? Given minimal energy and functioning limbs, a man could make an ounce or two a day on the streams; an ounce was worth $16 in trade or $5 to $12 in silver. Prices and wages were increasing rapidly. The only commodity to decline in price in June was real estate, which James Lick continued to accumulate on the cheap.

Brannan appeared in town in the first week of June with twenty pounds of gold ($5,120), the first profits from his mining camp emporiums. A few days earlier the schooner *Louisa* had sailed for Hawaii with two pounds of gold aboard; by June 17 the news would reach Honolulu.

The men with the best opportunity for instant wealth in 1848 were the tough and resourceful pioneers who had gravitated to California because it was a frontier, because there was plenty of good land there and a man could live as he pleased. It was ironic that the first gaudy spoils of the gold rush fell to them; they had come west not for plunder but to satisfy their yen for adventure and freedom. In time they were collectively labeled forty-eighters to distinguish them from the hordes of city and village folk who followed. Like James Marshall and Henry Bigler, they were self-contained, able to improvise a solution to a novel dilemma. Like John Sutter, they had befriended the Indians—not as equals, to be sure, but at least as fellow dwellers on the land with a right to live. Many of them learned Spanish, and some adopted Spanish names—the Vermonter Jared Sheldon, for example, called himself Joaquin.

There may have been a hundred of these men scattered through the Sacramento and San Joaquin valleys in the spring of 1848. Their reaction to the news of Marshall's discovery was characteristic; rather than gallop hell-bent to the sawmill or the Mormon diggings, they thought of the similar streams they knew. If gold lay on the bottom and banks of the American, then why not the Feather? It looked the same, it rumbled out of the same mountains at the same elevation, it curled around low gravelly bars and wooded outcroppings exactly as the American did. And why not the Yuba, Bear, and Cosumnes? Or the Mokelumne, Stanislaus, and Tuolumne? The forty-eighters knew all of these foaming, sparkling streams and more; they had watered their stock there, fished them for trout.

German-born Charles Weber, a San Joaquin Valley rancher since 1845, prospected first on the Stanislaus, panned color on the Mokelumne, and found his bonanza on Weber Creek, about ten miles over the ridge from Coloma. A Pennsylvanian named Jonas Spect was preparing to return to the East when he heard the news in April. He tried the Bear River and then moved north to the Yuba, where he opened the diggings in early June and stayed through the summer, abandoning his plans to return home.

John Bidwell, who owned a ranch in the upper Sacramento Valley, was at Sutter's Fort on business when he heard about the gold. He looked over the diggings on the American and headed for the Feather River, not far from his ranch, where his party of seven white men and fifty Indians cleared more than $70,000 in seven weeks.

All the valley ranchers depended on Indian labor. Weber employed hundreds of natives, paying them with food, clothing, and jewelry from his trading post. The Indians were taught to scoop dirt from the river bottoms and swirl it in a pan until color showed. The ranchers acted as overseers who selected digging sites and supervised the work.

Forty-eighters William Daylor and Perry McCoon, who ranched on the Cosumnes River, had several dozen Indians working for them when they made a rich strike in June in a ravine near Weber Creek; the site, the third important gold camp after Coloma and Mormon Island, became known as Dry Diggings, later as Hangtown, and eventually Placerville. Rancher Pierson Reading, whose sixty-five Indians gathered $80,000 on the Trinity River in July and August, was eventually forced out of his diggings by Oregonians who objected to his use of native laborers.

Reading's first pass at prospecting had come in the spring when he hired James Marshall as a kind of human divining rod. Many believed that Marshall had extraordinary powers as a gold finder—how else explain why he among all the forty-eighters had been the one to find it? Reading paid him $25 to prospect the American River between Mormon Island and the fort, but he came up empty.

In June Marshall took another prospector-for-hire job. This time he was supposed to find the source of the loose placer gold in the rivers. It had to come from somewhere higher in the mountains, the Californians reasoned, so there had to be a place near the headwaters where it was lying around in great chunks. Marshall and his clients climbed the rugged dividing ridge between the Middle and North forks of the American River. They crossed another ridge and prospected Bear River, finding only faint traces. It was the same on Deer Creek, a narrow stream that wove through a succession of ravines. They found no evidence of the rich bed of ore that would be discovered nearby more than a year later, giving rise to the bonanza town of Nevada City. Marshall plodded back to the sawmill, trailing his magic powers behind him.

Placer gold in the California foothills took the form of nuggets, flakes, and dust. The most ardently desired, of course, were the nuggets, which came in an infinite variety of water-worked shapes and in sizes ranging from bean to walnut. Flakes had been further eroded to thin pebbles of irregular shapes, while dust was composed of tiny particles resembling fine golden sand. Nuggets were often lodged in the seams of riverside boulders or in little pockets, while flakes and dust were more frequently found beneath layers of earth and clay, where time and the rivers had deposited them.

Henry Bigler and the novice prospectors at the sawmill had picked flakes and dust from crevices in the rocks with their knives, but more effective tools appeared soon afterward. The most pervasive was a slope-sided metal pan about three inches deep and perhaps 18 inches in diameter. The pan, commonly made of either tin or iron, was probably introduced in California by men who had seen it used in the low-yield gold mines of Georgia and North Carolina. European miners had used an identical device as far back as the sixteenth century.

The technique of panning took a little time to master. A miner first dug his paydirt out of the riverbed, gravel bar, or bank. He covered the bottom of the pan with dirt and then held it under water, swirling it in such a way as to create a little whirlpool within the pan. From time to time he raised it out of the water while continuing to swirl it. The constant motion eventually caused the clay, dirt and other lightweight particles to rise to the top and spill over the side, leaving only the heavier gold, sometimes mixed with a heavy black sand, at the bottom. The gold was then separated from the sand by heating the mixture in a pan over a fire. A miner might empty fifty pans in a full day of muscle-draining labor.

If pans were not available a willow basket or wooden bowl would serve. Mexican miners used a bowl called a *batea*. In dry diggings they emptied the paydirt onto a cloth sheet and then tossed it high into the air, allowing the wind to carry off the lighter particles.

Isaac Humphrey, the former Georgia miner who had teamed unsuccessfully with Sutter and Marshall, is credited with introducing the device that would soon become as common as the pan and was considerably more efficient—the gold-washing "rocker." The rocker was a wooden box, open at one end and closed at the other, about three feet long and half that wide. At the closed end was a hopper, a small tray with a perforated metal floor, and beneath the hopper was a slanting canvas "apron." Narrow wooden cleats called riffles were nailed across the bottom of the open end, and the entire contraption was mounted on rockers. Operating a rocker, or "cradle," usually occupied three men: one gathered likely dirt and shoveled it into the hopper; a second kept the dirt moving along the apron by pouring water over it; and the third rocked the cradle with a handle. The water washed out the lighter material and deposited gold-bearing sediment behind the riffle bars. Quicksilver, to which gold would adhere, was frequently placed on the bottom of the rocker. Heat would separate the resultant mixture.

Easy to build and light enough to ride a prospector's back, the rocker combined with the pan, pick, and shovel to form a minimal gold-digging outfit. A rocker greatly increased the amount of dirt a miner could wash in a day and thus improved his profits, even allowing for the addition of more men. Its major drawback was the fact that a substantial quantity of gold was washed out with the tailings, but this problem could be solved with a judicious blend of panning and rocking. The combination would remain the dominant mining method in California until early 1850.

Both Coloma and Mormon Island were overflowing with eager diggers by June. Henry Bigler complained that it suddenly cost 25 and 50 cents to get a shirt washed. A man passing through Mormon Island on June 17 noted that the diggers were clearing between $16 and $25 a day. There were so many tents on the riverside meadows that it looked like a military encampment. Those without tents improvised crude shelters out of piled-up branches and leaves; others slept in the open. During the day the valley echoed with the brain-rattling din of two tons of gravel clattering through two hundred tin pans and rockers. At night the campfires poked glowing holes in the blackness while weary men talked in low voices of finding the color and moving to new diggings. Occasionally a coyote, driven deeper into the hills by the advancing crowds, added his chilling cry to the night sounds of insects and rushing water.

The Mormons, faithful to their vows to their families and to Brigham Young, were preparing to buck the tide and head back to their new colony of Deseret on Salt Lake. They were going even if it meant turning their backs on California's glittering promise. Henry Bigler and two of his tough-minded brethren found a little valley east of Placerville where the expedition could assemble. Throughout late June the Mormon veterans rolled in with their wagons, their bands of horses and oxen, and their purses filled with gold. If they talked ruefully of leaving this El Dorado, none of them put it in writing. The main party started up the western face of the mountains in early July. On the Fourth they saluted Independence Day by firing a cannon they had acquired from Sutter, probably in lieu of wages.

Sutter had a special reason to celebrate the Fourth at the fort; a delegation of the military high command, including Governor Richard Mason and Lieutenant William T. Sherman, was camped outside his wooden gate. The officers had come up from Monterey via San Francisco and Sonoma. Along the way they had found mills idle, wheatfields abandoned to livestock, and houses empty. The fort was different: a constant stream of men flowed in and out, bragging about their dust; several stores and a hotel were doing a lively business; launches discharged cargo at the nearby embarcadero, including a timely shipment of wines and liquor.

Sutter was bubbling with joy; this was the kind of grandiose occasion that he loved. He was happiest, his friend Lienhard wrote, when his associates were "colonels, judges, or governors." And here was Mason, who was both colonel and governor. A steer and several sheep were slaughtered, invitations dispatched to neighboring ranchers, and tables set in the fort's largest room. Sutter, seated between Mason and Sherman, led the succession of toasts which followed an elaborate feast. He basked in the flattery of his eminent guests. The drinks included champagne, brandy, Madeira, sherry, and *aguardiente*. Everyone raised a patriotic glass, then another and another. In the morning Sherman could remember only that he and Captain Folsom had spoken for the army, that Sutter and others had perpetrated speeches, and that the lord of New Helvetia was "very tight." In a subsequent edition of his memoirs Sherman slyly changed "very tight" to "enthusiastic."

The governor's mission was to inspect the placer mines, and the next morning he and his sore-headed crew rode the twenty-five miles to Mormon Island. The river was low and the meadows were browning in the summer heat. They found about two hundred men working with pans and rockers, most of them standing knee-deep in icy water. After they made camp a number of the miners came by to talk. One asked Mason what right Sam Brannan had to tithe the Mormon miners as he had done through the spring. "Brannan has a perfect right to collect the tax," the governor replied, "if you Mormons are fools enough to pay it." Mason also took the opportunity to point out that the miners were all trespassers on public land and that the gold was the property of the U.S. government. He added hastily that the mining benefited the government and he would not interfere.

The next day Mason moved upstream to Coloma. Marshall, just back from his futile search for the source of the gold, obligingly answered questions and pointed out the spot in the tailrace where he had found the first flakes. He led Mason to a nearby dry ravine where pieces as large as four and five ounces had been found. On the seventh the Mason party, including the governor's black servant Aaron, crossed over to Weber Creek and encountered Antonio Maria Suñol, one of the few native Californians then working in the mines, and his thirty Indian laborers. Eight miles up the creek they found a mob of whites and Indians. The men working the streambed and its tributary gulleys were averaging two ounces a day. Trading posts and even eating places had already sprung up, charging three dollars for a plate of greasy food. Mason met Charles Weber and saw the hundred-yard-long gulley where Daylor and McCoon had made $10,000 in a week. "Hundreds of similar ravines," Mason wrote in his subsequent report to Washington, "are as yet untouched. I could not have credited these reports had I not seen, in the abundance of the precious metal, evidence of their truth."

Mason estimated that there were two thousand white men and as many Indians working the mines in July and that their total daily take was between $30,000 and $50,000. The miners' only worry, he reported, was that there was too much gold: the quantity would drive the price down. Mason also remarked on the astonishing absence of crime in the mines, noting that "no thefts or robberies had been committed in the gold district" despite the frequently seen piles of untended gold.

Mason returned to the fort on July 9, but his plans to push on to the Feather, Bear, and Yuba rivers were scrapped when he received an urgent message calling him back to Monterey. Before he left, however, he accumulated more outrageous statistics for his report: John Sinclair, a forty-eighter whose ranch was between Sutter's fort and the sawmill, had made $16,000 through his Indians' labor in five weeks; Sam Brannan's adobe store at the fort had taken in $36,000 in gold between May 1 and July 10. Sutter and Marshall appeared to be the only forty-eighters who were not getting rich.

The governor also collected several specimens of gold to supplement the report he would send to the Army Department, buying them from such successful diggers as Suñol, Sinclair, and Weber. One of the specimens came from a former unbeliever named Edward Kemble.

"ANOTHER bag of gold from the mines," Walter Colton wrote in his Monterey journal on July 18, "and another spasm in the community. It was brought down by a sailor from Yuba River and contains 136 ounces. . . . (I)t looks like the yellow scales of the dolphin passing through his rainbow hues at death." Three seamen from the U.S. Navy sloop-of-war *Warren* took one look and deserted, risking a flogging or worse. After a night of drinking they awoke the next morning on the beach, astonished to find that they were still within sight of their ship.

Soldiers stationed at the pueblo of Los Angeles got their first word of the discovery on the same day. For the many who were due to be discharged soon, the temptation was irresistible. They raced north. Among the few who stayed behind was Baltimore-born Lieutenant John Hollingsworth, who had enjoyed his California duty more than most. Hollingsworth was torn between the phantom lure of gold and the more tangible attractions of his friends Dolores, Gabriela, Francisca, Acadia, Josepha, and Doña Maria Ignacia. He held out until September.

So many men were deserting that the military commanders feared the collapse of their ability to govern. Mason issued a proclamation soon after his return from the mines demanding that civilians help capture deserters and threatening to arrest those who did not. He warned that the military might have to take over the mining district, overlooking the fact that his disintegrating force made this impossible. The navy commander, Commodore Thomas ap Catesby Jones, declared that "severe examples," presumably executions, might be necessary to preclude desertions. "No hope of reward nor fear of punishment," the commodore intoned, "is sufficient to make binding any contract between man and man upon the soil of California." The temptation was obvious: "Laboring men at the mines can now earn in *one day*," Mason wrote in his report, "more than double a soldier's pay and allowances for a month." He recommended a liberal furlough policy and a substantial pay raise. But nothing would stem the tide of desertion: army records show that 716 enlisted men abandoned their posts between July 1, 1848, and December 31, 1849.

Hawaii began to stir in late June and July. "If it isn't the land that flows with milk and honey," a Honolulu editor wrote of California, "it abounds with wine and money, which some folks like better." Nineteen vessels sailed for the Golden Gate between June and October. Trading ships carried the news to Oregon, and the farmers in the Willamette Valley began the trek south in late summer. The advance elements of Henry Bigler's Mormon caravan brought the message to Salt Lake City in July.

The dry season had set in; there would be no more rain until the late fall. Gradually the gulches would dry up, the streams would recede, the rivers would turn flat and languid. The dark emerald-colored velvet of the foothill meadows would turn pale brown and then wheat-gold. The canyon oaks would lean a little farther toward the river. Deer and grizzlies and coyotes and cougars would move to higher country where the streams still ran white and pine needles carpeted the forest floor. Antelope would move one shelf up, from the valley to the first terrace, maintaining a flat horizon so they could spot their enemies. Wild horses would surge across the dusty ravines and paw for grass in the fissures between rocks.

California was like a vast anthill aswarm with migrating bodies in this gilded summer of 1848. Governor Mason and Lieutenant Sherman encountered one of the more peculiar traveling companies on their way home to Monterey in mid-July: four Frenchmen and an Indian servant. The leader was a well-dressed, middle-aged man of aristocratic bearing. Their pack animals carried supplies for at least a month, including several bottles of wine. As it happened, the Frenchmen were setting out on exactly the same kind of mission that Mason was just completing, and for the same purpose—to report to their government on the gold district. The main difference was that the French would make a more thorough tour of inspection.

The leader, Jacques Moerenhout, was the French consul at Monterey. In a day when diplomats frequently served flags other than their own, Moerenhout had represented the Dutch government in Chile and the United States in Tahiti. A veteran of the Napoleonic wars, he was an artist, businessman, and gentleman. He was also representing a regime that had been deposed a few months earlier, but he didn't know it yet.

Moerenhout's little party rode to the Weber Creek diggings by way of the San Joaquin, Mokelumne, and Cosumnes rivers. On the Cosumnes he took tea with rancher William Daylor, a onetime British sailor now suddenly wealthy. Curious about everything he saw, Moerenhout even measured the circumference of the trunk of the oak tree he slept under: it was twenty-three feet.

They were relieved to find other Frenchmen at the camp. That meant they would at least eat properly. The animated bustle of the Dry Diggings reminded Moerenhout of "a village festival or fair in Europe." He shrewdly observed that the diggers were working only a three- or four-foot-wide channel in the middle of the ravines, which meant that plenty of paydirt was being ignored. The bigger chunks of gold, he learned, were found not in the gulches but on the hillsides. The average profit was three to four ounces a day, but "everyone goes to the richest places that are already known and all the rest is neglected." Rockers, which took a day to build, were now selling for $150 and $200.

The stock of the local trader, Moerenhout observed, ran to flour, sugar, rice, tea, wine, and brandy. He was appalled to find that the wine, "though quite ordinary," cost eight dollars a bottle. He also noticed one difference between the American-born miners and their Mexican or native Californian counterparts: the Americans brought plenty of provisions and stayed longer; the Mexicans carried less, settled for less, and quit sooner.

After nine days at Dry Diggings he moved over to Coloma and then Mormon Island, where the yield was down to an ounce and a half a day per man. He went on to Bear River and then to the Yuba, where the diggers had spread out for twenty miles along the banks and were earning an ounce to an ounce and a half. At Bidwell's Bar on the Feather he found Indians at work on the gravel bars and islands.

On July 28 he turned back toward the fort. His detailed letter to the minister of Foreign Affairs included precise estimates of the number of miners and the wealth produced at each of the sites he visited. He placed the number of miners at 1,000 at Dry Diggings, 350 on the American, 160 on the Yuba, 130 on the Feather, and 60 on the Bear. He calculated their harvest at $3 million for Dry Diggings, $600,000 on the American, $200,000 for the Yuba, $180,000 on the Feather, and $60,000 on Bear River—a total of more than $4 million by the end of July.

At Sutter's fort he saw "men on foot and on horseback, wagons going in and out, some bringing goods from the Sacramento landing, others taking them to the different mining regions." The courtyard was jammed with casks, boxes, bales, and rushing men. Sutter received the consul graciously and offered him a $2-a-day room at the fort's hotel. The only furniture in the room was two old chairs. Sutter told him that he was collecting $1,800 a month in rent from the hotelkeeper and tradesmen.

Moerenhout observed that a large number of men were sick with "fever." He had noticed it previously at the camps, especially on the Feather. The symptoms, which would become achingly familiar to thousands of miners, included diarrhea, general weakness, and a fever. Although it came in different forms and from different specific causes, the "fever" was a consequence of the living and working conditions in the mines—long hours in freezing water, the midday heat, and hasty meals of bacon and half-cooked biscuits.

The Frenchmen crossed mile after mile of fire-blackened grassland on their way back to the coast; careless travelers had kept the parched grass aflame for weeks. They ferried across Carquinez Strait and reached Monterey on August 16. The town was eerily quiet. It seemed as though everyone was in the foothills except Governor Mason and Reverend Colton. Colton was busy keeping a bonanza box score: one friend had made $5,300 in two months on the Yuba, another gathered $4,500 on the North Fork of the American. It was growing ever more difficult to keep the faith in Monterey.

THE UNITED STATES east of the Missouri River was still ignorant of the treasure in the California hills. Most Amerians thought of California, if they thought of it at all, as a distant and exotic province populated largely by Mexicans and grizzly bears. It had been acquired by conquest in an unpopular war, but only God and President Polk knew why anyone would want it. This attitude was about to undergo a profound change, but the change would be neither sudden nor particularly dramatic. The rest of the country would dawdle with the news even longer than San Francisco had; four months would pass before the skeptical East was finally convinced.

The first communications to reach the States after the gold discovery began to arrive around the end of July. The St. Joseph (Mo.) *Gazette* of July 28 published a letter from Charles White, the alcalde of San Jose, dated March 18. The letter, possibly carried to Missouri by the same expressmen who delivered Sam Brannan's booster edition of the *California Star*, listed gold as merely one among several recent mineral finds.

Kit Carson, carrying Brannan's *Star* as well as military dispatches, got to Washington on August 2. The great scout had weathered a brush with Utes and Apaches and still covered the 2,800 miles from Los Angeles in three months. One letter he toted was from Thomas Larkin, a longtime California businessman who was also the U.S. Navy agent in Monterey, to the New York *Herald*. Larkin, signing himself "Paisano," served as the *Herald*'s California correspondent. Dated March 30, his instantly obsolete letter reported that "mines are discovered in many places, but quicksilver is to enrich California beyond all other mines." It appeared on August 4. Other papers in New York, Philadelphia, and Washington published short items based on Larkin's letter in the following days.

On August 19 the *Herald* printed what purported to be a long letter from a member of the "New York Volunteers" who had gone to California during the Mexican War. The letter filled two complete columns. In fact a *Herald* writer had done a clever and unattributed rewrite of the "Prospects of California" article in the *California Star*. Like Victor Fourgeaud's article, the *Herald* story failed to mention gold until three-fourths of the way along. It described the lode, exactly as the *Star* did, as three feet below the surface and twelve to eighteen feet thick. The unmistakable tipoff came in the prediction of "a Peruvian harvest of the precious metals," the identical language that the *Star* used. Plagiarized or not, the *Herald* story caused no particular excitement.

The quickest, most perilous, and most remarkable coast-to-coast journey in 1848 was made by twenty-six-year-old U.S. Navy Lieutenant Edward Fitzgerald Beale, a dark-haired patrician from Washington. Ned Beale volunteered to carry military dispatches and letters from Commodore Jones, Thomas Larkin, and Walter Colton. The dispatches were intended for Secretary of State James Buchanan and Navy Secretary John Mason in Washington. He also carried a small amount of gold.

He set out from La Paz, Baja California, on July 29. He sailed across the Gulf of California to Mazatlán, then chartered a schooner to take him down the coast to San Blas. At San Blas he acquired a guide, a horse, four revolvers, and a sombrero.

Beale and his guide rode through the swamp along the coast and up into the bare, precipitous barranca country of the Sierra Madre Occidental range. In the mountains they were confronted by three bandits who turned tail when Beale drew his pistol. They outran another band of outlaws after a long chase. The only time they rested was the few moments it took to change horses. Near Guadalajara they saw what might have happened if the *ladrones* had caught them: eleven people lay dead on the ground, the blood still running from their wounds. They completed the four-hundred-mile ride to Mexico City in eight days.

Here the two men tried to rest for a few days, though Beale's nerves were stretched so taut that rest was difficult. Then they galloped out of the city and across the central plateau to the rugged ramparts of the Sierra Madre Oriental, which seemed bathed in a perpetual purple mist. Once more they had to race for their lives to escape pursuing bandits. They traveled through forests of orange and banana trees in the tropical foothills, then followed a trail between sand hills to Veracruz on the Gulf of Mexico. They had covered the 275 miles from Mexico City in just forty-eight hours, and they felt like it. Beale's guide collapsed in Veracruz. The lieutenant shed his sombrero and arranged passage to Mobile, Alabama, on an American warship.

THE SAN FRANCISCO *Californian* burst fitfully into print again on August 14; the editor warned that the paper would appear only occasionally during the "temporary suspension of business." In a wide-eyed account of the summer's developments, the journal reported that there were now about four thousand white men in the mines. The placers were so preposterously rich that "were we to set down half the truth, it would be looked upon in other countries as a 'Sinbad' story or the history of 'Aladdin's Lamp.'" Miners who did not clear $30 to $40 a day kept moving until they did. Prices were screaming out of sight. "Four months ago, flour was sold in the market for four dollars per hundred [pounds], now sixteen; beef cattle six, now thirty; ready-made clothing, grocer's and other goods . . . are at least double their original cost."

As yet there was hardly anyone who perceived a dark lining in the golden cloud over California. Most doubts were buried beneath the stunning statistics of success. One man who acknowledged a fugitive doubt or two was Navy Agent Thomas Larkin, whose letter to Secretary of State Buchanan was in Ned Beale's saddlebag. "Men and passions are unfavourable changed at these gold regions," Larkin wrote. Noting the rate of desertion and the evacuation of the towns, he added bleakly that "the future . . . prospect is not pleasant nor moral." Larkin was ambivalent; he had already made a quick trip to the mines himself, and his various business interests would soon make him one of the wealthiest men in California. But his New England conscience was aquiver: the gold delirium was leading to irresponsibility, imprudence, and worse; there was already a gambling house at Sutter's Fort, drunkenness was all too common, and prostitutes—"soiled doves," in the language of the day—would arrive before long. Larkin probably agreed with his stepbrother, who wrote from Washington that "there is something in the presence of the precious metals which seems to paralyze every kind of productive industry."

Some of the Californios had their doubts as well. Gold had not been discovered until shortly after the province passed from Mexico to the United States—might that be some sign, perhaps a warning? Don Luis Peralta, one of the California grandees, thought so. "God has given this gold to the Americans," he told his three sons. "Had he desired us to have it, he would have given it to us ere now. Therefore go not after it, but let others go. Plant your lands, and reap; these be your best gold fields."

The Californios were acutely aware, as was Lieutenant Beale in his mad dash across Mexico, that the two nations had been at war only a few months earlier. Bitterness lingered; the Californio miners would feel it, and so would the California-bound forty-niners who traveled across Mexico. The news that the treaty ending the war had been signed did not reach San Francisco until early August; it was celebrated with bonfires, a parade through the empty streets, and a rendering of "The Star-Spangled Banner" by a male chorus.

John Sutter, the man with the most to lose in the stampede for gold, had remained at the fort through July—collecting rent from his tenants and tribute from his distinguished guests, bullyragging his remaining Indians into harvesting wheat, and watching the disintegration of his dream. His control over New Helvetia was eroding daily; it was no longer the orderly village he had built but rather a lawless, brawling frontier outpost. "Anyone who could not protect himself with his fists was unfortunate," overseer Heinrich Lienhard remarked. Sutter's various business interests, including his mining partnership with Marshall, the sawmill, and a store at Coloma, were all foundering. His overhead was still formidable and he remained in debt. He suddenly decided to try prospecting.

In August he assembled a force of one hundred Indians and fifty Hawaiians and went to a deep gorge on the American River between Mormon Island and Coloma. His forty-eighter neighbors had made their piles in exactly this way, but not Sutter. "In a few weeks we became crowded," he wrote, "and it would no more pay, as my people made too many acquaintances"—presumably gamblers and bartenders.

His friend Lienhard found gold almost in spite of himself. Disgusted with his repeated failures, he took an angry swipe at a gravel bank with his pick, tearing a chunk from his leg as he did so. When he removed the pick he saw a trove of nuggets, which proved to be worth $260.

Sutter moved his company south to a stream below the Cosumnes

River which would later be known as Sutter Creek, but he did no better there. Again he blamed the "travelling grog-shops" for separating his men from their gold, but Sutter himself was their best customer. He spent his nights in brandy-fueled debauchery. The expedition was a total loss.

SUTTER'S eldest son, whom he had not seen for fourteen years, was waiting for him when he returned to the fort. John A. Sutter, Jr., known as August, was nearly twenty-two, a bright, energetic youth who possessed the business acumen that his father lacked. The younger Sutter had left Switzerland to join his father several months before the news of the gold discovery reached Europe. Sutter *père* had awaited him with ambivalent emotions. In letters to his friends he described his son with pride: well-educated and multilingual, he would doubtless make an "able clerk." And a good clerk, or business manager, was precisely what Sutter desperately needed: his financial affairs were a tangled thicket of debts, careless transactions, and sloppy books.

But Sutter was also apprehensive about encountering this son he had last known as a boy of eight. The youth was a living reminder of his deserted mother; his presence was an implied rebuke; indeed, he was barely legitimate—Sutter's bride had been nearly nine months pregnant with this very child on their wedding day. What would this boy who grew up fatherless think of the man he now found carousing drunkenly with Indian squaws? August got a whiff of his father's reputation even before their tearful reunion at the fort: in San Francisco he heard "strange reports and contradictory rumors" about Sutter's drunken carelessness and the "parcel of rogues" who preyed on him. Sailing up the Sacramento on a Sutter-owned schooner, August felt an apprehension as acute as his father's.

He soon discovered that the Sutter finances were even more muddled than he had feared. "Anything belonging to my father was at everybody's disposal," he wrote. The books had been neglected for six months. As a way of eluding his most pressing creditors, Sutter was persuaded to place legal control of his various properties and investments in his son's name. Soon afterwards he returned to the freedom of the mountains, leaving a game but bewildered August to cope with the creditors.

The distrust between a father and son who were strangers to each other intensified in the ensuing months. Sutter was paralyzed by his own ambivalence: he resented his son's decisions even as he respected them.

His greedy cronies, however, saw an opportunity to profit by driving the wedge between the Sutters even deeper.

Sutter had dreamed for years of creating a town on land he owned a few miles south of the Sacramento River embarcadero. The site was on high ground, which would protect it from the frequent lowland floods. The name, of course, would be Sutterville. But with the elder Sutter still in the mountains, the ubiquitous Sam Brannan persuaded August that the best town site was between the fort and the river, not at out-of-the-way Sutterville. Brannan explained that the sale of lots in the new town, to be called Sacramento City, would pay off the Sutter family debts, including $16,000 owed to the onetime Mormon elder himself. The lots indeed sold so rapidly that August was soon able to settle the major debts.

Sutter, returning home to learn that his cherished Sutterville had been abandoned, was infuriated. He refused to see his son. His self-serving "friends" promptly induced him to sign, drunkenly, a bond that in effect gave them most of his Sutterville property. At Brannan's suggestion these men then offered free building lots to any merchants willing to settle in Sutterville. With this as leverage, Brannan and his cohorts demanded that Sutter match the offer by giving each of them two hundred free lots in Sacramento. Overruling August's objections, Sutter capitulated. The result was that Sutter was euchred out of both Sutterville and a substantial chunk of Sacramento in one stroke.

By the end of the year Sutter needed to put some space between himself and the symbols of his shattered hopes. He had already sold the hotel at the fort. In December he disposed of his half-interest in the Coloma sawmill for $6,000. He and a chastened August left the fort for good a few weeks later and moved to Sutter's farm on the Feather River.

IT WAS possible to fail at the mines in 1848, as Sutter's melancholy experience showed, but it required an extraordinary combination of ineptitude and bad luck. Ineptitude alone was not enough; the hills and gullies were full of men who had blundered blindly into more money than they had ever known. They lived in a land where every ravine was rainbow's end. James Carson, the army sergeant who dreamed of marble castles and a battalion of virgins, was at Dry Diggings in the summer, certain that he was among "the happiest set of men on earth." And he probably was. No other men anywhere were making $50 a day by scraping rocks with their jackknives.

One of Carson's partners in bliss was a nearsighted British ex-sailor called Little Jack Swan. Little Jack had seen the world—China, India, South America, the Mediterranean, the Great Lakes—but he had never seen an Eden like this: "No one worked very hard," he wrote, "and round our campfires at night we would pass pleasant evenings singing and spinning yarns. Not a quarrel took place. . . . It was my first mining experience, and taking it in all, the happiest."

Swan watched a soldier gather twelve ounces one day before noon. A deserting sailor who had done equally well bought a barrel of whiskey and put a tap on it for the convenience of the camp. If a man tired of digging he could prospect the Indians: Carson saw Indians exchanging handfuls of gold for colorful handkerchiefs and shirts at Charles Weber's store; Swan sold a string of cheap glass beads to a native for seven ounces of gold ($112).

The only sand on the miner's tongue was the unsettling notion that somebody somewhere was making even more. There were constant rumors that a prospector had found the "fountainhead," the bed of gold in the mountains whence all veins, they believed, originated. In mid-August the enormously productive Dry Diggings were pronounced exhausted, although miners had worked only the centers of the ravines and the creek banks. Rumor was that the fountainhead was farther south. Carson, Swan, and two hundred more of the happiest men on earth rambled fifty miles across the dry, oat-covered foothills to the Stanislaus River.

The just-discovered diggings on the Stanislaus were the first in what would come to be called the southern mines. The north-south dividing line fell between the two great rivers of the central valley, the Sacramento and San Joaquin. The streams draining into the Sacramento—the Feather, Yuba, Bear, and American rivers—made up the northern mines. The northern camps were higher, greener, colder, and wetter, with deeper canyons and thicker forest cover. The rivers that emptied into the San Joaquin were the Cosumnes, Mokelumne, Calaveras, Stanislaus, Tuolumne, Merced, and Mariposa. Here the vegetation was sparser and the terrain became gradually softer, gentler, and more rolling.

In the first frenzied months the miners had concentrated on the Sacramento tributaries. But in midsummer Charles Weber sent a group of Tuolumne Indians to the Stanislaus with the promise that any gold they found could be redeemed in merchandise from his store. The Indians returned in August with enough coarse gold to send the colony at Dry Diggings scurrying south.

Reports of the new find sped through the state. Antonio Francisco Coronel, a Mexican schoolteacher from Los Angeles, was en route to Dry Diggings with a company of thirty when he heard the news from a priest at the San Joaquin River. The padre was carrying a bag of gold. Coronel, who would later become mayor of Los Angeles, turned toward the Stanislaus instead. He pitched camp in the main ravine, a deep chasm at the base of a high ridge, and was immediately confronted by seven Indians who coveted his saddle blankets and serape.

Coronel refused several sign-language offers—the Indians moved their thumbs down their sausage-shaped sacks of gold to indicate how much they would pay—but finally sold one blanket for seven ounces and another for nine. One of Coronel's men followed the Indians when they left that night, tracking them to another ravine about a day's ride away. The Mexican tried the ravine with his knife and quickly dug up three ounces, then raced back to tell Coronel. Coronel and his two Indian servants collected 45 ounces on their first full day of work at the new site, 38 the second day, and 51 the third.

Consul Moerenhout reported that another gulley near the Stanislaus yielded as much as $2,000 a day to two Frenchmen who spent most of their time picking loose gold off the ground. Sergeant James Carson, following the directions of a friendly Indian, meandered up a tributary stream of the Stanislaus to a point where he dug out 180 ounces in ten days; the creek was soon called Carson's Creek. His friend and fellow soldier George Angel found good diggings at a site later known as Angel's Camp. Even Little Jack Swan, who had no particular relish for the toil of gold digging, gathered three pounds—"something to take me to the coast" —and ambled home to his combination store/boardinghouse/saloon in Monterey, where it pleased him to learn that "a man that had been a month or two in the mines . . . was looked on as somewhat of an oracle."

In the years to come the tales that miners would tell each other about 1848 shared a reckless, joyous extravagance which surpassed anything in the boom times to follow. To be in California in 1848 was to be one of destiny's darlings. The land was so prodigal that exaggeration was impossible—every "stretcher" turned out to be true. Theft was unnecessary—it was easier to dig; poverty was a communal embarrassment and intolerable. The conviction was widespread that the mountains were a bank on which every man had a drawing account; if he came up short he need only seize his pick and pan and make a withdrawal. The story was frequently told of an 1848 miner dunned for a debt at an awkward hour of the night. In a rage he grabbed a lantern and marched to his claim, quickly washed out the amount in question plus interest, and hurled the dust in his creditor's face.

Another tale told of a woebegone sixteen-year-old boy, broke and weary and hungry, arriving at a ravine where thirty miners were cheerfully panning. He looked so gloomy as he watched the digging that one miner finally cried out, "Boys, I'll work an hour for that chap if you will."

An hour later the miners presented him with a hundred dollars in dust and a list of tools and supplies. They told him that they would stake a good claim for him while he went to buy provisions, but "then you've got to paddle for yourself."

The most famous of the 1848 yarns was first recounted by James Carson in a book published in 1852; gold-rush mythmaking began early. Carson's story, set in a camp on the American River, concerned a miner being laid to his final rest by a preacher who had drunk rather too liberally to the soul of the departed.

The miners knelt around the grave while the parson offered a garbled and extended prayer. Restlessly they ran their hands through the freshly dug earth. Suddenly a cry issued from one of the mourners: "Gold!" The preacher tentatively opened one eye and made a rapid assay: "Gold, by God, and the richest kind o' diggin's. The congregation are dismissed." Minister and funeral party fell to. Some time later they moved the remains of their lamented comrade to less likely diggings.

COLONEL MASON'S firsthand report of his visit to the mines, which would ultimately persuade both the government and the dubious eastern press that the gold accounts were not exaggerated, was ready by August 17. It was supplemented not only by the specimens Mason had acquired but also by a sealed Chinese tea caddy containing slightly more than 230 ounces of gold the army had purchased. To bear this vital cargo to Washington, Mason selected an artillery officer named Lucien Loeser, a newly promoted first lieutenant who was due for a trip home. Loeser was to sail to Payta, Peru, where he would board a British coastal steamer for Panama. He was then to cross the Isthmus and find passage to the States on the Atlantic side. He left Monterey on the chartered schooner *Lambayecana* on August 30.

By that time the other military courier, Navy Lieutenant Ned Beale, was halfway between Veracruz and Mobile on the sloop-of-war *German-town*. Beale's frayed nerves were almost back to normal. The voyage across the Gulf of Mexico was like a long siesta after his hell-for-leather sprint through Mexico. He arrived in Mobile in the first week of September. The final leg of his journey was by stagecoach and steamer to Washington, which he reached on September 16—exactly forty-nine days after he left La Paz.

Beale made news even before he arrived at the capital. On September 12 a short item from Mexico City appeared in the New Orleans *Picayune*, reporting his stop there in August. The story quoted Beale as saying that miners were clearing $70 a day with nothing more than a spade. He added that there were only twelve men left in Monterey in early June and ten in San Francisco. The rest had fled to the hills. The St. Louis *Union* reprinted the story with the comment that it was "evidently exaggerated."

Beale's gold specimens—the first to reach the East from California— were a sensation among his fellow stage passengers and the people in towns he passed through. One of the most inquisitive of the other passengers was Henry S. Foote, a U.S. senator from Mississippi. Foote was so impressed that he invited the young lieutenant to speak to the Senate.

Beale's arrival set off a chain reaction of news stories across the East and Midwest. His weathered saddlebags carried much more than official dispatches from Commodore Jones and Naval Agent Larkin; he also delivered long, informative, and somewhat hyperbolic letters from both Larkin and Walter Colton. Colton wrote to the Philadelphia *North American*, a paper he had once edited, and the New York *Journal of Commerce*. Larkin wrote several letters to the New York *Herald* over his correspondent's pen name, Paisano. In addition there were several letters from Larkin to Secretary of State Buchanan, most of which eventually surfaced in print.

Larkin and Colton were both middle-aged New Englanders and responsible government officials. Neither was apt to fall for a hoax or go off half-cocked. Yet what was a reader to make of these splashes of outrageous purple from the West? California seemed to have driven them loco. Compared with California, "Paisano" wrote in the *Herald*, "the famous El Dorado is but a sand bank." Mining "requires no skill. The workman takes any spot of ground or bank he fancies, sticks in his pick or shovel at random, fills his basin, makes for the water, and soon sees the glittering results of his labor."

Colton was equally vivid: his next-door neighbor gathered $500 in six days; "I know a little boy only 12 years of age who washes out his ounce of gold a day, while his mother makes root beer and sells it at a dollar a bottle"; "Your streams have minnows in them, and ours are paved with gold." Oh, California!—"It beats all the dreams of romance and all the golden marvels of the wand of Midas."

It was the facts that were outrageous. Larkin even tried to apologize in advance, writing that if he were a New Yorker he would scoff at such obvious fiction. Not surprisingly, editorial skeptics opened fire. "It needs some deposits of the precious metals to offset the howling sterility of nine-tenths of California," the Philadelphia *North American* commented, "but we will back a coal mine of Pennsylvania against all the gold mines of the new El Dorado." The New York *Sun* advised that the so-called gold was in fact mica, and the fever was "an unmitigated humbug in which knaves and fools were the partners." Most papers conceded that there was gold in California but suspected a bit of frontier gulling.

"All Washington is in a ferment" over the gold news, the *Herald* said. "It looks marvellously like a speculation to induce a rapid emigration, but then again, it is certified by the American alcalde at Monterey (Colton), and the American alcalde is a very proper man."

Larkin's letters were widely reprinted in Boston, St. Louis, New Orleans, Mobile, and elsewhere. His reports to Buchanan were milder in tone, but they gave the secretary plenty to think about: "Could Mr. Polk and yourself see California as we now see it, you would think that a few thousand people on one hundred miles square of the Sacramento Valley would yearly turn out of this river the whole price our country pays for all the acquired territory."

The flurry of excitement precipitated by Beale's arrival lasted about three weeks and then subsided. Newspapers in several cities reported a brief flaring of "emigration fever." A seventeen-year-old Philadelphia boy applied to the Navy Department for a post as dispatch bearer to California. A low-level civil servant in Washington requested transfer to California as a "timber agent." An Alabama clergyman sought a military appointment as a chaplain in California because his health required "a more congenial climate." Meanwhile the mania was spreading in other directions: an Oregon newspaper reported on September 7 that the territory was "convulsed" by gold fever; a ship carrying $2,500 in California gold arrived on September 12 at Valparaiso, Chile, inciting an outbreak in that lively port. Chileans—the miners called them *chileños*—were to play an important part in the gold rush.

By summer's end there were close to six thousand Americans, Mexicans, and Indians scattered along the sluggish rivers and dusty streambeds of the new Golconda. Their faces were leathery from weeks in the
sun. It never rained. The diggers panned their ounce or more a day and
spent it on whiskey and gambling and overpriced food. It was an unhealthy life, and an increasing number were coming home sick or dying
in the hills. The *Californian* counseled rest, temperate habits, wholesome
food, and warm bedclothes, but such sensible advice was lost in the smoke
of the mountain camps.

The gold country now stretched more than 250 miles from the Trinity
River in the north to the Stanislaus in the south, and restless prospectors
were expanding it daily. New camps had materialized on the Cosumnes,
Mokelumne, and Tuolumne. Every town in the state had been more or less
evacuated; even the amorous Lieutenant Hollingsworth, with his covey
of señoritas in Los Angeles, had broken free in mid-September and galloped to the Mokelumne. Almost everyone was digging successfully, and
a few were holding onto it, but the real bonanzas were in trade: San
Francisco merchants had already taken in more than $850,000. Sam
Brannan and the other businessmen had agreed at a September 9 meeting
to fix the value of gold at a firm $16 an ounce. The prospects were un-
limited: the *Californian* predicted there would be "profitable employment for 100,000 persons for generations to come."

Walter Colton could stand it no longer. He had remained dutifully
steadfast in Monterey while his neighbors got rich and his letters titillated
the East. On September 20 he set out for the Stanislaus to see for himself.

In the San Joaquin Valley he encountered a band of Californios who
gave him pause. They were ragged and hungry—"a more forlorn-looking
group never knocked at the gate of a pauper asylum," he wrote. Colton's
party gave them bread and meat but refused to accept payment, even
after the Mexicans produced a bulging bag of gold.

Arriving at the mines, Colton found the work arduous and the atmosphere feverish. "They who get less are discontented," he noted, "and
they who get more are not satisfied. Every day brings in some fresh report
of richer discoveries in some quarter not far remote. . . . Were an
ounce of diamonds to fall into one of our hands every day, we should
hold out the other just as eager and impatient as if its fellow were
empty." The food, especially jerked beef, was appalling: "When mois-
tened and toasted it will do something towards sustaining life; so also
will the sole of your shoe."

Colton was no miner, but he tagged along when a fresh rumor sent the herd of diggers stampeding to a new ravine. He was most impressed by their good-natured acceptance of failure. They came back at night, empty-handed, with brush heaps of kindling piled high on their heads as their cheerful shouts of greeting echoed down the canyon. "There is something extremely consoling in having the company of others," Colton reflected, "when we have been duped through our vanity or exaggerated hopes."

III

HO FOR CALIFORNIA!

ON THE WAY TO THE DIGGINGS

SHORTLY before noon on October 6, 1848, the steamship *California* slid lazily from her moorings on the East River in New York harbor and set sail on what would be a memorably tempestuous maiden voyage. Her destination was San Francisco via Cape Horn, but on the way the dowdy-looking vessel would call at Rio de Janeiro, Valparaiso, Panama, and several ports in Peru and Mexico. The captain would fall ill and be replaced. The engine would falter. A mutiny would be barely averted. And the passenger list would multiply from six to more than 360, dangerously exceeding capacity. The gold rush, in short, would overtake her.

At the moment, though, all that mattered was the bon voyage party. Off Bedloe's Island, where the Statue of Liberty would rise a generation later, a delegation of dignitaries climbed aboard the ship for champagne and speeches and a splendid meal. Insurance company presidents toasted the craft they had so graciously underwritten. Stylishly dressed ladies toured the two-hundred-foot-long ship with her twin masts and sidewheel and single smokestack. They peered into the empty staterooms, built to accommodate sixty passengers, and had a quick peek at the steerage quarters which could hold another 150. They may also have detected the livestock "closet," where sheep, pigs, and poultry were penned and butchered. The ship was well past Sandy Hook and cruising down the New Jersey coast by the time the *Orus,* a small steamer, retrieved the guests for the trip back to Manhattan. They loosed one final cheer from the deck of the *Orus* as the fine new ship steamed south.

The ultimate mission of the *California* was to inaugurate passenger and mail service by steamship between the east and west coasts by way of the Isthmus of Panama. The Pacific Mail Steamship Line, federally subsidized because it carried the mail, had been created only six months earlier. The *California* and two other steamers, the *Oregon* and the *Panama,* were to work the Pacific side, between Panama City and the west coast. Three other ships would ferry passengers between New York and Chagres, the pestilential village on the Atlantic side of the Isthmus. Across the sixty-mile Isthmus the passengers were on their own: they covered part of the distance in native-powered canoes up the Chagres River and part on foot or muleback along a narrow and often muddy trail. The *California* was the first of the Pacific Mail ships to roll off the ways. The timing, though coincidental, was perfect: east-west steamer travel began only weeks before the gold hysteria struck the East.

The *California* sailed during the last extended lull before the gold storm. Ned Beale had completed his daring scamper only three weeks earlier, and the papers had been full of the glittering tales of Larkin and Colton, but the eastern populace was not yet buying. Not one of the six *California* passengers was going there. Here was relatively quick and comfortable transportation for more than two hundred people to El Dorado itself—and no takers. The reason was visible in an item published in the St. Louis *Republican* on the same day that the *California* sailed. The story was commenting on some gold flakes recently received from California Governor Mason. It was gold all right, the paper conceded, but "such stories are usually greatly magnified and embellished by those who undertake to describe them. . . . Emigrants and settlers are wanted in California, and what is so captivating as these gold visions?" The *Republican* could not understand why a successful prospector would want to share his secret—unless it was for selfish gain. It would take two more months, Lucien Loeser's tea caddy, and President Polk himself to convince the East.

THE MIX in the mines began to change in early autumn of 1848. Men arrived from Hawaii and Oregon. The first caravans of Sonorans started north from the pueblos where Apaches constantly harassed them. Deserters from the army, navy, and merchant ships continued to swarm to the foothills. Most of the Mexican War veterans had by now either deserted, served out their enlistments, or taken long furloughs. The mines were filling up with strangers.

Inevitably they clashed. Early in October a murder was committed at the Coloma sawmill.

The mill had stood idle for several months, and miners now used it as a dormitory. Late one evening a drunken ex-soldier named Peter Raymond staggered into the building and began shouting for John Von Pfister, who apparently had some liquor. Von Pfister, a recent arrival from Hawaii, got up and seemed to placate the man, but Raymond suddenly seized Von Pfister's knife and stabbed him in the chest. Raymond was taken to Sutter's fort and locked up pending trial. A few days later he escaped and disappeared.

The incident reminded thoughtful Californians that they were without any real legal protection. There was no criminal code, no government besides the military, not even any guarantee that debts could be collected or contracts enforced. The few alcaldes, remnants of Mexican rule, represented what little law there was. At the same time, as the *Californian* commented, the state offered "unparalleled inducements to desperadoes, escaped convicts and the scum of the Pacific." Good citizens should unite, the paper urged, lest "red murder stalk through the land."

A few weeks later the rival *Star* reported that two miners were killed by Indians in the highlands between the Yuba River and the North Fork of the American. The Indians had reportedly been provoked by men from Oregon, who had been fighting redmen for years and viewed them with indiscriminate hatred. Both Marshall and Sutter, who enjoyed good relations with the Indians, mediated disputes between whites and Indians around this time.

For the dozens of independent tribes scattered through the California hills, these were the first skirmishes in a war without hope. The Maidu, Miwok, Yalesumni, and other foothill Indians had lived peaceably for centuries in communal societies which precluded the accumulation of individual wealth. Scorned as "Diggers" for their custom of digging edible roots and insects, they were mystified at first by men who dug not for food but for dust and rocks. Many forty-eighters recruited them as laborers, but the men who followed would destroy their villages and kill them on the flimsiest pretexts. In a year they would be all but invisible.

San Francisco was beginning to resemble a battlefield hospital. By mid-October the pale and weakened victims of various fevers were coming into the city by the launch-load. The lucky ones found rooms in the few hotels and boardinghouses; the others pitched tents or rigged makeshift shelters for minimal protection from the morning dampness and afternoon wind. The few available doctors charged an ounce or more for a visit. Carson, who could afford the best the city offered, paid a dollar for the privilege of sleeping on a bowling alley after it closed at 2 a.m.

Edward Gould Buffum, a just-discharged army officer and wide-eyed new arrival in San Francisco, stood on a city wharf and watched the parade of the enfeebled. Buffum was twenty-eight, dark-haired, and handsome, a renegade Quaker and one of a remarkable family of New England reformers. His father had been the first president of the New England Anti-Slavery Society, and his sister Elizabeth operated an underground railway station in Rhode Island, smuggling escaped slaves to safety. Another relative had resigned a seat on the Rhode Island Supreme Court rather than sentence a man to death. Young Edward was cut from a slightly different bolt of cloth: he fancied a career as a writer, and had worked several years as a reporter for James Gordon Bennett's New York *Herald*. The real affront to his Quaker family came when he enlisted in the New York Volunteers.

Buffum was so eager to be off for the mines that neither the season— it was already October 25—nor the pathetic procession of emaciated men returning to San Francisco daunted him. He and his two friends had their miner's outfits—shovel and ax and rifle, flannel shirt and corduroy pants and boots—and their tickets on an open launch up the Sacramento River. Unfortunately he had failed to reconnoiter the frail craft before boarding. It was packed to overflowing with merchandise for the camp trading posts, plus eleven passengers. "There was not room upon her deckless hull to stow a brandy bottle securely," Buffum wrote. At dusk they set forth upon the gray and heaving bay. For dinner they munched crackers and cheese. With evening came black clouds and a brisk wind which splashed spray over the boat's sides, which were barely above sea level. The trick would be finding a place to sleep.

"Sharper-sighted than my companions," he wrote, "I had spied out a box of goods lying aft that rose above the mingled mass around it, and upon which, by doubling myself into a most unnatural and ungentlemanly position, I could repose the upper portion of my body, while my heels rested on the chines of a pork barrel, at an angle of about forty-five degrees above my head. With a selfishness peculiar to the human race, I appropriated the whole of this couch to myself." Even so, he was presently roused by a fellow voyager who informed him that his "time was up"; the passengers had voted to take turns occupying his splintery bunk. But Buffum was nothing if not resilient; he possessed the indomitable cheerfulness of a besieged Quaker, and he was beating upstream to the most glorious adventure of his life.

California was a lodestar luring pilgrims from every direction. At the same time that Buffum's sagging launch was passing through Carquinez Strait, a company of exhausted and thirsty Oregonians were blinking in the welcoming sun two hundred miles to the north and enjoying their first glimpse of the Sacramento Valley.

The captain of the Oregonians was Peter Burnett, a forty-one-year-old lawyer and judge who had migrated west from Missouri in 1843. Burnett was a strong and capable man and a natural leader. He had organized a train of fifty wagons and 150 men in the Willamette Valley and equipped them with provisions for six months, then led them south past Goose Lake and across the rugged Cascade range. Near the western slope they were forced to cozy their wagons across a thirty-foot-wide natural bridge between two impassable ravines; it reminded Burnett of "an isthmus connecting two continents." They lowered the wagons with ropes to avoid a rock which blocked their descent into the great valley. Their final two days in the mountains were waterless.

The Oregonians stopped to rest at the ranch owned by Peter Lassen, a Danish-born blacksmith who had settled on Deer Creek, about a hundred miles upriver from Sacramento. Burnett moved on alone to the newly opened camp at Long Bar on the Yuba, where he found about ninety people, a single log cabin, and a cluster of tents. Long Bar was one of the first camps to recognize a "claim," the miner's exclusive right to work a particular piece of ground. Burnett paid $300 for a claim which measured twenty feet along the river and fifty feet back from the bank. He built a rocker and began clearing $20 a day within a week. After a month he had enough to pay his debts plus a six-month cushion. If mining was this profitable, he reasoned, then practicing law should be even better. Burnett washed his last dust in December of 1848. A year later he would become California's first elected governor.

Oregon was in fact losing most of its muscle to the mines. A few months earlier, many married men had declined to leave their homes to join a military expedition against Indians on grounds that they feared for their families' safety; the same men were now in California. Burnett estimated that about two-thirds of the Oregon males had hightailed it south to the gold country by fall.

Mexicans from the state of Sonora were arriving from the other direction. The first long caravan of Sonoran miners (many of them had mined gold in Mexico) filed out of Hermosillo in October and began the 250-mile trek to the border. Five thousand more Sonorans would follow during the winter, and by spring the biggest town in the southern mines would be named after their home state.

The initial shiploads of Chilean gold seekers had sailed from Valparaiso in September, even before the news appeared in the papers. In the first week of November a man arrived in Chile with $25,000 in California gold and the San Francisco newspapers, and the *chileño* rush was on. An editor wrote soon afterward that a ship which announced for California at 11 a.m. could book its available space by 2 p.m.

In the Atlantic, the sidewheeler *California* was still steaming south, in fact a bit too far south. The big steamer overran its first stop at Rio de Janeiro and had to backtrack before it docked on November 2. Captain Cleaveland Forbes had discerned several defects in the ship: the water closets were in the wrong place, the engineers' rooms were too hot, the pipes in the pantry leaked, and the livestock "closet" was so stifling that all the animals had suffocated. The captain himself also seemed to have a defect: his lungs were bleeding. Ship and skipper were both repaired during a twenty-three-day layover in Rio.

The only true innocents among the California-bound travelers of 1848 were the few hundred pioneers who had set out from Missouri in the spring. These were families going west simply to settle, with their furniture and farming tools and Bibles stowed in their wagons. They knew nothing about the gold, having left civilization behind at the Missouri River before the news arrived. There were two large wagon trains, one guided by the old trapper James Clyman and the other by Joseph Chiles, plus several smaller pack trains, one of which was led by Peter Lassen. Most of these emigrants encountered Henry Bigler and his eastbound Mormon caravan along the Humboldt River between Salt Lake and the Sierra Nevadas. The Mormons gave them the word.

They were nonetheless unready for what they found when they arrived. "My little girls can make from 5 to 25 dollars per day washing gold in pans," Michael McClellan wrote breathlessly to a friend in Missouri. "My average income this winter will be about $150 per day." McClellan, a member of the Chiles party, sold his trail-worn wagon and three yoke of oxen for $1,000. The biggest haul he had heard of was forty pounds ($10,240) in two days. "Gold is nothing more thought of than dirt," he wrote. "There is no credit asked or given, the transactions are all based on gold."

California fascinated and repelled him. A man was a fool to resist such a tidal wave of temptation, but what he knew best was farming. He allowed that he would stay until he made a fortune, which shouldn't take long, and then scoot back to Missouri. "I do not like this country," he declared. "I do not like the climate, and more than all I abhor and detest the society. I never expect to sow a seed or plant a grain in this country." Instead he bought a half-interest in the hotel at Sutter's fort.

Mining in the fall was a race against rain; through October and November the diggers worked with one eye on the sky. The coming of the rainy season transformed dusty gulches into freshets; placid streams became foaming cascades which swamped the paydirt in sand and gravel bars. Life in the camps became cold, wet, and miserable. The trouble was that the fall rains were impossible to predict in the Sierra foothills; they might come in late October one year and hold off until Christmas or even later the next. But there could be no mistaking their arrival when they did come: rarely did it rain for a refreshing hour or two or even a single day; it rained for day after drenching, hope-destroying day, swelling rivers and saturating valleys and making quagmires out of roads. Every day a miner could work gave him a little more insurance against the onset of the idle season.

The Reverend Colton tarried on the Stanislaus until mid-November, enjoying the color and music of the strangest life he had ever beheld. The nightly concert began with a clanging of kettles and pans as the miners attacked their cooking gear. Muskets thundered into the fire-softened night. At last there was only "the dirge of the pines, murmuring in the night-wind."

Colton watched the miners drifting from ravine to ravine like leaves in the wind. The sight propelled him into a spasm of alliteration: such a "restless, roving, rummaging, ragged multitude," he wrote, "never before roared in the rookeries of man."

Chester Lyman, like Colton a Yale-educated churchman, turned up at the Stanislaus diggings in the fall with a load of merchandise. Although he was delighted to have cleared $450 in a week, Lyman perceived that the real profiteers were the grogshop entrepreneurs, one of whom confided that he made $1,000 a day selling "the ardent" at $2 a shot. Gamblers had also arrived. The Mexican passion for gambling, especially for the card game called monte, was so intense that Colton concluded it was the only reason a Mexican mined—"the rallying thought which wakes with him in the morning, which accompanies him through the day, and which floats through his dreams at night." Monte was anything but complicated: the dealer, or "banker," turned over four cards; the players selected two and bet on which would come up first in the remainder of the deck. One of Antonio Coronel's friends set up a monte bank with a bowlful of Stanislaus gold, using a wool blanket for a table, and lost his entire stake in one night.

Wagonloads of provisions rolled into camp at intervals from the fast-growing town on the San Joaquin that Charles Weber had named Stockton. The prices were of course outrageous—$2 a pound for sugar, $4 for coffee, $20 for a quart of rum. Indians paid even more; cheating the natives was standard mining-camp practice. Lyman noticed that traders substituted a two-ounce weight for the regular one-ounce piece when dealing with Indians; this was known as a "Digger ounce."

Governor Mason and his aide Lieutenant Sherman, the future scourge of Georgia, also returned to the foothills in the fall, this time with a commercial objective. In partnership with two other men, the two officers invested in a Coloma store. They earned about $1,500 each in two months. Making a quick jaunt around the mines, Sherman found "many fine snug log cabins" at Dry Diggings and counted at least four women in the camps. One of them, a Mrs. Lucy Eager, told him she planned to stay until she had $20,000.

Sherman's military reflexes kept him alert for deserters, but he knew he could do nothing if he found any: manpower was lacking. It was cold comfort to learn that a half-dozen miners had hurriedly departed one camp the night he arrived. Navy men were abandoning ship too. Commodore Thomas Jones placed a newspaper ad which used the only language then understood. His headline was "$40,000—A New Gold Discovery." The patient reader learned that the navy would pay a bounty of $200 a head for the delivery of deserters, up to a maximum of $40,000, but there were no takers.

Crime was increasing as well. One man was shot and another knifed in the same Sutter's fort saloon within three weeks. Heinrich Lienhard said that a five-man band of horse thieves was operating out of the fort. Rustlers had thinned out the once vast herds of JAS-branded Sutter cattle.

The most appalling crime occurred in November in the sleepy little mission town of San Miguel, midway between Monterey and Santa Barbara. Three deserters from the ship-of-war *Warren* and two ex-soldiers methodically butchered an old settler named William Reed, three members of his family, and six servants. Reed, a genial ex-seaman, had made the mistake of showing off the gold he had earned by selling sheep in the mines. A posse chased the slayers to Santa Barbara and killed two; the other three were captured, tried, and promptly executed.

By late November both the rains and the exodus from the mines were in full flood. Colton went home to Monterey to meditate on what he had witnessed. The Californios on the Stanislaus abandoned their glorious canyon and decamped for San Jose. But none of this distracted Edward Buffum. He was just getting started.

Buffum's first foray into the mines was at Foster's Bar on the Yuba, a short distance upstream from where Peter Burnett was working at Long Bar. He found color, but the good claims all seemed to be taken, the labor was draining, and he had neglected to bring a rocker. He and his friends moved to Weber Creek, where they bought a cabin—"a little box of unhewn logs, about twenty feet long by ten wide"—for $500. "The terms, however, were accommodating, being ten days' credit for the whole amount." They were confident they could dig up the price in the allotted time, and they did.

Here at last was El Dorado. Buffum tasted the miner's rapture on his second day. He dug down to bedrock and found a crevice. "It appeared to be filled with a hard, bluish clay and gravel, which I took out with my knife, and there at the bottom, strewn along the whole length of the rock, was bright, yellow gold. Eureka! Oh, how my heart beat! I sat still and looked at it some minutes before I touched it, greedily drinking in the pleasure of gazing upon gold that was in my very grasp, and feeling a sort of independent bravado in allowing it to remain there." He finally succumbed and scooped it out, sprinted to his cabin and found he had made $31.

Buffum and his partners earned enough to pay off their mortgage in about three days. Then they heard that the take on the Middle Fork of the American, a wild province of steep cliffs and almost impenetrable canyons, was even greater. "The news was too blooming" to resist. Stopping at Coloma for supplies, they hiked thirty miles of trackless, roller-coaster terrain to the new diggings. The final descent was nearly perpendicular.

For once the rumors were true. The Middle Fork was even richer than Weber Creek, and empty to boot. Buffum had the sensation that "we had stolen away from the peopled world and were living in an obscure corner"—a secret garden of gold. They struck paydirt immediately: Buffum alone found $464 worth of nuggets and dust in a single day. He knew enough geology to realize that the rain washed the gold down from the mountains and that the ore rested "in any pocket or crevice that can prevent it from being washed further."

Buffum had been lucky as well as smart: in this area the severe rains had held off so far—but now they came. He crawled into a shallow cave and waited, "listening to the solemn music of the swollen river rushing rapidly by us and the big rain torrents pouring upon its breast." The rain continued without letup for three days, elevating the river by seven feet. They could see the water line from previous winters high up the canyon wall. On the fourth day they caucused and decided to leave, feeling like defectors from Paradise. Ruefully they began the rugged and slippery climb out of the canyon and the trek back to Weber Creek.

For all practical purposes the 1848 mining season was over. From November on a traveler risked snow in these mountains; shelter was essential. The majority of the five thousand–odd men who had dug gold during this spectacular year were back in the coast towns or the water-logged lowlands. They could use some rest. The best estimates are that their average profit was slightly more than $1,000 per man between June and November. The California hills had already yielded more than $3.7 million worth of gold.

But where had it gone? The most likely calculation is that about $1 million remained in California, most of it in the possession of Sam Brannan and other merchants. Nearly half of the gold was shipped to Chile and Peru in exchange for trade goods, another $400,000 went to the East Coast, and $300,000 to Britain. The remainder floated through the Golden Gate to such outposts of trade as Honolulu, Panama, and Mazatlán in Mexico. The bulk of California's first golden harvest now rested in the vaults of foreign businessmen.

LIEUTENANT Lucien Loeser, the army courier bearing Governor Mason's report and the tea caddy full of gold, stepped ashore on the levee at New Orleans on November 23. Loeser and his civilian companion, David Carter, arrived on the schooner *Desdemona* from Jamaica, the fourth vessel to carry them on their switchback course from Monterey. They had taken one ship to Peru, a second to Panama, crossed the Isthmus, and then sailed to Jamaica.

Governor Mason had taken the precaution of sending a duplicate copy of his report with another messenger, who left Monterey about two weeks after Loeser did. This second dispatch-bearer moved faster; probably crossing Mexico, as Beale had done two months earlier, he arrived in Washington on November 22, the day before Loeser and Carter reached New Orleans. Loeser, however, had the gold.

The New Orleans *Daily Picayune* published an interview with Carter which confirmed the rumored El Dorado. Carter's account accentuated the negative: digging was both perilous and laborious, he said, and "large numbers" of miners had perished. There was gold, true, but the stories of its abundance were exaggerated; in addition the gold was seriously harming California's economy. But to this gloomy report the *Picayune* annexed a reprint of the *Californian*'s August 14 article on the mines, which contradicted much of what Carter said. Did he say the work was man-killing? The *Californian* noted that "in one part of the mines called the 'dry diggins' no other implement is necessary than an ordinary sheath knife to pick the gold from the rocks." The New Orleans *Evening Mercury* found Loeser more sanguine: the lieutenant verified "the most glowing accounts heretofore received in the States." Loeser reported his arrival to the War Department by telegraph. The two men and their tea caddy then left for Washington.

The duplicate copy of the Mason report was immediately delivered to the lame-duck President, James Knox Polk. Polk, his health failing, had been denied renomination by the Democrats in favor of Senator Lewis Cass of Michigan. Cass had then lost the general election to the Whig candidate, the Mexican War hero Zachary Taylor—"Old Rough and Ready." Polk was preparing his final message to Congress when he received Mason's detailed confirmation of the gold discovery.

News of the Mason report's explosive contents leaked into the eastern press within days. The newspapers now shed their skepticism. The editors knew that Mason was no hysteric; he was the government's highest-ranking officer in California, a stolid soldier well-known in the capital, and a member of a preeminent colonial family. And Mason did much more than report a profusion of gold; he described the camps, cited prices, revealed the diggers' daily profits—all in specific and astonishing detail;

the numbers—preposterous but undeniable—banished any lingering doubts. The readers of the Albany (N.Y.) *Argus* got a sample of the new journalistic tone. Mason's reports, the paper said, told of "astonishing developments which would be incredible if not vouched for by him. . . . He thinks the quantity exhaustless, and that the amount which will be gathered there would pay the expenses of the Mexican War one hundred times over. . . ."

The New York *Herald*, in its review of the year 1848, would later pinpoint November 24, exactly ten months after James Marshall found the first flakes, as the day "California gold fever broke out in New York." The gold mania whirled through the East and South as it had raced down the California coast. Newspapers in one city after another—Baltimore, Boston, Philadelphia, Washington, New Orleans—reported a rising crescendo of excitement. Philadelphia had "a great many anxious inquiries about the shortest way and easiest mode of getting there." Boston was "rising to fever heat." In Washington the gold was "a prolific source of debate in the social circles of the city."

Excited groups of men clustered on street corners and argued about how to reach California. Ships advertised as ready for immediate departure. A hundred men assembled in Boston to form an "association" to travel to California and dig gold. Traders made plans to ship merchandise to the golden coast.

The country was now ready to read Walter Colton's florid letters with fresh eyes, and the Monterey chaplain delivered as if on cue. "The people are running over the country and picking [gold] out of the earth here and there," he wrote to the New York *Journal of Commerce*, "just as a thousand hogs, let loose in a forest, would root up ground nuts." Colton knew seven men who had gathered *275 pounds* on the Feather River, "so stick a pin there." He knew ten others who had made $1,500 each in a fortnight, "so stick another pin there. I know another man who got out of a basin in a rock not larger than a wash bowl, two pounds and a half of gold in fifteen minutes—so stick another pin there." And these *nouveau* nabobs were "plain matter-of-fact men, men who open a vein of gold just as coolly as you would a potato hill."

On December 1 the steamer *Falcon*, first of the three New York–to–Chagres ships to be ready to sail, fired up her boilers and chugged through the New York Narrows carrying ninety-five passengers for the Isthmus of Panama. This was only about half of the ship's capacity, despite the fact that the *Falcon* was the first Panama-bound vessel to depart New York since the onset of the gold fever. It was still early, but only slightly: the *Falcon* would be the last ship to leave the city without a full passenger load for many months. And this deficiency would be remedied in two weeks when she docked at New Orleans.

The *Falcon* was well protected spiritually: no fewer than four men of the cloth were aboard, all missionaries to the godless barrens of California. The New York *Tribune* explained that their goal was to "recall the attention of the multitudes rushing to that El Dorado to the fact that there is something more valuable than gold." They did not have to wait long to begin work. There was heavy gambling in the ship's saloon. Several passengers sinned shamelessly during an eight-hour stop at Charleston, South Carolina, landing in jail for drunkenness and staying there overnight. But the ministers rejoiced in the attendance at Sunday services on deck. At Havana the passengers enjoyed a military band concert and their rides in a "volante," a horse-drawn carriage with an apron discreetly draped between horse and passengers. Three days later they were in New Orleans, loading up with what one voyager described as "the most excited mass of moral floodwood that ever came down the Mississippi"; more than two hundred people jammed the ship for the nine-day cruise to Chagres. The New Orleans passengers, the *Picayune* observed, brought along a "liberal supply of the good things of life."

On December 5, President Polk delivered his message to Congress, and newspapers printed the text the following day. The news from California came midway through the speech: "It was known that mines of the precious metals existed to a considerable extent in California at the time of its acquisition," he declared (though he gave no evidence for this). "Recent discoveries render it probable that these mines are more extensive and valuable than was anticipated. The accounts of the abundance of gold in that territory are of such an extraordinary character as would scarcely command belief were they not corroborated by the authentic reports of officers in the public service. . . ." Polk urged the creation of a United States mint in California and recommended that Congress establish a territorial government to replace the military administration. He also passed on Mason's suggestion that soldiers on California duty be given a sizable raise. Polk would miss the subsequent acts in the California drama: he died in June 1849, at the age of fifty-three.

Loeser and Carter, carrying the tangible proof, finally reached Washington on December 7. Samples were promptly placed on exhibition in the library of the War Department, where reporters hurried to get a look. The New York *Tribune* man was convinced: "Any goose who could talk of 'mica' after seeing these specimens would not be worth noticing; it is no more like mica than it is like cheese." The bulk of Loeser's cargo was dispatched to the U. S. Mint in Philadelphia to be assayed. The next day Secretary of War William Marcy received a one-word telegram from his messenger at the mint: "Genuine." The gold was found to have an average fineness of .894, almost equal to the standard for coins. It was valued at $3,910.10. Marcy said that some of it would be used for military medals.

The Mason report was published in the *Tribune* and other papers on December 8. Lieutenant Loeser, interviewed by a New York reporter, confessed that he was relieved to be rid of the gold. The stock market rose across the board; Treasury notes were up to 7½ percent from a low of just over 2½. Thousands flocked to the War Department to view the samples on display. Editorials pulled out the few remaining stops. "Here is El Dorado, of which Ponce de Leon and his companions so vividly dreamed," the Philadelphia *Sunday Dispatch* said. Horace Greeley of the New York *Tribune* proclaimed the dawning of "the Age of Gold." "Whatever else they may lack," he wrote, "our children will not be destitute of gold." The Baltimore *Sun*, sounding a lonely, almost churlish note of lingering skepticism, wondered why anyone would leave California if it was all that rich. The *Sun* was the eastern counterpart of Edward Kemble's *California Star*.

Inevitably the tempo became too fast for mere facts, fantastic as the facts had seemed only a month earlier. Reports from California now spoke of "lumps the size of a man's hand" and "an inexhaustible supply." When a returned Californian named Joseph Cutting appeared in New Orleans in December, the *Picayune* noted casually that "gold can be had in California with less labor than in any other part of the world."

The editor of the *Scientific American*, a recently converted skeptic, wrote that "every 20th person we meet on the street is bound for California." The steamer *Oregon* was booked solid for her first voyage to Chagres. Even though the ship was to continue around the Horn to Panama City and San Francisco, most ticket buyers planned to cross the Isthmus and catch the northbound *California* on the Pacific side. Sailing-ship owners hurriedly fitted up their vessels for either the grueling, five-to-seven-month marathon around the Horn or the sprint to Chagres. The bark *J. W. Coffin* cleared Boston for Chagres on December 7. The schooner *Macon* left New Orleans for the Isthmus on the tenth, carrying sixty passengers. The bark *John Benson* sailed from New York on the eleventh with sixty more for Panama. After that sailings were almost daily.

Enterprising merchants realized that their bonanzas were already at hand. A Boston emporium claimed to have fifty clerks specializing in necessities for the California traveler. These included "Spanish or California cloaks" which doubled as blankets ($3.50 to $15), "Feather River mining coats" ($6.50 to $12), "Captain Sutter's long mining waistcoats" ($3–$3.50), "Isthmus bags" for pack mules, India rubber capes, and mosquito nets. Daguerreotype shops such as Matthew Brady's at 205–7 Broadway, New York, had a rush of customers who wanted a likeness to leave behind. Bakers and gunsmiths could not keep up with the demand for bread and weapons. An ad headlined HO! HO! HO! FOR CALIFORNIA! suggested sensibly that departing gold seekers should not forget "monuments and tombstones," currently available at reduced rates.

The speed and fervor of the response in the eastern cities suggested that men had hesitated only because the final, irrefutable confirmation provided by the President's speech had been lacking: now the time was finally ripe. The America of 1848 was a youthful and eager society, bursting with unproven confidence and bravado. New inventions, technology, and industries were blooming constantly. The Mexican War had added vast new territories to the nation, and the veterans of that war were newly home. And now came this irresistible opportunity for adventure, for success—for *action*. A similar gold strike at another time might have generated only a fraction of the excitement that gripped the East. The gold rush suited its time; it was a perfect confluence of the tangible and the intangible, the precipitating event and the welcoming spirit.

These were men with a righteous passion for democratic assembly; the impulse to organize now seized them by the thousands. Companies with between a dozen and 150 members—invariably male, predominantly youthful—quickly formed, complete with constitutions and bylaws and membership fees. The 150-strong Boston and California Mining Company, which included dozens of college graduates and professional men, began meeting in mid-December to discuss the purchase of a ship and supplies. Similar companies emerged in Hartford, New York, Albany, Virginia, and elsewhere.

"The gold mania rages with intense vigor," the New York *Herald* summarized on December 11, "and is carrying off its victims hourly and daily." The editorial added that another affliction had also arrived on the East Coast, this one from Europe. It was cholera, the often-fatal intestinal disease. "The cholera is entirely overlooked in this new excitement," the *Herald* remarked.

A WINTER carpet of green velvet spread over the Sacramento Valley. The frenzy of the past six months had not changed the appearance of the valley; it still looked fresh and lush and virginal. The only sign of man at the Sacramento River embarcadero, where the town of Sacramento would soon leap to life, was a single shanty built from the timbers of an abandoned ship. Groves of sycamores and live oaks crowded close to the riverbank and nodded over the three-mile trail to Sutter's Fort. The fort had degenerated into a cluster of grogshops and trading posts where wintering miners fetched supplies and drank brandy at 50 cents a glass. Ale sold for $5 a bottle, and a jovial artisan named Wadleigh was earning a fortune by making and selling tin pans at an ounce apiece. The atmosphere was raucously masculine: if a man offered to buy a stranger a drink the stranger accepted with thanks or risked a gunfight. The filmy fabric of law emerged only in the direst emergencies, and even then it bore little resemblance to civilized notions of justice.

In December a storekeeper known as "Philosopher" Pickett shot and killed an Oregonian named Isaac Alderman after an argument over a gate that Pickett had built. The alcalde promptly resigned. Sam Brannan called a public meeting to organize a trial. He was chosen to be the judge. When no one else was willing to be prosecutor, Brannan took that job too. A jury was empaneled and a defense attorney appointed. Judge, jury, witnesses, and defendant all drank freely during the trial, which ended in a hung jury. A second jury acquitted Pickett on grounds of self-defense.

THE *California* puffed into the beautiful mountain-rimmed harbor at Valparaiso, Chile, on December 20. The steamship's six-day passage through the Strait of Magellan had been an ordeal of sudden storms, precipitous tides, and long waits at anchor; at one point the ship dragged anchor and barely escaped running aground. Dozens of Chileans besieged the shipping agent for tickets to San Francisco, but Captain Forbes refused to accept any passengers; he knew now that there would be a mob waiting in Panama. The only man to come aboard during the short pause at Valparaiso was Captain John Marshall, who would soon replace the ailing Forbes as skipper. On December 22 the still-empty vessel sailed north, headed for Peru, Panama, and pandemonium.

OH! SUSANNA

BY BUNGO UP THE CHAGRES

THE CROWD on the old wharf at Salem stirred as they saw the three passengers climb to the quarterdeck of the crisp little bark *Eliza.* The ship, bound for California via Cape Horn, was a few minutes away from casting off. It was two days before Christmas. One of the boys on deck held up a hand and then the three began singing:

I came from Salem City with my washbowl on my knee . . .

People in the crowd smiled in recognition. The tune was "Oh! Susanna," the most popular minstrel song of the day. The words—most of them anyway—were their own; a group of young men from Salem had written them for the occasion.

I'm going to Californ-i-a, the gold dust for to see.
It rained all night the day I left, the weather it was dry.
The sun so hot I froze to death—Oh brothers, don't you cry!
Oh! California, that's the land for me.
I'm going to Sacramento with my washbowl on my knee . . .

The crowd fell still, listening to the eager voices. These were Salem boys, their boys. When would they see them again? California! California was the blank edge of the map, a territory perched on the fringe of the continent and the fringe of their consciousness.

I thought of all the pleasant times we've had together here,
I thought I ort to cry a bit, but couldn't find a tear.
The pilot bread was in my mouth, the gold dust in my eye.
And though I'm going far away, dear brothers, don't you cry!
Oh, California, that's the land for me,
I'm going to Sacramento with my washbowl on my knee . . .

Crewmen moved briskly along the railings, gathering in the heavy mooring lines. In moments the *Eliza* would be free and looking for wind. So would the boys from Salem. Full of themselves now, they sailed into the final verse:

I soon shall be in Francisco, and then I'll look all round,
And when I see the gold lumps there I'll pick them off the ground.
I'll scrape the mountains clean, my boys, I'll drain the rivers dry,
A pocket full of rocks bring home, so brothers, don't you cry!
Oh! California, that's the land for me,
I'm going to Sacramento with my washbowl on my knee.

The song, in this and a dozen other versions, would almost instantly become the anthem of the gold rush, the marching music for a restless and leaderless army. Now, as the tune's final words died on the water, the crowd ashore erupted in cheers. "Let's give them three times three," someone shouted. The waving throng responded with three cheers three times in succession. Within minutes the little craft was gone, out of sight, headed across Massachusetts Bay on a seventeen-thousand-mile voyage to the other side of the world.

These Americans beginning the rush west were willing to believe that they could do anything they put their minds to. Hadn't they just won a war? Wasn't the country prosperous? Weren't the signs of progress—the railroads, the steamboats, the telegraph—everywhere around them? Now they had the breadth of a continent in which to flex their muscles and stretch their arms. Why, the gold in California was no more than they deserved. Why else would it lie undiscovered so long, eluding the Mexicans, as if waiting for the Yankee eyes of old Jim Marshall? A man had to be a fool or, worse, a ne'er-do-well, to ignore a chance like this. They thought of themselves as "go-ahead boys." Obey the impulse and go! He who hesitates is stuck behind the plow, chained to the counter at the dry-goods store, locked behind the bank window. The gold discovery, a British diplomat wrote home, was producing one of those popular manias that sporadically seized a people "so passionately addicted to all money-making pursuits as the Americans."

The westering bravos were a crazy quilt of contradictions. Their infatuation with democracy, in principle and especially in form, was extravagant; they loved to convene, to caucus, to associate and incorporate; yet their democratic tolerance was invariably restricted to the white-skinned and English-speaking. They were expansionists who believed in America's "Manifest Destiny," yet most were home lovers who had never traveled more than a hundred miles from their birthplace. They honored the Sabbath and proclaimed their faith, even as they reached for the whiskey and cut the cards. Like Americans before and since, they were both idealists and materialists. Their love of country was intense: nothing pleased them more than a patriotic oration, the flossier the better. They bragged interminably. And they were, often enough, as generous as their land.

Gold was not just the dominant subject of this Christmas season in the East, it was the only subject. Newspapers were filled with it. Ministers preached about it. Teachers discussed it with their classes. Stockbrokers gambled on it. Merchants cashed in on it. It was a tide which engulfed everyone. Nothing remotely like it had ever happened in America.

A West Point professor named Boynton drew overflow crowds to New York's Broadway Tabernacle with a series of three lectures on "The structure and formation of the earth," particularly its gold-bearing zones. The climax of Boynton's talk (admission 25 cents; illustrated with paintings) came when he declared that there would be gold in California for at least another one thousand years. This precipitated a thunderous ovation. Boynton advised would-be argonauts to travel in companies of ten or more for safety's sake.

The ministerial theme was the moral shortsightedness of "hasting to be rich." "Gold will not save you any of the pains that go to make life honorable," the Unitarian Nathaniel Frothingham told his Boston congregation on December 17. There was no honor in poverty, the pastor added, but "gold cannot gild a disgrace, it cannot bribe the fate of the next hour. . . . Sickness and sorrow will make no exchanges with it."

There were plenty of merchants willing to make exchanges. A newspaper advertisement with the headline GOLD! GOLD! HURRAH FOR CALIFORNIA! turned out to be huckstering "Wright's Indian vegetable pills," good for almost any malady in any clime. Other ads extolled wax taper matches, portable sheet-iron houses, money belts designed for gold, and "California saddles." The most bizarre offering was a concoction called California Gold Grease, which sold for $10 a box. The purchaser was directed to apply the grease liberally to his body and then roll down a gold-spangled hill; "gold and nothing else" would adhere to his skin.

Exporters made a more direct bid for California gold. A New York *Journal of Commerce* survey of California-bound cargoes in December found that El Dorado would soon be deluged with 3,000 pieces of calico for dresses (for fewer than a thousand women), 12,000 Panama hats, 30,000 pairs of shoes, and enough broadcloth to clothe the populace for five years. There were also a hundred lace veils which, as the *Journal* noted helpfully, might also be used as sieves in gold washing.

The ships now sailing daily were laden with passengers, their hastily assembled outfits, trade goods, and a few items to smooth the troubled waters: the brig *Saltillo* left Boston on December 22 with seventeen passengers plus several crates of champagne, brandy, gin, whiskey, wine, and cider. The New England men preferred the route around the Horn; they had spent their lives in sight of the sea and were familiar with its moods; the Horn voyage was also cheaper. The *Eliza* and her trio of choristers set sail from Salem on the twenty-third, the same day that the steamer *Crescent City*, bearing New York *Herald* correspondent Stephen Branch, 129 other men, and one woman steward, departed lower Manhattan for Panama. On Christmas Eve came the departure of the *Neumpha*, carrying the first delegation of gold hunters to choose the Mexico route so swiftly traveled by Ned Beale. The bark carried eighty-one well-armed adventurers for Veracruz.

From the beginning there were men of substance on the passenger manifests. The cost of the voyage—from as little as $150 for the Cape Horn trip to $420 for first-class passage via Panama—eliminated most laboring men. Eventually the gold rush would attract all classes, but at the outset the voyagers were likely to be merchants, self-employed artisans, farmers with a savings account, or professional men like Elisha Oscar Crosby. Crosby was a thirty-year-old New York lawyer whose clients included the owners of the Pacific Mail line, a connection that wouldn't hurt him when it came to getting from Panama to California. On Christmas morning he found himself among a cold, forlorn, and snow-spattered crowd on the deck of the undersized old steamer *Isthmus*, about to sail for the unknown terrors of Panama from Cortlandt Street pier in New York. Crosby had read accounts of the Isthmus which made it sound like a quagmire of death and disease, but his fire was up and his motor running. "They might as well have attempted to stop a band of wild horses," he wrote in his journal.

The *Herald* published the first of four special issues on California on December 26, complete with an enthusiastic map which put the distance from Monterey to the Coloma sawmill at twenty-five miles (it was actually 165). *The Gold Regions of California*, a 25-cent paperback guidebook by New York *Tribune* writer G. G. Foster, was already on sale in New York bookstores. Foster's was a cut-and-paste compendium of California facts and lore, the first and best of dozens of similar guides to appear during the winter. The author struggled bravely to maintain his perspective, but repeatedly slipped into hyberbole. Gold digging was hard work, he noted, but anyone up to it could collect "a competency for his old age and a handsome legacy for his children." He also fretted about the effects of American civilization on bucolic California: "With our magnificent cities, plantations, schools, colleges, manufactories, newspapers and mechanics' shops will doubtless go lawyers and licentiousness, prostitution and petty larceny, smallpox and the venereal, rheumatism and intemperance, and the whole horrid train of civilized vices and diseases." It was a grim prediction, and it was realized in almost every particular.

Three Weeks in the Gold Mines, by "Henry Simpson," which also appeared before the year was out, was the first gold rush hoax. Seasoned with just enough fact to be plausible, the book recorded the wanderings of a discharged army veteran who found gold wherever he looked, including a piece "as large and as thick as my double hands outspread." The unidentified "Simpson" repeatedly betrays his ignorance of California geography, but few eastern readers knew enough to doubt him; the book was still being taken for fact a generation later.

"Who should go to California?" Horace Greeley's *Tribune* asked itself in late December. Not the well fixed or those with families, it said, nor the nervous or overly fastidious, but "young men of moderate means and resolute energies," either single or with adventurous wives. "Give the first chance at the gold region to those who have as yet had no chance elsewhere." The Panama route was the easiest, the *Tribune* said, providing one had money and a ticket; with little reliable information to go on, the paper recommended the Mexico crossing via Veracruz as the best of the overland routes; the Oregon and Santa Fe trails were both tedious and perilous.

The great majority of men now embarking for California were traveling in companies. These associations operated on the principle of each member's contributing an equal sum and each receiving an identical share of the profits. The main advantage of traveling in company was the safety in numbers, especially on the overland routes. It also offered an apprehensive adventurer the comforting assurance that he would be looked after. In addition it was a way to raise enough front money to buy a ship and supplies and often trade goods as well.

Most companies had elaborate "articles of association" similar to those of the Brothers Mining and Trading Company of New Haven. The articles specified a membership fee of $200, established a system of self-government, demanded good moral character and physical condition, and forbade liquor, gambling, and labor on the Sabbath. The directors would procure a ship and provisions. Every member would put his daily take in the general fund, from which the profit would be distributed evenly and regularly. Many companies permitted proxy agreements whereby a man with capital bankrolled an impecunious would-be miner in exchange for half his proceeds.

The company names were a litany of American places. They proclaimed the roots of the migrating mass: the Green Mountain Mining and Trading Company, the Wisconsin Blues, the Rhode Island Hope, the Shawmut and California, the Nantucket, the Mattapoisett, the Niagara and the Kennebec, the Cayuga and Charlestown and Sag Harbor. Some took the names of their ships—the Emily Bourne company, the Sarah Parker, the Naumkeag—while others identified themselves with heroes—the Kit Carson Association, the Frémont company. A few chose names for their masculine, adventurous sound—the Wolverine Rangers, the Cape Ann Pioneers, the Helltown Greasers.

Albert Lyman of the Connecticut Mining and Trading Company copied his group's roster into his journal. The catalog of ages, occupations and marital status presents a fair picture of a gold rush company: the oldest of the 25 members was fifty, the youngest twenty-one; 16 were in their twenties and 7 more in their thirties; 8 were married and 17 single; they were predominantly artisans—brassworkers and sailmakers and joiners and mechanics, along with two clerks, two doctors, a manufacturer and a solitary "gentleman." The surnames were overwhelmingly Anglo-Saxon. The skipper of their schooner, Charles Falkenburg, was only twenty-three.

THE GOLD MANIA had by now become an international phenomenon. The first reaction of the British press had been to denounce the gold reports as "Yankee humbug," but the editorial blessing of the London *Times* converted the faithless and sparked a rush. A Royal Mail steamship sailed in the second week of January with more than a hundred shovel-toting passengers for Chagres. At least five companies were immediately formed. "John Bull has been actually mad, crazy, and bewildered," a Liverpool correspondent wrote. "Nothing is heard or talked about but the new El Dorado."

The diehard British debunkers either snarled or turned to satire. "The people that believe these things are only fools," the Liverpool *Mail* sneered, "who . . . richly deserve to be cheated." What was billed as "a new gold song," to the tune of "Yankee Doodle," appeared on January 6:

> *Now's the time to change your clime, give up work and tasking:*
> *All who choose be rich as Jews, even without asking.*
> *California's precious earth turns the new world frantic:*
> *Sell your traps and take a berth across the wild Atlantic.*
> *Every one who digs and delves, all whose arms are brawny,*
> *Take a pick and help yourselves—off to Californy . . .*
>
> *How this flush of gold will end we have statements ample;*
> *Perhaps a few sacks they will send, only for a sample.*
> *But we hope this golden move really is all true, sirs.*
> *Else will Yankee Doodle prove a Yankee doodle doo, sirs.*
> *Every one who digs or delves, stout and tough and brawny,*
> *Buy a pick and help yourselves—off to Californy.*

The first French mention of California gold had appeared in November. In January a ship was announced for San Francisco, and a company, "Expédition française pour les mines d'or de Sacramento," was selling shares. The gold rush would ultimately carry off Frenchmen by the thousands, many of them the beneficiaries of a grandiose lottery; the French in turn would have a great impact on California. Halfway around the world in Australia, the first ship of gold seekers sailed from Sydney on January 9; the second followed twelve days later.

Newspapers in the eastern United States began to publish state-by-state roundups of gold rush news in mid-January. They reported that twenty-three ships carrying 1,356 passengers left eastern and southern ports in the five days between the twelfth and sixteenth of January. A group from Springfield, Massachusetts, planned to sail across the Gulf of Mexico and then up the Rio Grande River to Paso del Norte, later known as El Paso; no one told them that the upstream Rio Grande was often nothing but mud or dust. The graceful *Greyhound* of Baltimore, one of the first of the streamlined new clipper ships, was loading freight and passengers for what would be the quickest trip around the Horn in 1849—only 112 days. Other ships were considerably less promising. The directors of a Massachusetts insurance firm, having inspected several California-bound vessels, declined to sell life insurance to passengers for the gold coast.

The voyagers themselves sometimes had intimations of disaster. A New York *Herald* reporter witnessed a poignant scene at the January 16 sailing of the bark *Peytona*. A beautiful young blonde, perhaps seventeen years old, "with remarkably rosy cheeks, a lip the bee might swoon on, and soft dark eyes," was staring intently at a youth leaning over the taffrail. Tears rolled down her cheeks as the ship began to move. She stretched out her hands and "in a most thrilling, plaintive whisper, said, 'Charley, ain't you sorry now?'

"The color fled from Charley's cheeks," the *Herald* man wrote, "his pale lips quivered a moment, and then he turned, without speaking, to hide himself and his tears in the cabin."

Prominent names appeared on the passenger lists. Scions of several fine old New York families—Livingston, Schermerhorn, Beekman—sailed in the *Christoval Colon*. Caleb Lyon, a well-known poet and later diplomat and governor of Idaho Territory, was on the *Tarolinta*, along with New York publisher Jonas Winchester. The financier Sam Ward was going out to establish a bank in California. Twenty young men from the "first families" of Lowell, Massachusetts, departed on the bark *Oxford*.

The *Edward Everett* carried the 150 lucky members of the Boston and California Joint Stock Mining and Trading Company, the best organized and best equipped of the early companies. The Boston men were young—120 of them were under thirty—and capable: there were 4 doctors, 15 other professional men, 8 whaling captains, a number of businessmen, and 76 mechanics. They bore such Yankee names as Bradford, Webster, Phelps, Curtis, Wingate, and Pratt. They had named their ship after the president of Harvard College, who would subsequently become a U.S. senator and the greatest orator of the day. The ship's cargo holds contained a small steamboat, four steam engines, the frames of two houses, wagons and shovels and wheelbarrows and enough food for two years.

The Sunday before they sailed the Boston boys attended a special service at the Ashburton Place Church. They listened, squirming in their seats and sneaking glances at each other, as speaker after speaker admonished them to remember their heritage. One company member, a former journalist named William Thomes, left an irreverent account of the service:

"The Rev. Mr. Kirk . . . said we were going to a far country where all were in ignorance and sin and we should take our Bibles in one hand and our good New England civilization in the other and conquer all the wickedness that stood in our path. We promised to follow his advice. Mr. Abbe . . . gave to each of us a Bible. He told us when the good books were presented that we were going to a strange, immoral country and that we must take our Bibles in one hand and our New England civilization in the other and implant our principles on the soil. The Hon. Edward Everett . . . made us a present of 100 volumes as a library and in his letter conveying the gift said, 'You are going to a strange country. Take the Bible in one hand and your New England civilization in the other and make your mark on the people and country.' "

On the thirteenth the Bible-burdened *Everett* picked her way through the floating ice in Boston harbor and headed out to sea before an Arctic wind. Two-thirds of the passengers were almost immediately seasick.

THE STEAMSHIP *California*, eighty-three days out of New York, eased alongside the sandbar pier at Callao, Peru, on December 28. A burst of cannon fire announced her arrival. There were more fireworks as soon as the ailing Captain Cleaveland Forbes went ashore.

Forbes, who had refused to accept any passengers in Chile, learned that his company's agent in Peru, the Connecticut Yankee Richard Alsop, had sold sixty-nine tickets to California. Forbes, expecting a crowd when the ship reached Panama, saw trouble on the horizon, but Alsop promised that the Peruvians would sleep on deck if necessary. The ship's surgeon, Dr. A. B. Stout, thought that "influence prevailed," but he gave no specifics.

The gold fever had developed slowly in Peru. Governor Mason's emissary, Lucien Loeser, had brought the first word when he passed through in October. Two ships had sailed for California since then, but another had advertised and then canceled after a disappointing response. Many of the *California* ticket holders were British and American expatriates. Another was a wealthy landowner named Villanul, who booked passage for himself and a thirteen-man work party. The ship sailed on January 10. Panama City was a week away.

The steamy, green-carpeted Isthmus was about to begin its second incarnation as a golden highway: three centuries earlier the Spanish conquistadores had named it the *camino real*—the royal road—as they bore Peruvian treasure to the Caribbean side for shipment to Spain. Columbus had probed the Isthmian coast in his quest for a route to the Indies. Francis Drake and Henry Morgan had plundered its shores.

This narrow knot of land between the Pacific and the Caribbean blazed with the colors of the tropics and teemed with life. The forty-niners' route took them forty miles up the languorous Chagres River from the fetid village of Chagres on the Caribbean, then switched to a land trail through dense thickets and over jagged hills before emerging onto the broad savannas near Panama City. The thick and vivid vegetation beside the river was unlike anything these cold-country Yankees had ever seen. "Every shade of green, sombre and bright, mingles with rose-red, purple, white, yellow, orange, blue and pink in an endless varying kaleidoscope," wrote the historian Hubert Howe Bancroft, an 1852 Panama traveler. "Solemn palms, thick-leaved mangoes, bold majestic teaks and bounteous bananas are linked by crimson-blossomed parasites." The rain forest pressed so close to the river that its branches sometimes formed a canopy, protecting travelers from the burning afternoon sun. Silent crocodiles lolled on the muddy banks and lazily eyed high-stepping flamingoes.

Voyagers debarking at Chagres joined together in groups of between three and eight to hire twenty-five-foot-long canoes called bungos for the upstream trip. Awnings made from bamboo leaves and canvas shielded the rear of the boats from sun and rain. The easygoing, mahogany-colored boatmen kept their boats close to shore, cradling long poles against their bare shoulders and pushing them off the bottom. At intervals they would startle their passengers by shedding their loincloths and leaping into the dark water for a *baño*. An Isthmus guidebook warned gold seekers that it was sometimes difficult to persuade the boatmen to resume their stations after one of these refreshing dips.

The Chagres carried the pilgrims upriver to the thatch-and-bamboo high-country villages of Gorgona and Cruces, where the palms and broad-leaf evergreens gave way to tableland amid dark and rolling ranks of mountains. The rainy season here was from May to December, and during that time it rained at some point practically every day. A sodden blanket of humidity covered everything—drooping trees and brightly hued parrots and chittering monkeys, mud-choked gulleys and mangrove swamps and trailside huts. Steam rose from the water. The sense of inertia was palpable.

At Cruces, where the river veered north and travelers transferred to mules, the natives thought at first that the Yankees had come in conquest and drove their animals into the mountains. It took five days to persuade them to retrieve their horses and mules and rent them to the gringos. The twenty-mile trail to Panama, which the Spanish had once paved with stones, was now a tortuous up-and-down path so narrow in some places that it was passable by only one sure-footed mule at a time. The original stones had collected in mounds. The Spanish had chosen the straightest possible line: "It seems to lead directly over the hills in every case," an American wrote, "sometimes almost perpendicular."

American entrepreneurs had contemplated a railroad across the Isthmus even before the gold discovery, and American diplomats had gained transit rights across Panama in an 1846 treaty. Construction would begin in late 1850, and with the laying of the final track five years later it would be possible to cross the Isthmian corridor in four and a half hours. But in 1849 the Panama jungle was a largely unknown province where the accepted conventions of American life did not apply. One guidebook claimed that the combination of tropical fruit and alcohol would produce "fermentation in the bowels" and almost certain death. The Victorian Americans were repeatedly shocked at the casual dress of the tropics, where the women sometimes wore "a poor substitute for the Edenic apron." Everything—from the vegetation to the tropical sunsets— seemed overripe.

Because of its higher cost the Panama route attracted a slightly better-heeled clientele than either the passage around the Horn or the overland trek by pack or wagon train. The Isthmus was the path of New York brokers, Philadelphia lawyers, Boston bankers, and Mississippi River gamblers. But the Isthmus also reduced every traveler to the same level of discomfort and aggravation.

By early January the first wave of forty-niners was already in Panama City, the ancient Spanish port on the Pacific which was now a city of about eight thousand. Passengers on the *Falcon*, the first ship of gold seekers to arrive, paid $40 for the three-day bungo ride to Cruces. Their bill for a night in a hammock at a riverside hut was $2 each, but the inn-keeper accepted the quarters they proffered without question. Their hosts also charged 50 cents for a chicken but $2 for the pot to cook it in.

The colors and sounds and smells of the jungle impressed them as strange and gorgeous and alarming, mostly alarming. "The equator chil-dren are yelling and squalling in the contiguous hut," wrote the New York *Herald*'s Stephen Branch, who had arrived on the *Crescent City*. "The pigs are squealing, the ducks cackling and the reptiles on the banks are breathing the most frightful sounds. Before me is Jamaica rum, cocoanuts, oranges, lemons, sugar cane and other poisonous substances." A dozen water snakes had to be evicted from the boat after a stop ashore. "The alligators brought their jaws together so fiercely as to make the forest tremble." They slept in the boat or in bamboo huts, wrapped in their blankets. Insects marched boldly across their bodies.

One Isthmus traveler sent this advice to his friends in New York: "First, stay at home. Second, if you go to California, take any route but this. Third, if you insist on crossing the Isthmus, bring but one trunk, weighing not more than 125 pounds. You should also bring tea and sugar, hard bread, and ham enough to last you from Chagres to Panama. Fourth, ten cent pieces, as many as you can get transportation for; eight of them make a dollar." He was not the first to discover that the American dime was indistinguishable from the Panamanian *real*, worth 12½ cents.

Another Panama veteran filed a dissenting opinion in Branch's *Herald*. He saw no suffering, this writer said, "that is not surpassed by a twenty-mile ride in the spring upon any of our Western prairies. . . . It certainly is not as easy traveling as by railroad to Rahway, but on my

word, sir, taking the novelty and excitement of the thing into consideration, it is quite as agreeable."

On the Pacific Coast, Panama City was fast filling up with Americans
awaiting the *California*'s arrival. There may have been seven hundred
there by mid-January—the 350 passengers from the *Falcon* and *Crescent
City*, plus at least that many more from the first half-dozen sailing ships.
Cholera began to assail them; the *Falcon* had brought the plague from
New Orleans. Much of the sickness was blamed on the tropical fruit or
liquor. Failing to understand its true cause—bacteria contaminating the
water—the emigrants called it "Panama fever." Many men, unable to
find lodgings, pitched tents outside the city's stone gate. They exchanged
rumors: the *California* had been lost at sea; the ship had sailed directly
for San Francisco from Peru; it was loaded with South Americans. It was
now obvious that all those waiting in Panama would not be able to get on
the ship if and when it ever came. Sixty of the itchiest among the impatient horde jammed themselves aboard a ninety-ton schooner and took
off. Everyone else waited for the *California*.

The steamship shuddered to a stop about two miles off Panama on
January 17; inshore shallows precluded a closer anchorage. The jubila-
tion among the men ashore, who could see the single smokestack from the
sea wall, lasted only as long as it took the first lighter to arrive with the
news that there were already sixty-nine passengers from Peru aboard.
The Americans immediately exploded in anger and indignation. Many of
them had purchased through tickets to San Francisco before they left
New York; the earliest arrivals in Panama had booked passage to California through the local agents of the Pacific Mail line, who had booked
the ship to capacity and beyond, then suspended sales. No one in Panama,
including the agents, knew that a third of the berths had already been sold
in Peru.

But they knew now. Bands of furious passengers stormed the office of
the ticket agents and demanded that the Callao passengers be removed.
The crowds, unaware that many of the offending passengers were in fact
Americans, howled at the injustice of permitting foreigners to beat them
to American gold. They also insisted that their tickets gave them priority
because they were purchased earlier. The Peru passengers, aware of the
rising temperature on shore, wisely refused to leave the ship.

The Americans turned instinctively to Brevet Major General Persifor
S. Smith of the U.S. Army, who was en route to Monterey to replace
Colonel Richard Mason as commander in chief of the fast-dwindling
Pacific military force. The general, the highest-ranking American officer

in Panama, rushed to their aid. "The laws of the United States inflict the penalty of fine and imprisonment on trespassers on the public lands," he proclaimed in a written statement. "As nothing can be more unreasonable or unjust than the conduct pursued by persons not citizens of the United States, who are flocking from all parts to search for and carry off gold belonging to the United States in California; and as such conduct is in direct violation of the law, it will become my duty, immediately on my arrival there, to put these laws in force."

Smith's declaration was dubious law supported by dubious logic, and he lacked the troops to back it up. It was also the first formal expression of the nativist bigotry that would prevail in the California mines. For the moment, though, the threat to foreigners seemed to placate the mob, some of whom had already talked of raiding the ship and throwing the interlopers overboard.

A protest meeting on the nineteenth drew three hundred aroused men. They elected officers, established committees, and adjourned to write irate resolutions. The shipping line offered a compromise: a chartered sailing vessel would carry the excess passengers. This pleased no one; who wanted to risk the vagaries of wind and sail if he could travel under steam? A second meeting was held to approve the resolutions and condemn the ticket agents.

Finally it was decided to move the Callao passengers out of the staterooms and steerage compartment and install them on the open deck. Tiers of berths were hastily constructed on the hurricane deck. The first-class staterooms, with their mirrors, toilet stands, and damask curtains, were turned over to the Americans.

With the foreigners exiled to the deck, the scramble for places in the steamer reached a climax. Many passengers scalped their tickets at three and four times their original cost; one man offered $1,200 for a $100 steerage ticket. Some bribed their way aboard. Others bid against each other for nothing more than a place to stand on deck. The New York lawyer Elisha Crosby presented a letter from his clients, the steamship company proprietors; the ticket agent gave him a box of food and a Mexican hammock which he slung in the ship's rigging. The cargo hold was filled with temporary berths. Men made themselves as comfortable as they could in lifeboats or atop piles of cable. When the ship at last steamed off on February 1 she carried 365 passengers, about 150 more than capacity, and a crew of thirty-six. At least that many more watched morosely from the shore.

"The ship was filled to cramnation," the now incapacitated Captain

Forbes wrote in his log, "with passengers and stores and everyone looking out for himself with peculiar aptness." There were high-quality men aboard, he observed, but "we also have many of the scum of creation—blacklegs, gamblers, thieves, runners, and drunkards." A few of the latter may have been known to passenger Malachi Fallon, the former jailer at the New York Tombs. There was also a Panamanian stowaway named Sylvie.

The passengers formed themselves into messes for their meals. One of the deck dwellers would collect containers of food and deliver it to his group. "The grab game is practiced at every meal," Forbes wrote; he noticed a minister moving a dish of peas toward his plate while saying grace.

The ship watered at Acapulco, then steamed on to San Blas and Mazatlán. The stowaway was discovered and put in irons, precipitating a mutiny by his protectors, the boiler room stokers. A new crew of firemen was taken aboard at Mazatlán, where hundreds of disappointed Mexican gold seekers watched the *California* depart on February 15. California itself was now less than a week away.

EDWARD BUFFUM, chased from his fabulous strike on the Middle Fork of the American by high water, plodded disconsolately over the hills to Coloma. Arriving gold-heavy but hungry, Buffum and a friend spread a cloth on a storekeeper's counter and bought a few groceries for breakfast. When they finished they called for the bill, which proved to be a document so memorable that Buffum saved it. It read as follows:

One box of sardines	$16.00
One pound of hard bread	2.00
One pound of butter	6.00
A half-pound of cheese	3.00
Two bottles of ale	16.00
Total	$43.00

The first heavy snow of the winter was falling by the time Buffum got back to his Weber Creek cabin in January. He and his partners passed their time reading, playing cards, and talking gold. Then, on the twenty-first, Buffum the New England Quaker suddenly found himself involved in the first gold rush lynchings.

The incident began with the seizure of five men for the attempted robbery of a Mexican gambler at Dry Diggings camp. The five were tried by an impromptu jury of miners, found guilty, and sentenced to thirty-nine lashes each. Buffum, hearing of the excitement, arrived just as three of the flogged men, two Frenchmen and a Chilean, were charged with another robbery and attempted murder at the Stanislaus diggings. By now the three were stretched out in a nearby cabin, unable to stand, but the mob went ahead with their second trial without them. A jury of two hundred men convicted them again.

"What punishment shall be inflicted?" shouted the man chosen as judge.

"Hang them," a miner bellowed. The others roared their approval.

A slight, dark-haired figure mounted a stump. Somewhat to his own surprise, Buffum heard himself protesting the lynchings "in the name of God, humanity, and law." The liquor-fueled crowd shouted him down with threats to hang him too.

"Thirty minutes only were allowed the unhappy victims to prepare themselves," Buffum wrote. They were hustled into a wagon; ropes were knotted around their necks and thrown over a limb; they tried to speak, but none knew English; the drunken, screaming mob was beyond listening anyway. "A black handkerchief was bound around the eyes of each; their arms were pinioned, and at a given signal, without priest or prayer-book, the wagon was drawn from under them and they were launched into eternity." Dry Diggings had become Hangtown.

The dapper French consul, Jacques Moerenhout, was wintering in San Francisco. From the waterfront he could see some thirty windjammers bobbing in the tide, lying where they had been deserted by their crews. The city's population was edging past two thousand. The Parker House, which would be the first of its grand hotels, was rising on the south side of the old plaza at a cost of $3,000 a week; the bricklayers alone earned $20 a day. Owner Robert Parker of Boston would recoup his investment by renting rooms to gamblers at astronomical rates. Houses and stores were going up haphazardly. Persistent rain turned the dusty streets into rivers of mud. Moerenhout's letters to Paris urged the shipment of liquor, food, weapons, and ready-made houses—a shopping list for an impatient and masculine population.

One midwinter arrival in San Francisco was Domingo Ghirardelli, an Italian-born candymaker who had owned a store next to James Lick's piano factory in Lima, Peru. Ghirardelli would try mining, storekeeping, owning a hotel, and running a restaurant before he returned to making chocolate candy. The lots that Lick had begun buying up at $16 a year earlier were now worth $15,000. Eggs sold for $4 a dozen. The few women in town could earn between $5 and $8 for washing a dozen shirts, though hardly anyone owned that many. Young editor Edward Kemble purchased and merged the town's two newspapers into the well-written weekly *Alta California*, which first appeared in January.

Peter Burnett, the lawyer who had led a caravan of Oregonians into the gold country, was selling Sacramento city lots for August Sutter and watching the gaudy parade at the fort. In a letter to a Missouri friend he described one newly rich young man who wore a long black cloak which he liked to unfurl "like a flag to the passing breeze, that he might catch the admiring gaze of the passersby." Another equally dashing miner preferred to march in front of a tavern with a large bell in his hand; "at short intervals he would stop and jingle his bell as much as to say, 'Look here, *this is me!*' "

Burnett became president of a citizens' group which met in early January to discuss the first steps toward statehood. Another active member was the entrepreneur Sam Brannan, who spoke against the extension of slavery into California. The Californians wanted a temporary government which would commence immediately and remain in effect until Congress voted statehood. One thing troubling them was the steady increase in crime. The most recent outrage was an attack on two German miners en route to San Jose in December: three bandits killed one and wounded the other while stealing $8,000 in dust. The assailants were quickly captured, tried, and hanged in San Jose. Burnett's band of concerned citizens, along with similar groups in other towns, called for the election of delegates to a convention to form a provisional government; the convention would ultimately assemble at Monterey in September.

Sonorans streamed into California through the winter. "The whole state of Sonora is on the move, passing us in gangs daily," a U.S. Army officer wrote from the Colorado River in December. Unlike other emigrants, the Mexicans brought their women and children; they expected to return home after a season of gold digging. Many were grubstaked by *padrones* in exchange for a' share of their dust. Most of the estimated five thousand Mexicans who moved north during the winter traveled in large, well-organized caravans which sometimes stretched for a mile across the horizon. One caravan encountered by a German miner was broken into three divisions: the *padron*, his majordomos and gringo guests made up the first section; in the second group came the *cargadores* who looked after the supplies; the *arrieros*, cattle herders, were in the rear. The men carried lassos, canteens, and machetes. Occasionally they played a game in which one rider would try to dismount another by pulling his horse's tail. At night they tended their stock first, then ate and smoked around the campfire, letting the fire die if there was no danger from animals.

Governor Mason, Walter Colton, Lieutenant Sherman, and the other residents of Monterey maintained a daily watch for the *California*. They had arranged for a cannon salute when the steamer came in view. On February 22 the army officers held their annual Washington's Birthday ball at the new stone schoolhouse Colton had built. The party went on till nearly dawn. The officers were at breakfast the next morning when they heard the cannon.

"A RESIDENT of New York coming back after a three months' absence," the *Tribune* commented in late January, "would wonder at the word 'California' seen everywhere in glaring letters, and at the columns of vessels advertised in the papers as about to sail for San Francisco. . . . He would be puzzled at seeing a new class of men in the streets, in a peculiar costume—broad felt hats of a reddish brown hue, loose, rough coats reaching to the knee, and high boots. Even those who have watched the gradual progress of the excitement are astonished at its extent and intensity. . . . The business part of the city presents a spectacle of extraordinary activity. Boxes, barrels and bales crowd the sidewalks, and hundreds of drays convey to the wharves the freight now being stored away in seventy vessels for the Gold Region. . . ."

"Do you know the meaning of the word 'California'?" one high-booted argonaut asked another.

"No, what does it mean?"

"It comes from the Indian words *kali*, which means 'gold,' and *forna*, which means 'wouldn't you like to get some?' "

Washington bureaucrats were decamping for the Pacific like so many fugitives. The rumor was that President-elect Taylor and Senator Henry Clay had already shipped from New Orleans for San Francisco. The government might have to move to the Sierra Nevadas.

Day after day the stories filled the papers and flew through offices and taverns and coffee houses, inflating as they went. Larkin wrote that he had heard of a twenty-five-pound nugget. Soon Larkin had *seen* a twenty-five-pound nugget. Then there were twenty-five-pound nuggets lying loose, free for the taking.

Resistance was futile; a man had to go, to take part somehow, lest he wonder forever what might have been. "You will be tried as you have never before been tried," a Rhode Island preacher warned a departing company. "I tremble for the result. Strive to rise above circumstances. Be men." A minister in Northampton, Massachusetts, reacted more directly: he organized a company and lit out. A joint stock company of a hundred Methodists-for-California accepted applications in New York.

The routes west were delimited only by the pilgrims' imagination. Two young brothers from Portland, Maine, set out afoot from St. Louis in January with no more supplies than they would take on a hunting trip. A Philadelphian reportedly forged $30,000 worth of banknotes and then had himself boxed and taken aboard a ship as merchandise to elude police. Members of a cautious group from Danvers, Massachusetts, chipped in $10 each to supply one digger who was to proceed to the mines, "procure the ore and forward it home." A man in Rochester, New York, hired a clairvoyant to accompany him to California, help him find gold, and heal any incidental ailments. Many inquired about the overland party to be guided by the legendary Kit Carson. Carson, who knew nothing about it, was wintering on his New Mexico ranch while the *Tribune* ran a serial recounting his western adventures.

"The class of our citizens which is leaving us for El Dorado is of the better sort, well-educated, industrious and respectable," the *Tribune* noted. "The rowdies, whom we could well spare, cannot as a general thing fit themselves out for so long a voyage." Ninety-six of the better sort were aboard the ship *Pacific* when she left in a blizzard on January 23, bound for more than her share of travail and adventure. One passenger was Jacob Stillman, a physician who would later establish a hospital in Sacramento. Another was a thirty-five-year-old Manhattan commission-house merchant named Mark Hopkins.

January 25 was the busiest day yet on the eastern docks: five ships sailed from New York, two from Boston, and one each from Baltimore and New London; in all more than six hundred passengers embarked for San Francisco that day. Horace Pond, a twenty-four-year-old doctor from Castleton, Vermont, was probably the most lugubrious man among them.

Pond, a somewhat delicate youth, was worried about his chances— not of finding gold, but of survival. Writing to his father on the eve of his departure, he mentioned the possibility that he might be "taken away." He said he had purchased a life insurance policy and sent it home. He asked to have his photograph copied "without fail" and sent to a girl named Jane.

He continued the letter as his ship, the *William Ivy*, was towed out of New York harbor by a steamboat. He apologized for not sending any presents to his sisters but promised to "make it up in gold dust later." "We are making out to sea rapidly," he wrote in mounting excitement. He asked that someone look after his pets. "Now I am interrupted by a call for the doctor to drink a toast. . . . We are now opposite Long Island. . . . Now I hear some sporting about our live pigs aboard as to who shall feed them and kill, etc. We also have foals aboard and a bitch bull terrier. . . . I must bid you all goodbye." Hastily he sealed the letter and handed it to a crewman on the steamboat just before the boat headed back to the city.

A handbill appeared on New York streets on February 2 over the name of Mrs. Eliza Farnham, a pillar of Christian righteousness most recently employed as the matron of female inmates at Sing Sing prison. Mrs. Farnham's proposal was at once extraordinary and splendidly logical: she wanted two hundred single women to go with her on a civilizing mission to California. Only "intelligent, virtuous and efficient" women need apply.

Mrs. Farnham was convinced that a shipload of good women—potential wives and mothers—was the surest check against the rampant debauchery of masculine California. She demanded that applicants be at least twenty-five years old and possess "satisfactory testimonials of their education, character, capacity, etc." plus $250. They would sail around the Horn on a chartered ship, a veritable bark of angels. The San Francisco *Alta California*, hearing of the plan several months later, applauded any effort "to bring a few spare ribs to this market." Before recruiting could get fairly under way, however, Mrs. Farnham fell ill. The mission had to be delayed. More disappointments would follow.

In England a more devious mind was at work. Henry Vizetelly, a twenty-nine-year-old London printer, conceived the idea of a well-documented book about an Englishman's adventures in the gold country. The fact that no such Englishman was at hand did not deter him. Relying on a descriptive account of California by the explorer John Frémont plus newspaper articles, Vizetelly wrote a ninety-four-page book in ten successive evenings. He called it *Four Months Among the Gold-Finders in Alta California*. The author was a fictitious J. Tyrwhitt Brooks, M.D. The completed manuscript was sent to London printer-bookseller David Bogue, who was in cahoots with Vizetelly, and printed in a fortnight.

London reviewers were unanimously enthusiastic. "Here is a gentleman who knows all about it!" the *Times* exclaimed. "A live Englishman who has set foot in the diggings, has had his hand in the washings, has scratched for the dust until his back ached . . . and in fact gone through a regular Californian experience in less than no time at all." Despite the literal truth of the *Times*'s last observation, Vizetelly had in fact done his work artfully; the book was true to both the physical circumstances and the spirit of 1848 California. Dr. Brooks hears one miner declare that the gold "beats Joe Dunkin's goose-pie and apple sarse." He points out that trading is more lucrative than mining. Marshall, Mason, and Sutter all appear in the narrative. "It is easy to get gold here," the doctor concludes accurately, "but very difficult to keep it."

The book was a sensation. Success in England led to other editions in Europe and the United States. Even the most careful historians accepted it as authentic; the great California historian Hubert Howe Bancroft relied heavily on it in his account of the 1848 mines. Vizetelly, later a well-known London journalist, confessed his imaginative construction in an 1893 autobiography, but as recently as 1976 the estimable Dr. Brooks was still showing up as a vivid and trustworthy source.

The New York–to–Chagres steamers *Falcon* and *Crescent City* were back in New York in late January, ready to haul a second wave of impatient ticket holders to the Isthmus. The *Crescent City*'s 305 passengers maneuvered their luggage aboard during a morning-long snowfall on February 5. Trunks, crates, and people were jammed together on the muddy deck. The travelers wore their California best: passenger T. T. Johnson saw "a Broadway topcoat, boatman pea jacket, Western hunting shirt, and Mexican blanket." One man carried a large, balloon-shaped rubber life preserver.

The atmosphere was festive. The crowd on the wharf pelted the passengers with snowballs. Spectators on the deck of another docked ship joined in. The *Crescent City* passengers returned fire, then attached a white handkerchief to an umbrella and waved it in surrender. "Is anyone on the dock dead broke?" a passenger shouted. "I am," someone yelled. The passenger flung a half-dollar into the cheering crowd.

THE PANAMA ROUTE was the swiftest—unless one credited an intriguing proposal which appeared a few weeks later. AIR LINE TO CALIFORNIA, the handbill said. "The aerial locomotive will leave the city positively on the 15th of April, on its first trip to the gold mines. Passage $50, wines included. Baggage extra." The trip would take three days.

The man behind this astonishing scheme was Rufus Porter, a Yankee tinkerer who was already homing in on the principles of powered flight. Porter had designed an eight-hundred-foot-long steam-powered craft with a startling resemblance to a modern dirigible. He promised that it could carry up to a hundred passengers in a 180-foot-long compartment at speeds of sixty to a hundred miles per hour. An "arrow-proof" rubber skin would be stretched over a frame of spruce rods; hydrogen gas would keep it aloft. Porter had already published the specifications in the *Scientific American*, a journal he had founded in 1845.

Porter's flirtation with power-driven flight was one of dozens of similar episodes in a career of extraordinary creativity and dogged obscurity. He almost willed his own obscurity: he was a brilliant and original painter who rarely signed his work, a prolific inventor who often sold his inventions without patenting them. The unifying threads in his life were spontaneity and mobility—he made it up as he went along, and he never stopped moving. At one time or another he was a successful musician, painter, writer, mechanic, and inventor. He could fix a clock or design a plow, write a sonnet or an essay, paint a barn or a portrait.

He grew up in Massachusetts and Maine, finishing his formal education at twelve. By seventeen he was supporting himself playing the fife, drum, and fiddle. At twenty-four he was an itinerant portrait painter, walking up and down the East Coast with a gaily decorated cart. Characteristically, he devised a way to speed up the artistic process. He built a camera obscura to reflect the features of his subject onto a sheet of paper. He could then trace the outline, fill in the details, and produce a portrait in fifteen minutes.

He next became a landscape painter and muralist. He crisscrossed New England, stopping to paint the walls of a home or tavern, returning now and then to his wife and family in Billerica, Massachusetts. His career as a painter was interrupted by frequent seizures of inventiveness. He developed a rifle with a revolving cylinder, the precursor of the revolver, and sold it to Samuel Colt of Hartford for $100. The sight of his wife working at a scrub board inspired him to design a washing machine. A dozen or more of his creations exist in some form today: the rotary plow, a trip hammer, an icemaker, a municipal fire-alarm system, a sewing machine.

The *Scientific American*, launched when he was fifty-three, was a showcase for his remarkably versatile mind and talents. He offered schematic drawings of his inventions, including a steam-powered automobile and a workable elevated railroad, anticipating the New York

"el" by twenty years. He published a column on how to paint and another
on how to do dozens of practical things—one note explained "how to get
a ring off your finger." But journalism too lost its appeal, and he sold
his interest in the paper within a year.

None of Porter's inventions ever made him rich, or even comfortable
for very long. His son described him as "improvident." He lacked Yankee
shrewdness. He was an idea man, self-contained and self-motivating; his
attempts to sell his ideas were long on scientific detail and short on
salesmanship.

The idea for an aerial locomotive first occurred to him in 1820. He
said that he was inspired by the notion of liberating Napoleon from
captivity on the island of St. Helena. He built his first model in 1833,
offering to split the patent claims with anyone who would back him, but
there were no takers. In 1841 he tried again, and this time he said he
would settle for 10 percent if someone would come up with the money
to build it. Again, nothing. He built and exhibited another model in
1847. Then came the gold rush.

But powered flight proved to be too much for even the feverish gold
seekers to believe. Only two hundred of them bought tickets, far short of
the number needed to finance construction. The sarcastic reaction of
Porter's friends at the *Scientific American* was typical: "Just think of it—
to see a vessel 800 feet long flying thro' the firmament to California . . .
we intend to put down our name for the *second* trip."

A few years later Porter actually succeeded in selling some six hundred shares in his airship at $5 each. Setting up shop on a field in Wash-
ington, D.C., he constructed a 160-foot-long vessel sixteen feet in diameter,
covering it with varnished linen. He built a sixty-foot-long passenger
saloon complete with seats and glass windows. He installed the engines
and fastened the rudder in place. Then he discovered that the varnish
had so weakened the linen shell that it was beginning to disintegrate.
Before he could repair it a violent storm struck the craft and damaged the
framework. Vandals slashed its skin. Money was gone, winter was coming
on—and the sixty-year-old Porter was left to stare at the tatters of his
dream.

Porter could have used the skills of a contemporary who was also trying to profit from the gold mania: Phineas T. Barnum. The impresario,
then operating his famous American Museum on Broadway, was looking
for a veteran of the California mines to lecture eager eastern audiences.
In March he met G. D. Gilman, just in from California. Barnum asked

Gilman to give a short talk. He wanted him to stand next to a table containing a twenty-five-pound lump of gold.

"As you are talking you can handle it," Barnum explained. "Just pass your hand over it now and then. . . . If they get the idea that that's the kind of lumps they may find, a fortune's made, and we'll share it."

"But what a perfect humbug that would be," Gilman blurted.

Barnum gave him a reassuring pat on the shoulder. "My dear sir," he said, "the bigger the humbug, the better the people will like it."

LIEUTENANT William Tecumseh Sherman raced to the Monterey wharf and peered out through the morning fog. He could just barely make out a ship's outline. Excitedly he commandeered a rowboat and ordered two soldiers to take the oars. Naval Agent Thomas Larkin, the man whose letters had thrilled thousands of easterners, suddenly appeared at his side and asked to go with him.

Sherman and Larkin scrambled up a Jacob's ladder onto the crowded deck as the *California* cruised slowly toward shore. Sherman was immediately surrounded by old friends, mostly fellow officers. They bombarded him with questions. One of the first concerned the coal supply in Monterey; the ship was out of fuel.

The passengers spilled out amid the white-walled buildings of the old Spanish port. Crewmen formed gangs to cut wood for fuel. The Californios, who had never seen a steamship, stared at the vessel, amazed at its ugliness. It quickly developed that many of the new arrivals were ready for business. They "appeared quite in their element" at a Mexican gambling house, ex-soldier William Ryan wrote. Several had their own roulette tables and dice. Others offered clothes, tools, and weapons for sale. A tavern owner cleared $2,000 in two days. The most successful gamblers, Ryan noticed, were "quiet-looking fellows with sharp eyes," many of them from New Orleans. An extra supply of coal was finally found on board after three days of wood cutting. The ship left for San Francisco at 7 a.m. on February 27.

The *Alta California* had prodded San Franciscans to give the ship a tumultuous welcome. "Let us show the newcomers that this is a 'land o' cakes,' " the paper urged. Crowds spread along the bay shore and across the crests of the hills as the ship steamed through the Golden Gate on the morning of the twenty-eighth. Warships in the harbor thundered a twenty-one-gun salute. Hundreds of sailors swarmed onto the yards and rigging of their ships. The steamer listed to starboard as passengers hurried to the railing to stare at the ramshackle city.

General Persifor Smith, Elisha Crosby, and the other passengers were loaded onto small boats for the last few hundred yards. The bay looked like "a great mud flat" to Crosby. Their first steps in the promised land were across the boulders at Clark's Point. Within hours the entire thirty-six-man crew, save Captain Forbes and a single engineer, deserted.

California at last! One passenger held out a half-dollar to a man standing on the rocks and asked him to take his valise to a hotel. The San Franciscan drew two half-dollars from his pocket and threw them at the newcomer's feet. "Carry it yourself," he said.

THE ARGOSY

ROUNDING THE HORN

SUDDENLY a heavy blow struck the starboard quarter and careened the ship over on her side, throwing those on the weather side out of their berths and across the lower deck against the staterooms opposite. The dim lights which usually hung above the tables were put out. A crash was heard overhead—chains rattling and falling, sails madly flapping, yardarms snapping and masts breaking; for a few seconds the noise was terrific. . . ."

The ship *Henry Lee*, bound for California via Cape Horn, was three weeks out of New York when the storm splintered two of her masts on March 11. Aboard were the 122 men of the Hartford Mining and Trading Company—farmers and machinists, shoemakers and blacksmiths, harnessmakers and upholsterers. These were landsmen. Their only acquaintance with the violence of the sea was by reputation. The rocky soil of their

Connecticut homeland was harsh and stingy, to be sure, but it was as stolid as faith and as predictable as an old friend—"as sure as sunrise," they liked to say. There was an awful strangeness about a storm on the ocean; even the sounds were unfamiliar.

The Hartford Company men were craftsmen, men who could build and fix things. They were also New Englanders: they aspired to good order, good citizenship, and sobriety. Each had signed a solemn pledge of temperance. Strict rules (lights out at ten, no smoking in the 'tween-decks sleeping area) regulated their shipboard behavior. They planned to vote in the upcoming Connecticut election and tabulate the returns in spite of their isolation; their patch of the Atlantic would be just another precinct. They had transformed their vessel into a floating New England village, tidy and righteous and tight as a tick.

The chronicler of the *Henry Lee*'s voyage, a printer from Bloomfield, Connecticut, named Linville Hall, described their reaction to the storm: "The cry of alarm from those below, as they endeavored to reach the hatchways in the darkness, falling one over another, was terrible. Some were silent and made no effort to extricate themselves from their berths. . . . Some were praying; others paralyzed with fear; others were calm and silent. One man, beside himself with fear, was endeavoring to put one foot into his coat-sleeve."

At dawn the next day the deck was a tangled and soggy mass of canvas, shattered wood and rigging, but they were still afloat and the storm was past. The task now was to clean up the mess and repair the damage, a job that landsmen understood. They unpacked their tools and went to work, pausing only on Sunday to sing a hymn of gratitude ("Safely through another week, God has brought us on our way . . ."). In twelve days the masts were repaired and the *Henry Lee* was once again shipshape, running before the southeast trade winds toward Rio de Janeiro.

The armada of windjammers bearing the men who called themselves Californians around Cape Horn was by and large a nautical disgrace. Hulks once condemned were summoned back to wobbly service. Dozens of rickety whalers were hastily fitted out with tiers of hammocks and pronounced ready for the six-month voyage. The San Francisco customhouse eventually reported that 15,597 people arrived via Cape Horn in 1849, as against 6,489 who came across the Isthmus. Astonishingly, not one of the more than five hundred weary ships that left the east coast in 1849 sank and all but a few dozen of the passengers survived to step uncertainly ashore at San Francisco. Within a few years the sleek and elegant American-built clippers would cut the time of the journey to ninety days, but in 1849 the clipper fleet on the Horn route could muster only a half-dozen ships. Most seagoing forty-niners traveled in square-rigged, blunt-sterned tubs which shipped water in even a modest swell and rolled hideously in a storm.

There were four main types of sailing vessels: (1) ships, which were three-masted and square-rigged; (2) barks, on which the forward two masts were square-rigged and the rear (mizzen) mast rigged fore-and-aft; (3) brigs, with two square-rigged masts; and (4) schooners, with two masts rigged fore-and-aft. The twenty-eight-ton schooner *Toccao* of Cape Cod, which carried five passengers and a crew of four, was the smallest craft to negotiate the Horn in 1849. More typical were the dimensions of the bark *Canton*, which sailed from New York in March with the Island City company on board: the ship was 93 feet from bow to stern, 24 feet wide, and 10 feet deep; she weighed 198 tons. The forty-eight passengers had to be nimble just to keep out of each other's way.

On most ships the voyagers had to provide their own diversions. They scanned the horizon for whales and porpoises, played cards, wrote in their journals, read, fished, organized debating societies and prayer meetings, fought and gambled and muttered about the food. They speculated end-lessly about how much gold they would gather and how long it would take. And they fretted about arriving late. "It was impossible to get rid of the absurd notion," one passenger wrote, "that the whole country would be appropriated before we had set foot in it, and that we should thus be in the awkward predicament of a dilatory guest who arrives only in time to be tantalized by sight of the fragments of the feast."

The trip usually began as an adventure, settled quickly into tedium broken by spurts of conflict, and deteriorated into a dreary ordeal. For a shipload of men in their twenties, each one convinced that he was on the high road to fortune, a windless day was agony; the long equatorial calms were unrelieved torture. The ships normally sailed southeast from the Atlantic ports until they were within a few days of Africa, verified by the frequent appearance of red desert dust on deck. There they picked up the northeast trade winds which swept them briskly through the horse latitudes and into the eight-hundred-mile-long equatorial doldrums. A few degrees south of the equator they finally found the southeast trades which carried them into Rio, the customary first stop.

The Bostonians aboard the *Edward Everett*, still clinging to their

Bibles and their New England civilization, probably lived more comfortably than anyone else on the Cape Horn run. The organizers of the Boston and California Company had thought of everything—the ship had a dispensary, a board of health, a police force, and a weekly paper, among other amenities—but they thought of food first. While men in other companies turned surly after a dozen straight meals of salt pork or salt beef, the men of the *Everett* enjoyed such delicacies as cheese, potpie, applesauce, and plum pudding. They could snack between meals from a barrel of hardtack.

To remind themselves of home the Boston men attached familiar names to the corridors in their between-decks dormitory: there was Beacon Street, Ann Street, Riggers Row, and even the North End. They educated each other in weekly lectures on geology and other scientific subjects. The two ministers aboard took turns preaching on Sundays. On holidays and other special occasions the company might enjoy a concert by its own orchestra of four violins, four flutes, and several guitars.

The grim character of life aboard the brig *Osceola,* which sailed from Philadelphia three days after the *Everett* cleared Boston, was far more typical. The *Osceola*'s journal keeper was thirty-year-old Samuel Upham, a thin, sharp-featured former countinghouse clerk. Upham, who later became a newspaperman in Sacramento, brought along three gold-washing machines.

Grumbling about the *Osceola*'s food, particularly among Upham's companions in the steerage compartment, began the first week. They complained that the portions were skimpy and poorly cooked. Several days of rain exposed leaks in the deck which dripped directly onto the top bunks in steerage. But the real calamity came when the captain jettisoned the cargo stored on deck—most of it belonging to the passengers—to ease the ship's burden. Over the side went Upham's gold washers, several trunks and valises, crates of brandy, casks of vinegar and other food, and the frame of a house. Several passengers had left all their baggage on deck. One man managed to salvage a cask, only to learn to his sorrow that it contained pilot bread and not brandy.

"The reality of a sea voyage," Upham decided, "speedily dispels the romance." Complaints about the food precipitated an indignation meeting as they neared the equator. More rumbles were provoked when the captain, whose name was Fairfowl, flogged a crewman for what the passengers considered a trifling offense. When Fairfowl decreed that there would be no more potatoes for the men in steerage, Upham branded him "a sea-tyrant totally unfit to command a passenger vessel." The ship was "a perfect *Hades*."

The only relief came when they sighted another California-bound ship, which turned out to be the *Croton* of New York. A "jollification" ensued. Boatloads of passengers visited back and forth, sampling each other's food and drink and comparing grievances. The *Osceola* apparently had the edge; Upham noted that one of his fellow sufferers offered $150 to anyone from the *Croton* who would trade places, but there were no takers.

The passengers bet on anything—checkers, poker, backgammon, dominos, euchre, monte, penny pitching, what their latitude was, what they would have for dinner, or who would be the first to sight land. A week before they reached Rio the despotic Fairfowl finally relented and increased their rations. Upham could now relax in the tropical sun, but it was too hot. It would be all right, he wrote, "if I could only divest myself of flesh and sit in my bones for an hour or so."

The chief hazards of the Horn voyage, in order of their appearance, were seasickness, unpalatable food, and boredom. John Angell, a passenger on the *Pacific*, may have established some sort of gold rush record by vomiting twenty-seven consecutive days. The "Californians," however, hardly ever said it that way; seasickness to them was invariably "casting up accounts"; a passenger on the *Sweden* cast up his false teeth with his accounts. The nadir may have been reached by the white-faced forty-niner on the *Bonne Adele* who admitted that "he didn't care a darn, he'd just as lief live as die."

Food was a universal complaint. "I really believe that I can drink or eat anything and be content if I ever get on shore again," wrote one despairing voyager. One indignity they were subjected to was lobscouse, a hash of salted meat, potatoes, and hard bread. A critic called it "seven baskets full of the fag ends of dinner from the day before." Another was hushamagrundy, tentatively identified as two parts turnips, two parts codfish, and three parts parsnips. The travelers' rancor was often focused as much on quantity as quality. "The beans are three to a quart of hot water, with a small piece of rusty pork," wrote Moses Cogswell of the *Sweden*. "The tea tastes like ground autumn leaves." Dandy funk, which was seabiscuit cooked in molasses with raisins and cinnamon, was the favored dessert along with plum duff, which resembled a cobbler.

Variety vanished as the voyage stretched on. By the final weeks on the Pacific side most companies were down to salt meat and fish, rice and beans and hardtack. Too often they had to share even that with bugs and worms.

Jammed into cramped sleeping quarters, pinned to a motionless sea for days and even weeks on end, weary of reading and writing and gambling and even talking, men grew desperate for something to do. Linville Hall sketched this scene on the *Henry Lee*'s deck late on an 1849 afternoon:

"There are on the hurricane deck, at this moment, twenty-five persons, four of whom are playing backgammon; two, chess; four, checkers; one reading . . . , one on his side sleeping soundly; two are on their backs, and three on their faces, musing; one is whittling; two are a little separate, engaged in conversation, three are overlooking the plays; two are sitting cross-legged looking at me while writing this note." Letting his gaze wander slowly beyond the hurricane deck, Hall saw two men in a longboat pulling each other's legs; several were on potato bins, guessing ages; a man on the stern polished a dirk while three others supervised; six were high up the mizzenmast; twelve watched a checkers game near the wheel; seven stared at the sea.

Practical jokes helped to alleviate the ennui. On one ship a goat was stuffed into an oilskin coat and nudged into the captain's cabin. On another a passenger who could imitate the skipper's voice amused himself by issuing senseless commands to the crew. A canvas bucket was tied to the leg of a sleeping passenger and tossed overboard, nearly jerking the victim over the side.

Crossing the equator called for an elaborate ceremony. A seaman dressed as King Neptune, often crowned and carrying a trident, would mysteriously appear on deck. One by one the unfortunate neophytes were called forward, lathered with soap and grease and shaved with a crude wooden razor, then dunked in a tub of salt water. Vows were sometimes extracted from them: "Do you solemnly swear that you will never eat brown bread when you can get white? That you will never kiss the maid when you can kiss the mistress? That you will not drink water when you can get wine?" A gift for the king, preferably something bottled, would exempt a passenger from the ritual and enliven the subsequent party.

The most unrelenting foes of shipboard tedium were probably the twenty-five high-spirited Harvard students, banded together as the Old Harvard Company, who had shipped aboard the *Duxbury* of Boston. The Harvard boys had fun with everything, even their own complaints. The first issue of their handwritten newspaper, the *Petrel*, presented their version of "Oh! Susanna": "Oh, Ship Duxbury, you are the ship for me, you are the greatest humbug that's floating on the sea." The *Petrel*'s contents ran to doggerel, undergraduate humor, and stylish bitching. A want ad requested a set of dentures for a passenger who had lost his original teeth chewing hardtack. The "Committee on Three Meals a Day" announced its motto as "Bread or Blood." An irritating fellow passenger was the target of a poem called "Ask Loveland":

> *Who on the house at night doth stand*
> *And argue with a big fat man*
> *On what they neither understand,*
> *Ask Loveland . . .*
>
> *Who is the man, who is so neat*
> *That when we're catching water sweet*
> *Goes on the house to wash his feet*
> *Ask Loveland . . .*

The *Petrel* also reported that some passengers were so disheartened by the poor food and slow progress that there was talk of an expedition across the Andes from Rio to the Pacific. Later in the year a party of Frenchmen actually tried this, leaving their ship at Buenos Aires and trekking to Valparaiso, Chile, but when they arrived the ship had already come and gone.

A sensitive traveler could find rapture in the voyage in spite of everything. The sea was an unfailing wonder, as glorious at sunrise as at moonrise, as captivating in glassy tranquillity as in mountainous fury. The small-town boys, refugees from deciduous forests and village greens, gazed at it tirelessly, cocked their heads and stared, studied it like a slate at school, returning at dusk and again at midnight, then again at dawn. The twenty-six-year-old Moses Cogswell, son of a New Hampshire barkeep, stood alone on deck at 2 a.m. on a March night and watched the ocean "boiling and foaming in its rage. It resembled an ocean of flame. I never saw so sublime a sight." Night was his favorite time on deck. "Gloom ahead, the rush of water, the glistening wake, invisible sailors, the helmsman with his light"—his imagination could transform the shadowy sea into the familiar woods and fields of home.

Cogswell was something of an innocent. His bright eyes lit up a slightly cherubic face framed by long dark hair. His father had died a year earlier, and Moses had drifted down to Boston and a job selling building materials. The gold rush seized his imagination—the adventure and novelty, the romance of it as much as the potential profit. With other New Hampshiremen he had joined the Roxbury and Sagamore Mining Company and sailed from Boston on the 650-ton *Sweden*, named in honor of the Swedish soprano Jenny Lind.

Moses liked the camaraderie. "It is almost impossible to sleep late," he wrote cheerfully, "for each one has something to say. An occasional dry joke will set the whole uproarious with laughter." The food was barely digestible, the skipper a barnacled savage, and the sleeping area looked like "a second-hand dry-goods shop," but he still came up smiling. As the *Sweden* sailed down the east coast of South America he tried to evoke the feeling he found so thrilling: "The cold autumn wind, the dull heavy rolling of the ship, the loud and boisterous laugh of my companions, the ribald jest, the merry song, the squeak of flute and violin, the heavy tramp of feet on deck, the rough stern voice of the mate giving orders . . ." Cogswell listened to the crew singing "A Hundred Years Ago" as they reefed the topsails in a storm. "How fearfully wild and grand it rang out, mingled with the raging of the elements."

A few days later the *Sweden's* crewmen spotted the *Magnolia* of New Bedford and commenced a race which continued past midnight. "The moon shone very bright," Cogswell wrote, "and the white sails reflected its pale light, casting a bright shadow on the rushing waves beyond. I never expect to see a more beautiful sight." Passengers on both ships cheered as the *Magnolia* finally pulled ahead to stay.

The two most popular stopping points on the Atlantic side of South America were Rio and the island of Santa Catarina, five hundred miles farther down the coast. Santa Catarina had a lovely crescent-shaped harbor ringed with adobe cottages that gleamed white in the sun. Thick shrubbery and wild fruit trees climbed the surrounding hills. Even before they went ashore the Americans encountered vendors in small boats selling melons, pineapples, bananas, and milk. Lively Rio assaulted their senses. The long silence of the sea gave way to a babel of sound. "Imagine all the blackbirds you ever heard," one man wrote, "with a sprinkling of a few thousand crows, and four or five hundred jackasses, all in one crowd and all in full chorus." On closer investigation the voices proved to be almost unanimously male; women were hardly ever seen in the street.

The beautiful pastel-tinted city beneath Sugar Loaf mountain was full of Americans; eighty-six California-bound ships had called there by the end of March. The adventurers bellowed greetings to each other across the water. "Who won the Sullivan-Hyer fight?" shouted a man who had set sail shortly before a much ballyhooed prizefight between Yankee Sullivan and Tom Hyer in Maryland. "Hyer—in sixteen rounds," came the reply.

The forty-niners spilled out of their ships and rushed to the Pharoux Hotel, the favorite American gathering place, to compare times on the first leg of the voyage. The *Christoval Colon* had made it in 51 days; Samuel Upham's *Osceola* took 49; the *William Ivy* needed only 42. In April the westering vessels were joined in the harbor by the storeship *Lexington* from California, carrying $300,000 in gold from the Sierra placers.

The city charmed them. They trooped by the palace of Dom Pedro II, the bearded twenty-four-year-old emperor, and rode mule-drawn carriages to the emperor's luxuriant gardens. They stared at the aqueduct which delivered the city's water supply, toured the cathedral, and tried to understand a play in Portuguese ("We came out as wise as we entered," a playgoer remarked). They were startled to learn that restaurants kept live chickens on the premises and needed only thirty minutes to convert them into a meal.

The people of Rio struck them as sober and courteous and even austere. Dr. Jacob Stillman of the *Pacific* noted that they "never laugh heartily, never hurrah, and very rarely get drunk"—peculiar behavior indeed. The *Henry Lee's* Linville Hall found the locals "wonderfully forbearing" and wished that his countrymen would emulate them; many of the rowdier Americans got an inside view of a Brazilian jail.

Slavery was a subject that most forty-niners avoided, but the ardent abolitionists among them were offended by the Rio slave market. Schooners from Africa deposited their wretched cargoes across the harbor at Preia Grande, anchoring at night to avoid British warships; the British regarded slave traffic as piracy. Ezekiel Barra winced as he watched a line of twenty blacks toting 120-pound sacks of coffee from a warehouse to a waiting ship. Samuel Upham saw overseers with pointed sticks supervising slave laborers at the Rio slaughterhouse.

The interlude at Rio also offered the most bitterly aggrieved voyagers their first opportunity for formal complaint. Dr. Stillman and the other passengers on the *Pacific,* in particular, were seething. The trouble had begun with the skipper's refusal to honor an agreement by which first-class travelers were to get the same food as he did. The irascible Captain Tibbets had responded to passenger protests by threatening to set fire to the powder magazine and blow up the ship. He had posted a notice promising to clamp any troublemakers in irons.

The passengers were further incensed to learn that their ship carried cheese, butter, flour, and pickles in the cargo holds while they ate repetitious meals of salt pork, beans, and hardtack. Tibbets told them he would keep the better provisions as long as he pleased; they learned later that he planned to sell them in San Francisco.

By the time they had been at sea a month the mutterings had become mutinous. The passengers quietly discussed their legal position if they seized the ship by force. Among those urging caution was the thin and taciturn Mark Hopkins, who would later be the quiet member of the Big Four builders of the Central Pacific railroad. Stillman thought the problem lay as much in the customs of the sea as in the captain's personality. A seaman "is never asked to do anything, but he is damned to do it," he wrote. "The master damns the mate, the mate damns the second mate, and the second mate damns the sailors. . . . Our captain, having passed his life among seamen, is incapable of treating passengers any other way." Hopkins suggested that they see U.S. diplomatic officers in Rio.

A delegation of passengers filed a complaint with the U.S. minister and the American consul as soon as they landed. Tibbets appeared conciliatory, but that night they learned that he had quietly cleared customs and planned to sail immediately. The passengers rushed to the consul's home and then to the residence of one of the emperor's chamberlains to get an order restricting the ship to port. The American officials relieved Tibbets of his command, after an investigation, a few days later. "Outraged humanity has triumphed," Stillman exulted.

The melancholy Horace Pond, the young doctor who feared that he wouldn't survive, wrote his father from Rio. He said he had been severely seasick: "There is no use of my trying to describe this long continued scene of suffering, it is sufficient for me to say I suffered." Still his ship, the *William Ivy*, was among the swiftest—"we're bound to beat any." Rio de Janeiro was "peculiarly wild and romantic," but he would have none of the exotic Southern Hemisphere fruits: "I would not exchange the apple for any fruit I have yet seen." His yearning for home was apparent in every line. He wondered whether they were making sugar yet back in Vermont, and added that he hated to say good-by so far from home. He asked his father not to sell his horse. But young Pond's

pessimism was colliding with a newfound confidence and sense of adventure. "I feel that if I ever live to get there and one year after I can make
my fortune," he wrote. "I shall be full of yarns, as the sailors say." Then
apprehension stole up on him again—"if I live to return."

The Harvard boys aboard the *Duxbury* staged a mock trial a few
days out of Rio. The defendant was charged with violating a Brazilian
prostitute. One witness testified that the accused complained of "great
irritation about the unmentionables," while another swore that the defendant had claimed a married man could be pardoned when this far
from home. A third witness refused to answer questions for fear of in-
criminating himself. It appeared that the judge was in a similarly delicate
position, but his honor found the prisoner guilty anyway, sentencing him
to treat all hands.

On the Atlantic once again, the ships of the golden armada drove
toward the Southern Cross and their rendezvous with the most daunting
stretch of ocean on the planet, the perpetually storm-lashed waters off
Cape Horn. "Doubling the Cape" could be an endless ordeal by wind and
wave. Slate-colored clouds rolled furiously up from the southwest on gale
winds, flailing the puny windjammers with snow and sleet and hail and
forcing them to reef sails and tuck themselves into the angry sea and
wait. There were days when storms pushed the little ships so far eastward
that passengers on some vessels seriously debated continuing in that direction and trying the Cape of Good Hope instead.

The conventional navigational strategy for rounding the Horn was
to sail far enough south to avoid being driven ashore by the westerlies
and southwesters, and then to skitter northwest to the sanctuary of the
Pacific. A ship under heavenly auspices might make the passage of
the Horn in a week, but most of them needed thirty days and more. The
storms were so constant, and the intervening calms so fleeting, that the
sea never truly yielded to tranquillity; something was forever stirring.
The generations of sailors who had felt their vessels dancing birdlike atop
the waves knew this part of the southern sea as Cape Stiff.

For the argonauts the struggle around the Horn was unrelieved misery.
The waves crashing over the bow sent water through the hatches and
leaky decks to the passenger holds below. A man simply resigned himself to being wet. Pitching and rolling were so constant that formal meals
were suspended; men filled their trays at mealtime and prowled their
ships for a calm place to eat. The winter sun peered over the horizon and
modestly retired after a scant five or six hours—"as if ashamed of its

own dullness and stupidity," Moses Cogswell wrote. It was difficult to keep a lantern lit and almost impossible to read or write; the penmanship of the few who tried to maintain their journals was given to sudden swoops and long tangents.

Jacob Stillman and his shipmates on the *Pacific* tried to sleep by lashing themselves to their berths or wedging their bodies between berth and bulkhead. "Sometimes the ship would continue so long on her side that we would fear that the next wave would finish her," he wrote. "We would stare into each other's faces like owls, and as she righted would relapse again into drowsy indifference. Now and then the ship would rebound and tremble as though we had struck an iceberg. This would be followed by the rushing of water across the deck and a heavy roll." A passenger who ventured topside in what passed for daylight was knocked to the deck and slid face down to the railing, breaking his nose and shattering his glasses. At least two ships lost men overboard. "These times have harmonized our minds on one point," Linville Hall wrote, "that some other way to California is preferable." "There is such a thing as too great an intimacy with the ocean," another forty-niner concluded.

The alternative to the rough ride around the Horn was the shorter but more perilous Strait of Magellan, a U-shaped waterway first sailed by the explorer who gave it his name in 1520. The strait tapered to a width of less than two miles amid the fjords and steep cliffs on its western leg, a channel too narrow for most of the overloaded arks of 1849 to maneuver in. The terrain along the eastern section was barren tableland which climbed a succession of terraces to the southern spur of the Andes. Patagonian Indians, whom the forty-niners believed to be cannibals, built villages of wigwams on the windswept barrens and hunted seals and otters from canoes.

A ship trying the strait had to contend with fog, sudden squalls, headwinds, unpredictable currents, a shortage of safe anchorages, and short-lived but ferocious storms called williwaws. Only about a dozen vessels in the forty-niner fleet attempted the strait; one took seventy days to travel its three hundred rugged miles. The steamer *California* ran into so much adversity on her maiden voyage through the strait that it rendered her skipper "sick with anxiety"; the ship lay at anchor for most of her six-day passage. The one outpost of civilization along the strait was a Chilean penal colony at a village aptly named Port Famine.

The gales that raked the strait could lift a schooner from the water and slam it ashore. A ship optimistically named the *John A. Sutter* was driven aground in a squall and abandoned. The bark *Hebe* of Baltimore and the schooner *John Allyn* of New Bedford were nearly wrecked as well. Both were anchored near the first narrows when Indians wishing to trade appeared on shore. Men from both ships went ashore in boats, but before they could return a sudden storm caused both vessels to drag anchor and drift helplessly back toward the Atlantic. Eleven men in the *Hebe*'s boat were swept out to sea, where they were picked up by another ship two days later. The first mate and a passenger from the *Allyn* were taken prisoner by the natives. A ransom of five bottles of rum and five pounds of tobacco bought the release of the passenger, but the officer was held for ninety-seven days before he escaped.

Albert Lyman of the *General Morgan* was one of the few forty-niners to explore the Patagonian mainland. On one safari he came upon a herd of some five hundred deerlike, fawn-colored guanacos loping across the treeless plain. Naturally he shot one, as well as a gray fox and an animal he described as a "three-foot-long rabbit." When he and his fellow hunters surrounded an ostrichlike bird called a rhea the creature fell dead from fright. Lyman and his friends collected mussels, watercress, and wild celery. They also found a chest filled with the five-year-old papers and clothes of an unfortunate English seaman.

Lyman was either lucky with weather or more curious than his contemporaries. He found a lonely beauty in this strange and silent land. He and his mates discovered a twenty-foot-high cross on an uninhabited island. As the *General Morgan* neared the Pacific the passengers played host to a band of stocky, copper-colored and curious Indians, then evicted them for showing too much interest in the ship's fresh meat supply.

THE WELCOME serenity of the Pacific inspired bold innovations in maritime recreation. Several passengers on the *Pacific*, attaching a harpoonlike weapon to twenty fathoms of line, set out in a small boat to hitch themselves to a whale. After an hour they succeeded, but they regretted it almost immediately. The whale, pulling them ever farther from the ship, jerked them around as if the boat were a piece of cloth. The amateur Ahabs had neglected to bring a knife to cut the line. Their initial exhilaration subsided into chastened aggravation and then fear before the whale turned back toward the ship, enabling crewmen on a rescue boat to seize the line and permit the whale to escape.

With the Horn behind them, the voyagers felt entitled to another rejuvenative break. Talcahuano and Valparaiso, a pair of sailor's delights midway along the Chilean coast, were ideally equipped to receive them. Talcahuano, by two hundred miles the southerly of the two, was a village of mud huts and tile-roofed shanties tucked between a long bay and steep green hills. Its principal natural resource was its blackeyed, pigtailed whores. Samuel Upham of the *Osceola*, who arrived on May 14, discovered that there were no available beds ashore except those with girls in them—"they being the only persons authorized to take in strangers." Upham was among the few forty-niners who mentioned the girls in his journal; the diaries were usually intended for home consumption. But even Upham could not quite bring himself to be explicit. Reporting that several fellow passengers went with the girls, he wrote that they "followed the directions of the landlords."

In Talcahuano Upham learned that eleven other gold rush ships carrying about a thousand men had arrived in the preceding two weeks. He also found out that he had gained fifteen pounds (to 145) since leaving Philadelphia—in spite of the sorry shipboard meals. Watching a procession of mourners bearing the elaborately carved coffin of a Chilean infant, he thought of his daughter, the "golden-haired darling I left behind me," and wept.

Valparaiso, with a population of about thirty thousand, was more imposing. Merchants from many nations sold their goods in handsome white-walled waterfront stores. There were orange and almond orchards, gardens of giant geraniums, and fine homes on the cliffs behind the city. There were also squalid grogshops among the three hills that sailors had named Fore Top, Main Top, and Mizzen Top for the topmasts on a windjammer. Olive-skinned women beckoned from dark doorways. Argonaut Luther Schaeffer of New York took a disapproving look around and clucked that the people "appear to care more for their temporal comforts than their spiritual interests."

The Americans swaggered through the streets, a Valparaiso newspaper said, "with the aplomb of ancient Romans in a foreign city." They paid twice normal prices for fruit and curios, galloped donkeys down the cobblestoned alleys, pored over months-old New York newspapers at the reading room, and stared at the natives. The well-provided Bostonians on the *Edward Everett*, who made their first port stop at Valparaiso on April 29, drew lots to decide who went ashore first. The earnest tourists on the *Everett* had studied Spanish aboard ship and practiced for several days before they arrived. They were astonished to find that the citizens of Valparaiso did not understand their own language.

A smaller delegation from the 1849 argosy called at the romantic isle of Juan Fernandez, four hundred miles west of Valparaiso. This thirty-six-square-mile volcanic outcrop was Robinson Crusoe's island; Daniel Defoe had based his famous tale on the experiences of a Scottish sailor named Alexander Selkirk, who lived there alone from 1704 to 1709. The island, like the Black Rock Desert in northwest Nevada, had more visitors in the year 1849 than at any time before or since.

The Yankees found a few thatched huts occupied by about a dozen Chileans and a single American, a Maine-born former whaler named Pierce. Peaches, pears, figs, and other fruits and vegetables grew wild; horses, dogs, and goats released by earlier settlers ran free. The Harvard sports from the *Duxbury* idled away a day fishing and chasing wild goats. A group from Dr. Stillman's *Pacific* inspected the twelve-foot-deep cave near a grove of peach trees where Selkirk had lived. The visitors left with their casks filled with good spring water and as much fruit as they could carry.

The Cape Horn route was by any measure the safest path to California in 1849. While hundreds perished from disease in Panama and thousands died of cholera on the long trek across the plains, the number of fatalities among the seagoing forty-niners was probably fewer than fifty. Most deaths were due to disease, which in some cases had developed before the voyage. The victim was normally covered with a tarp and dropped overboard. His possessions were burned to preclude contagion. Scurvy killed several, including six from a single ship, but it was nothing like the scourge that had been feared at the outset.

Between ten and twenty men died in the sea. William Beecher, a passenger on the *Clarissa Perkins*, described what happened after one argonaut fell into the Pacific: "Boards were hove overboard and ropes. He made out to catch one of the boards which kept him up. The current was taking him astern very fast and in less than 15 minutes he could hardly be seen except as he came to the top of a wave, but we could hear him holler very plain. A boat was cut loose. . . . After the boat was gone an hour there were signs of a hard squall and the captain made signals for her to return. The wind and rain came. They found the piece of board but they couldn't find the man." The victim was identified as George Little, an unmarried confectioner from Philadelphia.

By the Fourth of July the *Edward Everett* and the *William Ivy*, carrying Dr. Horace Pond, were only two days' sail from San Francisco. Linville Hall and the *Henry Lee* were just north of Juan Fernandez. The Harvard lads on the *Duxbury* were not far from the equator off Peru.

Moses Cogswell on the *Sweden*, Samuel Upham on the *Osceola*, and Jacob Stillman on the *Pacific* were all at about the same latitude off Central America. Every ship celebrated the holiday.

The *Osceola*'s program included music by the "Oh Susanna Serenaders" and a speaker whose liquor-loosened tongue malfunctioned in midspeech, precipitating a hasty adjournment. On the *Pacific* there were several volleys of gunfire, a reading of the Declaration of Independence, and considerable stomping around deck in semimilitary style. The abstemious patriots on the *Henry Lee* had a whole pie each, a dance on the lantern-lit deck, and several dozen toasts with cold water—"the best Fourth I ever remember," Linville Hall testified.

At noon on the festive day the ships *Henry Lee* and *Loo Choo* came in sight of each other. The captains grabbed their speaking trumpets and shouted over the waves:

"Ahoy, ahoy, what ship's that?"

"The *Loo Choo*, from Valparaiso last, five days out, ninety-five days from New York there. What port did you sail from?"

"New York, one hundred and thirty days out. What time did you have round the Horn?"

"Pretty good, what had you?"

"We had an ugly time—forty days. Any news from California at Valparaiso?"

"Yes, good news. Plenty of gold. No women. Pleasant passage."

"Thank you. Same to you."

A fortnight later the *Pacific* and the *Osceola* had a similar encounter. Stillman and the other *Pacific* passengers rowed over for a visit while Upham and the *Osceola* men cheered from the railing; they had heard that the *Pacific* was lost. The two groups mingled excitedly on deck, had dinner together, and parted amid a chorus of hurrahs from both sides.

The last leg of the journey was a long, slow passage to the northwest until the ships were abreast of San Francisco Bay but still several hundred miles west, sometimes halfway to Hawaii. This enabled them to fill their sails with the prevailing westerlies and race down the homestretch before the wind.

The tedium was most oppressive during the last few weeks. Fellow passengers who seemed tolerable enough a month earlier were now unbearable. Fights broke out over trifles. The menu was more drearily monotonous than ever. Even the chipper Moses Cogswell, the most wide-eyed and uncomplaining of travelers, at last reached his limit. Cogswell was tired of men who wanted to get in their trunk as soon as someone sat on it, tired of grumblers, tired of scroungers and swearers. Nothing interested him anymore, not reading or writing or watching the sea or eating or sleeping.

His ship, the *Sweden*, had made no shore stops at all. By June the New Hampshiremen had been at sea so long that Cogswell wondered if he might have dreamed the reports of California gold. On July 8 he gave this woeful accounting of his situation:

"A dead calm sun, exactly overhead. Prospect dark and dreary. Temper cross, unaccommodating . . . Body in a perspiration. Mind neither one thing or another. Occupation, learning Spanish. Companion, sick with the mumps. Victuals, potted meats and duff. Drink, lime juice and rain water. Novelty, a large shark . . . Ideas, none in the market. Friends, few and far between. Wishes, to once more get on land. Determination, to get gold. Hopes, again to see home. . . . If any vessel makes a longer passage than we do, I pity them."

Then came the electrifying announcement that they were only a few days from their destination, and everything changed. The men were suddenly busy mending clothes, making wooden chests for their gold dust, sharpening knives and shovels, packing and repacking their gear. The transformation was total. "Although we have had nothing to do for five months," Cogswell wrote, "we now seem to have work enough for a month."

The *Sweden*'s passengers got their first glimpse of the California coast on the afternoon of August 2. The next morning they missed the Golden Gate twice in the fog but found it the third time, finally dropping anchor at 3 p.m. Cogswell's company sent two scouts to the mines while the rest looked for work in the city. Within a week he was earning $20 a day for helping to erect a house.

The *Pacific* sailed through the Gate on August 5. Jacob Stillman was ecstatic: "What hills!" he wrote. "What an entrance! What a bay spread out!" A few moments after they anchored a familiar figure came aboard. It was their old nemesis, Captain Tibbets. After his dismissal in Rio he had returned to New York and then traveled to San Francisco via the Isthmus. Tibbets uttered a single enigmatic sentence: "Now, gentlemen, you are in California, and you can go on shore as soon as you please."

The fretful Dr. Horace Pond had stepped ashore at San Francisco a month earlier. He wrote home that miners were averaging from $8 to $12 a day and that doctors were doing even better. He could hardly wait to get started for Sacramento. "All I have to say is if I have my health I am going to get rich." The excitement around him made it difficult to think. "Keep up good courage," he wrote, "until you hear worse news."

He reached Sacramento in late July. On August 1 he suffered an attack of "billious remittant fever." A doctor was called when his condition worsened. He complained of an earache on the eleventh, then lapsed into delirium. The doctor applied mustard and poultices of bread and milk, but to no effect. Poor Pond died on August 16. A friend wrote his father that Horace's pulse was racing from the moment he became sick. "The doctor and all of us attributed this to extreme nervous excitement and a conviction that his disease would prove fatal." Horace might well have worried himself to death. They buried him at Sutter's fort.

VI

THE EASY WAY

IN PANAMA

PANAMA was aswarm with Americans. The departure of the *California* on February 1 had left several hundred men feverishly awaiting the arrival of her sister ship, the *Oregon*, which had steamed out of New York more than two months after the *California*. Each day another troop of impatient Yankees passed through the stone gate on the city's landward side. Their eyes scanned the Pacific for the steamer that would speed them to El Dorado. Some were armed with through–to–San Francisco tickets they had purchased in New York; others had booked passage through the unloved Panama agents; but most of the waiting throng were both ticketless and worried. As yet only a few dozen had been stricken with cholera and fever—the number would increase sharply when the rainy season began in April—but many were running short of cash and frittering away more with each wasted day.

The forty-niners jammed the few sleepy hotels and boardinghouses. They dickered for sleeping space in the balconied rooms above adobe stores and taverns. Still suspicious of tropical fruit, they spurned the orange vendors on the quarter-mile-long main street. A motley village of multicolored tents flapped into existence in the wooded fields outside the gate. Panama appeared to be occupied by a raucous, exuberant army in flannel, but this was an army that opened shops, started a newspaper, traded with a zest approaching frenzy, staged auctions, and set up gambling houses. There hadn't been this much activity in the old Spanish treasure port since the buccaneer Henry Morgan ravaged it in 1671.

Halted by the long delay between steamships, the go-ahead Yankees hissed and fizzed like a stalled locomotive with its throttle stuck. They marched dutifully through the benchless cathedral with its twin pearl-spangled spires. They walked the sea wall, staring aggressively at the horizon. They hurried through the small, bone-littered cemetery. They organized hunting trips and attended cockfights. They fretted and fussed and fought and complained.

They also did their best to transform languid Panama into a tropical extension of home. They celebrated American holidays, convened lodge meetings, passed resolutions of protest, and held Sunday services. They even established a fund to help the sick. "You would suppose yourself in Pittsburgh," forty-niner Jabez Lewis wrote. By the time the *Oregon* bobbed into view on the morning of February 23 there were more than a thousand men trying to get aboard. The ship could carry 250.

On the previous day the Americans had managed a reasonably splendid birthday salute to George Washington. Theodore T. Johnson, a recent arrival who owned a ticket on the *Oregon,* was awakened on the twenty-second by the sound of drums and gunfire. Stumbling sleepily to his balcony, he peered past a line of red tile roofs and beheld a ragged procession of three to four hundred Americans. A uniformed band played "Hail Columbia." Johnson noticed several buzzards overhead as the parade moved to the residence of the United States consul in ninety-degree heat.

Johnson, a thirty-year-old Philadelphia exporter, was himself a gold rush phenomenon: he made the quickest round trip of 1849 and produced the first genuine book by a returned argonaut. His time in transit was astonishing, particularly when compared with the normal duration of a journey by Cape Horn or the overland trails: he left New York on February 5, reached Chagres on the fourteenth and Panama on the twenty-first, sailed in the *Oregon* on March 13, and arrived in San Francisco on April Fool's Day. He stayed for exactly one month, visiting Coloma and Sacramento and meeting both Sutter and Marshall, then sailed back to Panama on May 1. On June 26 he was home in Philadelphia. Total elapsed time: 141 days. He completed his book in September and published it a few weeks later. Surprisingly, it proved to be a careful and richly detailed narrative, one of the finest by an Isthmus traveler. His one great adventure behind him, Johnson returned to his quiet life as a prosperous Philadelphia businessman and wrote no more.

In Panama Johnson visited a bathhouse where he was given soap and a towel and assigned to a bamboo hut. Inside were three jars of water, each large enough for the immersion of a foot. He ogled the winsome Panamanian women: "A loose chemise ascends unwillingly, or rather hangs provokingly," he wrote, "from the short-sleeved shoulder." With hundreds of others he spent part of every day squinting hopefully down the trail from the town gate, searching for the animals bearing his luggage.

Bargaining and trading for tickets on the *Oregon* intensified as the March 13 sailing date approached. The ship lay at anchor in the bay, just beyond the inshore shoals. Since every ticket had long ago been sold, the only way a traveler could get one was to find a scalper. Steerage tickets with a face value of $100 went for $400 and up. More comfortable cabin accommodations, which sold originally for $200 and $250, were proportionately higher. The patricians who chose the Isthmus passage could afford the inflated prices, but the majority faced the prospect of another agonizing wait for the next steamer or a long and chancy cruise by windjammer.

Clutching their tickets, Johnson and the other *Oregon* passengers assembled on the beach below the sea wall on the twelfth. One by one the passengers climbed onto the bare shoulders of native porters who carried them through the breakers to waiting boats for the ride to the ship. Hundreds of their recent friends, trying bravely to convince each other that there was gold enough for all, watched forlornly from atop the wall, then turned back to the now intolerable city. At five the next morning the *Oregon*'s wheel began to turn. After a stop at the nearby island of Taboga for water, coal, and fruit she finally slipped over the horizon.

William M'Collum, who had headed west to escape the treadmill of life in Lockport, New York, was among those left ashore. M'Collum had sustained his spirit during his three weeks in town by the dogged pursuit of novelty. He had spent one day investigating the orange and tamarind groves on Taboga, where much of Panama's produce was grown. Another day was given over to an exploration of the ruins of Old Panama, the original city destroyed by Henry Morgan's freebooters, now thickly overgrown with jungle plants. He had studied a bowlinglike game played by the natives and tramped the bush in search of wild hogs. But now he was running out of diversions. After the *Oregon* sailed his days turned tedious and repetitious; he was frozen in place like a bug pinned quivering to a laboratory board. M'Collum's Tuesdays became indistinguishable from his Saturdays: he took a saltwater bath, strolled the streets, wandered into the forest, returned to his ten-man room for a siesta, got up for a four-o'clock dinner, and watched for ships until dark. Then it was cards, reading, or an occasional fandango. A brawl erupted at one fandango when some Americans patronizingly tossed coins on the floor and disrupted the dancing. Pistols and knives were drawn but no one was killed.

The mood of the Americans gradually turned more desperate. M'Collum and ten other men in his twenty-man company fell ill at about the same time. Alternately sweating and shivering, they lay on their bunks in the two small rooms they shared. After eight days a man named Harrington died. The others arranged for an Episcopal service and buried him amid palms and cocoa trees west of the city. A week later two of the Lockport men decided to return home.

By the end of March there were close to two thousand Americans in Panama. The last of the three Pacific Mail steamers, the *Panama*, would not arrive until early May, by which time the *Oregon* would be back for another load and the *California* would be on her way as well. But the men sweating it out in Panama had no idea when another steamer would arrive. All they could do was scramble for berths in the few available sailing ships, contrive to spend as little of their poke as possible, and fume.

The delay was too much for many of them. Dozens waited as long as they could and then gave up, loading their trunks on the hardy little Panama mules for the walk back to Gorgona. An Ohio newspaper reported that every mail brought news of more men back from Panama. Several sailed south along the South American coast, hoping to find a California-bound vessel in Peru or Chile.

Desperation impelled a few daredevils to take to the sea in nothing more than long canoes with built-up bulkheads and improvised masts. At least three such boats set out from Panama in March and April of 1849. One was dismasted almost immediately and returned the same day; a second managed to get a few hundred miles up the coast of Central America before its crew was forced to quit; a third boat, incredibly, carried six men all the way to San Francisco. The craft had two masts, a canvas half-deck, and raised sides. The crew made frequent stops for food and water. The boat turned up later on Feather River in the mining country.

Another out-of-patience group bought a fifteen-foot iron lifeboat on the Atlantic side of the Isthmus and carried it twenty miles on their shoulders. Casting off from Panama, they apparently got as far as Mazatlán before they decided to beach the boat and transfer to a French bark. The French vessel was subsequently driven aground in a storm with a loss of twenty lives, including two of the iron boat sailors.

Passage in sailing ships hastily modified for the California trade was not much better. Many were converted whalers, coalships, or even fishing boats. Speculators made a fast profit by purchasing them and cramming them with passengers at $150 or $200 each. John Letts of Staten Island, New York, said he saw one schooner so crowded that the owners "appear to have taken the exact measurements of each man and filled the vessel accordingly." The outraged passengers would not permit the captain to weigh anchor until they found and locked up one of the owners. Then they agreed among themselves that the latest ticket buyers would leave the ship.

The *Alexander Von Humboldt,* a coal storeship which had been languishing in Panama for five months, sold 440 berths at $200 apiece. On going aboard the passengers found that nine of them were stuffed into each six-foot-square compartment. A delegation marched ashore and forced the owners to remove 80 men, 40 to get down to the announced maximum and 40 more for punishment. Even with the reduced load, New Englander Julius Pratt wrote, "we were packed more densely, had less accommodations for sleeping and were served infinitely viler food and water than inmates of the worst jail."

Collis Huntington, who would also become one of the Big Four railroad builders, was among those shoehorned into the *Humboldt.* The twenty-seven-year-old Huntington had Sam Brannan's gift: he could turn a profit while treading water. On his own since he was fourteen, he had eventually settled down to run a successful store in Oneonta, New York. He brought a stock of goods with him to Panama and promptly went into business, buying and selling whatever paid well. "A lot of companies came there and quarreled," he wrote many years later. "They came to me; they all seemed to come to me. I used to buy them out." While his countrymen wrung their hands and stared out to sea, Huntington shrewdly bought a schooner on the South American coast and shipped in beef, potatoes, and sugar from nearby ports. He was already amassing California gold: he left Panama $4,000 heavier than he arrived.

Darius Ogden Mills, a twenty-three-year-old Buffalo banker, was another Panama profiteer. Mills perceived that there was money in shipping if he could only find a ship, so he took a British steamer to Callao, Peru, chartered a bark to carry a hundred men to California, and pocketed the profit. Mills was so eager to reach San Francisco that he set out in a rowboat when his ship was becalmed several miles off the Golden Gate. He eventually became California's leading banker, a man so unfailingly successful that "the luck of D. O. Mills" became a California axiom for prosperity.

By late April the bloom of excitement was long gone for the Americans stranded in Panama. Gamblers had commenced separating them from their thinning bankrolls. The melancholy spectacle of men auctioning off their possessions to pay their way home became common. "Many have lost all and many more are poor," Jabez Lewis wrote home to Mississippi. "There is a perfect hazing and cutthroat game played here." And the stakes were higher than money: there were already thirty fresh graves in the American cemetery.

The *Oregon,* the second steamship to reach San Francisco from the Isthmus, glided between the mustard-washed hills bordering the Golden Gate on April 1 with streamers flying. The shipboard mood of breathless anticipation had heightened during the stops at San Blas, San Diego, and Monterey. At San Blas the passengers listened entranced as an eastbound Californian told of "hundreds of pounds—vast quantities—immense heaps" in the Sierra foothills. At San Diego they were told that all but seven of the town's males were at the mines. At Monterey the ship's carpenter swam ashore and disappeared.

Aware that the *California*'s crew had absconded nearly en masse, *Oregon* skipper Richard Pearson anchored across the channel at Sausalito under the guns of the U.S. man-of-war *Ohio.* Crewmen he considered potential deserters were shackled. Several other crewmen and at least one officer managed to desert anyway by capturing a dinghy and rowing ashore.

Passenger T. T. Johnson let his gaze sweep over a town of some three hundred unpainted houses plus an uncounted number of tents. Dozens of abandoned ships lay creaking in the cove. Calico, silk, and furniture were piled on the beach in neglected heaps. Quart bottles of gold dust perched on the tables at gambling houses. Johnson plucked some small change out of the mud where high rollers had scattered it and bought himself a three-dollar breakfast.

GORDON'S California Association seemed to be among the most promising of all the gold rush companies. George Gordon was a sophisticated young Britisher with formidable business and scientific skills, a "practical geologist," maybe a touch too clever but undeniably attractive—"the handsomest man I ever saw," in the words of a man who didn't particularly like him.

Gordon had a new way to California. The alluring broadsides he distributed in Philadelphia and New York in early 1849 described a route across Nicaragua by way of the San Juan River, Lake Nicaragua, and a sixty-mile hike on a "well-traveled carriage road" to the Pacific. His company would provide everything: oilskin tents, hammock beds, field stoves, gold-washing machines, crates of tools, and an ample larder including ham, sausage, preserved fruit, potatoes, rice, and coffee.

Gordon's party would travel to Nicaragua by chartered ship and climb the river in a little steamer they would bring along. His agent would have another ship waiting at Realejo on the Pacific. The entire trip would consume "50 to 60 days at farthest." Gordon's plan appeared sound and the man himself seemed solid; his wife and five-year-old daughter Nellie were accompanying him. The only rub would be finding a ship at Realejo, which was not one of the busier Pacific ports, but Gordon was especially persuasive on just that point: his men were even now seeking a ship in Panama and Acapulco; passage money and provisions would be refunded if no vessel materialized.

Roger Sherman Baldwin, Jr., a recent Yale graduate and the son of a U.S. senator from Connecticut, enthusiastically climbed aboard along with three of his classmates. Young Baldwin airily waved aside his father's objections in a letter shortly before they sailed in February: "It is too late now—my passage is engaged and money paid and I must try it. If you never hear from me again, consider that there are no mails from Realejo."

Gordon and his 116 confident recruits sailed into the harbor at San Juan on March 11. A village of forty or fifty thatch-roofed huts amid palms and coconut trees, San Juan looked like a healthier Chagres. The boys unloaded their cargo, taking special care with the steamboat *Plutus*, which was to carry them upriver and across the lake. They installed the boiler and engine and tried to start it, but it failed to catch. They tried again. Nothing. Gordon said that it might take a few days. They settled in.

Baldwin wrote his mother after a week, proudly reporting that they had eaten alligator steak and roast boar but adding ominously that "Gordon's Line is a humbug." The men read and played cards, hunted and fished, and took an occasional kick at the *Plutus'* boiler. One journal keeper allowed that "considerable hilarity" prevailed in the evenings.

After three weeks Gordon gave up on the steamboat and hired a fleet of bungos to take them the 120 miles to Lake Nicaragua. The shores of the San Juan were dense with vines and giant-leafed plants, brightly colored birds and the strange trilling sounds of the jungle. They glided through tunnels of overhanging moss and listened to the roars of tropical cats. The real menace was closer: "The mosquitoes are so infernal thick," wrote H. C. Logan, "that you can kill at the very lowest calculation one million with a blow."

They reached the lake in a week and transferred to larger boats for the 120-mile cruise to Granada, a city of some fifteen thousand. Here the Yale men found rooms in an abandoned convent while Gordon hustled to the coast to complete arrangements for a ship. Baldwin's morale, if not his confidence in his leader, was still high. A letter home in May described Gordon as "a man who combined with a little of the knave a great deal of the fool." The Englishman had "overreached himself" and "wasted most of our funds." He had been unable to find a ship on the Pacific side. Still, life in Granada was no bed of nails: girls delivered trays of oranges to their convent digs; "all Granada keeps open house for us"; and Baldwin said he had already declined "two offers of marriage." He and his friends lingered for five weeks before proceeding on muleback to the capital city of León, where they were startled to find themselves designated the president's personal bodyguards. Each of them was given a room in a large house fringed with orange trees and jasmine.

Gordon finally found a brig at Port Union, a short distance up the coast from Realejo, but he was $2,250 short of the charter fee. He asked each man to chip in another $20 and aimed a special appeal at the affluent Yale men, who grudgingly responded. By now the company's discontent was phasing into disaffection. "I shall go forward the first opportunity that offers," H. C. Logan wrote to his brother, "and Gordon may go to the devil, for he is decidedly the greatest humbug of the day."

The association's point men got to Realejo in late May. Here, to their astonishment, they ran into more forty-niners, the first they had seen since they left New York. A group from New Orleans had turned up there after leaving their disabled Chagres-bound ship in Belize, British Honduras, and traveling by mule train to Realejo. On June 2 there was another surprise: the iron boat that had set out from Panama rode up on the beach; the sunburned occupants stocked up on food and water and sallied forth once more.

Two more weeks passed with no sign of Gordon's brig, which was supposed to meet the company at Realejo. When a ship at last floated into view it turned out to be a southbound Ecuadorian brig. Logan and three others defected and shipped out for Panama.

The cloud over Gordon finally lifted on July 2, nearly four months after he arrived in Nicaragua. Another ship appeared at Realejo, not the mysterious brig he had bargained for but the hundred-ton *Laura Ann*, and he hurried to make an offer. He told Baldwin and his cohorts that this was their last hope. The price was $3,500 cash. He was unable to resist a final teaser: "The captain and supercargo have both recently been working in the mines, and their specimens look most tempting." Baldwin and his friends came across with more money, then piled their luggage into a farmer's cart and headed for the coast. "There is really now some prospect of our getting off," Baldwin wrote to his family. He had paid little attention to a crucial line in Gordon's urgent plea: "In this brig," the promoter had said, "we must expect to be something crowded, but it is this or nothing."

PANAMA was the clean-fingernails route to California, the way of the wealthy, the well-educated, and the fastidious. Jessie Benton Frémont, the twenty-four-year-old wife of the explorer, hurried across Panama in 1849 while her husband was barely surviving a winter crossing of the San Juan Mountains in Colorado. New Orleans gambler Jack McCabe and his mistress, Irene McCready, one of the earliest San Francisco madams, traveled the Isthmus. So did whole caucuses of past, present, and future politicians: ex-Congressman Thomas Butler King of Georgia; former Ohio Congressman (and future California Governor) John Weller; and onetime Mississippi Congressman (future California Senator) William Gwin. A New Orleans correspondent wrote only half facetiously that at one point there were 600 lawyers idling in Panama, 400 of whom expected to be California congressmen; he added that 17 were already campaigning for governor and 21 for U.S. senator.

Some of the well-bred Isthmus travelers were young men whose only acquaintance with labor had come as spectators; digging for gold would be a revelation for them. One such youth was twenty-two-year-old Howard Calhoun (Cal) Gardiner of Sag Harbor, New York, who arrived on the steamship *Crescent City* in late March. "I had never done any work that required more effort than occasionally to split wood for my mother or perhaps dig a post hole," he later confessed. California would be his crucible of manhood.

Likable, self-effacing Cal Gardiner belonged to the aristocracy of Long Island. His family had owned what is still known as Gardiner's Island, off the eastern end of Long Island, since 1638. As a boy he swam in Gardiner's Bay. He grew up in an atmosphere of comfort, piety, and culture; his father was a Presbyterian minister, his mother a writer of both prose and poetry. Cal himself was well read in both the classics and contemporary literature. Sensitive and buoyant, he joined the rush to California at the first opportunity; the thought of being left behind was intolerable.

His first night on the Chagres River was the most miserable of his life. His bunk was a dried bull hide stretched between poles in a sweltering hut. Fleas made sleep impossible. The insects plus the squalid stench of the place finally drove him to sleep in the bungo. By early April he was a part of the milling mob of Americans in Panama. He watched the natives celebrate Easter by hanging and burning an effigy of Judas Iscariot "to the great amusement of the multitude."

On April 23 the Panama horizon watchers spotted the ship *Sylph*, a three-hundred-ton ex-whaler out of Fair Haven, Massachusetts. Speedily converted to a passenger carrier, the *Sylph* sold 191 tickets at $300 each in an hour. Among the buyers were all of Gardiner's companions, but not Cal; he had misunderstood the time of the sale and failed to show up. He got aboard anyway with a friend's ticket; the friend, who came from Fair Haven, knew one of the ship's officers. The *Sylph* sailed on May 9. By that time the Americans in Panama were dazed with excitement: the steamers *Oregon* from San Francisco and *Panama* from New York had arrived on successive days.

BAYARD TAYLOR, who reached the Isthmus in July, could also afford to travel first class. But unlike Gardiner, Taylor had a trade; he was a writer for Horace Greeley's New York *Tribune*. At twenty-four, the slender, long-haired Taylor was the most gifted journalist to take part in the 1849 migration.

Raised in a family of Quaker farmers, Taylor had parlayed his talent and an engaging personality into a precocious career as a travel writer. His book of European sketches, *Views Afoot,* had won him literary celebrity at twenty-one. A collection of poems appeared two years later. Taylor was traveling to California as a professional writer with the intention of producing a book about his trip. His friend George P. Putnam had already agreed to publish it.

Curious, personable, and brimming with energy, Taylor was a perfect gold rush correspondent. In addition his travels in Europe had given him a perspective shared by few of his fellow wayfarers. He could sketch what he saw with the soft brush of a few words, as in his first view of the tropics at Chagres: "A heavy cloud on the sea broke out momently into broad scarlet flashes of lightning. . . . The dark walls of San Lorenzo, the brilliant clusters of palms on the shore, and the green, rolling hills of the interior leaped at intervals out of the gloom, as vividly seen as under the noonday sun."

Taylor was startled to hear his Chagres River boatman sing "Oh! Susanna"; the anthem had become international. On the trail from Gorgona to Panama he encountered a Mississippian with cholera; the disease by now had killed hundreds of Panamanians and Americans. The stricken man attached himself to Taylor's party and rode into Panama in agonizing pain which was dulled only slightly by a bottle of claret.

Lucky Taylor spent but a day and a half in Panama before boarding his steamship. The Yankee influence had not abated: "nearly half the faces seen were American, and the signs on shops of all kinds appeared in our language." He estimated that seven hundred Americans sought space on the steamer. A lottery was devised to apportion the fifty-two available tickets. This quieted the crowd, he noticed, "though there was still a continual undercurrent of speculation and intrigue." The simmering resentments broke into the open a few weeks later with charges that the shipping agents were arbitrarily delaying steamship departures so they could sell high-priced tickets on sailing ships they had chartered. This amounted to extortion, a resolution said, of "those whose poverty and suffering in a strange country ought to entitle them to aid rather than . . . oppression."

IT WAS a grim irony that the forty-niners who traveled the Panama route, unarguably the quickest and easiest path to California in 1849, suffered some of the most severe hardships. The only argonauts who endured worse were the overland parties on the western deserts. The most hapless Panama voyagers were those who impatiently jammed themselves aboard unseaworthy and poorly equipped vessels for the final 3,500-mile leg of the journey to San Francisco.

Collis Huntington, Julius Pratt, and the 358 other passengers on the German-built *Alexander Von Humboldt* knew they were on such a ship before they escaped the Bay of Panama. It took three weeks just to do that. Alternately flailing against adverse winds and stymied by calms, the ship needed forty-eight days to sail the fifteen hundred miles to Acapulco. They almost ran out of food. Pratt and nineteen passengers disgustedly left the ship, yielding their places to innocents ashore who had crossed Mexico on foot and horseback. Pratt was gambling that he could somehow get aboard a steamer at Acapulco.

The *Humboldt* drifted so far west in quest of favorable winds in the Pacific that the captain considered putting in at Hawaii. Six passengers perished of various diseases. George Payson, who had rounded the Horn on the *Magnolia,* saw the *Humboldt* as she neared San Francisco, one hundred days out of Panama. The sagging bark struck Payson as "an out-and-out vagrant, a beggar born and bred." Passengers "swarmed black as ants out on the bowsprit, they clustered like bees in the rigging. . . . [The] matted heads that looked at us over the bulwarks seemed almost as thick as a pile of coconuts." In San Francisco the *Humboldt* got what she deserved: condemnation.

The entrepreneur Collis Huntington began doing what came naturally as soon as he touched land. He negotiated a deal to enlist passengers on a Sacramento schooner at a commission of a dollar a head. This earned him $84. A week later he made his first and last pass at gold mining. "I tried mining as thorough as any man did in this country," he wrote afterwards. "I worked nearly a whole day in the mines and I made up my mind it would not pay me. I came back to Sacramento to start in business."

The hundred-ton schooner *Dolphin,* which left Panama in January with forty-five men aboard, was an even shabbier vagrant than the *Humboldt.* The ship leaked, her rigging was rotten, and she was short of drinking water. Most of the original passengers defected in Mazatlán, but there were so many anxious Yankees on shore that sixty-eight were aboard when she set off again. One was James McClatchy, later a prominent newspaper publisher.

About two-thirds of the way up the Baja California coast the exasperated *Dolphin* passengers took a vote and forty-eight elected to get off and walk. Each was given a half-bottle of water, half a pound of rice, and two pieces of hardtack—all that could be spared. Splitting into small parties, the men jettisoned most of their baggage and trekked through cactus-choked ravines and dry streambeds, constantly searching for water. When one dropped from hunger and exhaustion, the others revived him with the meat of a dead horse. They traded for corn and pinole at a coastal village. A few miles farther north they found the dilapidated *Dolphin;* the remaining passengers had finally given up.

Ragged and weary, the first of the *Dolphin* survivors straggled into San Diego on June 22, three and a half weeks after they started. Only one died in Baja. Later in the year twenty-three passengers from the little schooner *San Juan* had a similar ordeal but had to walk even farther; it took them fifty-one days to make San Diego.

THE MEN of George Gordon's once eager band lay in a breezeless torpor off Guatemala. Gordon had been right: their ship was "something crowded." The *Laura Ann* was also something wretched. One passenger described her as "an old-fashioned tub of a vessel, and slower than justice." Shortly after leaving Realejo they learned that they had lost nearly half of their water through leaks from the cedar tanks. They had to endure the tropical summer becalmed and limited to a quart of water a day. Part of their meat had spoiled too. "The smell would sicken all but a California emigrant," Roger Baldwin wrote. Gordon, who may have glimpsed the potential for disaster, had stayed behind in Nicaragua to arrange a lumber shipment.

Running dangerously low on both food and water, the *Laura Ann* inched up the Baja coast. The menu dwindled down to wormy biscuit, weevil-fouled rice, and beans that hardened as they boiled. "I would have been thankful for the mush grandfather feeds his hogs," Baldwin wrote. Spying a little green valley, they tried to send a boat ashore for water but were driven back by the surf.

Deliverance came a few weeks later. Still off Baja, they ran their boats on shore in a fog and stumbled on a pool of fresh water. A Peruvian brig appeared and anchored next to them. The brig turned out to be loaded with food. The Gordon men bought flour, cheese, sugar, lard, and other groceries. They found cattle grazing in a nearby valley and bought some for beef. The valley was an Eden of plants and wildlife; Baldwin gathered thirty kinds of wild flowers. The *Laura Ann*'s officers and crew liked it so well that all but the captain deserted. Passengers took over their jobs.

Three weeks later they landed at San Francisco. It was October 4; the "50 to 60 days at farthest" had stretched into eight interminable months; the voyage from Nicaragua alone took seventy-eight days.

Baldwin, weakened by an attack of dysentery, wrote home the day he arrived: "It was a bad business, our connection with his 60-day line. I feel that I have lost everything by the delay." Then he took a look at the place he had been so avid to see: "Such another city never was and never will be," he wrote. "Sharpers, swindlers, speculators, gamblers and rogues of every nation, clime, color, language and costume under the sun are here. . . . You can conceive nothing of this country. No account that you have ever read can give you half an idea. Double everything, and believe that then you know not the half."

CAL GARDINER was better outfitted for the last lap of the trip to California than most Panama travelers. As a boy he had watched whaling crews fitting out in his native Sag Harbor and learned what was important: he boarded the *Sylph* in May with a sawdust-filled mattress, a large tin pot, a pan, and eating utensils. At meal times he stood in line with his tinware while a steward ladled food onto whatever receptacle the passengers presented. Some had only a coconut shell or a cleated board.

The *Sylph* sailed a circuitous course, first swinging south to the Ecuadorian village of Atecames to load wood and water and then heading northwest in search of the trade winds. Cal spent his days high in the ship's rigging where he could read in peace and relative comfort. He borrowed *The Three Musketeers* from a crewman and read it three times.

Shipboard meals demanded a sturdy stomach. The staples were salt pork and eighteen-month-old hardtack flecked with weevils. As for the butter, passenger Hiram Pierce wrote that "the sight is sufficient without the smell." When Cal saw a man secrete a newly baked shortcake on a shelf above his hammock he was able to silence his Presbyterian conscience long enough to snatch it and eat it. That evening the outraged baker accused another man of appropriating his shortcake and appealed to the squirming Gardiner for corroboration. Cal judiciously allowed that the evidence was circumstantial and that "the defendant was entitled to the benefit of the doubt."

By the Fourth of July they were about six hundred miles west of Baja California. The patriots on the *Sylph* prayed, sang, and orated at each other and then dived into a banquet of bean soup, plum duff, boiled rice, and no fewer than twenty-one doughnuts each. Gardiner listed the day's potables: "Agua frio, tea, wines impossible, whiskey ditto, individual contributions freely authorized."

On July 16 the passengers were summoned on deck for the burial of Corydon Bristol of Troy, New York, a father of two who had been ill for several weeks. A short service was read after which the canvas-shrouded body was dropped over the side. Ten days later the *Sylph* entered San Francisco Bay.

Cal went ashore alone. The $400 he had started with was now down to $6, and he lacked a tent. A man hailed him and invited him to "test" some brandy he had bought. Cal complied, then tested it again. The next day he confronted his own dearth of marketable skills, passed himself off as a carpenter, and got a job at $12 a day.

BAYARD TAYLOR left Panama on the steamship *Panama* the day before Gardiner went to work in San Francisco. If Taylor had any shortcoming as a gold rush chronicler, it could only be a kind of excessive good cheer; he was good-natured to a fault, optimistic by temperament, and uncritical about most of what he saw in California. The greedy boorishness he encountered at the *Panama*'s dining table furnished an example: Taylor qualified it even as he deplored it. "A dish of sweet potatoes vanished before a single hand," he wrote. "Beefsteak flew in all directions"; half the passengers stuffed themselves while the other half went without. "I believe the controlling portion of the California emigration is intelligent, orderly, and peaceable," he wrote, "yet I have never witnessed so many disgusting exhibitions of the lowest passions of humanity as during the voyage." Taylor may have been the first to try to characterize the 1849 emigrants as a whole. Like many who wrote later, from a longer perspective, he was ambivalent.

Only two groups of men on board provoked Taylor's unequivocal enmity: gamblers and self-pitying sufferers. He had heard of four loutish gamblers who used the altar candles in a Panama church as cigar lighters. These sports ran monte games on the *Panama*'s quarterdeck until they were chased off by the captain. The other type—"miserable, melancholy men, ready to yield up their last breath at any moment"—yearned for sympathy. Taylor thought they would prefer being buried alive with only their heads above ground.

At Acapulco the *Panama*'s boat to shore was turned back by a column of Mexican soldiers on the beach; word of cholera in Panama had led to a quarantine of ships from the Isthmus. This came as a stunning blow to Julius Pratt, who had abandoned the doddering *Alexander Von Humboldt* in Acapulco and was now struggling to get aboard a steamer. Pratt was running in circles on the beach like a tormented terrier; what was bedeviling him was the fact that he could *see* the ship but couldn't reach it. He bought a small boat but the troops refused to let him leave shore. Then he found a canoe and simply took it, frantically pushing through the surf while the owner's dog yapped in protest. This fizzled too: "Our last ray of hope flickered . . . as the water came rushing up through a great seam in the bottom." Pratt and his friends walked miserably up the beautiful beach and watched the steamer's lights disappear around a point. It would take him two more months to get on a steamship.

Taylor discerned a change in the passengers' moods as they neared San Francisco: "Their exhilarant anticipations left them, and were succeeded by a reaction of feeling that almost amounted to despondency." The unknowns and uncertainties of this strange new land suddenly loomed before them.

The ship cruised through the Gate, around Telegraph Hill, and in sight of the slats-and-canvas city on August 18. A gun announced her arrival. Taylor scrambled up the steep bank from the bay and collided with the afternoon wind. "On every side stood buildings of all kinds, begun or half-finished. . . . Great quantities of goods were piled up in the open air. . . . The streets were full of people, hurrying to and fro, and of as diverse and bizarre a character as the houses." Noticing a fellow passenger selling copies of his newspaper, the New York *Tribune*, for a dollar a copy, Taylor rummaged through his trunks and found his first nugget—twelve *Tribunes* he had stuffed amid his gear. He sold them to a vendor for $10, a profit he calculated at four thousand percent. Horace Greeley would have been proud.

REVEILLE ON THE RIVERS

STEAMER *Antelope* LEAVES FOR SACRAMENTO

MOST Americans who dreamed of California in 1849 could find a way to get there. A trip to the golden land was feasible; it was within the range of their possibilities. It demanded time, money, planning, courage, stamina, vigor—it was a venture for the young and strong, to be sure, but it was a manageable idea, as ten years earlier it would not have been. California had been part of Mexico in 1839. The few American vessels that stopped there were either whalers or merchant ships trading for hides and tallow. Steamship passage via the Isthmus of Panama had not yet begun. American civilization in 1839 halted at the Missouri River;

beyond lay the void, the realm of darkness, the province of the painted
Plains Indians and the bold mountain men who trafficked with them. The
average schoolboy's knowledge of American geography had advanced
only slightly since Lewis and Clark's explorations in 1804–6.

But all that had changed in the decade preceding 1849. Frémont had
plunged into the void and come out the other side with maps, scientific
data, and an eagerly read journal which lifted the curtain from the trans-
Missouri West. Plain farmers from Illinois, Ohio, and Tennessee had
traveled the Oregon Trail with their families and settled in the luxuriant
valley of the Willamette; James Marshall and a few other Oregon settlers
had drifted down to California. Brigham Young had guided his perse-
cuted flock to sanctuary on the Great Salt Lake, and Sam Brannan had
led a seagoing congregation of Mormons to San Francisco. Battalions of
eager young men like Edward Buffum and James Carson had marched
through Mexico as soldiers and conquerors and lingered on in what was
still known as Alta California. Americans had leaped a continent in the
1840s, spreading the fabric of Yankee civilization until it lay like a
tattered and windblown tent over the vastness between Florida and
Oregon. The forty-niners would peg it down on the Pacific.

The way west was no longer a mystery. There were dozens of ways
west. Besides the sea route around the Horn and the land-and-sea journey
through Panama there were the main overland trails and their variations:
the Oregon Trail out of Independence or St. Joseph on the Missouri, up
the Platte and on to South Pass, then forking southwest to the Humboldt
River and California; the Santa Fe Trail that John Sutter had traveled,
southwest out of Independence to Santa Fe and then to the Colorado and
Los Angeles; the Mormon Trail from Kanesville (later Council Bluffs)
on the Missouri, up the north bank of the Platte and on to the Salt Lake.

The men in the river towns of the East and Midwest gathered at the
dry-goods store or the firehouse through the winter of 1849 and discussed
the possibilities. For them the trip would start by river, however it ended.
They looked on the rivers as New Englanders viewed the sea—as the
high road to everywhere. Riverboats cruised the Ohio, the Illinois, and
the Monongahela, the Arkansas, the Missouri, and the Mississippi. They
linked the mushrooming cities on the rivers, Pittsburgh and Cincinnati
and St. Louis, Louisville and Memphis and New Orleans. A Pennsylvanian with a yen for gold could travel by river steamer all the way to
Independence or St. Joseph via the Ohio, the Mississippi, and the Missouri. The fare was about $15. For a little more he could transfer to a

southbound boat at Cairo, Illinois, and go on to New Orleans and thence Panama. But those were only the most obvious choices. Gathered around an atlas on a long January night, a group of argonauts could shift their eyes south and spot a half-dozen more ways to El Dorado, and at least a modest case could be made for each.

There was Mexico, for example, which narrowed enticingly as it dipped southward. Mexico had been the route of Lieutenant Ned Beale, the swiftest of the gold rush couriers. Beale had crossed the waist of the country from San Blas to Veracruz via Mexico City, and his experience had vividly illustrated both the strengths and weaknesses of this route. The main advantage was that most of the country along the trail was settled; a traveler could obtain food, water, and livestock. The chief disadvantage was the distinct likelihood of robbery or worse in the eastern or western spurs of the Sierra Madre mountains; Beale had eluded three separate attempts.

A more northerly Mexican trail ran from Tampico on the Gulf to Mazatlán or San Blas on the Pacific. This 550-mile route through sparsely settled and often rugged country was used by relatively few forty-niners. Several companies set out from the mouth of the Rio Grande River on the border and crossed the dry, dun-colored highlands of Nuevo León, Coahuila, Chihuahua, Durango, and Sonora before returning to the States at the Colorado River. If outlaws were the chief hazard on the Mexican routes, there was also the danger of antigringo hostility in the aftermath of the recent war.

Texas offered several possibilities. Starting from the Gulf ports of Galveston, Port Lavaca, and Corpus Christi, wagon roads led through well-watered farmland to Austin and San Antonio, then across the un-settled and partially explored reaches of west Texas to El Paso, Tucson, and a linkup with the Santa Fe Trail. One major talking point for the Texas trails was that they stayed north of the border and thus avoided touchy foreigners. Another was the mild climate, which permitted an early start and eliminated the risk of being snowbound in high mountains like members of the unlucky Donner party only three years before.

Texas newspapers, savoring the commercial potential, saw even more advantages for the Lone Star trails: "the free air of the prairies," for example, which "bids defiance to the diseases of crowded seaports or the pestilence-breathing marshes of the Isthmus. The abundance of game protects the hunter from the dread of famine, cool streams assuage his thirst, and scattered mots [sic] of timber afford a grateful shelter from the noonday heats." The booster ads failed to mention just how scattered those cool streams and "mots of timber" were, of course, just as they overlooked the alarming fact that the Texas routes crossed the territories of two of the most formidable Indian tribes in the West, the Comanches and the Apaches.

Arkansas presented still another avenue. Riverboats steamed up the Arkansas River from its junction with the Mississippi to the head of navigation at the neighboring frontier villages of Fort Smith and Van Buren, which were as far west as Independence and St. Joseph. From Fort Smith a fur traders' trail took emigrants along the Canadian River across present-day Oklahoma and the Texas Panhandle to Santa Fe. On the map, this route looked more direct than the trails from either Missouri or Texas, an impression cleverly underscored by its promoters: "American people," the Arkansas State *Democrat* commented, "do not usually reach a point in a roundabout way which can be gained by a direct approach."

The greatest coup for the Arkansas route was achieved somewhat less directly. A U.S. senator from Arkansas splendidly named Solon Borland persuaded the War Department to order a military escort—the only such escort in 1849—for travelers from Fort Smith. The presence of a troop of cavalrymen could allay any number of apprehensions—Indians, starvation, and the danger of getting lost, among others. The dragoons could banish almost every anxiety, in fact, except the weather, so inevitably it was the weather that produced the most serious obstacle on the Arkansas road: heavy spring rains turned the Canadian Valley near Fort Smith into a quagmire which took weeks to get through.

A forty-niner who consulted the growing library of guidebooks to learn about land routes to California was as likely to be misguided as guided. Lansford Hastings, a longtime California promoter, dashed off a snappy summary of the mid-Mexico route which made it sound like a pleasure jaunt: from Veracruz, "by stage, three days, to the city of Mexico; thence by stage, six days, to Guadalajara; thence on horseback, five days, to Tepic; thence on horseback, two days, to St. Blas; thence by water, twelve days, to California." This optimistic itinerary ignored both the cordilleras and the bandits they harbored plus the low likelihood of finding a boat on the West Coast, but Hastings had a history of giving bad advice: in 1846 he had directed the Donner party to a fatally prolonged "cutoff" across Salt Lake Desert. Fayette Robinson, another guidebook author, fell back on vagueness: the overland emigrant should "seek the most practicable route," he suggested helpfully; the traveler would find a particular trail junction "at a certain point," but he wasn't quite sure where.

Information on the Texas and Arkansas trails was the skimpiest, often consisting of nothing more than newspaper advertisements or third-hand reports from anonymous army officers. The Oregon-California trail, the best known and most heavily traveled, was the best documented as well. The Missouri River outposts had been the jump-off points for a generation of self-sufficient trappers and traders; the adventures of men like Kit Carson, "Broken Hand" Fitzpatrick, Andrew Sublette, and the Robidoux brothers had already passed into American folklore. Mountain men like Jim Stewart, Antoine Robidoux, and Jim Kirker could still be found on the Missouri; all of them would guide overland companies in 1849. Because of them the Oregon Trail guidebooks, especially those published in the West, were full of the details a traveler needed: the whereabouts of good grass and water; the distances between good campsites; advice on how to deal with different Indian tribes; descriptions of poisoned springs and difficult river crossings.

The best overland guidebook was a fifty-six-page pamphlet by St. Louis newspaperman Joseph Ware. Ware's book answered most questions and anticipated almost every dilemma. He advised the Missouri emigrants when to leave (by May 1), what size traveling parties worked best (no more than fifty men), what kind of wagons to take (strong but light), and exactly how much food they needed: expect everyone to eat twice as much on the trail as they did at home, he said. He urged that the wagons be formed in an oval at night, that a leader be elected after a few days on the road, and that the train move out by 4 a.m. daily. It was Ware's best estimate that the total cost for provisioning a wagon and four people for the journey was $670.78, or $167.69 each.

It was certain, Ware wrote, that emigrants would "meet with difficulties and trials." The greatest trial would prove to be neither Indians nor starvation nor storms but a scourge that no one could have anticipated: cholera. By midwinter the epidemic had already spread from New Orleans along the Gulf coast to the Rio Grande; by early spring it had invaded the Arkansas; by late April and May, when the great heaving, clanking, and cursing army would at last roll out from the Missouri, cholera would be with them.

JOHN WOODHOUSE AUDUBON was the kind of man who charmed mothers along with their daughters. The thirty-six-year-old son of the

naturalist John James Audubon was handsome, even dashing. As a youth
he had played the fiddle on a Mississippi riverboat. Yet he was also sober
and cautious. A gifted painter and student of wildlife like his father,
Audubon rarely took a stride in any direction without careful consideration of the consequences. He hesitated for several days before he agreed
to join the California company led by Colonel Henry L. Webb, whose
brother James edited the New York *Herald*. When Audubon finally did
sign on he was immediately placed second in command.

Webb, a Mexican War veteran, envisioned a crisp, military-style company which would start from the Rio Grande bottomlands and move
briskly across northern Mexico by way of Monterrey, Chihuahua, and the
Gila River west of Tucson. His ninety-eight men, many of them New
Yorkers with only the slimmest acquaintance with the outdoors, were
issued woolen uniforms with brass buttons. They set up camp in early
March near the village of Rio Grande City, 125 miles upstream from the
river's mouth. Webb ordered them to align their tents in the military
fashion, ignoring the fact that this placed some tents on mud and others
on sand. The temperature was close to 100°. Webb then went off on a
mule-shopping trip to Mexico, leaving Audubon in charge.

Audubon happily set about gathering specimens of the local fauna;
for him, the chance to see and describe a whole new world of wildlife
was the greatest attraction of the journey. He soon found several birds
he had never seen before: "a new thrush, a beautiful green jay, a new
cardinal . . . two new woodpeckers and a little dove." He spread the
skins to dry and permitted himself to enjoy the sense of physical well-
being he felt simply in being there. His only major worry was the $27,000
in company funds which Webb had entrusted to him; he didn't like holding it.

Three days later a company member named John Lambert, a lawyer
from Connecticut, suddenly fell ill. Lambert was retching violently and
suffering from stomach cramps, diarrhea, chills, and fever. Audubon
helped the doctor rub mustard on the sick man's chest and gave him
spoonfuls of brandy. The doctor suspected cholera. Lambert died fourteen
hours after the initial attack.

Cholera killed quickly and miserably, usually through a loss of fluid.
Audubon's men probably picked up the bug in New Orleans, where they
had stopped en route, or in one of the towns along the Rio Grande, where
dozens had already died. Hamilton Boden, a strong, well-built youth,
was stricken the following night. His convulsive retching burst the blood
vessels in his face, streaking his nose and forehead with violet ridges.

Two other men were seized with cramps and were soon dying along with Boden. The rest of the now terrified company took the opportunity offered by a passing riverboat to pack up and flee upstream to the town of Roma. Audubon and a few volunteers stayed behind with the sick.

Now calamity struck from a new direction. Moving his beleaguered little band into Rio Grande City, Audubon turned over about $15,000 of his burdensome cash to a bartender for safekeeping. In the morning, after burying two more cholera victims, he asked for the money. It was gone. Audubon's men seized the barkeep and chained him to a mesquite bush, then grabbed a suspected accomplice. They eventually recovered about half the money.

The hideous disease continued to ravage the company. Two of the group who fled to Roma died. The number of deaths in the company would reach ten before the plague passed. The majority, including Audubon, recovered after a miserable few days, but the company was permanently scarred. Nineteen men decided they had had enough of the golden trail and took passage back to New Orleans. Colonel Webb suffered through a painful night and decided to join them. Even Audubon's spirits sagged when he found only eleven men able to stand by a friend's fresh grave.

At last Audubon himself gave up. He and the remnants of the company waited at Roma for a steamer to take them downriver. When no boat arrived for several days, Audubon began to have second thoughts. The men had regained their health. Audubon saw that they were merely dispirited, not defeated; the disease had run its course; why not try it? He delivered what he described as "a little address," urging them on, and forty-eight agreed to follow him.

No other company of 1849 endured such an ordeal before their first day on the trail: their leader was gone, $7,000 stolen, and half the original roster had either died or defected. Audubon spent another four weeks disposing of excess baggage and closing company business in Texas. The diminished group finally moved out on April 28.

THE CROWDS began converging on the Arkansas River villages of Fort Smith and Van Buren in early March. Every steamer disgorged more flannel-shirted men with their wagons and equipment. Everyone was furiously busy: bakers filled large chests with pilot bread; horse and mule dealers set up shop on every vacant piece of ground; the daguerrotypist confronted a line of men who wanted their picture taken before they left;

hotels and saloons were filled to bursting with excited men loudly declaiming on their imminent wealth. A renowned Kentucky horse tamer known as the Whisperer amazed the street throngs with his ability to subdue a horse by rubbing its nose and murmuring softly; the secret was a tranquilizing substance on his hand. Frontiersmen in fringed buckskin stared skeptically at greenhorns in heavy overcoats and wide-brimmed "California hats." Well-dressed Indians from the Cherokee and Choctaw nations drew curious glances from the newcomers. An emigrant wrote from Van Buren that the price of mules varied from $35 to $60. "The traders here get their stock from the Creeks and Cherokees," he reported, "who get them from the Comanches, who steal them from the Mexicans."

Most of the arriving emigrants were farmers or village dwellers from the South. Some brought slaves. In addition there were northern men who had come by riverboat from Ohio and the East. One of the richest and best-organized aggregations was the sixty-five-strong Knickerbocker Exploring Company of New York. The Knickerbockers set forth on March 26 to the chorus of their company song: "Hy, ho, away we go, O'er the Rocky Mountains, O!" A Tennessean en route to Fort Smith drowned when he fell overboard from the sternwheel steamer *Kate Kirkwood* on the Arkansas. The money belt he wore, containing $500 in silver and gold, caused him to sink like a cannonball.

In all about three thousand emigrants assembled in the Arkansas towns. The largest band was the Fort Smith and California Emigrating Company, composed primarily of men from the Arkansas Valley. The Fort Smith train was so unwieldy (479 people in seventy-five wagons) that it had to break up into smaller groups. They departed in early April, accompanied by the eighty-man military escort commanded by Captain Randolph Marcy, which was to ride with them as far as Santa Fe. The rules drawn up by the Fort Smith company suggested a feminine influence. In addition to the customary requirements for extra livestock, tools and food, each member had to change his underwear weekly and carry at least three pounds of soap.

Of the several families traveling with the Fort Smith Company, the most visible was probably that of Dr. John Conway of Little Rock. Conway's party included his wife, ten children, and a slave, but the Conway who caught everyone's eye was seventeen-year-old Mary, a vivacious raven-haired beauty. Mary's presence guaranteed that military assistance would never be far from the Conway wagons.

Cholera stole onto the Arkansas in late March. Seven passengers on the steamer *Pennywit* died on the trip up from New Orleans; soldiers prevented the vessel from tying up at Van Buren. On April 12, the day after the Fort Smith company left, another steamboat arrived with several cholera cases aboard. Two passengers perished as soon as they were brought ashore. In the ensuing weeks the disease spread through the frontier settlements to the Indian villages, killing dozens. An outbreak on board the New Orleans steamer *Robert Morris* in April killed three crew members and five other men, including the president of a New Orleans–based company. Two of the victims were given an elaborate Masonic funeral in Little Rock.

The grass in the Canadian River Valley, the most important variable in determining the time of departure, was judged high enough to graze by the first of April (a month earlier than the Missouri grass was ready). Most of the Arkansas bands moved out in April, a few days ahead of the cholera, though stragglers continued to leave for several weeks afterward. Unusually heavy spring rains were drenching the valley almost daily. By late April the main body of the Arkansas migration was axle-deep in mud.

THE CHEROKEES who lived just west of Fort Smith in what is now eastern Oklahoma felt the lure of gold too. They had adapted so thoroughly to the dominant culture by 1849 that they published their own newspaper, practiced Yankee-style agriculture, and even gave their children American names. The Cherokees had a special interest in gold: they had been driven from their Georgia homeland in the wake of an earlier gold discovery. In addition they held a card that whites could only envy—they were on friendly terms with their red brothers on the plains.

"Shall we Cherokee not take advantage of the times and be found trying to get to this glorious country?" Cherokee editor James S. Vann asked in early 1849. The question inspired a series of meetings and eventually, in April, the formation of a gold company, which included Vann, fourteen other Cherokees, and more than a hundred whites from Arkansas. On April 24 they set out overland from Grand Saline, near present-day Salina, Oklahoma. The five slaves in the party were owned by Cherokees.

EVERYTHING about San Francisco in the spring of 1849 "savored of transition," one resident wrote. There was a dreamlike, ephemeral quality about this city of tents and unpainted shanties and abandoned ships and foreign-looking people. Nothing seemed to have any permanence or solidity; the place appeared to have been thrown together in a few days for the urgent purposes of the moment, and it would probably vanish just as abruptly when the moment passed. Mexicans, old settlers, Chileans, passengers just off the Panama steamers, Hawaiians, Oregonians, ex-soldiers, Australians, and Californios flowed through the streets in an unending stream—bragging, trading, planning, and shouting to be heard over the wind.

The bulking hills around the city, wet with recent rain, were at their greenest in early spring. The bay seemed to change color as the sun made its daily circuit, from green-gray in the morning haze to silver-spangled blue in the brightness of midafternoon. Permanent or not, this was a spectacular site for a city. The ramshackle town, the scurrying men and the glistening backdrop seemed somehow all of a piece; they blended. William Ryan, a recently discharged soldier who had once been a portrait painter, tried to sketch the blend in words: "All is bustle . . . boats going to and fro; rafts slowly discharging their cumbrous loads; porters anxiously and interestedly civil; all excited; all bent on gain; ships innumerable in the bay; mountains around; a clear blue sky above; and the bright waters dancing in the sun, until they touch the horizon in the distance."

The illusions that men brought with them doubtless tinted their perspective. "Oh, if I am to believe what is said," a young Frenchman wrote to his mother, "all one has to do is to stoop and pick up gold. . . . It seems to me as though I am under the influence of an enchanted sleep." With many more bodies than bunks in San Francisco, any other kind of sleep was impractical anyway.

A venerable resident, a San Franciscan for twenty-seven months, wrote that the newcomers appeared to believe "that when they arrive at San Francisco they are 'thar,' and that all they have to do is to take a pick and shovel and commence digging." This was followed in rapid succession, he said, by anxious inquiries, perplexity at the replies, and discouragement. Many "either determine to return home, or accept situations as clerks, inspectors of customs, or in fact anything."

If a man needed any help over the pass between perplexity and discouragement the gamblers were there to guide him. A friend of Ryan's advised him solemnly that the only people making any money were traders, speculators, and gamblers. The Baptist minister O. C. Wheeler, who had arrived on the *California* at the end of February, wrote in dismay to his eastern headquarters that the volume of vice in his immediate vicinity threatened to "make my whole head sick and my whole heart faint."

The most popular game was monte, the disarmingly simple old Mexican standby. Enormous sums were wagered; Ryan heard about a new arrival from the States who promptly made $20,000 and boarded a ship back to Panama two days later. Stories of losses of that magnitude were more common: the most familiar tale told of the bewhiskered miner coming to the city with his brimming bag of dust, losing every atom of it, gratefully accepting a drink on the house, and shuffling back to the diggings. Such incidents undoubtedly happened frequently.

The talk was that many of the gamblers had been in Mexico with the American troops. Others had worked on the Mississippi and at New Orleans. They were obviously experienced. Ex-sergeant James Carson listened in wonder to one gambler's come-on: "Here, gentlemen, is the monte bank that will stand you a 'rip.' Walk up, you chaps with the long bags o' dust, just bet what you please, it'll all be paid—pungle 'er down. If anyone gets broke I'll give him money to get a big drink, sure! Stake up to win a fortune. I don't belong to the aristocracy—I don't, I'm just a plain old devil like all of you. . . ."

The tide of sin had been rolled back only an inch or two by Reverend Wheeler and the other newly arrived clergymen. "All my powers are demanded in efforts to save men—pulling them out of the fire," Wheeler wrote. The completion of the lavish Parker House hotel in early spring was a victory for the enemy: gamblers paid as much as $1,800 a month to rent a room for their tables. Chilean harlots congregated in "Chilecito," an unsavory neighborhood near Telegraph Hill, while white prostitutes worked the Portsmouth Square area. Cafe owners hired women to pose nude, in various suggestive positions, on special platforms in their dining rooms.

No one was prepared for San Francisco prices. The most expensive commodity was probably lumber, which was freighted down from Oregon and sold at $400 per thousand board feet. A small room rented for $50 a month; board was $16 to $21 a week, about ten times what it cost in the East. Barbers charged $2 for a shave. Hats that cost $20 a dozen in New Orleans went for $10 each. By April, however, enough goods had arrived by sea to drive prices down. Storage rates of 10 to 20 percent a month forced merchants to sell their stock at auction.

Sam Brannan, the renegade Mormon who owned businesses in both

San Francisco and the budding metropolis of Sacramento, was making so much money so fast that Brigham Young wrote to inquire if a tithe might be forthcoming for "the Lord's treasury." Brannan's reply to the prophet's messenger clearly invited damnation: "You go back and tell Brigham," he said, "that I'll give up the Lord's money when he sends me a receipt signed by the Lord."

The fast-moving Philadelphian T. T. Johnson tarried only a few days in the city after his April 1 arrival on the *Oregon* before boarding a schooner for Sacramento. His boat paused at Benicia on Carquinez Strait, a village of two frame houses and a dozen tents where town lots were now selling for $1,000. At Sacramento he found some fifty houses and stores amid the oaks and sycamores along the river. Many stores were little more than booths made from scrap lumber and canvas. The prices were even steeper than in San Francisco: a six-shooter brought $100.

Johnson encountered the still lordly John Sutter, "a perfect and most courteous gentleman of the old European military school," on the road to the fort. Sutter, just back from a tour of nearby Indian *rancherías*, was already an anachronistic, dimly romantic figure, overwhelmed by the rush of events he had helped launch. Rustlers had stolen most of his livestock. "The people looked on my property as their own," he wrote a long time afterward. "I had not an idea that people could be so mean."

The rift between Sutter and his son August had widened. Each felt betrayed by the other. August railed at his father for his besotted irresponsibility; Sutter stormed at his son for selling his land to pay debts. Sutter eventually forced August to transfer control of his property back to him.

Sutter's Swiss friend Heinrich Lienhard, who had sometimes slept on the floor of Sutter's room at the fort, listened to the old man's midnight ravings about his son and later scolded him for them. Sobbing with shame and sorrow, Sutter grabbed a pistol and threatened to shoot himself. Lienhard wrenched the gun away, only to find that it was unloaded.

August asked Lienhard to travel to Europe to collect the rest of the Sutter family—his mother, Anna, two brothers, and a sister—and bring them to California. Lienhard discreetly obtained the consent of the elder Sutter before he agreed to go and then, in June, departed.

The fort had become a combination casino and bazaar. Johnson noticed both a bowling alley and billiard table on the grounds as well as gambling rooms, saloons, and stores. Pack animals pranced restlessly in a large corral. The editor Edward Kemble, his *Alta California* prospering in San Francisco, had just arrived with a hand press to inaugurate Sacramento's first newspaper, the *Placer Times*, providing an excuse for an eggnog-and-champagne soirée. Indians and rough-looking miners idled in the central courtyard.

Johnson joined a caravan heading up the American River to Coloma, where he found about twenty wooden houses and many more tents. Dozens of men worked the banks and bars near the recently reopened sawmill with rockers, pans, long-handled shovels, picks, and trowels. Johnson was surprised by their silent intensity. "They seemed averse to all conversation," he wrote. He saw a miner drop a small flake of gold worth perhaps $3. When he scooped the piece off the ground and returned it to him, the miner stared at him in astonishment. "Stranger, you are a curiosity," he said at last. "Guess you ain't been in the diggin's long. Better keep that for a sample."

Johnson spent only a week in Coloma before returning to the fort, but it was a week of bloodshed and bedlam. Many of the Coloma miners were migrants from Oregon with a long-standing enmity toward Indians. Through the winter and early spring the Oregonians and the generally peaceful foothill tribesmen had clashed sporadically. Early in April two members of a seven-man company of Oregonians returned to their diggings on the American River's Middle Fork to find the camp ransacked and their companions missing. They found bloodstains amid their littered provisions.

The two men told their story in Coloma, where a posse was immediately formed under the leadership of John Greenwood, the half-caste son of mountain man Caleb Greenwood and his Indian wife. The posse burst upon an Indian *rancheria* on the river and opened fire, killing and scalping four men. A second expedition murdered perhaps twenty more Indians and brought another eighty back to Coloma as prisoners. Over the shouted-down protests of James Marshall and other old residents, seven braves were selected to stand trial for the murder of the five Oregonians, whose bodies still had not been found. Johnson watched as the Indians were marched to a triangular patch of ground in the middle of Coloma. New York *Tribune* correspondent Samuel Osgood, who was also present, described what happened next:

"They broke and ran, some toward the hills and others toward the river. The word was given to fire, and two immediately fell. . . . The others who had fled to the hills were overtaken and stabbed with bowie knives. Of the two who plunged into the almost freezing waters of the

American Fork, one was shot. . . . The other swam to the opposite shore, but was prevented from landing by two mounted men who threw stones at him until . . . he sank to rise no more."

This barbarous incident brought to an end the Indian-white harmony that had marked the first year of work in the California mines. No longer would large bands of Indian miners toil for white ranchers, exchanging their dust for clothes and jewelry at inflated prices. The inoffensive California Indians who had worked along with Sutter, Marshall, Reading, and the others now withdrew, leaving the placers to the whites and their firepower. An article in Kemble's *Placer Times* reported in May that the Indians, fearing further white attacks, were in full flight.

The Indian exodus was symptomatic of a change in the mines that was just beginning to be felt. The men arriving now were townsmen, farmers, and city dwellers from the settled states, strangers to each other and to the easygoing, live-and-let-live tempo of pre–gold rush California. The forty-eighters were retreating from the mines along with the Indians. These newcomers were too single-minded, too intense, too full of anxieties and resentments, and in too damned much of a hurry. All they seemed to want was to get their pile and get out. They distrusted Indians, Mexicans, or anyone else who looked different.

When forty-eighter James Carson returned to Stockton and the southern mines in the spring of 1849, he found the old camps "filled with human beings. . . . A hundred flags were flying from restaurants, taverns, rum-mills and gaming houses." He learned for the first time what a mining claim was; in 1848 a group of miners simply worked where the dirt was richest, sometimes four or five men to a hole. The gold came more readily in 1848. "We made piles easy and we spent them *tambien,* for we expected it was to continue so forever," Carson wrote. But the crowds of 1849 were afraid that it wouldn't, and they brought not only their claim law but also their suspicions and their biases and their hasty homemade justice, stampeding anyone in their way. The Indians were merely the first victims.

Another change from 1848 was the disappearance, for the most part, of the easy bonanzas. The first wave of diggers had skimmed off most of the obvious treasure, and it was no longer possible to pluck gold off the ground as Antonio Coronel had done so casually on the Stanislaus. But plenty remained. A lone miner named Hudson created a sensation when he turned up at Coloma in the spring with a mule-load of gold. A column of men followed at a polite distance when he left town, trailing him to a gulch so rich that a teenaged boy subsequently dug out seventy-seven ounces one day and ninety the next. The unhappy Hudson yielded to the inevitable only after trying to discourage the intruders with tales of the ferocious grizzlies in the vicinity.

Mining remained a hard and unhealthy life. "I have seen men living for days without any other food than flour mixed with water formed into a kind of dough and baked in ashes," a Californian wrote in April 1849. The result was a high incidence of disease, especially scurvy.

Edward Buffum was making four ounces a day on the Middle Fork of the American River when scurvy overtook him in March. While wintering in Placerville he had heard of several scurvy deaths; the fresh vegetables or vegetable acids which would combat the disease were unavailable. His first symptoms were swollen and bleeding gums, followed by so much swelling in both legs that he was unable to walk. Growing weaker by the day, Buffum sent a friend to try to obtain some salts, but he failed.

Finally his legs began to turn black. The ever optimistic Buffum was at the point of despair. "Above me rose those formidable hills which I must ascend ere I could obtain relief," he wrote. "I believe I should have died, had not accident discovered [a] remedy." A friend found a little cluster of beans growing wild. Buffum boiled the sprouts and lived on them and spruce bark for several days until his strength returned. Then he legged it over the hills to Coloma and switched to a diet of fresh potatoes (at $3 a pound) until he recovered. Soon afterward he quit the mines for Sacramento and San Francisco.

T. T. Johnson returned to San Francisco by schooner in the last week of April. He polled his twenty fellow passengers and found that the most successful was toting $7,500 in gold; Johnson himself hadn't stayed long enough to fill his pockets. On May 1 he boarded the *California* for Panama and home. His ship picked up more passengers at Monterey, among them Colonel Richard Mason, the former military governor whose report had confirmed the gold discovery for the President and the nation at large.

THE LARGEST foreign contingents in the volatile California mix of the spring of 1849 were Mexicans from Sonora and Chileans. Sonorans had migrated north in such numbers that their headquarters in the southern mines, first known as Sonorian Camp and later as Sonora, now contained an estimated five thousand people, making it the most populous town in the mining district. Chileans were so numerous that Americans indiscriminately lumped all Latins together as *chileños*. All classes of Chileans had been arriving by sea since late 1848. Wealthy dons brought squads of peons to do their digging, antagonizing the gringos by filing claims in the names of individual laborers. T. T. Johnson met one group of indentured Chilean workers on Weber Creek in April; another band of thirty peons was camped on the Yuba at the same time.

An advertisement in a Chilean newspaper in February sought "two hundred young girls, white, poor, and of irreproachable conduct, not altogether destitute of grace and beauty, to be shipped to CALIFORNIA, and to be there honorably married to the thousands of North Americans and other foreigners who have made their fortunes in the mines." The girls who answered this ad, placed by "a respectable merchant whose name we cannot at present give," probably landed in the cribs of Chilecito.

Conflict between whites and Latins flared in April. A group of Americans at Coloma, taking their justification from General Smith's proclamation in Panama that the mines were restricted to U.S. citizens, chased off the Mexicans, Chileans, and Peruvians in the vicinity. The Anglos made no distinctions among Spanish-speaking miners; native Californians were routed along with the others. In May a party of American miners near Jamestown on Woods Creek took umbrage at the presence of a Mexican flag and forced the offenders to haul it down.

Antonio Coronel, the Mexican-born Los Angeles schoolteacher who had harvested a fortune on the Stanislaus the previous summer, made the mistake of moving north to Hangtown in 1849. One Sunday he saw a posted notice ordering all noncitizens to leave within twenty-four hours and threatening violence to those who disobeyed. Coronel and the other foreigners gathered together and stood fast until the threat passed. A few days later a Frenchman and a Spaniard were seized and accused of stealing four pounds of gold. Coronel protested that both men had good reputations and sufficient money, with no reason to steal. He raised five pounds among his friends and turned it over to the leader of the vigilantes, who promised a reply in a few hours. Before the appointed time the two were hanged.

Two days later Coronel prudently moved to another camp, but it was no better there: marauding bands jumped the claims of Spanish-speaking miners at will. Coronel suspected that part of their motivation was jealousy—the Sonorans were more successful miners. In addition the number of thieves and other criminals was increasing, and there was no effective law to check them. Coronel went home to Los Angeles. "For me," he concluded bitterly, "gold mining is finished."

Most of the Spanish-speaking men who stayed in the mines settled in Sonora and the south, where their numbers offered security. But in time they too became casualties of nativist bigotry. Persecution of Mexicans and especially of Californios drove another wedge between the early settlers and the forty-niners. Pre–gold rush Californians like Walter Colton had learned to cherish the Californio life-style: "There are no people that I have ever been among," he wrote, "who enjoy life so thoroughly as the Californians. . . . Their hospitality knows no bounds; they are always glad to see you, come when you may; take a pleasure in entertaining you while you remain; and only regret that your business calls you away." Between the open-handed liberality of the Californians and the sharp-eyed shrewdness of the Yankees, Colton had no trouble making a choice: "Give me the Californian." James Carson was another admirer: "If happiness, in the full sense of the word, was ever enjoyed by mankind," he wrote, "it was by the old settlers and inhabitants who were here before the discovery of gold."

THE NEW YORK *Tribune*'s column "Golden Chronicles" reported in March that new overland companies of gold seekers were organizing in Buffalo, Ithaca, Binghamton, Boston, Pittsburgh, and elsewhere; some were traveling by way of Independence and the Oregon Trail and others via Texas. The classified columns were filled with announcements of ship sailings, gold washers for sale ("guaranteed to wash 10 times as much sand with less labor than any other machine"), overland companies seeking members, and such miscellanea as "California life insurance" and fifteen-by-twenty-foot portable iron houses which could be erected in a day. The only jarring note came from Maine, where the *Tribune* found enthusiasm waning: "The town of Machias, which was to have been represented at the mines by six or eight citizens, will now probably send few or none, the adventurers having been deterred on the eve of departure by the gloomy side of the picture presented in the later accounts from California." The gloomy side doubtless included high prices, lawlessness, and disease in the mines.

In Lynn, Massachusetts, the fifty-two members of the Lynn Sagamore

and California Mining and Trading Company donned full-dress uniforms for their leave-taking: dark gray suits and caps trimmed with silver
lace, hunting boots, rifles, swords, life preservers, and a brace of pistols
per man. A swivel gun was mounted on one of their wagons. The departure of a seven-man party from Warren, Ohio, inspired this salute from
an apparently untraveled editor: "Men who can muster the courage and
fortitude enough to start on such a journey have endured more than half
the hardships of the trip." In South Ottawa, Illinois, a twenty-six-year-old
man shot himself when a last-minute hitch thwarted his plans to start for
California.

The British were still divided. The *Athenaeum* told its readers excitedly that "America is now discovered, as it were, a second time," while
the *People's Journal* warned of immense speculations, immense losses,
madness, and ruinous habits. The French were untroubled by doubts. For
France, undergoing a period of political and economic turmoil, the gold
rush offered an escape for political outcasts and jobless workers. One of
the earliest of several French gold companies, La Californienne, was
organized in April with a capital investment of a million dollars. The
company's prospectus promised that "from very careful, conservative
estimates, every . . . share should double its value every year." A
Parisian shop announced a line of California fashions including a
"chapeau californien" of taffeta or crepe.

In Washington, D.C., one of the most remarkable men to join the gold
rush was making his final preparations in late March. Joseph Goldsborough Bruff, the leader of the Washington City and California Mining
Association, was nothing if not fastidious. Bruff had studied several possible routes before choosing the overland trail out of St. Joseph. He had
already dispatched advance parties to acquire wagons and mules. Now,
in his own controlled and undemonstrative way, he was itching to get
going.

Bruff was forty-four, older than most of his fellow emigrants, and the
father of five. At the time of the gold discovery he was a draftsman for
the War Department's Bureau of Topographical Engineers at a salary
of $1,000 a year (slightly more than an ounce a week). Black-haired and
erect, he was a strong, self-reliant, and disciplined man and something
of a perfectionist. He had spent two years as a West Point cadet and
several more as a merchant seaman before settling into government
service. Bruff combined the military man's dedication to duty and honor
with a reflexive kindness. He was also artistic; as a cartographer he had

drawn the first map of Florida a few years earlier. His enunciation of the Washington company's purpose was characteristically straightforward and cautious: "We go as a body of energetic gentlemen, to enrich ourselves, if possible, by every honorable means." He had a second goal in mind as well: through sketches, scientific observations, and a precise journal he would compile a "perfect guide" to the overland trail. The journal he eventually produced was by far the most intimate record of any yet found.

The sixty-four men of Bruff's company, decked out in gray frock coats and striped pants, assembled on the morning of April 2 at Lafayette Square, across Pennsylvania Avenue from the White House. A military band played marches as they paraded on the square and then formed a column in front of the mansion. Bruff and the others trooped up the steps and entered the great hall to be presented to President Taylor. "Old 'Rough and Ready' received us in his blandest and frankest manner," Bruff reported. Bruff explained, the company's plans, probably in more detail than the President really needed, and late in the afternoon they boarded a train for Cumberland, Maryland, the first leg of their journey to St. Joseph.

Twenty-year-old William Johnston, who had set out from Pittsburgh a few weeks earlier, was in many ways Bruff's opposite—eager, impetuous, inexperienced, and happy-go-lucky. An exuberant, blundering youth, he was as careless as Bruff was disciplined. Johnston's California expedition had taken shape during winter-night talks with his friends in the back room of a drugstore. It seemed to him that he had always wanted to go to California, a place of "peculiar, inexpressible attractions." He spent his last night in Pittsburgh amid the more tangible attractions of the neighborhood girls at a dance. Then he and his companions took a steamer for St. Louis and Independence.

The gold rush placed a tremendous strain on affections. Henry Crandall, a twenty-two-year-old clerk in a Greenwich, New York, dry-goods store, had succumbed to gold fever during the winter. Mary Mills, his inamorata, was unable to talk him out of it. Henry's boss advanced him $500 for the trip in exchange for half his profit. On March 5 the lovers parted, both promising to write faithfully and both knowing that it might be six months before they received a letter. Henry stopped in Troy, on his way down to New York, to have a picture taken for Mary.

Henry wrote first from Baltimore, a week after he left home. "We all 'feel our oats' and act more like children let loose from school than

men on a desperate adventure," he said. He asked if she liked his picture
and said that he looked at hers daily. Five days later he wrote from
Pittsburgh, wondering who had been sitting next to her at church meetings
since he left and pointing out that he expected to be in St. Louis for ten
or twenty days, time enough "to receive twenty letters."

But there were no letters in St. Louis, where the Mississippi looked
to him like "one big mud puddle, dirty enough to give you the cholera."
"I almost wish I could be left behind," he confessed, but it was too late
now. On April 14 he reached St. Joseph, which he described to Mary as
a town of two thousand people, two churches, and four hotels. He was
assigned to cook for his fifteen-man company, "for how long I cannot
say, but probably during good behavior." There was no letter at St.
Joseph either, leaving Henry to his lonely tent and his melodramatic
imagination: all he was facing, he wrote as he prepared to set out on the
plains, was four months in the company of "wild and treacherous Indians
lurking for plunder. . . . Will you write me at San Francisco by the 1st
[of May]? Do, dear Mary, and every month after, is the last request
from—your Henry."

Henry's jump-off point of St. Joseph was the most raucous of the
frontier outfitting towns. Hotels, saloons, gambling houses, streets, and
even churches were thronged from late March on. The din was incessant,
a mixture of hissing and clanking steamboats, lowing cows, braying
mules, shouting men, and the tinny tones of organ-grinders. Most of the
gathering argonauts pitched tents on the undulating prairie around the
little town, creating a canvas village which came alive at night with campfires, music, and laughter. The few who were able to get rooms at $1 a
day at such hotels as the Edgar House complained of meager meals and
filthy sheets.

Mountain men who had roamed west out of St. Joseph for years advised the greenhorns that the grass was commonly not high enough to
graze until late April. This year a cold spell in April meant that it would
be May before they could set out. Burdened with time, impatient men
filled the taverns and spilled into the streets. "This place is the scene of
more drunken fights and gambling and drinking than any other place on
the frontier," seventeen-year-old Lucius Fairchild wrote home to Wisconsin. "The streets are in commotion all of the time and it is best for
sober men to keep back." A youth from Washington died after he swilled
a pint of brandy without pausing for breath to win a bet. Quarrels erupted
in some of the waiting companies; several members of a large band from

Pittsburgh became so disgusted that they sold their mules and went home. A correspondent for a St. Louis paper reported that easterners were particularly "out of fix" in St. Joseph because of their unfamiliarity with livestock and the outfits needed for overland travel. "The Missourians are skinning them most horridly," he wrote. "Every day has its own price."

By the time J. Goldsborough Bruff and his Washington company reached St. Joseph near the end of April, there were at least three thousand emigrants watching the grass grow on the east bank of the Missouri. Fairchild was surprised to see so many families among them; the journey would inevitably be longer and harder for them. Cholera visited the town in April but mercifully killed only seven. Many hurried up their preparations in the mistaken belief that the plague would not pursue them onto the plains.

Long lines of wagons formed at the two ferries which crossed the river at St. Joseph and the two others several miles above them. Working from early morning until midnight, the four ferries could transport some 150 wagons a day. "From the principal street in St. Joseph," Bruff wrote, "down 300 yards, crossing a bridge to the riverbank, was one dense mass of wagons, oxen and people." Two teamsters shot each other to death in a dispute over who was ahead in line. Estimating that the delay at the crossing might be as long as a fortnight, Bruff proposed that his company move their blue-topped wagons to another ferry ninety miles north, and the members agreed.

The most important decision an overland emigrant had to make was whether to use mules or oxen to haul his wagon. There were good arguments for each: oxen were cheaper, more easily handled, less likely to stray; they were less fussy about their diet and in an emergency they could be eaten. Mules, on the other hand, traveled much faster—a mule team could make up to forty miles a day where oxen might travel only fifteen. Mule partisans argued that they needed less water; the ox lobby replied that mules were unmanageable. Most forty-niners opted for economy and manageability and bought oxen. For a skillful teamster, however, particularly a Missourian—William Johnston said that "Missourians understood mules as though they were blood relations"—mules were probably the better choice.

Overlander wagons were strong, light, and small, perhaps ten feet long by four feet wide. A team of three yoke of oxen could pull more than a ton of tools, salt pork, jerked beef, pilot bread, and other provisions— Joseph Ware's guidebook set the maximum load at 2,500 pounds. The wagons lacked both springs and brakes, but their iron wheels could be chainlocked to slow them going down steep hills. In a pinch the wagon bed could be caulked and used as a raft. The bows supporting the canvas cover were usually made of hickory. Many forty-niners painted exuberant names on the canvas: "Lone Star," "Live Hoosier," "Wild Yankee," "Gold Hunter."

The wagon traveler's greatest apprehension was Indians. Most Americans of the time equated Indians with danger, and Frémont and other writers had warned them to beware of the redmen. "Never allow an Indian to come within your lines under any pretext," Ware cautioned. "They seldom have a good object in view." As a result every emigrant wagon was an arsenal of rifles, pistols, and knives. The weapons turned out to be a greater hazard than the Indians. Dozens were killed or wounded in shooting accidents, while contacts between red and white, though sometimes larcenous, were for the most part nonviolent.

The merchants of Independence, ninety miles downstream from St. Joseph, had been outfitting overland parties for two decades. Even though St. Joseph was a few days closer to the main Platte River road, Independence attracted the largest number of emigrants in 1849. Part of the reason was advertising: agents from Independence passed out handbills to emigrants coming upriver from St. Louis.

Independence offered thirty stores, twenty blacksmith shops, enough mules and oxen to transport a major army, and an unlimited complement of gambling houses and other temptations. Eager young Bill Johnston arrived there on March 15, more than a month too early, and set about acquiring mules and useful information. It struck him that everything in Independence moved fast—people jostled each other, animals contested for the right of way—except the grass, which "grows with provoking slowness." Rain began to fall regularly in late March; for two weeks it rained about half the time; then came a day of sunshine, followed by a snowstorm.

By mid-April the most impatient of the Independence companies were beginning to move out. But trail-wise veterans like Edwin Bryant, who had crossed to California in 1846 and served briefly as alcalde of San Francisco, preferred to wait a while yet. So did Jim Stewart, a forty-year-old Scotsman who was guiding Johnston's party. Rumors of cholera raced through town. A lone pedestrian turned up with the news that he and his bulldog had walked all the way from Maine and planned to foot it the rest of the way as well. A man from Elmira, New York, was shot in the groin when he inadvertently got between two duelists; the assailant pleaded guilty to assault and was fined one dollar.

Johnston was counting the days; by April 24, when he dolefully watched a uniformed company from Cincinnati depart in iron wagons, he calculated that he had been in Independence thirty-nine days and had gained fifteen pounds. Two days later the first elements of Edwin Bryant's group moved out, and two days after that Johnston was at last on the road.

The only venture in mass transit across the plains in 1849, the "Pioneer Line" of twenty six-man coaches, left Independence on May 16. The line's promoters were a pair of entrepreneurs from St. Louis named Turner and Allen. Their advertisements claimed that the covered, mule-drawn carriages would reach California in sixty days. Passengers were issued army rations and permitted a hundred pounds of baggage. The 120 available tickets quickly sold out at $200 each.

The shadow of cholera appeared on the Missouri in April. The course of the disease seemed to defy logic and predictability: most river steamers made the St. Louis–to–Independence run with no sign of cholera, but others became floating infirmaries. Philadelphian Isaac Wistar was on a boat which lost eighteen men to the contagion. The dead were wrapped in blankets and placed on deck until they could be buried ashore. Alonzo Delano of Ottawa, Illinois, later a well-known humorist, heard the awful cry, "the cholera is on board," on his second day out of St. Louis. His boat stopped at a lonely riverside clearing to bury a man from Virginia. Three men on the steamer carrying Bostonian Reuben Shaw were struck down, and four more of Shaw's party died after they reached Independence. The plague swept through the crowded town in the first two weeks of May, carrying off at least thirty-four victims. The worst would come still later, among the masses toiling up the Platte in their wagons.

By early May the great migration was on the move. The more impetuous among them had been creeping forward since the middle of April, feeding grain to their stock while waiting for the grass to rise. The men in the lead reasoned that the best strategy was to get in front where the forage was good and stay there. The first company out of Independence, a pack train, pushed off on April 14; the earliest to set out from St. Joseph left five days later. One of the lead bands was a party of Kentuckians, described by a man who encountered them as "all old men, gentlemanly and affable and full of enthusiasm."

Daily the overloaded, clanking wagons rolled out onto the prairie, digging deep ruts in the soft earth. Some men rode alongside on saddle horses, while others stayed in the rear with the extra stock. The ambience was festive; most felt relief to be finally moving as well as excitement. Lovesick Henry Crandall set out on May 2 to the now familiar strains of "Oh! Susanna": *"I'm going to San Francisco and then I'll look around, And pick up all those lumps of gold a-laying on the ground . . ."* Lucius Fairchild walked twenty miles back to St. Joe from his company's first encampment to get off one final letter from the settlements. J. Goldsborough Bruff and the Washington City company, slowly working their way up the east bank of the Missouri, were among the last to turn toward the setting sun; they finally crossed the river on June 2, 3, and 4.

A surprising number of overland emigrants perceived, if only vaguely, that they were part of a grand and historic adventure. Dozens brought journals and faithfully recorded each day's events. Others chronicled their trip in a kind of continuous letter home which might not be mailed until they reached California. The migration setting forth on the Platte River route in April and May was the largest ever seen in America to that time. The best estimate puts the total at about 22,500, a number equal to the population of a good-sized 1849 city.

At least one of them viewed the impending journey primarily as an opportunity to have a good time. Joseph Hamelin, a whimsical young Missourian, bade farewell in his journal to "sweet home, kind friends, pleasant faces, soda water, ice cream, feather beds and girls." Observing that most companies marched off with bylaws forbidding liquor, Hamelin proposed that his do the same. He suggested that the members promise to abstain with the following exceptions: "unless wet or dry, too warm or too cold, sick, or wanted it."

THE COURSE OF EMPIRE

FORDING THE SOUTH PLATTE

THE CAMP is astir well before first light cracks the prairie night. A man emerges from a canvas wall tent and shuffles sleepily off for water. A rattling coffeepot brings a protesting groan from somewhere inside a wagon. Someone lights a candle. The grass is damp, sweet-smelling. The dim and shadowy forms of picketed animals rouse themselves heavily and nuzzle the moist earth. It is too early for the birds and too late for the insects; nature is still.

The crisp snap of the fire lures the last shift of night guards. They squat and talk softly as they wait for their coffee. One gnaws on a chunk of hardtack, another lights his pipe. Bacon sizzles in an iron pan.

The guide—alert, even-tempered, self-contained—studies his map in the firelight. "Catch up, catch up," he shouts after a few minutes. The men pull on their boots and retrieve their animals, buckling them into harness. Tents are hurriedly wrapped around poles and stowed in the wagons. The sky pales to a hazy dark gray. Laughter comes from a cluster of men on horseback, heading for the rear to tend the extra stock. The last of the cooking gear is packed, the fires covered with dirt.

The lead wagon squeaks and creaks as it peels off from the circle, its tar bucket swaying from a hook at the rear of the wagon bed. The animals readily find the grooved and grassless trail and begin their rhythmic trudge: *clop-a-ta-clop-a-ta-clop*. Only a few men ride in the wagons; the others are astride horses or walking alongside, rifles slung over their shoulders.

The sun arcs above the prairie behind them like a ring of fire. Ahead they see another train of wagons, cresting an invisible rise on the plain like a line of schooners at sea. Sharply outlined puffs of dust are suspended in their wake like distant brown-leafed trees. The wagons might be two miles off or five; the vast sprawl of the prairie confounds a man's judgment of distance.

The pedestrians scan the short grass for snakes and prairie dogs and sweep their eyes along the horizon in search of alien intrusions: this is Indian country. The prospect of a confrontation with the redmen tightens the belly with fear and excitement. Every bend in the trail, every stream, every grove of scrawny trees holds the potential for adventure. Everything about this unmarked land is new to them. They see it with pilgrims' eyes, fresh and full of wonder.

Yet they must not dawdle. Nature has written their timetable and charted their route. Their road is fixed not by grade but by the availability of water and forage. They could not leave Missouri until the grass was up in May (unless they brought their own feed). They have to cross the Sierra Nevadas before October's first snow; the story of the Donner party is still vivid in their memories. To be safe, they should average fifteen or twenty miles a day. Laze around the fire, get lost, stop too long for repairs, and you might miss out; the gold might not wait.

The guide starts looking for a campsite with good wood, good water, and good grass in mid-afternoon. If he's lucky he finds two of the three. The wagons lumber in and form a ragged oval. The animals are unhitched and allowed to graze within the oval. Fires are built for each mess of five or six men.

The first sentries take their posts outside the perimeter of the wagons at dusk. The other men sit around the fires talking, whittling, sometimes singing or playing a scratchy fiddle, sometimes just listening to the night sounds: owls, crickets, the long lonesome cry of the coyote. One by one they withdraw from the fire's circle and dive into their blankets. A guard, startled by a sudden animal movement, fires his rifle and immediately feels like a fool.

Late at night the wind rises. A casually staked tent begins to flap and thump the ground. A spring storm strikes with sudden and savage force. Rain slams onto the canvas tents and wagon covers like a shower of gravel. The shallow moats they have dug around their tents overflow; water soaks their blankets. Horses rear as a flash of lightning streaks the sky. Guards try to calm them. Then it stops, as precipitously as it began. The men arise in a quagmire, but the stars are back out. Every trail rut is an oblong pool of brown water. Fresh new buds are peeping over the gray-green grass. The land is once again refreshed. "Catch up, catch up," the guide cries, and the men splash through puddles to fetch their animals.

"THE ICE is at last broken, and the inundation of gold diggers is upon us," the correspondent of the St. Louis *Republican* wrote on May 18 from Fort Kearny, a year-old army post on the Platte River 317 miles northwest of Independence. "The first specimen, with a long pick-axe over his shoulder, a long rifle in his hand, and two revolvers and bowie knife in his belt," appeared in a yellow-topped wagon on May 6. "Up to this morning 476 wagons have gone past this point, and this is but the advance guard." He added that several overland companies had already broken up because of arguments.

The correspondent, probably an army officer, was both impressed and amused by the passing cavalcade. The migration contained "the best material of our land," he wrote, along with a fair share of knaves and fools. "Several horses and mules have changed hands; but, as it is in Indian country, the poor Indian must bear the blame.

"The last arrival on the frontier is a solitary foot traveler, who says he has come all the way from Maine. . . . He is accompanied by a savage-looking bulldog, has a long rifle over the shoulder, on the end of which he carries his baggage, in a small bundle about the size of your hat. He has no provisions, but gets along fairly well by sponging on his fellow travelers. He says he wants but a hundred meals to carry him through, and he rather guesses he'll find Christians on the road enough to supply him."

Eight days later the same writer updated his census of the Platte River migration to 2,527 wagons bearing more than ten thousand persons;

wagons had been constantly in view for two weeks. Heavy rain had persuaded several to turn back toward home, and three men had already died
in shooting accidents. But in his opinion the greatest hazard to the emigrants was their own careless overloading. He had seen wagons sagging
under portable sawmills, anvils, feather beds, rocking chairs, and other
impedimenta. "Soon it was found that the loading was too great for the
teams," he wrote, "and now overboard goes everything. The road is lined
with various articles—even gold vases and gold washers are abandoned
by the roadside."

Young Bill Johnston, one of the greenest of the greenhorns of 1849,
was in the vanguard of the migration. His company of Pittsburgh men
guided their mule-drawn wagons out of Independence even before the
grass was up, using corn for feed in the meantime. They began to jettison
their excess on the second day; out of the wagons went a plow, lead, nails,
clothing, two bushels of beans, and a "fair-sized library," gifts to a surprised Shawnee farmer and his family.

The prairie was alien terrain to city-boy Johnston. On his first night
on guard duty he nervously waved an ax at a dark, menacing form which
turned out to be a fellow sentry. His guard shift every other night meant
the loss of two hours' sleep; the worst watches were from ten to twelve
and twelve to two. His horse stumbled while crossing a stream and injured
a leg. A few days later he acquired a sorrel pony in a trade with a band
of Potawatomi Indians, but he was without a mount again when he
realized the pony was too light to ride.

Johnston's company arrived at the Kansas River crossing, the first
major obstacle on the Independence trail, on the sixth day. They lowered
the wagons down a steep embankment by tying them to a tree, then
muscled them onto a ferry operated by two enterprising Indians. Joseph
Ware's pocket guide noted that the toll was a dollar per wagon, but by
this time the Indians were collecting two dollars a wagon, 25 cents per
mule, and 10 cents a man. The river, fordable in dry years, was bank-high
because of the recent rainstorms.

On May 9 they plodded up to the junction of the Independence and
St. Joseph trails, a few miles west of present-day Marysville, Kansas.
Only now, gazing out at the long, snaking column of wagons on either
side of the point where the trails merged, did they realize the scale of
the movement they were a part of. "For an indefinite number of miles
there was an unending stream of emigrant trains and dust," Johnston
wrote. "It seemed as if the whole family of man had set its face westward."

The Pittsburgh men hankered to put the rest of the family behind them. On the same day that they reached the junction they found a message in a notched stake reporting that the pack train headed by G. W. Paul, which was leading the emigration, was only nine days ahead of them. "Our daily task . . . will be to get past those in advance of us," Johnston wrote in his journal. Now it was a race.

Johnston noticed an increase in the number of roadside graves as they pushed northwest through the well-timbered valley of the Little Blue River. Some were marked with boards or sticks, others with buffalo skulls bearing a chalked inscription, but most were only mounds of earth elevated a few inches above the plain, unmarked to conceal them from Indian grave robbers. Cholera was tracking them across the prairie.

Their twice-a-day meals of "oatmeal mush, bacon sides with pilot bread fried in the fat, and coffee" were already becoming stale. Their favorite was bean soup, which required two and sometimes three campfires to boil; between fires the soup gathered dust on a hook at the rear of a wagon. They were in Pawnee territory now, but few emigrants saw the once dangerous Plains tribesmen except in their imaginations. Smallpox and recurrent skirmishes with the Sioux had left the Pawnees with little more than their villainous reputation.

The company struck the Platte River at Grand Island. The mud-caked banks of the Platte—"the coast of Nebraska"—had been the pioneers' route west for a generation; the river was the first important milestone on the trail to California. But at close range the Platte looked like a broad, gray-brown scar on the prairie, a band of lifeless-looking water striping the treeless land. It was wet, but that was about all. "Ugliest river I ever saw," one forty-niner allowed, "a mile and a half wide and thick enough with mud to cut into chunks."

On May 15 they stopped at Fort Kearny, but only long enough to write letters home and ogle a Mormon girl whose parents kept a boardinghouse there. The post, established to protect emigrants from Indians, was a charmless compound of low sod buildings housing a hospital, powder magazine, bakery, stables, and a few platoons of semimutinous troops. Rain drummed down on them almost daily, turning the trail into a soggy morass and drenching clothes, blankets, and even food. One morning they tried to cook breakfast in the tent with their sheet-iron stove, but the dense smoke forced them to settle for cold pork, hard biscuits, and river water.

The trail held to the south branch of the Platte beyond the fork in the river one hundred miles west of Fort Kearny. Immense herds of buffalo now grazed just beyond rifle range. White-tailed antelope, swift enough to elude all but expert hunters, bounced through the rising grass. Hundreds of prairie dogs popped their heads above ground as the wagons rumbled past their villages. Johnston, now mounted on a portly mule, accepted the challenge of a pair of friendly Sioux squaws to race their ponies and, to the hoots of his friends, finished a bedraggled third.

On May 21 they reached the ford of the South Platte, here about three-quarters of a mile wide and belly deep, with a quicksand bottom. Several hundred Sioux were camped on the south bank. The Indians crowded curiously around the wagons, opening boxes and picking through their baggage until the emigrants became tense and irritated. Then Johnston had an inspiration.

He remembered that they had brought a bag of tin horns, harmonicas, mirrors, and other trinkets to trade with Indians. Grabbing a horn, he demonstrated his tooting technique to an attentive audience of natives and then held the horns to the lips of several old men (the younger ones were off fighting Pawnees) while they puckered and blew. The response was hysteria. "They danced about in great glee in knots of ten or a dozen," he wrote. Johnston let on that he would not object to a few pairs of moccasins in return. "They showered them at my feet as fast as I could pick them up. . . . Very soon the whole tribe was in a perfect uproar."

The next day they labored over the jagged hills between the north and south forks of the Platte and emerged at Ash Hollow, a welcome grove of ash trees shading a fine spring at the foot of a steep hill. From here the trail passed through a strange, surreal landscape of lone rock outcroppings like Courthouse and Chimney rocks and high bluffs beside the North Platte. Wood was scarce, but there were plenty of dry buffalo chips (*bois de vache*, the French trappers called them), which burned almost as well. Still racing, the Pittsburgh boys arose at 3 a.m. to get the jump on a competing train only to discover that their rivals had moved out even earlier. They made thirty miles on May 28, pausing along the way to sample the foul whiskey dispensed by a member of the famous Robidoux family of trappers at his trading post at Scott's Bluff.

By now all the petty aggravations of life on the trail—the soggy blankets and redundant meals and nights on guard and dust and bad water, the stubborn animals and the inevitable friction between the men— had merged into a single chronic sore which afflicted everyone; even the good-natured Johnston was getting touchy. He could probably get along without any more criticism of his cooking, he reflected, even if it was a little clumsy of him to knock over a pot and put out the fire. The resultant uproar caused him to quit his cooking assignment in a huff, grumbling that "some men are natural faultfinders." Domestic chores gave him trouble. One morning he stacked a pile of dirty clothes on the bottom of a shallow, fast-moving stream, placed a boulder atop the pile and went off to do something else. He returned to discover that both clothes and boulder had disappeared.

They rolled into Fort Laramie, a fur trappers' depot which would soon be purchased by the army, on May 29. The fort was thirty miles inside what would later become Wyoming. Here they tossed their surplus bacon onto a mound of discarded food as high as a haystack, helping themselves to leathery slabs of cured buffalo meat in exchange. Five more days brought them to the ferry across the two-hundred-foot-wide North Platte operated by Mormons from Brigham Young's colony on the Great Salt Lake. Here at last they left the Platte, which had gradually turned into a tree-bordered high-country stream, and headed overland for their next landmark, the Sweetwater River.

This was the homeland of the Crow Indians, who had recently lured an emigrant away from his camp and divested him of horse, clothes, and valuables. They heard a rumor that twelve Crows led by a white man had robbed another emigrant party after pretending to approach in peace. The trail along the slender blue Sweetwater climbed steadily but almost imperceptibly. On June 9 they spotted snow on the peaks of the Wind River range to the north. The following day they rode through sleet and freezing rain to the gentle elevation in the sagebrush plain that marks the Continental Divide at South Pass. Ice coated their wagons.

Johnston and his companions were now closing in on the leaders of the migration. They had traveled 915 miles, nearly half of the distance to the Sierra foothills, in forty-three days. But no one felt festive, at least not yet; most of them were wheezing and coughing with the colds they had caught on the miserable forty-third day.

IT WAS an army of the young that trooped up the Platte Valley in the spring of 1849. Bill Johnston at twenty was probably a little below the average age, but not much. J. Goldsborough Bruff's Washington City company was more elderly than most, yet forty-four of its sixty-four members were thirty or younger; five were teenagers. Isaac Wistar of Philadelphia was at twenty-two the oldest of the sixteen men he started with. The migration was also overwhelmingly male. There is no reliable count of the number of families who took to the trail in this gold-frantic year, but an emigrant writing from Fort Laramie on July 1 reported that only a hundred of the 5,500 wagons which had passed carried families.

The great majority of overland gold seekers were white, Protestant, and American-born. Many—perhaps a fifth of the 1849 total—were frontiersmen from Missouri, the Far West of the day; the gold rush would have a strong Missouri flavor from now on; the word "pike," which evolved in California into a synonym for hick or hillbilly, originally referred to a citizen of Pike County, Missouri, which borders the Mississippi below Hannibal. Many other overland emigrants were from Ohio, Illinois, Iowa, Wisconsin, Kentucky, or Indiana. Easterners and southerners, with easier access to the Cape Horn and Panama routes, were the minority. Europeans were almost invisible, although there was at least one overland company of Englishmen. A few blacks, mostly slaves accompanying their owners, joined the migration. John Banks, a slavery-hating farmer from Albany, Ohio, met a slave named James Taylor while ferrying the Missouri at St. Joseph. He was bound for California, Banks wrote, in "the hope of redeeming a wife and seven children. Success to him."

Like their counterparts on the Panama steamers and the windjammers off South America, the forty-niners on the trail came from the more respectable reaches of society. They were better educated and better off, on the average, than their neighbors back home, many of whom did not attempt the trip because they could not afford it. They were farmers and shopkeepers, clerks and artisans, teachers and students, ministers and bankers and journalists. A disproportionate number were doctors, primarily because many companies actively recruited physicians and offered them tempting inducements such as free membership or an exemption from routine camp chores. "If any suffer from sickness," one forty-niner wrote, "it will not be for want of medical advisers."

Most emigrants, particularly the westerners and Mexican War veterans, were used to working with their hands and were at least minimally competent in the outdoors. Still there was a sizable delegation of softhanded urban greenhorns like Bill Johnston, men whose adventures prior to this one had come from books. The lessons of the trail would come hardest for them.

The youthful forty-niners often reacted to the freedom of life on the plains like suddenly liberated schoolboys. With no one to nag them to wash or shave, they could be cavalier about personal hygiene; besides, a beard hid their fresh-cheeked youth. "Everyone who can turn out a hair on his face makes a parade of it," wrote Missourian Joseph Hamelin. The race for gold was among other things a dispensation from church attendance for the duration. It was an opportunity to drink and curse with the men and to brandish unfamiliar weapons while talking knowledgeably of the "accursed Injuns." Much of it—the novelty of encountering a new slice of country every day, the thundering bedlam of a buffalo chase, the warm brotherhood of the campfire, the stunning and exotic beauty of the land—must have been pure joy, the stuff of winter dreams in the pale-walled parlors of home. Whatever else it was, it was fun. There were chores, to be sure, there were always chores, but there were also mornings and evenings when a man wanted to open his mouth and drink in the enchantment that he felt, when he could taste the sense of freedom and limitless possibility that derived from the land itself.

The sight of a woman on the trail was electrifying. Joseph Hamelin scribbled a valentine in his diary when he met several women at the Robidoux trading post at Scott's Bluff: "My little old heart went pit-a-pat, it did." He even lapsed into lecherous if unmelodious verse: "I venerate a petticoat, a garment of mystical sublimity, whether of rustic, silk or dimity." The presence of women in camp usually demanded a celebration. Niles Searls, a Missouri lawyer traveling on the Pioneer Line commercial train, was captivated by the "vocal concert" staged by a group of women at their campsite near the Sweetwater.

With or without women, music was the favorite diversion on a star-capped prairie evening. "The boys are in fine spirit," one journal keeper wrote. "We have had a serenade tonight, music from fiddle and camp kettle." With a little luck the brandy wagon man, who peddled his stock at 50 cents a glass, might come by to fuel the revelry. Occasionally a man was overcome by the impulse to dance, even if his only available partners wore beards and muddy boots.

These were men who had spent their lives close to home. They thought of their journey as a sort of extended business trip, which would detain them no longer than the brief time necessary to gather a pile and hurry home. In their minds they had not really left. They pined not only for their families but also for the familiar contours of small-town life. Joseph Hamelin was amazed at how thrilled he was to run into a fellow townsman along the Platte, even though he hadn't been especially fond of the man back home in Lexington, Missouri: "Here the sight of a familiar face, even though slightly doggish, is respected."

The sense of loss was felt even more deeply by those left behind. The ardent Henry Crandall of Greenwich, New York, who had written his last plaintive letter to his girl friend Mary Mills on the eve of his departure from St. Joseph, was camped with his company at Chimney Rock on June 7, the day that Mary mailed her first letter to him.

Mary's letter was in verse. She described a picnic, the formation of three new schools, and a wagon accident before she permitted her feelings to flow:

Well, anybody reading this
Might safely judge I prize a kiss!
I always did, and more so now—
For I don't get one anyhow . . .

For I was NEVER more alone—
Forgive me if you hear a moan;
I just have nothing else to do
But spin, and work, and think of you.

The dreads that crept into the emigrants' night thoughts came in a dozen phantom forms. Despite the isolated forts and trading posts they were crossing largely unknown territory. Who could know every hazard that waited beyond the glow of the fire? Rattlesnakes, for example. Bostonian Reuben Shaw believed with the ardor of the ignorant that rattlers "were always on the offensive and hunting for prey and could spring six or eight feet and fasten their fangs in the flesh of their victim, causing death almost instantly." But there is no record of an overland traveler dying of snakebite. Nor was anyone killed by wolves, another overrated danger on the plains—though one man passed a few nervous hours trapped on a ledge.

The emigrants knew that they could drown at perilous river crossings such as those on the North Platte and the Green, and dozens of them did. They could linger too long in the valleys and let snow catch them in the high Sierras. Their cattle could stampede. The livestock could die of alkali poisoning, thirst, starvation, or plain exhaustion, leaving them to scuffle for themselves the rest of the way. They could of course die from cholera or other diseases, but that was a known and acceptable risk that they also faced at home. Perhaps the fear of disease should have daunted them—they knew about the cholera epidemic before they set out—but it didn't. On the contrary, doctors of 1849 viewed a long journey as therapy for any number of ailments, and scores of patients traveled west with medical blessings. So did several elderly people, most of whom survived.

What frightened them most—petrified them, stalked their imagination—was Indians.

For the most part it was an unjustified fear, rooted in half-remembered accounts of distant massacres and the overripe tales of greenhorn-baiters. The western tribes, to their ultimate sorrow, did not yet perceive white men as threats to their survival. Reactions to whites varied widely among different tribes, depending on their status and needs at the moment and their previous dealings with white men. The Pawnees of the eastern Platte Valley were cruelly reduced in both numbers and influence; Bruff ran into a party of emaciated Pawnees who begged him for bread. The Sioux, who would ultimately become the terrors of the plains, were wary but at least superficially friendly. The Crows, farther west, were potentially troublesome.

Mischievous rumors and false alarms flitted from company to company. John Banks of Ohio heard a rumor on the Little Blue River that Pawnees had killed twenty-two men; no evidence ever turned up. A company of heavily armed Virginians flattened themselves on the ground to take aim at a reported Indian war party crossing the Platte; the war party turned out to be six large elk.

Isaac Wistar was one of the few forty-niners with a genuine Indian story to tell. Wistar was alone on horseback, hunting buffalo, when he encountered a party of Pawnees near the Little Blue in late May. The Indians immediately split into two bands on either side of him and gave chase, firing both bullets and arrows. Wistar dashed between the flanking groups and galloped wildly to a swamp close to his halted train, where he dismounted and led his horse through. The Indians pulled up at the sight of the wagons, made a few "insulting gestures," and vanished.

British-born Sarah Royce, sharing a wagon with her husband and infant daughter, was traveling with a company close to the rear of the migration when they were confronted by several hundred Indians who demanded that they pay a toll. The Americans caucused and refused. The captain ordered the men to show their weapons and keep going. Mrs. Royce described what happened next:

"The drivers raised aloft their long whips. The rousing words—'Go long, Buck,' 'Bright!' 'Dan!'—were given all along the line, and we were at once moving between long but not very compact rows of half-naked redskins, many of them well-armed, others carrying but indifferent weapons, while all wore in their faces [an] expression of sullen disappointment mingled with a half-defiant scowl. . . ."

AS ALONZO DELANO explained it, his doctor ordered him to join the gold rush for his health. A "radical change" was essential, he was told, to salvage what remained of his decrepit forty-two-year-old frame. His distinctive nose, which projected from his homely face like a jagged ledge of granite, was doubtless beyond repair. A few years later, flourishing under the restorative California sun, Delano was able to describe himself with some pride as the ugliest man in the state.

Born in Aurora, New York, Delano had drifted west to South Bend, Indiana, and later to Ottawa, Illinois, where he became a mildly prosperous storekeeper. His engaging personality and self-deprecating wit, which endeared him to his neighbors and fellow merchants, eventually led him to a career as a humorist and one of the best of California's first generation of writers.

But in mid-May of 1849 Delano was a man in distress: he suffered alternately from chills and fever; his company of fifty downstate Illinois men, trying a "cutoff" north of St. Joe which was supposed to save ten days en route to the Platte River road, was lost and alone after two weeks on the plains; the almost constant rain made it feel more like November than May.

The only charm of this adventure thus far had been the sight of so much fresh meat on the hoof—elk and antelope—but the animals had eluded the company sharpshooters. They did bag a solitary raccoon. Delano noted the recipe: "Parboil an hour to take out the strong musk, then roast it before the fire on a stick. While it is roasting, walk ten miles, fasting, to get an appetite, then tear it to pieces with your fingers."

On May 20 their point men finally spied the main trail out of St. Joseph; instead of gaining ten days they had lost thirteen. Cold and wet weather dogged them at Fort Kearny, but the worst storm yet came on the twenty-ninth. Wind-borne rain whooshed through tents and wagons as if they were made of paper. Hundreds of unstaked cattle bolted and disappeared. Sleep was impossible. In the morning the camp was a shambles, and a hard rain continued throughout the day. "Distance, nothing," Delano wrote at the end of his diary entry for May 30. Several ox trains lost so many animals—seventy out of a hundred in one company—that they considered turning back. "It was a kind of *terra firma* shipwreck," Delano observed.

By early June the men in the company had settled into a comfortable rhythm. Their oxen were making from fourteen to twenty miles a day. The storms finally abated. Delano was dismayed to discover that some emigrants had deliberately fouled their excess baggage before jettisoning it, so that others could not use it: sugar had been doused with turpentine, flour mixed with dirt and salt, and wagons and clothing burned.

They disappointed a band of Sioux they encountered at Ash Hollow by refusing their requests for whiskey. Two days later the company found a Sioux burial site. The body, wrapped in a blanket and buffalo skin, rested on a wooden rack in the branches of a hackberry tree; a tin cup, moccasins, and other articles had been placed on the body for use in the afterlife. Delano later learned that "some Goths from Missouri wantonly cut the limbs away and let the body fall."

Delano's health was finally improving; he was now able to walk the length of a day's drive and take his regular turn on guard. And the countryside was becoming more interesting. From a distance the high, water-sculpted cliffs at Scott's Bluff resembled "castles, forts, towers, verandas and chimneys," though on closer inspection the bluffs looked more like "bare, shapeless, waterworn rocks."

Fort Laramie, which the company reached on June 12, was built on the same lines as John Sutter's fort in the Sacramento Valley. A single two-story building overlooked a square courtyard bordered by a series of rooms backing on a surrounding wall. Knots of emigrants compared Indian stories in the plaza. Dozens of abandoned wagons, offered for as little as five dollars each, stood outside the whitewashed adobe walls. Here the Illinois men voted to divide into two groups—one with eleven wagons and twenty-nine men, the other with twenty-one men in six wagons. The reason was forage; grass at their campsites had frequently been too skimpy for the herd. Delano joined the smaller caravan.

Riding ahead to scout the North Platte crossing a few days later, he and another man came upon a sign posted on a board near a marshy meadow. "Look at this, look at this," the notice commanded. "The water here is poison, and we have lost six of our cattle. Do not let your cattle drink on this bottom." Alkali-charged water would be a serious hazard to their livestock from here on. The only antidote was vinegar or bacon forced down the throat of the suffering animal.

They found two makeshift ferries about four miles apart on the river; a man from New Orleans, charging five dollars per wagon, had gone into competition with the Mormons. Delano counted more than 250 wagons waiting in line at each site. The ferries were actually several canoes lashed together and covered with enough planks to support a wagon. A long rope was fastened to each end and anchored on either bank. Groups of straining men tugged the rope to pull the craft through the strong current. The ferries frequently capsized, dumping men and wagons over the side. One man fell overboard and was swept away as Delano watched; seven had drowned in the previous few days, and more than two dozen would die here before the year was out. One emigrant wrote that the crossing site seemed "like a battlefield."

The long procession of wagons was a cavalcade with a constantly shifting cast. A train might begin with 25 wagons, lose 12 in the first month, and gain another 8 later. Dozens of companies collapsed in dissension. Many men abandoned the trek when their animals gave out— Delano watched two turn back from Ash Hollow—or after a calamity such as the loss of a wagon. Some pulled ahead of their companies and joined faster caravans; others forsook their wagons and switched to pack trains. "As near as we could ascertain there were about a thousand wagons before us and probably four or five thousand behind us," Delano wrote.

Delano's band slogged up the Sweetwater toward South Pass in late June, past high tableland and flat-topped conical peaks, red buttes and oddly shaped granite hills, sagebrush plains and alkali ponds and long benches "like huge embankments for railroads or canals." Here he met one of the romantic adventurers whose lives enthralled and mystified the Americans of 1849—a long-haired, buckskin-clad mountain man. The man had left the States eighteen years before. He lived with three or four squaws and several children in a cluster of cabins on the Sweetwater. He was between thirty-five and forty and well-educated, "with a pleasing countenance and mild blue eyes." Delano, who felt acutely his separation from his own wife and two children, asked the man if he ever missed his family and friends back home.

"Oh yes," he replied, adding that he had started to return five years ago but had changed his mind. "I look at my responsibilities," he said, "and I give it up. . . . I think I will go sometimes, but I may never do it. Who would protect my children?"

The company camped just west of South Pass on the afternoon of the twenty-ninth. Delano, still thinking of home, climbed a high hill for a last look at "the Atlantic waters, which flowed towards all I held most dear on earth." He stood there for a long time, letting his emotions rise and subside, involuntarily stretching out his arms as if to embrace his family.

But all he could see were "barren reaches of tableland, the bare hills and desert plains of the Sweetwater, while long trains of wagons with their white covers were turning the last curve of the dividing ridge."

CHOLERA was the forty-niners' cruelest enemy. The epidemic had moved from New Orleans up the Mississippi to St. Louis, a way station for almost all overland emigrants, and then accompanied them to the outfitting towns on the Missouri. In St. Louis alone the disease was blamed for an estimated four to five thousand deaths. The full impact of the plague struck the emigrants as they passed up the Platte Valley in May and June. "From Independence to here is a graveyard," a Michigan man wrote from Fort Laramie. Nearly every company lost at least one member to the scourge; dozens lost more. An Ohioan wrote home that he saw an average of four fresh graves each day for the first 170 miles. "Today we saw a grave in which three emigrants are buried who died with cholera in 10 hours after they were taken," Virginian Vincent Geiger reported. Journalist Bayard Taylor later estimated the total number of cholera deaths among 1849 emigrants on the various trails at four thousand.

The 120 passengers on the Pioneer Line, who had ponied up $200 apiece to be transported to the gold fields in relative comfort, endured a particularly severe siege. A teamster known as "California Bob" died just as the train was about to leave Independence on May 15. Two passengers—one from Connecticut and the other from Toronto—succumbed two days later. The most faithful journal keeper in the company was Niles Searls, a twenty-three-year-old law graduate who had recently moved from New York to Cass County, Missouri. Searls saw the first cholera symptoms in his friend Charles Sinclair on May 21.

Sinclair, who came from Ann Arbor, Michigan, seemed to respond to medicine; he was able to continue traveling. Searls sat up with him all one rainy night in the leaky wagon where he lay, trying to keep the water off his head. On the twenty-seventh a doctor told Sinclair that the cholera had passed, but he continued to decline. Searls encouraged him and tried to keep him warm, but he worried that it was too late. By the thirtieth Sinclair was so feeble he could neither travel nor speak. Searls and another man stayed with him at their campsite when the train pulled off. He died that afternoon. His friends wrapped him in blankets and buried him on a slight rise on the prairie.

The company lost three more men to cholera before it reached Fort

Kearny on June 8. By then the passengers were not only frightened but disgusted with their slow progress: they complained angrily that there were too few mules for their heavily loaded carriages. The Pioneer Line's travail was only beginning.

The emigrants passed the contagion to the Indians. In early July Captain Howard Stansbury of the U.S. Army noticed a peculiar absence of activity around the Sioux encampment at Ash Hollow on the North Platte. These were the same Indians that Bill Johnston had met earlier. Impelled by curiosity, Stansbury and a few other soldiers investigated. They found the bodies of nine Sioux warriors with their weapons and other possessions piled around them. The camp was deserted.

Stansbury noticed a small tepee "of rather superior pretensions" set slightly apart. Inside lay the richly dressed body of a pretty Indian girl of sixteen or eighteen, Stansbury learned later that the Sioux had dressed her for death and then abandoned her while she was still alive. Later a party of white men had also seen her alive, but they too had deserted her.

The callous abandonment of the sick was all too common along the trail. Several overland diarists tell of finding cholera-stricken men who had been deserted by their panicky comrades. Their companions were fearful that the disease would spread and too impatient to waste time waiting for those who could not travel. Often they left the sick man with food and medicine; some survived to join new companies; others were cast aside with nothing.

The most tragic story involved Joseph Ware, author of the popular pocket guide to the overland trail which advised emigrant parties to cultivate, among other graces, "a spirit of civility and accommodation." Ware had joined a company somewhat behind the bulk of the emigration and had fallen ill a short distance east of Fort Laramie. Alonzo Delano learned what happened next when he ran into an old Illinois friend on the Humboldt River in August. Ware's colleagues, he was told, "barbarously laid him by the roadside without water, provisions, covering or medicine." Unable to walk, Ware crawled a mile off the road to a pond and lay there alone for two days. Delano's friend found him there, just barely alive. Two days later he died, denied the opportunity to travel the road he had described so well for others. "We assure you that you will be tried to the utmost," Ware had written of the trail, "in view of the appalling obstacles to be surmounted—but never despair."

The most common cause of argonaut deaths besides cholera was their own carelessness, particularly in handling weapons. Nowhere was the greenhorn quality of many forty-niners more obvious. "I confess to more fear from careless handling of firearms than from any external foe," one emigrant fretted. He had just watched his company doctor shoot himself in the hand while picking up a rifle.

In one company, a canvas wagon cover brushed against a rifle and caused it to discharge and kill a passerby. Another man was shot while holding a trunk cover as a target for an inexpert marksman. A teenaged member of a Missouri caravan thought it would be fun to wrap himself in a white blanket and try to sneak up on the guard during the middle watch. The sentry fired after hailing him several times, wounding the youth in the arm and side. Several people were gravely injured when they fell under wagon wheels. Dr. Caleb Ormsby of Ann Arbor saw three victims of such accidents at Fort Laramie hospital in late June; in one case the heavy iron wheel had run over a man's head.

Given the special character of this body of men—they were young and impatient, heavily armed, frequently on each other's nerves, and unhindered by any law beyond their own company bylaws—it is surprising that the road west was not ankle deep in blood. But murders on the trail were rare. It is at least possible that the constraints of their own governments-on-wheels—the risk of banishment or worse—dissuaded them from serious acts of mayhem, but it seems more likely that the reason was the absence of most of the time-tested motivations for murder. Greed was hardly a factor, for example, when great mounds of excess food and other supplies were stacked by the roadside for the taking. The scarcity of women precluded jealousy. What was there to kill for? Pride, perhaps, or cumulative aggravations—but a fistfight could usually ventilate those tensions.

Delano heard about an exception at Fort Kearny. In the quaint language of that Victorian day the provocation was a "gross insult" to an emigrant's wife by another company member. She was probably raped. The outraged husband promptly shot the offender to death (another account says he killed him with an ax). He then consented to be taken to the fort for an investigation in which he was "honorably acquitted."

Expulsion was the most common punishment for serious bylaw violations. A company on the North Platte sentenced a man to be beaten and banished for theft. A member of a Kentucky train was ousted after injuring a man in a knife fight. Others were expelled after shooting incidents. One man was hounded so mercilessly for falling asleep on guard that he quietly packed and left. Some crimes doubtless went undetected. An Ohio diarist saw a grave on the North Platte with the inscription, "John Brown, found in the river June 19, shot in the head."

J. GOLDSBOROUGH BRUFF missed nothing. Meticulous, careful to a fault, encyclopedically well prepared for the journey west, the forty-four-year-old leader of the presidentially blessed Washington City company filled the thickest travel notebooks of 1849. Bruff researched everything. Those were not just wild flowers blooming on Cottonwood Creek, they were gooseberries and prairie peas. The Pawnee chief who embraced him "with the warmth of an affectionate bear, and smelling just as odoriferous," was no anonymous sachem but rather the nephew of the old chief "Chiricherish," and Bruff knew who he was when they met. He had noted the name during his preparations in St. Louis. "I took out my pocket memorandum-book"—one imagines him squirming out of the chief's bear hug, brushing himself off, and licking the end of his pencil after removing the notebook—"and found the name of 'Chiricherish' among the old and principal chiefs of their nation. When I pronounced the name the chief was struck with astonishment and delight, and wished to look on the page as if he could read." Bruff had been a friend of the Pawnees since he passed out bread, bacon, and tobacco to a starving band he met in the Platte Valley.

As a draftsman and mapmaker for the Bureau of Topographical Engineers, Bruff was well known to the officers at Fort Kearny. On June 17 he sent his card ahead to the fort to announce his arrival, appending a militant couplet on the back: *Our banner flutters in the breeze, In spite of Sioux and black Pawnees.* His old friends were more gratified to see him than he had hoped; a rumor of his death by cholera had preceded him.

Bruff supervised an overhaul of his mule-drawn wagons at the fort, discarding some provisions and repacking the rest. He had breakfast with the post commander, Lieutenant Colonel Benjamin Bonneville, a colorful veteran officer whose western explorations had been the subject of a book by Washington Irving. Shortly after Bruff left Kearny the St. Louis *Republican* correspondent took one final census of the migration: 5,516 wagons had passed through the fort and an estimated six hundred more had traveled the Mormon Trail on the north bank of the Platte. He also had a question—"Can this vast crowd succeed in crossing the mountains in safety?"—and a discouraging answer: "It cannot. The leading trains will doubtless succeed, but those behind will find the grass gone and their heavy teams must then fail." The writer was probably thinking of trains like Bruff's Washington company, which was already more than a month behind the leaders. On the day that Bruff departed Fort Kearny Bill Johnston's Pittsburgh company was fording the Bear River only four days short of Salt Lake City.

Bruff maintained a steady and sensible pace. His men frequently rose before four and traveled several miles before stopping for breakfast. They regularly took a long midday break, which gave Bruff a chance to make his weather readings, sketches, and journal notations. On June 22 he left his deputy in charge and struck out alone to hunt. He had an adventurous day: he saw a pack of coyotes—"a moving mass of dark forms and pointed ears"—bagged an antelope, eluded four painted Indians, and captured a coyote cub. The buffalo hunts he had witnessed, he wrote, were frequently harder on the hunters than the hunted—"men were charged by wounded bulls, unhorsed, and many badly hurt, the horses generally running off with the band of buffalos. . . ." Some men were dismounted so far from their camps that they were missing for days. On the twenty-fourth he ran into another old friend in a New Orleans company which included several women. Their hunters had been luckier; Bruff and his friend dined on buffalo soup.

Bruff faithfully recorded the inscription on every graveboard he saw. The entries became more frequent after he passed the forks of the Platte: Lemuel Lee of Vandalia, Illinois, aged 64, died June 3, cholera; Captain Pleasant Gray, Huntsville, Texas, 43, died June 9, cholera; C. Taylor, Tennessee, cholera and typhus; Rachel E. Pattison, aged 18, June 19, 1849.

Strict and correct in dealing with the men in his company, Bruff was a soft touch for anyone in need. His code demanded that the strong help the weak, particularly women and children on the trail. At Ash Hollow he met a group of several men and two women traveling in only three wagons. Fearing an attack by Indians, they asked Bruff if they could join his company for security. "We took the little party under our wing," Bruff wrote. "Seem to be very clever people."

On July 2 he reported that his men, now nearing Courthouse Rock, had put 429 miles between themselves and the Missouri. A grave marker he found that day bore the most poignant inscription he had seen yet:

Jno. Hoover, died, June 18, 49
Aged 12 yrs. Rest in peace,
sweet boy, for thy travels are over.

CALIFORNIA was daily becoming a more heterogeneous blend. The San Francisco *Alta California* estimated the non-Indian population at roughly thirty thousand by the end of June. More than 10,600 novice Californians had arrived in the preceding eleven weeks, 6,450 from Mexico and the rest from the shores of the Pacific: Chile (1,350), Panama (1,251), Hawaii (370), Peru (227), even Tahiti (120). About 2 percent of the newcomers were women, the majority from Mexico and South America. The great bulk of both the land and sea migration from the East would not reach the coast until August and September.

The mecca of the moment was the southern mines, especially the diggings on the Tuolumne and Stanislaus rivers. A New Orleans *Picayune* correspondent wrote in June that miners on the tributaries of the San Joaquin were collectively removing a thousand pounds of gold a day. "Whenever a miner gets less than an ounce a day," he reported, "he thinks he is not paid for his labor and seeks some better place." The writer calculated the Latin American population in the region at about eight thousand. "They keep up all the customs and habits of their country— bullfights, chicken-fights, dancing, gambling, etc. on Sundays and feast days."

William Daylor, a onetime English seaman who had discovered the Weber Creek diggings in 1848, was working the Stanislaus in May. It was "the hardest work I have ever undergone," he wrote, but the most vexing part of it was that everyone but him seemed to be striking bonanzas. Three men found a nugget worth $278 below Jamestown. Another group gathered five and a half pounds in two days. A party of Mexicans dug out $2,200 on Woods Creek. Daylor, averaging about an ounce a day, figured that it would improve when the rivers began to fall.

Sonora, the metropolis of the southern mines, weaved through the narrow, twisting valley of summer-dry Woods Creek. Wild oats and live oak trees grew on the tawny hillsides above the creek. The valley floor was pitted with deep holes alternating with mounds of dirt. The Mexican miners, many of whom had their families with them, had transformed the rickety camp into a vivid outpost of their own Sonora. William Perkins, a twenty-two-year-old Canadian who got there in late June, thought he had never seen a more beautiful or romantic spot. The tents and brush shelters were "decorated with gaudy hangings of silks, fancy cottons, flags, brilliant goods of every description." Gold- and silver-plated saddles lay on the ground. Mexicans in multicolored serapes mingled with Peruvians in white cotton ponchos and Chileans in dark wool. Perkins saw tables packed with *dulces*, sweetmeats, cooling beverages with snow from the Sierra Nevada floating in them, cakes, dried fruits, hot meats, and pies. The outdoor gambling tables, covered with a scarlet cloth, were piled high with coins and buckskin bags of gold dust.

If Latin-flavored Sonora was the hub of the southern mines, go-ahead Yankee Sacramento was plainly the capital of the northern diggings. Despite the temporary vogue for the southern streams, the *Picayune*'s man reckoned that four-fifths of the arriving gold seekers still lit out for Sacramento and the north. Edward Buffum was flabbergasted by the metamorphosis in Sacramento since his last visit six months before. Houses had spread over the flats between the thick-trunked oaks. Tall-masted ships were moored on the river. Cabins and tents had sprouted around the long-isolated fort.

Sam Brannan opened his gaudy new City Hotel with the roar of a cannon and a grand banquet in June. Brannan had spent the huge sum of $50,000 to transform John Sutter's old grist mill into a porticoed pleasure palace where one could eat, drink, gamble, and sometimes sleep. A large dormitory room was equipped with four tiers of bunks against the walls, a hairbrush chained to a mirror and a single, rarely used toothbrush.

Canvas-roofed bars and gambling houses crowded together near the river. The most notorious was the Round Tent, where "naked, unmasked depravity" was said to prevail. The Stinking Tent, which took its name from the odor of a former ship's sail which served as its roof, had a similar reputation. "There is not a house in the town where ardent spirits are not retailed," William Ryan clucked. He exaggerated by at least one: a minister launched semiregular services in June.

Coloma appeared to be in a lull after the Indian episode in April. Brigadier General Bennet Riley, the new military governor, had ordered a detachment of troops into the area to keep the peace. High water hampered digging here and in the rest of the northern mines until late spring. The sawmill where it all began was once again running night and day and selling boards at $400 per thousand feet. Newcomers invariably gaped at the tailrace where Marshall had glimpsed the first color. The discoverer himself tacked notices on trees, still making a futile effort to establish a preemptive claim to the land around the mill.

The toilsome labor of gold mining was a distasteful revelation. Most of the aspiring miners who arrived in the spring had traveled the Panama

route. They were not acquainted with work as arduous as this. James
Tyson, a Baltimore doctor, tried it for a few days at Placerville and concluded that "none but a laboring man is fit for the business." Tyson wisely
returned to doctoring, which yielded as much as four ounces ($64) for a
visit. Hundreds of men ended their mining careers almost before they
broke in their equipment.

New Yorker James Delavan drifted from Coloma to the Middle Fork
of the American to the Yuba in May and June. He spent most of his time
watching from a disdainful distance. At Fords Bar on the Middle Fork
he saw four men using a diving bell to prospect the bottom. Two pumped
air into a hose manned by a third. The fourth scanned the bottom from a
window on the bell, tugging a cord when he wanted to be moved. Delavan
found Hawaiians working a variation of the same principle on the Yuba.
They dove to the bottom with crowbars and containers they filled with
dirt until the frigid water forced them to quit. But Delavan's biggest surprise was his discovery of two women at Big Bar on the Middle Fork. It
was even whispered, he wrote, "that a knife and fork had been seen."

The government of this lively province remained ineffectual and
largely invisible. Political power in California was suspended awkwardly
between the obsolete military government left over from the Mexican War
and the highly vocal democrats arriving daily. The skeletal legal system,
a holdover from Mexican rule, was fast becoming irrelevant. California
lacked both a civil and criminal code; crimes were sketchily defined and
contracts legally unenforceable.

The newcomers were ardent believers in the participatory politics of
Jacksonian America. They wanted to be a fully recognized part of the
Union, and now; it was unthinkable to them that free adult male Americans should be ruled by a military commander administering foreign
laws. The least they expected was that Congress would promptly establish
an interim territorial government.

But in May came the shocking news that Congress had extended the
federal revenue laws to California while neglecting to provide any kind
of government whatever. A wave of indignation rolled across the foothills
and valleys. Not only was this taxation without representation, an irate
San Franciscan wrote to the New York *Herald*, but the betrayed Californians were left "to find, feed, clothe and govern ourselves, while our
pockets shall be emptied to support a government which yields us no
protection." The idea of secession was bruited about in the mines: "As
Congress had done nothing for us," the angry letter writer pointed out,

"a general determination began to appear that we should do something for ourselves."

The complaint was legitimate, even if congressional inaction was the result not of a paralysis of will but of the delicate balance between slave and free states in the Union. Representatives from the slaveholding states wanted to be certain that the Free-Soilers did not take advantage of the antislavery sentiment of most Californians to gain a numerical superiority in Congress; there would be no statehood for California without a corresponding addition to the proslavery side.

General Riley, the military governor, chose this volatile moment to issue a heavy-footed proclamation proposing a convention to organize a government. Riley's assumption of civil authority—"in accordance with instructions from the Secretary of War"—inflamed the fragile sensitivities of the San Franciscans. They would set up a government because it was their right as free and democratic Americans to do so, not because some tin-star general told them to. Edward Buffum was in town when the governor's fiat was posted on June 10. He found that a majority of the citizenry regarded Riley's move as "an unjust usurpation of power," and he agreed with them.

The steamer *Panama,* the third Panama steamship to reach San Francisco, chugged into the harbor in the midst of the furore with a cargo of help. The *Panama,* as it happened, was topheavy with politicians. Passenger Thomas Butler King, a former congressman, was carrying secret instructions from President Taylor to aid in the formation of a state government. Another ex-congressman aboard, William M. Gwin, had already announced that he would be California's first U.S. senator when statehood was achieved. John Weller and Fred Low, both future California governors, were also on board. So was Mrs. Jessie Frémont, daughter of Senator Thomas Benton and wife of the noted explorer (and later California senator) John Frémont.

With so many politicians at large, a public meeting was inevitable. It was held at Portsmouth Square on June 12. King and Gwin, among others, spoke out for the immediate formation of a state government. Peter Burnett, steadily emerging as a leader in the drive for statehood, spoke of Californians as a "commercial, civilized and wealthy people without law, order or a system to protect and secure them." They would form their own government, with or without Washington and with or without the presumptuous Governor Riley. The next step would be an election in August to choose delegates to a constitutional convention.

But neither politics nor anything else could overshadow commerce for long. It was a time, as San Francisco newspaperman Frank Soulé wrote a few years later, when "everybody made money, in spite of himself." Every kind of business in the city flourished. Sam Brannan, James Lick, Thomas Larkin, and others had already amassed fortunes in trade and real estate. Ships brought more customers every day: three vessels sailed through the Gate on the first of June, nine more anchored the next day, and six—including the Baltimore clipper *Greyhound*—on the day after that. The city's population would hit five thousand by July.

One of the most popular business speculations was the sale of lots in towns existing only on paper. Dozens of invisible towns with names like Plumas, Oro City, Eliza, and Vernon surfaced in newspaper ads. A town called "New York of the Pacific" in the Sacramento–San Joaquin Delta had more pretensions than most. The *Alta*'s ad on May 17 spelled out the town's assets: rich soil, fine climate, pure water, a deep harbor. Lots, streets, and no fewer than three public squares had been laid out; "there is not in all California a point combining so many advantages for business purposes." Dr. James Tyson, passing the site shortly afterwards, found it "barren and desolate" without a single visible structure.

The town of New York eventually materialized, sputtered along for a couple of years, and disappeared. Considering the reputation of the local mosquitoes, it is surprising that it lasted that long. A company of Boston men spent one long night there in combat with mosquitoes of "terrible size and ferocity." Ever afterwards, whenever New York of the Pacific was mentioned, "a ghastly smile would overspread their countenance" and they would beg to be excused.

IX

THE UNYIELDING LAND

JUNCTION OF THE GILA AND THE COLORADO

BY THE FOURTH of July the great caravan of California-bound
wagons, mule trains, and footsore emigrants was a frieze extending
from the Platte Valley eight hundred miles west to the sage-specked banks
of the Humboldt. With the exception of the slowest stragglers, no emigrant
train clanking through the prairie solitudes was more than a day's travel
from at least one other company. An uninformed stranger watching from
a slice of rimrock, looking down on the endless procession of tiny wagons
inching across the vastness, might have wondered what catastrophe had
precipitated such an exodus. It seemed as though all of America was on
the move.

Thousands of men were still in Panama, cruising uneasily up the
Chagres River or anxiously awaiting a Pacific steamer. Thousands more

were crammed into the storm-battered armada strung out along a necklace-shaped track of ocean with Cape Horn at the bottom. Dozens of companies were scrambling over the mountain spine of Mexico. Others were scattered through the deserts and canyons and summer-dry washes of the Southwest. Ships packed with Germans, French, and Britons were running before the wind into the Atlantic sunset. Chilean aristocrats were coming, and so were Australian convicts. The lucky minority—mainly passengers on the first Panama steamers, the earliest packers to cross Mexico, and voyagers from the Pacific ports—were already wandering wide-eyed in Ophir. Everyone else was in transit.

The American forty-niners celebrated the Fourth wherever they were. It was, most of them agreed, a grand time to be a Yankee, and the beckoning hills of the newest territory under the flag merely gilded their already robust patriotism. Sailing up from Panama on the *Niantic*, John Letts of Staten Island, New York, beheld a revelation on the Fourth: "At 12 o'clock we felt a slight breeze, and the mist rose like a curtain, displaying to our astonished vision the coast of California." The ship was only a few miles off the Golden Gate, and on entering the harbor the next day the 240 passengers cheered wildly at the sight of the Stars and Stripes on a U.S. warship. "Our patriotism at this particular time was not of a nature to be smothered into silence," wrote Letts.

Silence was never a danger. Most overland companies began the holiday the way that J. Goldsborough Bruff's men did at Chimney Rock on the Platte—with a fusillade of rifle fire. Bruff loosed an oration—"by request," he explained—and the subsequent feast included pork and beans, buffalo steaks and stewed dried apples, the last contributed by the women in a neighboring train.

The Wolverine Rangers, a company of Michigan men camped just east of Fort Laramie, set an even more elaborate table. The Rangers aligned their wagons in parallel columns fifteen feet apart and spread the wagon covers across the intervening space to form a marquee. Thus shaded, they sat through a prayer, a reading of the Declaration of Independence, an enthusiastic speech, and a concert. The rewards included ham, buffalo, gingerbread, three kinds of pie, corn bread, johnnycake, pudding, and lemonade.

And whiskey. The toasts were the most entertaining part of the program. Joe Hamelin's band of Missourians, halted at the North Platte ferry, drank gratefully to "the health and happiness of Miss Elizabeth Mills, to whom we are indebted for the catsup." The last toast which

Hamelin recalled clearly saluted "Henry Clay—Ashland his home and Dr. Dudley his family physician."

Bill Johnston and his Pittsburgh hotspurs were in too big a rush to celebrate much. They spent the Fourth on the road, driving through the broken country near the headwaters of the Humboldt. In the evening they persuaded a reluctant lawyer to deliver an address, then learned that he had been secretly rehearsing. Alonzo Delano, camped on the Green River, watched an impromptu murder trial deteriorate into a drunken and inconclusive melee. The defendant finally left in disgust.

John Audubon and his men lay over for the day at their campsite amid the dusty ramparts of the Sierra Madre Occidental range in Mexico. Audubon had an American flag which had been given to him by one of the company's cholera victims. His men rigged the flag to the highest tree at their camp, shot and roasted a wild heifer, and sang operatic arias. The Frémont Association, a band of New Yorkers traveling across Texas, entertained each other with a music-hall revue of comic songs and recitations. One member recited "Rollo's Address to the Peruvians."

The patriots already in Sacramento celebrated with fireworks and oratory at the grove of oaks which later became the site of the state capitol. Men were dispatched to nearby encampments to round up women for a ball at Sam Brannan's new City Hotel. They managed to find eighteen to dance with the two hundred champagne-swilling male guests. A merchant at Coloma had a handsome pine in front of his store trimmed and converted into a flagstaff for the Fourth. Miners gathered around it to listen to an antislavery speech. Afterwards they voted to bar Mexicans and Chileans from the Coloma diggings.

A few miles down the South Fork of the American River, a former Philadelphia minister named Daniel Woods suffered through his first full day of gold digging on Independence Day. Spreading God's word was never like this. The reverend passed the glorious Fourth "digging one hole after another, washing out many test pans, hoping at every new attempt to find that which would reward our toil—and we have made ten cents each."

THE GOLD SEEKERS crossing Mexico, Texas, and the Southwest traversed a land with different demands, terrors, and satisfactions from those on the South Pass route. The Mexican passage was at once exotic and extreme; the terrain varied from palm-shaded coastal lowlands and

dense tropical rain forests to perpendicular red-brown peaks and broad
sandy deserts. The country could be crossed via Mexico City and Guadalajara to the sea in four or five weeks. Farther north, the trek across mountains and dry plains to the Colorado River could take as long as six
months. The great danger was thirst on the desert *jornadas* in Chihuahua
and Sonora and beyond the Colorado in California. The Comanches and
Apaches, boldest of the southwestern tribes, were another potential peril.
The imponderable was the attitude of the Mexican people, so recently at
war with the heavily armed men who now walked their roads in peace.

One's apprehensions were never altogether still on the Mexican trails.
Bandits, a threat to emigrants traveling in small groups, roamed both
spurs of the Sierra Madre. Rumors flowed among the Americans that the
Mexican government had banned firearms and military-style organizations among foreign travelers. The countryside itself seemed to be waiting
in ambush: "Everything is thorny, even the grass is pointed . . . and
all the insects are venomous," one traveler wrote. Racial and religious
prejudice increased the tension. Few forty-niners bothered to conceal their
contempt for a people they considered dirty, shiftless, and priest-ridden.
The insensitive Yankees antagonized their hosts by wearing their hats in
church and traveling on religious holidays. Even as worldly and tolerant
a trespasser as John Audubon confessed to a "hatred of everything
Mexican."

The joy of the trip for Audubon had eroded back on the Rio Grande,
where he had buried ten of his men. After that his journey was less an
adventure brimming with possibilities than an ordeal he was obliged to
finish. Audubon himself suffered a mild attack of cholera after a month
on the trail. Another man from his company perished from the disease
on the edge of the western mountains. His men were hooted as they rode
past a Mexican cavalry garrison. Rustlers in another village tried to
stampede his horses.

Only the lure that had drawn him originally, the chance to observe
and describe nature in a fresh setting, could revive his spirit. Audubon
alone among the wayfarers of 1849 could watch a gliding, heavy-winged
hawk and write, "he had two white bands on his tail—could it be *Falco
lagopus?*" He was thrilled by the richly colored wild flowers of the Sierra
Madre, scarlet lilies and cinnamon-stemmed laurel and pink sweet williams. "I am so enchanted with the wild beauty all about us that I could
almost stay months to enjoy it," he wrote in late June. "It is all new to
me . . . the plants, trees, rock, all strange, and as we take our horses
to [a] beautiful creek to drink, curious fish come to look at their noses."

Audubon's enchantment faded when his company emerged from a month in the mountains and entered the dry mesquite plains and sand hills of Sonora. Many of his men fell ill when they passed from "an atmosphere like that of Maine" into searing desert heat. An eight-day journey over desolate hills brought them to the hostile little village of Altar, about seventy-five miles southwest of the present international border at Nogales. They looked like beaten soldiers. "Half of us are on foot, our clothes are ragged and torn, and we have lived on half rations, often less, of beans and what we call bread," he wrote. "Several days we were 20 or 24 hours without water, no grass for our horses, and inexpressibly weary always." The villagers refused to sell them food. A few days later they ran out of beans. All they had left was bread and water.

In late September they reached the Pima Indian settlement on the Gila River not far from present-day Phoenix. Here they fortified themselves with corn and melons raised by the friendly Pimas as they prepared for another grassless and waterless march. Vegetation was limited to "a few cottonwoods and scrub-willow" and the creosote plant, "the accursed emblem of barrenness and sterility." Audubon's mules were now so jaded that they could carry only a hundred pounds. The only cheering note was that no one was ill and no one was quitting—victory enough in his ravaged company. In mid-October they reached the Colorado River. They had one more desert to cross.

THE CHOLERA EPIDEMIC which had besieged Audubon's men on the lower Rio Grande assailed Mexico through the spring and summer. "We have seen scarcely anything but suffering and death," an American traveler reported in March. Dozens of emigrants died, but casualties were even higher among Mexicans. In Monterrey the terrified residents massed in a religious procession to pray that they be spared. Saltillo, a city of six thousand in the foothills of the eastern mountains, was losing some sixty people a day to the plague in May. It was worse farther west in Durango, where estimates of the deaths ran as high as five hundred a day. Church bells pealed incessantly.

Violence between Americans and Mexicans was surprisingly rare, given the volatile combination of Yankee arrogance and Mexican pride. The Mexican government, undoubtedly mindful of the thousands of Sonorans already in California, placed no special restrictions on American travelers. Most Mexicans treated the intruders with courtesy if not affection. But inevitably there were clashes. A dispute over an innkeeper's

bill near Tepic resulted in a gunfight which killed an American. A brawl
in a San Blas cantina left a Mexican dead and several more wounded.
Forty Yankees were jailed in Mazatlán for recklessly firing their weapons
in a plaza.

Flannel-shirted Americans and their sore-backed mules and mustangs
were weaving westward on a dozen different routes through Mexico. By
late spring there were probably as many as nine thousand gringos in the
country. The 150 men of the Manhattan and California Overland Association, outfitted in red shirts and high boots, crossed from Veracruz to
Mazatlán in two months. Their only scare came when they neglected to
remove their wide-brimmed hats during a religious ceremony in Mexico
City, provoking sullen rumbles from the crowd. They found an American
brig in Mazatlán and sailed into San Francisco in May.

The Defiance Gold-Hunters Expedition of Defiance, Ohio, struggled
across southern Texas and the high dry plains of Coahuila to Chihuahua,
suffering so severely from thirst that some men drank their own urine.
One went mad. Their losses included a half-dozen cholera victims, a man
who shot himself in the side, and another who wandered off and never
came back. The survivors made it to the Colorado River in five and a half
months. Some companies cut southwest to Durango and emerged on the
Pacific at Mazatlán or San Blas. A pack train which included Daniel
Woods, the Philadelphia pastor who was to pan a dime's worth of dust
on the Fourth of July, traveled from Tampico to San Blas by way of San
Luis Potosí and Guadalajara in five weeks.

Woods was impervious to the charms of Mexico. He found a bullfight
he attended to be "disgraceful and cowardly butchery"; a fandango was
"a lazy shuffle accompanied by music." He was appalled to learn that
the rooms at wayside inns were without beds or any other furnishings,
though not without an occasional tarantula. The food was too spicy, and
the liquor made from the maguey plant was vile. The countryside was
more felicitous: the coastal plain near Tampico was greened in "perpetual spring"; the mountains west of Guadalajara concealed sparkling
streams and dense stands of reassuring pines.

But the mountains also concealed villains. The high passes and switchback trails between Guadalajara and the Pacific were bandit country.
Woods's company heard that three hundred armed men were waiting to
waylay them in a gorge. Fortunately soldiers also patrolled these mountains, and the Americans were told that troops had recently killed several
desperadoes in a shootout. As if in confirmation, they rounded a bend
and saw three bloated corpses hanging from a gallows in a fire-blackened

field. A sign over the scaffold identified the dead men as robbers and murderers.

Foreshadowing the destiny of most gold rush companies, the members of Woods's caravan broke into factions when they arrived at San Blas in April. Some ended their journey on foot, walking up the coast of Baja California after abandoning the dilapidated twenty-three-ton schooner they had chartered. Woods was luckier; he found a British bark and sailed into San Francisco Bay in late June.

THE WAGON TRAINS leaving the Arkansas River outposts of Fort Smith and Van Buren set out on a well-worn trail through the territory of the "five civilized tribes"—the Cherokee, Choctaw, Chickasaw, Creek, and Seminole nations—in present-day Oklahoma. The trail split off from the Arkansas not far from Fort Smith and headed west along the Canadian River, past Indian farms and scattered trading posts and through the forest known as the Cross Timbers.

The foe on this route was mud. The extraordinarily wet spring which was making travel difficult in the Platte Valley made it almost impossible along the Canadian. "It was nothing unusual," a Mississippian wrote home in late April, "to see ten or a dozen wagons mired down in less than half a mile, and a portion of the road was so boggy that it was necessary to unhitch the mules from our wagons and drag them through by main strength." A Louisiana argonaut reported that the constant toil and hardship had splintered most company organizations, proving that man in adversity was a "weak, wavering, peevish and mutable thing." An Arkansas company lost their wagons and animals in a flash flood and had to turn back.

The gold seekers slogging up the Canadian were far less numerous than those on the Platte, but they were nevertheless a formidable force: a U.S. Indian agent stationed about 150 miles west of Fort Smith said in June that he had counted between fifteen hundred and two thousand people. They were generally "a substantial class of citizens," he remarked, though most lacked "any very definite idea of what they will do." The most impressive aggregation was the 479-strong Fort Smith and California Emigrating Company, which fell in step with its military escort beyond the westernmost trading post in mid-May. Here the trail climbed from the lowland mire to the sparsely timbered and wind-scalloped prairie.

The younger officers in Captain Randolph Marcy's army detachment were smitten instantly by the Fort Smith Company's most decorative member, the winsome Mary Conway. The seventeen-year-old Mary, who was traveling with her parents and nine brothers and sisters, looked ravishing even after a day on the road. Lieutenant James Simpson watched enraptured one afternoon as the bonneted Mary dismounted from her splendid black horse. "A veil thrown carelessly aside," he wrote, "she is listlessly twirling a switch and giving heed to the conversation of a young emigrant who is sitting contentedly at her feet." The other women were busy preparing the evening meal.

Officers and emigrants competed for Mary's smiles. Simpson seemed to have an edge when he discovered a sixty-foot-high mound of rock looming out of the plain and promptly dubbed it "Rock Mary," but before long the leading contenders had narrowed to two recent West Point graduates, Second Lieutenants John Buford of Kentucky and Montgomery Pike Harrison of Indiana. Both proposed marriage. Mary accepted the twenty-three-year-old Harrison, whose sixteen-year-old brother Benjamin would grow up to be President. The young couple sought her parents' permission to have a wedding on the trail, but the Conways asked them to wait until their arrival in California. The trouble with that was that the troops were accompanying the caravan only as far as Santa Fe, whereupon they would return to Arkansas. The Conways suggested that young Harrison might obtain a leave and come to California later.

The Fort Smith emigrants passed out of Indian Territory into Texas at the end of May. Their road now lay straight west to the horizon, unimpeded by hill or tree. Plum thickets tumbled down the riverbanks. Dark herds of buffalo coursed slowly over the plain like the wind-driven water of a shallow lake. On June 8 an emigrant woman gave birth to twin boys, named Dillard and Marcy for the civilian and military commanders of the expedition. Oddly, the emigrants on the Arkansas trail were spared the scourge of cholera that carried off so many on the Platte. A traveler writing at the end of April said that there had been just three deaths on the trail. Only a few more were recorded the rest of the way. The suffering on this route would come not from disease but from thirst on the western deserts.

New Mexico and the Texas Panhandle were the northern range of the nomadic Comanches, the jewel-bedecked cavalrymen who were feared throughout northern Mexico and the American Southwest. The Comanches, who measured a man's wealth by the number of horses he owned, were probably the most daring horsemen in North America. In the 1840s their power and influence in their territory were at a peak. Comanche raiders swept through the Mexican states of Chihuahua and Durango like an all-consuming pestilence, killing ranchers, kidnapping women and children for slaves, stealing livestock and food. They were forever on the move. Once the Spanish had persuaded a band of Comanches to settle down and try farming, but they had failed to take into account the Comanche custom of moving to a new camp after the death of an important man. The Indians abandoned their farms when the first such death occurred.

Comanches had murdered Jedediah Strong Smith, the greatest of the early American mountain men, on the Cimarron River in New Mexico. Brightly dressed warriors had plundered a several-hundred-mile-long strip on the Rio Grande only a few months before the first gold seeker wandered into Comanche territory. But in those few months their leader had died, and his successor promised Texas pioneer Jesse Chisholm that the bloodshed was done. Chisholm said that the Comanche chief had appeared bewildered when told that large numbers of whites would be crossing his land, and no doubt he was. But no chief was prescient enough to see that the forty-niners were merely the advance guard; in a decade the lordly Comanches would be fighting for their survival, and in two decades they would be conquered.

It would take longer to subdue the other great nomadic tribe of the Southwest, the Apaches. Their domain lay mainly to the west, in Sonora and present-day Arizona, and they would retain their wary, bristly independence longer than any other American tribe. Apaches would resist the Yankees with the same implacable hostility they had shown to both Spanish and Mexicans. The exasperated Spanish had given up trying to befriend them and embarked on a campaign of extermination, but the Apaches, as always, had refused to quit. By 1849 the states of Chihuahua and Sonora were offering bounties for the scalps of the estimated five to six thousand Apaches. Americans in Arizona would do the same a generation later.

The Apaches, who operated in small, autonomous, and unpredictable bands, generally ignored the forty-niners. The few reported confrontations were mysterious and inconclusive. One emigrant became separated from his company and ran into three Apaches who told him in Spanish that they liked Americans and delivered him back to his caravan. But two other forty-niners were killed in their blankets by Apache rustlers on the Rio Grande. Another decade would pass before relations between Ameri-

cans and Apaches, poisoned by repeated American betrayals, would
harden into the mutual savagery that persisted until the surrender of
Geronimo in 1886.

Curiously it was the peaceful, agricultural Pimas, descendants of a
people who had farmed the Gila Valley for thousands of years, who
defended themselves against the Apaches most successfully. The Pimas
were warmly admired by Americans for their friendliness, honesty—
"almost to a fault," one emigrant noted—and industry. They had per-
fected an intricate system of flood-water irrigation that enabled them to
produce corn, beans, squash, melons, pumpkins, wheat, and other crops,
which they cheerfully exchanged for clothes and manufactured goods.

A stopover with the successful and attractive Pimas—"every movement was a specimen of native grace," a young New Yorker exclaimed—
made it difficult to sustain the comforting illusion of Caucasian superiority. U.S. Army Lieutenant Colonel W. H. Emory, who visited the Pima
villages in 1846, gave up the attempt. The Pimas, he wrote, "surpassed
many of the Christian nations in agriculture, [were] little behind them
in the useful arts, and immeasurably before them in honesty and virtue."
These remarkable Indians would eventually be decimated like so many
others, but in a different way: settlers dammed and diverted their water
for their own use, an act that ultimately desiccated both the Pima paradise and the Pimas.

Mary Conway and the rest of the Fort Smith Company met a band
of Comanches near the Pecos River in New Mexico in June. Captain
Marcy exchanged moist greetings and professions of friendship with the
chief, enduring his embrace "for the good of the service" and dispensing
pipes and tobacco to the gaudy warriors. The showier braves wore beaded
blankets and bright red leggings along with large earrings and bracelets.
Long buffalo-hair braids ornamented with silver disks hung from their
hair. Marcy learned that the three hundred Indians in this band owned
some 2,500 horses and mules, most of them formerly Mexican, along with
several Mexican slaves.

Marcy and his officers sat with the chiefs in a circle, surrounded by
some five hundred emigrants and soldiers. When the formalities were
over, Marcy noticed his Delaware Indian guide Black Beaver in animated
conversation with the Comanche commander. Marcy, a twenty-year army
man, asked him what the trouble was.

"He say, captain, he bring two wife for you," Black Beaver replied,
pointing to two girls sitting nearby.

The embarrassed Marcy, ignoring the guffaws from the crowd, told the guide to explain that white men limited themselves to a single wife. Black Beaver passed this on and then turned back to Marcy.

"He say, captain, you the strangest man he ever see," Black Beaver translated. "Every man he seen before, when he been travelin' long time, the first thing he want, *wife*."

The line of Fort Smith wagons clattered onto the narrow and adobe-walled streets of Santa Fe a few days later. The 250-year-old Spanish settlement was the most important crossroads in the Southwest, the principal way station on the Arkansas route and the terminus of the old traders' trail which John Sutter had once traveled from Independence. Forty-niners began to pour into the town in early May. The deluge continued through the summer: as many as three thousand arrived via the Canadian River and perhaps another 2,500 on the trail from Missouri.

Santa Fe, though part of the United States, was still a Mexican frontier town—"a little of the hardest place I was ever in," one forty-niner wrote. Many emigrants swapped their wagons for provisions and pack animals in the crowded plaza. The Americans tentatively explored the cantinas and gambling houses and were startled to see women gambling alongside the men. Guitar music from fandango parlors continued late into the night. The residents, a man from Little Rock wrote, "are the poorest-looking people I ever saw. They subsist principally on mutton, onions and red pepper. The proportion of poor to rich is about one thousand to one." A favorite local diversion was to release a chicken in the plaza. Hundreds of mounted men then chased the terrified fowl through the streets until it was caught.

The unwieldy Fort Smith Company finally broke up in New Mexico. The only explanation came in a hasty letter from Mary Conway, written after they left Santa Fe in July: "Some got to disobeying orders and Captain Dillard resigned, which split the company all to pieces." The Conways, now traveling with about two dozen other wagons, drove south down the Rio Grande toward the village of Dona Ana, where they would turn west for Tucson and the Gila River trail. Mary's fiancé, Lieutenant Harrison, galloped off on an expedition against Apaches; the young couple said good-by along the Rio Grande in July, and the troops headed back toward Arkansas.

The road to the Gila led the emigrants on a steep climb across the Continental Divide at Guadalupe Pass, near the point where Arizona, New Mexico, and Sonora now converge. Passing through the dusty pueblo

of Tucson, the Americans noticed Mexican soldiers stationed there to protect the inhabitants from Apache raiders. Beyond Tucson lay a ninety-
mile *jornada* to the Gila. The trail crossed a sun-scorched mesquite plain
with little grass and no water except that which collected after the in-
frequent rains. John Durivage, a young correspondent for the New
Orleans *Picayune*, toiled across this barren expanse in early June. It
struck him as somehow surreal: dead still except for the clatter of
hoofs, lifeless, "a perfectly blasted heath." At one point he fainted, fell
from his mule, and made up his mind to die of thirst beneath a stunted
mesquite. But his black servant rode to his rescue with a canteen of water
from the Gila, only four miles away. When his mule sniffed the river
"she pricked up her ears, gave one long bray and struck a bee line for the
Gila directly through the thick chaparral, I hanging on her back like
death." The mule plunged her head into the river and raised it only when
her sides were distended.

The Conway family passed through the village of the amiable Pimas
and on down the Gila Valley in September and October. At a campsite
on the Gila they found a written notice on a board nailed to a mesquite
bush. Nearby were two graves. The notice gave a brief summary of the
only trail execution of 1849.

The marker identified the murdered man as Elijah Davis and his
slayer as George Hickey. Both were teamsters with a company from
Clarksville, Arkansas. The two men had quarreled "about something of
no importance" while herding oxen on September 4. The argument boiled
into a fistfight won by Davis. The enraged Hickey then stabbed Davis in
the heart. He was immediately seized by other members of the company.

That evening the Clarksville men selected a judge and jury and
conducted a trial. The verdict was guilty, the sentence death by firing
squad. The next morning the entire company voted to sustain the jury's
decision. Twelve men were chosen by lot as a firing squad. Six rifles were
loaded with ball and powder and six more with powder only. A blind-
folded man drew the weapons from a stack and handed them to the executioners. Hickey died instantly. They buried him next to his victim, tacked
up the notice, and moved on.

The Conway wagons, minus several oxen and most of the possessions
they had started with, reached the Colorado River on October 24. A week
earlier the remnants of John Audubon's threadbare band had left the
river to start across the final ninety-mile desert to Carrizo Creek. Mary
Conway may have been the only forty-niner whose reputation preceded
her; Lieutenant Cave Johnson Couts, who commanded a company of

soldiers at the river, had been saving a bottle of molasses and a lump of sugar for her for three weeks. She was apparently worth the wait: the lieutenant took supper with Mary and her mother and escorted the family for several miles when they left. "An angel in such wilds!" he exulted in his journal. "May you wed your true love and may the Lord take a liking to you." The lieutenant's blissful benevolence did not extend to the rest of the emigrants, who pestered him constantly with questions about the trail and requests for food. "I was never in my life so annoyed," he complained.

The Colorado was about two hundred yards wide with a five-mile-per-hour current where the emigrants crossed. During the summer each group built their own raft, but by October the army was operating a ferry at $4 per wagon and 50 cents a person. The tall and muscular Yuma Indians who lived on the river swam the livestock across for a toll of one shirt per animal. The emigrants passed bands of Sonorans returning home from the diggings. For them there was an additional charge; the new U.S. Collector of Customs for San Francisco, who crossed the Colorado in October, ordered Lieutenant Couts to impose a gratuitous tax on Mexicans taking gold out of the country.

The last ordeal was the Colorado Desert, its desolation broken only by a few sulfurous wells. John Durivage called it "the Sahara of America." Mules sunk to their fetlocks in the heavy sand; "the hot air was laden with the fetid smell of dead mules and horses." Audubon thought it was the bleakest landscape of his melancholy trek: "not a blade of grass or green thing of any kind relieved the monotony of the parched, ash-colored earth." One emigrant found the bodies of three men who had dropped beside their mules.

When at last they hobbled into San Diego the survivors of the Gila Trail looked like a battalion of beggars. Hollow-cheeked, eyes empty of hope, they trudged into the beautiful little port in tatters. The writer Bayard Taylor met some of them when his steamer stopped at San Diego in August—"men lank and brown . . . with long hair and beards and faces from which the rigid expression of suffering was scarcely relaxed."

John Audubon's travail came to an end in the luxuriant San Felipe Valley in late October. The valley seemed an Eden of glades and great oaks and delicious little streams; he even found some grapes. A few days later he stood on the tiled piazza at the Mission San Diego and watched the breakers slam against the beach, thinking about the men he had left back on the Rio Grande.

Mary Conway and her family got to San Diego at the end of Novem-

ber. During the winter she received the devastating news that Lieutenant
Harrison had been killed by Indians in Texas. By May she was married
to a ship captain.

THE DAY of the mountain man was past. By 1849 the self-sufficient
adventurers who had explored and trapped through the western wilderness had either died or scattered to isolated ranches and jobs for wages in
the frontier towns. The most enterprising among them had opened trading
depots on one of the emigrant trails where the greenhorns couldn't miss
them. Jim Bridger's stockaded trading post, a combination fort and supply
station, sat in the lovely Blacks Fork Valley in what is now southwestern
Wyoming, about midway between South Pass and Great Salt Lake. "Old
Gabe" Bridger, still lean as a musket in his mid-forties, was there to greet
Bill Johnston and the rest of his fast-moving Pittsburgh company when
they arrived on June 15.

The travelers purchased a steer, buffalo robes, and a roll of butter,
but the real luxury for young Johnston was the chance to sit in a chair
while the courtly, Virginia-born Bridger cordially answered their questions about the trail to Salt Lake City; he himself had been the first white
man to see the lake. His Indian wife—"a stolid, fleshy, roundheaded
woman," Johnston thought—stayed in the background. Joe Hamelin,
who pulled into Fort Bridger a few weeks later, described its interior as
"an odd mixture of squaws, pigs, chickens, cats, and rough-looking men."

The Pittsburghers had selected the Salt Lake route over an alternative
trail which crossed the Green River farther north and then followed the
Bear River Valley into present-day Idaho. Their main consideration, as
always, was speed, but they soon realized that the Wasatch mountains
were anything but a shortcut. One day they forded the same stream
twenty-eight separate times. The trail was alternately hub-deep in marsh,
overgrown with shrubbery, or blocked by immense boulders. Descending
the western side, they tied their wagons to trees and lowered them a foot
at a time down nearly vertical cliffs. The interminable drudgery exhausted both men and animals.

Johnston was still having trouble looking after himself. Before going
on guard one night he changed out of his wet clothes and left them by
the fire. He returned to find his only extra pair of boots burned to cinders
and his corduroy pants scorched.

On June 23 they pitched their tents a mile from Brigham Young's two-year-old settlement in Salt Lake Valley and decided to take a couple of days off. Like most Americans of the time, the Pittsburgh men regarded the polygamous Mormons with both self-righteous intolerance and lecherous curiosity. The Mormons, who had been terrorized and driven from their homes in the States, were leery but polite. They also viewed the forty-niner visitation as an economic bonanza. "The saints, like sinners, seem disposed to make all they can out of us," a New Yorker commented. Within hours of their arrival the men from Pittsburgh were bartering coffee and bacon and sugar for butter, milk, and cheese; Johnston was only too happy to hire a willing Mormon woman to do his laundry.

The next morning, scrubbed and shaved and dressed in linen and broadcloth for the first time in months, the boys went to church. Johnston conceded that it was not piety nor even curiosity that inspired their devotion, but rather the prospect of seeing girls. Unfortunately the fetching maid he sat next to turned out to have a husband and baby.

The Salt Lake stopover was for most emigrants an almost idyllic respite. It came at a perfect time: they were slightly more than halfway to their goal. Brigham Young's sermons might offend them ("nonsense and bombast rarely equaled," one listener wrote), but the pause gave them a welcome break in the routine and a taste of the social life they missed so acutely. Given a feeble resistance to temptation, a man might linger for three months like Joe Hamelin did, even if it meant switching his course from the Humboldt River to a more southerly route to avoid the mountains. Hamelin was a delightful rarity among forty-niners: he enjoyed himself wherever he was. The girls of Salt Lake City filled him with "a feeling of alloverishness," he reported, though he observed that far too many of them appeared to be pregnant. It was his impression that Mormon couples could divorce "by agreement to disagree," so he thought he might marry "on six months probation, as Methodists take new members." Becoming friendly with several Mormons, he attended dances and went on picnics where they drank whiskey punch and swam in the briny lake. You had to "towel fast," he wrote, "or you're encrusted." He had so much fun that he stayed until November and fancied himself an apprentice Latter-Day Saint. He even composed a prayer thanking the Almighty for showing him such a good time in Salt Lake City. "And some folks think I never pray," he added.

The emigrants who were in town on July 24 watched the Mormons celebrate the second anniversary of their entrance into Salt Lake Valley with a day-long extravaganza. Cannonades and band music jolted them out of their blankets in the morning. At nine o'clock a parade stepped off from Brigham Young's house. There were twenty-four young men in white carrying copies of the Declaration of Independence in one hand and sheathed swords in the other, twenty-four white-clad girls crowned with rose wreaths, and twenty-four old men known as the "silver greys." The young people sang hymns amid the roar of cannons. The forty-niners, unable to resist, wheeled their wagons into the procession and waved affably to the cheering crowds. The party concluded with a banquet for seven to eight thousand people, including some two hundred convivial gold seekers.

Among the spectators were the Cherokee Indians who had left their farms outside Fort Smith three months earlier. The Cherokees, who arrived in the valley on the festive day, had taken a unique route: starting near Fort Smith, they had driven north 250 miles to the Santa Fe Trail, detoured west into modern Colorado, and then cut north again along the base of the Rocky Mountains until they reached the California trail near Fort Bridger. A second band of Cherokees, setting out from the same territory, lost eight of their fifteen men to cholera.

Bill Johnston and the Pittsburgh boys tore themselves away from Salt Lake City after only two days. They drove north on a road looping around the top of the lake, avoiding the broiling salt flats to the west. Most 1849 emigrants accepted the Mormons' advice that they shun the salt desert; the few exceptions paid the price in parched throats, dead animals, and abandoned wagons. Johnston and his companions were flabbergasted to discover that the Fort Bridger–Salt Lake City road had cost them precious time; other companies had pulled ahead of them. They had chosen the route at the suggestion of Louis Vasquez, whom they met near South Pass. Vasquez, as a partner of Jim Bridger, was hardly a disinterested guide: he shared in the profits from the Fort Bridger trading post.

Johnston spied one of the headwater streams of the Humboldt trickling through the tall grass on July 5. The next fortnight was a feverish sprint down the disheartening little river the emigrants came to call the Humbug. They drove the weary mules relentlessly: 36 miles on the fifth, 40 on the seventh, 40 more on the eighth. They moved out as early as 2:30 a.m.— "stealing the tail of night," Johnston said, "to lengthen the day." The country was empty and unyielding: clumps of sage and greasewood littered the dry plain on either side of the warm gray river, thinning on the aprons of the bare dark hills. They were now in a flat-out race with at least two other wagon trains. On the seventh the other two passed them as they stopped for their evening meal. The Pittsburgh men hitched up the mules and pushed on by moonlight, passing the halted wagons of their rivals and moving ten miles ahead. Johnston, careless as ever, couldn't find his blankets for four days. Sand fleas harassed him. He spurned an offer from a "Digger" Indian to trade a cooked rat—tail, entrails, and all—for tobacco.

Daily the landscape became more forbidding. The river narrowed to a milky, foul-smelling stream so filled with alkali that even mules rejected its water. At last they came to the sink where the Humboldt abandoned all pretense of flowing and vanished into the ash-colored earth. Together with the jagged peaks beyond, the forty-mile desert between the sink of the Humboldt and the Carson River was the most severe test on this trail; it was here that they would "see the elephant," a popular expression of the day which meant to learn or gain experience by enduring great hardship. Later in the summer the desert would resemble a vast boneyard of animal skeletons mixed with the jettisoned belongings of a thousand wagons. The swifter companies like the Pittsburgh train managed best, but the crossing was a nightmare for everyone who experienced it.

Johnston's company set forth on the evening of the fifteenth, stopped for four hours at midnight, and plowed into the heat of the next day with their water casks empty. The hot wind felt like "a blast vomited from a stygian furnace." Dark and alluring pools of water shimmered before them in the haze: mirages. When they stopped they brushed aside the surface sand and rested on the cooler layers underneath. In midafternoon they reached the Carson; men hurtled down the steep banks and wallowed happily in the water. Two hours later they moved off for the final pull over the mountains.

When they passed a wagon train in the Carson Valley Johnston was convinced that they were finally the lead caravan; he knew of only two pack trains ahead of them. The Carson led them up the eastern flank of the high Sierras until boulders and fallen trees clogged the trail. The mules quivered, planted their hoofs, and strained at their harnesses. Aching men unloaded supplies from the wagons and pulled the empty beds up the steepest cliffs with ropes. For three days they climbed continuously, each ridge higher than the one before. Fields of hard-packed snow lay in the shade of the tall pines. The Pittsburgh men survived the grueling struggle to the summit without injuries or loss of equipment; many in the caravans to follow would not be so fortunate.

Abruptly they started down. On July 24 Johnston was amazed to see that "we no longer had mountains to climb." They were at long last in the gold-spangled western foothills. They may even have been the first wagon train in, as Johnston later boasted, but the probabilities are against it. A July 24 news item from Sacramento in the *Alta California* said that Missouri River emigrants were already arriving daily. Some packers had been in town for five or six days. Johnston and the Pittsburgh boys had done superbly all the same: they had survived the trip without a fatality, made it through with mules and wagons intact, and finished in eighty-eight days. He even had a pair of boots left, the ones he was wearing.

ALONZO DELANO could not remember a more disagreeable birthday than this one. On July 2 he turned forty-three. He was probably too damned old for a trek like this, yet here he was walking across a god-forsaken sagebrush plain to the Green River, walking all night and all day to reach water, and he was miserable. Ware's guidebook identified this forty-three-mile stretch as "Sublette's Cutoff," but the only thing it cut off was Delano's circulation. He gave out five miles short of the Green and collapsed in a wagon, wondering if he would ever see forty-four.

Delano's Illinois company had spurned the self-serving advice of Louis Vasquez and chosen the northerly route rather than the road to Salt Lake. A good case could be made for either trail: the Salt Lake road had mountains but no deserts; it offered places to reprovision and a chance to stare at Mormon girls. The Sublette route had its *jornada* but it also had the garden-green Bear River Valley, the most inviting piece of property on the entire trail; the Green River had to be ferried, true, but most of the route beyond it lay close to good water.

The company waited three days for their turn on the two-wagon ferry operated by the ubiquitous Mormons, but the ride across the dangerous, fast-moving river was short. Snow-hooded peaks nudged the clouds in the middle distance. A trapper they met told them that heavier and later-than-usual rains this year had produced the most abundant grass crop in his memory. This phenomenon, which they had first observed on the Platte, would ultimately be the salvation of the overland stragglers; a dry year would have brought on a catastrophe.

The sight of the Bear Valley, narrow and steep-walled and fringed with wild flowers, seemed to energize Delano's middle-aged legs. He clambered to the top of a fifteen-hundred-foot-high cliff where he sat on a snowbank and beheld a panorama embracing four seasons: "Winter, with its snow, was under us," he wrote. "A few feet farther down the mountain plants were just starting from the ground; next the flowers and straw-berries were in bloom, while at the foot the growth of summer was parched to autumn dryness." The date was Friday, July 13, but his only bad luck came when he met a dense cloud of mosquitoes in a ravine.

The Bear Valley was the probable scene of one of the most infamous incidents of the migration, set down by Ohio emigrant John Banks in his journal a few days after Delano passed through. The major characters were an Illinois minister named Lancaster and his teenaged son, a couple named Jenkins, and their ripening daughter Alice. As Banks told it, the Reverend Lancaster and Mrs. Jenkins developed an attachment on the trail that left no room for her husband Thomas. At the same time Lancaster's son Henry lusted after Alice Jenkins. The only solution seemed to be to get rid of Jenkins, and young Lancaster and a companion agreed to do the dirty work.

Pretending that they had found gold some distance from the road, they lured Jenkins into an ambush and shot him, then ran back to the trail screaming "Indians." But they neglected to make sure that he was dead. Jenkins, only slightly wounded, limped to another train and revealed the sordid truth. Lancaster senior and junior were promptly captured, tried on the spot, and sentenced to be left on the trail without food or animals; they later turned up in Salt Lake City. Jenkins and his wife continued to travel together in what had to be the chilliest wagon on the trail.

Delano's company turned south where the Oregon and California trails parted at Raft River. In previous years most wagons had kept on the road along the Snake to the emerald promise of Oregon, but not this year. West of the creek-sized Raft, near the cluster of water-grooved granite palisades that the emigrants called City of Rocks, they came to another junction. Here the trail from Salt Lake City merged with the California road. Now, for the first time since South Pass, all but a tiny minority of the forty-niner trains were once more traveling the same trail. It was a sort of wilderness homecoming. Delano found one of the most welcome amenities of the journey nearby: the emigrants who preceded him had established a reading room inside a shaded circle of rocks. Newspapers lay on the rock seats together with a posted request to "read and leave them for others."

Camped near the headwaters of the Humboldt on July 26, Delano met a lone hiker who told him that he had started the trip as a first-class passenger on the Pioneer Line of spring carriages. The brisk prospect of "sixty days to the diggings," the stranger said, had disintegrated into a succession of disasters with himself among the victims. Cholera had struck first. Then it became obvious that the carriages were overloaded. They switched to lighter wagons at Fort Laramie, but still their progress was agonizingly slow. They agreed to cut the baggage to seventy-five pounds each and to reduce the number of wagons. The man told Delano that many had to walk from then on. He and others, "trusting to luck and the emigrants," had set out on their own.

Niles Searls, who stayed with the Pioneer Line, watched several demoralized passengers succumb to scurvy and other diseases on a diet of rancid bacon, moldy flour, and coffee. The last of their food ran out on the Humboldt. The twenty-four-year-old Searls, who would later become Chief Justice of the California Supreme Court, fell ill at Humboldt Sink. He worried that he might be destined to "play Moses by looking at the Promised Land and never entering" it. More dead than alive, he and the other Pioneer Line survivors finally staggered across the Sierras into California in a sleet storm at the end of September.

The story told by the Pioneer Line passenger suggested a truth borne out by the scenes that Delano was now encountering daily: the journey launched in hope and the tang of adventure was now a stark test of survival. The sight of men traveling alone on foot had become common— "Walker's Train," the forty-niners dubbed them. These people had lost their animals through carelessness or bad luck. Now they were forced to proceed with only what they could carry and were often reduced to begging food or a ride. Most wagon drivers helped when they could, but many were worried that they might not have enough for their own needs. On July 29 Delano met another pedestrian, "with a lame leg and a cancer on his hand," limping toward the long-sought Humboldt.

Ware's guidebook, relying on the descriptions of John Frémont, led emigrants to envision the course of the Humboldt as a rich and verdant highway to the mines, "beautifully clothed with blue grass, herds grass, clover and other nutritious grasses." For the weary and dispirited men toiling toward the salvation it promised, the Humboldt was the cruelest disappointment of all. An Iowan named John P. Grantham ventured a poem about it:

> . . . *From all the books that we have read*
> *And all that travelers had said*
> *We most implicitly believed*
> *Nor dreamed that we should be deceived,*

That when the mountains we should pass
We'd find on Humboldt fine blue grass;
Nay, that's not all, we learned moreover
That we'd get in the midst of clover.

Nay, more yet, these scribbling asses
Told of "other nutritious grasses";
But great indeed was our surprise
To find it all a pack of lies . . .

Delano's band started searching for a way off the river almost as soon as they struck it on July 30. Besides the poor grass and water there was the persistent irritation of Indians, who tried repeatedly to rustle their horses and cattle. In early August they heard about a new cutoff which avoided the final fifty miles of the Humboldt and the dreaded forty-mile desert; accounts of the hardships beyond the sink had begun to drift back along the trail. The new road was known as Lassen's Cutoff for its chief promoter, California rancher Peter Lassen. This route was supposed to offer good grass and water, an easier road through the mountains but more belligerent Indians. It also led to Lassen's ranch (and putative townsite) in the upper Sacramento Valley. It sounded good to Delano and the Illinois men; on August 15 they arrived at the turnoff and voted to try the new road.

Unknowingly Delano was heading into one of the most desolate reaches of North America, then and now—the Black Rock Desert of northwestern Nevada. Named for a basaltic outcrop which reared up incongruously at its center, the desert was the desiccated alkaline bed of a long-dead lake. The only available water came from boiling springs and a few feeble wells. Grass was all but nonexistent. The company wheeled thirty-five miles across this steaming waste before they realized their dilemma; by then it was too late to turn back.

The heat stole the strength from their legs. Starving animals dropped by the dozen; he saw a dying ox try to brace its legs to keep from falling; another was boiled when it fell into a pool. Nothing broke the horizon but wisps of stunted greasewood and bare-sided mountains. A four-day trek left them near collapse, but past the worst of it.

The mountains still separated the train from the golden rivers. The cliffs were less precipitous this far north, but the men had to beat their way across a long succession of benches, beautiful high valleys, and tim-

bered passes. Gradually the pines gave way to oaks. They reached a
branch of the Feather River on September 10, and a few more days
brought them in sight of the Sacramento Valley.

Ahead of the train as usual, Delano stumbled down the last hill and
came to a rude cabin. He was startled to find himself unable to speak.
"I felt lost and bewildered," he wrote, "at seeing men and women moving
about at their usual avocations." He could manage only grunts in response
to questions. After an hour he was able to ask where the emigrants were
camped. "About a mile below," came the reply.

He walked along a stream until he saw a broad grassy field. Hundreds
of cattle grazed contentedly. Suddenly there was a white tent, then three
more, then dozens of them. Wagons were everywhere. Scores of voices
blended into a collective hum. He heard his own among them—it was
working again. He was home at last.

THE DUST-EATING laggards in the rear of the migration were there
for one of only two reasons: either they had a problem—their wagons
might be overloaded, their animals weak, or their stops too frequent—
or they chose to be there. J. Goldsborough Bruff and the Washington City
company chose to be there.

The disciplined and deliberate Bruff was not a man to be rushed. He
would no sooner hurry into a careless or hasty mistake than he would
convert to Buddhism. Bruff knew what to do and how to do it, what he
could expect from his animals and where the water was. Men—impatient,
irrational, vain and frivolous men—were more difficult. There were times
when he could not understand them. The time might come when he could
not control them. Lieutenant Colonel Bonneville had given him fair warning at Fort Kearny: leading an overland company was "a most trying,
thankless, and unenviable task." It would turn out to be all of that and
more.

Bruff's code did not permit men to abandon civilized behavior simply
because they had abandoned civilization. When a man died, for example,
he was given a funeral. Most companies dug a hole for their dead, said a
prayer, and hurried on. But when the first Washington City man fell to
cholera on July 8, Bruff carved a headstone and footstone, ordered the
men to don clean uniforms, and orchestrated a funeral procession complete with a dirge. When a company "guard-sergeant" punched another
man, Bruff instantly convened a drumhead court and broke the offender
to the ranks.

Bruff focused sharply where others merely glanced. Finding a pile of jettisoned bacon near the North Platte ferry, he methodically removed the fat and discolored chunks from his own supply and replaced them pound for pound with choice cuts from the pile. The waste on the road appalled him: he saw mining tools, water kegs, wagon beds, even a new Gothic bookcase. His men broke up the bookcase for firewood.

Almost alone among the throngs on the trail, Bruff disapproved of the American penchant for writing on any accessible hard surface—trees, rocks, buffalo skulls, even gravestones. "The singular feature is that of marking initials, for instance A.S.S.," he wrote slyly, "as if every one should know who he was." The most prominent rock slabs, such as Independence Rock on the Sweetwater River and Names Hill on the Green, were covered with so many initials and dates that a straggler had trouble finding a spot. Even Bruff could not resist Independence Rock, though he probably told himself that he was thinking only of the historical record. He searched out a bare place and wrote, "The Washington City Company, July 26, 1849." Six days later, he reached South Pass, the western limit of the cholera epidemic of 1849. He was still keeping a stately pace; Bill Johnston was already playing monte in Sacramento.

Bruff's company, like many other overland trains, had a pet dog. Dogs had once been a fighting issue on the trail. A few years earlier the members of an Oregon caravan, worried that barking hounds might betray their location to Indians, had voted to destroy every dog in the train. The dog owners succeeded in overturning the decision, but not before twenty dogs had been killed. Forty-niner hounds had it easier. Bruff's big yellow dog Bull hit on a comfortable routine: he begged breakfast from one of the messes in the morning, then trotted ahead of the wagons and found a place to nap until the train came up. The pet of another company became so sore-footed that they made leather moccasins for him.

Scores of 1849 diarists observed that life on the trail invariably elicited the worst in men. A dispute over the weight of a load of cargo or whose turn it was to get firewood could magnify under the cumulative pressures of the journey into a free-for-all. Bruff's militaristic discipline and unbending personality undoubtedly riled many of his men. He in turn was surprised to see that some, "whom at home were thought gentlemen, are now totally unprincipled."

Resistance to his autocratic leadership developed slowly. Bruff's journal entries on the dissension were generalized sputters: "A few villains . . . threw obstacles in the way of my operations and evaded the correct performance of duty"; later, "a small set of evil-disposed and turbulent

fellows . . . take advantage of anything to affect my reputation and to
annoy me." Three-quarters of the company's members, he wrote, were
"intelligent good men." As for the other one-quarter, they had a constitutional remedy: the company bylaws mandated a reelection of officers on
August 14, a date which found them in the Bear River Valley near the
present Idaho-Wyoming line. The company voted out every officer save
one—the president himself, thus vindicated.

Their Indian encounters had been friendly, and Bruff the military
man was mildly disappointed. A skirmish on the prairie might well have
been therapeutic: "I could have had no objection as its effects on the
company would have been beneficial." But instead it was one amiable
powwow after another. He met the Snake chief Washakie, a legendary
friend of the whites, near Beer Springs. The best-known member of
Washakie's tribe was Sacajawea, the "Bird Woman," who had accompanied Lewis and Clark. The chief, a straight-backed, elderly man wearing a blue frock coat buttoned to the chin, approached Bruff while he was
conferring with his men, extended his hand, and said "How do?" Then
"he placed himself on my right, standing very erect, with his hands
folded on his breast and his back against the wagon. . . . He was a chief,
found I was and [was] holding a council, and desired a place in it."
Bruff had seen another sign of racial harmony two days earlier. A cross
over the grave of a squaw killed in a fall bore the legend, "Calm be her
sleep and sweet her rest. Be kind to the Indian."

The weather was becoming cold at night though still warm in the afternoons; Bruff awoke on several mornings with his long hair frozen to the
saddle he used for a pillow. The road down the Humboldt was cluttered
with signs of the crowds on the trail: a well-preserved wagon, left by its
owner for anyone who wanted it; a grave marker telling of a death by
bowie knife; a band of Mormons en route to Zion; a detachment of
soldiers headed for Fort Hall on the Snake—Bruff learned that several
had deserted. The men in a Kentucky company found a poignant letter
fluttering in the brush on the Humboldt trail. It was written by a young
girl staying with relatives in New York to her emigrant father in Independence. She asked him to write a poem for her. "Pa you write very good
poetry and no one here knows it," she wrote. The biggest excitement for
the Washington City men came when they discovered two caravans carrying women; one was from Michigan and the other Wisconsin.

Bruff's research, which had not failed him yet, convinced him that the
Lassen route would avoid both the worst deserts and the steepest moun-

tain passes. The company unanimously endorsed his decision. On September 19 he guided the first wagons to the right at the fork, toward the Black Rock Desert which Alonzo Delano had crossed a month before. It was Bruff's first mistake.

"JUST ARRIVED—San Francisco be damned! Further particulars in my next."

The opinion of the Bostonian who scrawled these lines home in early July was hasty, to be sure, as well as terse, but one wonders about those "further particulars." Was he too rushed to describe them? Or had he not had time to enjoy them yet?

The Bostonian's quick judgment probably represented the majority view among fresh arrivals in the summer of 1849, especially New Englanders. Like an unkempt relative, San Francisco made a poor first impression. It was not like Boston, certainly, nor New York nor Philadelphia. The prices were of course absurd. Sharpers seemed to own the place. The weather was awful: foggy every morning, windy every afternoon. The populace was—well, motley, not excepting the Yankees—"the worst-looking set of Yankees ever known," observed Moses Cogswell of New Hampshire, an August arrival on the *Sweden*. Cogswell, the youth who had found such sublime beauty in the ocean voyage, would die after only six months in California.

San Francisco was the most exciting city in the world in the summer of 1849. Life telescoped there: a man lived a year in a month. Everything seemed outsized, speeded up, overdrawn. John Letts, who had watched the mist lift from the golden coast on the Fourth of July, was dumbfounded to see the frame of a house unloaded from a ship in the morning and the same house erected and fully occupied that night.

The atmosphere was most feverish on the waterfront, especially when a steamer arrived. John Durivage, the New Orleans reporter who had struggled across the southwestern deserts, got on the *California* in San Diego and landed in San Francisco in July. He recorded the babel he heard as his ship tied up:

"What's the news from the States?" "Twenty-one dollars a week without lodging at the Parker House." "Is the gold all gone?" "Started back last week with all his family in perfect disgust." "A common cradle and tin pan is all you want." "Have you seen my brother?" "You have to dig from two to twenty feet, sir, and stand up to your waist in water."

"Where's the post office?" "There's gold in the mines plenty but it's very hard to get." "The sun's powerful hot and the rivers still high."

Durivage, who had a taste for cities, felt at home immediately. He found it a "delectable place."

Stephen Massett, a singer and comedian who called himself "Jeems Pipes of Pipesville," gave the city's first concert in June. The program of ballads, recitations, and impressions concluded with his "celebrated Yankee Town Meeting," in which he played all seven parts. The front row, "reserved for ladies," was occupied by four doves of dubious repute.

Respectable women were difficult to locate, but hope persisted. Word of Eliza Farnham's plan to deliver a shipload of certifiably good women had arrived and been greeted with an enthusiasm approaching hysteria. The eager Californians had no way of knowing that Mrs. Farnham's bold venture had already fizzled; she was en route around the Horn with only three potential wives in tow.

The only positive effect of the absence of women was a corresponding absence of snobbery, at least in the opinion of newly arrived *Osceola* passenger Samuel Upham. "Mrs. Grundy has not yet arrived," he wrote, "and consequently social and society lines have not been strictly drawn." In fact nothing much had been strictly drawn, least of all the law. The city was adrift in a kind of legal limbo. An alcalde appointed by the military governor was nominally in charge, but there were few laws and fewer policemen. Each man had to protect himself and his property. Inevitably the foreigners were the first to suffer.

A gang of bullies and thugs called the Hounds, many of them ex-soldiers from New York, had been harassing Chileans and other Latin-Americans in the city for months, stealing from Chilean merchants and beating any who resisted. Early in the summer a number of *chileños* evicted from the mines began to drift into town, settling into the tent village of Chilecito at the base of Telegraph Hill. The Hounds grew bolder. When an American was shot during a confrontation between a crew of Hound "enforcers" and a Chilean merchant, the Hounds had all the pretext they needed for a raid on Chilecito. It came on Sunday, July 15.

The Hounds spent the day drinking and parading in their uniforms to the music of a fife and drum. In the evening some fifty or sixty men descended on the Chilean barrio—looting, ripping down canvas tents, and flailing with clubs and fists. The screams could be heard at the wharf where the *California* had arrived that afternoon. The torch-lit marauding continued through the night to the eerie accompaniment of the fife and drum. Two men were shot, one of whom later died, and more than three dozen others injured. The loss in gold dust and other property exceeded $9,000.

The San Francisco gentry, who had ignored the Hounds prior to this, were at last aroused. Alcalde Thaddeus Leavenworth summoned the frightened townsfolk to a public meeting at Portsmouth Square the next day. Sam Brannan moved that a subscription be collected for the victims. Amid what one correspondent called "a terrible excitement," a force of 230 volunteers was hastily formed to pursue and arrest the marauders. Seventeen men were seized and locked up on the warship *Warren* by night-fall. Two more were captured later.

On the following day the crowd selected two judges and a twenty-four-man grand jury which speedily returned indictments for robbery, riot, assault, and other crimes. Nine men were convicted, two of them receiving sentences of ten years at hard labor in either the District of Columbia prison or at a site in California (as yet without a prison) to be chosen by Governor Riley. The other seven received lighter penalties. The effect of the sentences was not imprisonment but exile; several of the convicted men were banished from the land of gold and shipped to the quieter East.

At the end of July the *Alta* totted up the arrivals by sea for the month and came up with 3,565 men and 49 women. The newcomers were now overwhelmingly American—961 had sailed from New York, 922 from Boston, and 812 from Panama; fewer than 500 from Mexico and South America. There was also a faint signal of things to come: eight voyagers arrived from China.

The Boston arrivals included the 150 superbly equipped members of the Boston and California Joint Stock Mining and Trading Company. They sailed into port on the *Edward Everett* a week before the Hounds' rampage. Still clutching their Bibles in one hand and their New England civilization in the other, they lingered only a few days amid the fleshpots of San Francisco before they discreetly moved on to Benicia and Sacramento.

The company foundered almost immediately. Still flaccid from their long voyage, they set out on a hard, waterless twenty-mile hike on the first leg of a trek to the Mokelumne River diggings. They were unprepared for either the heat or the aridity of the California summer; they didn't even fill their canteens at the start. Dozens gave out and threw themselves miserably on one of their three wagons. Their confidence evaporated, and shortly after reaching the Mokelumne they voted to disband. Sale of their ship and the trade goods they brought netted a dividend of $160 for each member on his original $300 investment. But the magic in the word "California" was gone forever. "The company dissolved after about two days' digging," one member wrote home. "Half of them would not work."

X

MAGIC LANTERN COUNTRY

GROUND SLUICING

OSQUITOES. Mosquitoes like they had never seen before, like *nobody* had seen before. So damned thick they cast a shadow. Why, a man passing through the San Joaquin Delta on his way to the southern mines put his hat on the end of a stick and held the stick in the air and then slowly lowered it. Sure as sunrise the hat stayed where it was, held up by a swarm of mosquitoes. And they were burlier than their eastern relations too. Young John Cowden of Danville, Pennsylvania, alleged that they were "nearly big enough to carry brickbats under their wings to sharpen their bills on." Hyperbole was only natural: California was a continual astonishment. A man needed three more senses and a new language to describe this country.

What was it like, this land at rainbow's end? The forty-niners had dreamed of it for so long that the illusion, the California of the mind, had merged with the reality of the place with no line of demarcation. In their first giddy weeks they were helpless to distinguish what they saw from what they had read or imagined; the facts were as fantastic as the most preposterous fabrications. A newcomer composing a letter home could never be certain if he was reporting what he knew, what someone else knew, or what no one knew. Cowden, writing with the accumulated wisdom of ten days' residence, gravely advised his cousin that "any young man who can't get along in this country, aye make money, where any kind of labor is worth 10 to 15 dollars per day . . . had better be dead." As it happened he was right about the money, and much closer than he realized about the alternative: wealth and death were the poles of the California gamble; the difference was that the odds against wealth were a great deal higher.

Cowden, who arrived on the brig *Osceola* in early August, knew that he would never have been satisfied with himself if he had stayed home. He went directly to the Mokelumne River diggings, "now thought to be the best, though it is all a lottery"—his father had ponied up $500 for his lottery ticket. The trip to the southern mines was a succession of surprises. Merchants in Stockton left their stock lying outside their canvas shops. "Very few ever think of stealing in this country of plenty" (the embittered John Sutter might have given him an argument, but this was generally true in the summer of 1849) "and those who do so are immediately strung up. There is a gallows still standing here upon which a man by the name of Mickey was hung about two weeks ago, for some small theft, I believe robbing a washerwoman." (Mickey was probably a murderer; the most common punishment for theft was thirty-nine lashes.) Cowden also noticed that the communal give-and-take he had grown up with in his Susquehanna Valley village was absent in El Dorado: "Everybody here attends only to his own business and cares but little what his neighbors do or say."

Chastened but still exhilarated, Cowden resumed his letter after a week on the Mokelumne. He wrote that he was working from 5 a.m. until 1 p.m. with a break at eight o'clock for breakfast. It was too hot in the afternoon for anything but a siesta. He and his companions dug a hole about ten feet deep and fifteen feet square, washing the dirt in a rocker until they reached bedrock; this they attacked with pick and crowbar. "Digging wells or cellars at home would be play alongside of digging into these hills and rocks." Still, they had already taken about six ounces from their hole—the largest flake was shaped like a toad—the air was clear and pure, and he had never felt better.

"The young lady at Elmira who expressed a desire to see John Cowden," he wrote, "can be gratified at present only by coming out to Californy, and by enquiring at the upper hole close to the hill on the Upper Bar of the Mokelumne diggings. She will find him there or at his tent during all hours of the day. If she is handsome, accomplished, with a good disposition and reasonably rich I shall be glad to see her."

The elation that Cowden felt was shared by thousands of bug-eyed neophytes scattered through the sun-parched hills. E. G. Waite, prospecting a few hundred yards from Cowden on the Mokelumne, thought that "the very color of the earth, covered with wild oats or dried grass, suggested a land of gold." Their initial euphoria had as much to do with freedom, adventure, and raw excitement, with liberation from the bonds of duty, as it did with the promise of wealth. It was a life "as free from restraint as the air that came through the soughing pines," Waite wrote. The necessities were pick and pan, shovel and rocker, tent and blanket, bread and bacon and beans. The luxuries were coffee and tea and dried peaches and women.

John Letts, the Staten Islander whose ship had breached the offshore fog on the Fourth of July, thought that every rock he saw on the North Fork of the American River was tinged with yellow, and even the camp kettle "appeared to be gilded." Every day there was a new bonanza story to fuel their fantasies. Letts heard that a miner in his camp took out $1,500 in an hour, a report he chose to believe "to keep the necessary elasticity in my suspenders." Waite averaged nearly $150 a day for seventeen days on the Mokelumne. Miners at Placerville, who had previously concentrated on the dry ravines running down from the hills, switched in the summer to the ground beneath their cabins along Weber Creek. To their amazement, it proved as rich as the ravines. One man found gold worth $2,000 beneath his doorstep. Three Frenchmen removed a stump from the trail to Coloma and dug out $5,000.

A letter from two prosaic Missourians working the Feather River showed that no fantasy was too farfetched: "Now I will tell you what we have done since we got here: we have worked eight days and have made $16,000. . . . Board is worth $10 a day, and rough at that. There are a great many in the gold diggings at work, some are making fortunes and some are spending fortunes. A man who will half work can make a great fortune in three years. . . . My advice to you is to come and make your fortune while it is plenty, but leave your family."

Inevitably the rapture of the first few weeks fluttered and faded. It was replaced by the unsettling realization that the work of gold digging was wretchedly laborious, that sickness and death were all too common, and that prices were so high that it required a promising "pile" just to keep going. The gold was there, but the cost of extraction was extravagant. William M'Collum of Lockport, New York, summed it up aptly: "The abundance of the gold in California has not been as much overrated as the labor of procuring it has been underrated." Missourian James Douglass put it more plainly: "All the gold a man gets here, he gets by hard licks."

M'Collum and hundreds of other would-be gold miners retired from the diggings after a brief but painful apprenticeship, in his case lasting but five weeks. Slowly the belief began to emerge that the only men suited for success in the mines were those with steel muscles and the staying power of an ox. A corollary belief arose simultaneously: trade was the way to riches; not only did a merchant accumulate more gold for less effort, but he could usually manage to hold on to most of it.

John Letts made the transition from miner to merchant after a dispiriting few weeks in which his earnings consistently lagged up short of his expenses. On mature reflection he decided that the rocks that had at first appeared to be tinted with gold now seemed "about the same color as those in the states." Letts trekked to Sacramento, hired a cook at $50 a week, and loaded a wagon with merchandise for his store and cafe at Mormon Bar on the American. He also bought a horse, only to learn to his dismay that "California horses cannot trot." Like many another creature in this fast-paced land, his mount could only gallop.

Nearly everyone felt obliged to make at least a perfunctory pass at mining while the weather held. The patrician Cal Gardiner of Sag Harbor, Long Island, the youth who had filched a neighbor's shortcake on the cruise to San Francisco, settled in at Hawkins Bar on the Tuolumne River in late summer. Shaded by handsome live oaks, the five-acre flat he shared with some two hundred other prospectors was one of the loveliest camps in the foothills. Chaparral and manzanita flecked the side of the mountain which rose abruptly behind them. The river shimmered at their feet.

The atmosphere in camp was friendly—Cal found that the earlier arrivals were cheerfully willing to advise newcomers—but somewhat discouraging: the miners were just getting by. He and his friends began digging at a grass-covered ledge jutting into the river. They noticed flakes of gold on the roots of the grass they pulled up, but in their innocence they thought this was normal. After a few hours they gathered up their tools and their gold and cooked supper. When they weighed out their take at the local store the next morning they were dumbfounded to see that it totaled $20. They raced back to the claim, but it was too late. A neighbor, noting the gold-specked roots as well as the greenhorns' failure to secure their claim by leaving their tools on it, had jumped it. They could do nothing but curse their own stupidity. The claim eventually proved to be the richest on Hawkins Bar.

Doggedly they searched out another spot, which yielded enough to cover expenses and leave a little for their treasury, a thirty-ounce glass bottle which bore a succession of labels at regular intervals on its surface. From bottom to top, the labels read "half rations," "pork stew," "pork and beans," "roast beef and potatoes," "plum duff," "canned turkey with fixings," and, at the summit, "oysters with ale and porter." "The line of dust seldom rose above plum duff," Gardiner wrote, "and never actually receded to half rations. The average height was at pork and beans." After six weeks of pork and beans they decided that they would do better if they divided their six-man party and separated. Cal and two companions set off on a twenty-mile hike for the diggings at Sullivan's Creek.

The rough trails through the foothills were becoming crowded with mules and wagons and high-booted men on the move. The traffic on the road outside Sonora reminded one Connecticut prospector of New York's Broadway or Main Street in Hartford. The miners' lives took on a recurrent rhythm—two or three weeks in the diggings, a trip to Sacramento or Stockton or Coloma for supplies and a visit to the gambling tables, then back to their drawing account on the rivers. The towns harbored the pleasures they had vowed to resist, and were therefore irresistible. In Stockton the eating tents alternated with gambling tents along the main street. Coloma was filling up with so many hotels and gambling houses that the morose James Marshall frequently decamped on solitary expeditions. Sometimes he was trailed by men who suspected that he was sneaking off to a treasure trove known only to him.

Sacramento probably offered the most temptation per square yard. All that was required of an aspiring casino entrepreneur was a tent, a few tables, and a pouch of gold dust. Gaming houses popped up like mushrooms after a summer rain. The infamous Round Tent displayed erotic pictures on its canvas walls; the Plains decorated its interior with paintings of familiar scenes from the overland trail; the Humboldt, the Mansion, the Diana, Lee's Exchange—the lantern-lit clubs marched up and down the lettered streets perpendicular to the river. In the first few months the professional gamblers were the most powerful interest group in Sacramento; viewing the establishment of a town government as a potential threat, they were able to round up enough friends to defeat the first attempt to pass a city charter in September.

But a miner could do more than sin in Sacramento. He could buy or trade a horse, stock up with canned goods for the rainy season, acquire a pan or a rocker at Collis Huntington's store, and spend his poke on a team to transport the lot. He could consult one of the numerous "lawyers," who may or may not have gone to law school, or "doctors," whose knowledge of medicine might well have come from lingering around a drugstore. Missourian D. H. Moss complained that the town was overrun with such "professionals"—"a fellow will stretch his tent here and mark over it, 'Hospital.' " Peter Burnett confronted an old friend who had declared himself a physician and demanded to know what qualified him to dispense medicine and wisdom. "Well, not much," the man conceded, "but I get all I can do, and I kill just as few as any of them. I never give them anything to hurt them."

The city-reared forty-niners, men like the impetuous Bill Johnston of Pittsburgh, were attracted to the color and bustle of the gold-country towns. Johnston rode past the "Meals at All Hours" sign at Sutter's fort and into Sacramento on July 29. The Round Tent, with its string orchestra and its cut-glass bowls filled with cigars and lemons and peppermints, particularly impressed him. Having raced all the way from Independence, he now decided that he was in no hurry to go to work in the mines; first he wanted a look at San Francisco.

Two facts about the brimming metropolis on the bay appear in almost every journal and reminiscence: the annual rent collected by the Parker House hotel (between $110,000 and $175,000, most of it from gamblers), and the presence of Chinese (the first few hundred emigrants from China arrived during the year). Johnston, who dallied in the city for a few weeks in August and September before making his prospecting debut at Mormon Island, noted that there were "many Chinese mechanics" in town.

By mid-August the Cape Horn armada was gliding past gusty Fort Point and around the bend to the bay at a rate of a half-dozen ships a day: Mark Hopkins and Dr. Jacob Stillman arrived on the *Pacific* on the fifth, the New York aristocrats on the *Christoval Colon* pulled in on the seventh, the Harvard cutups on the *Duxbury* on the twenty-second. The Panama steamers were now making regular runs up the coast—New York *Tribune* writer Bayard Taylor came in on the *Panama* on the eighteenth. Day after day the newcomers spilled off the ships and added their voices to the urban din. Launches cast off for Sacramento and Stockton. Newsboys hawked the thrice-weekly *Alta California* and its new rival, the *Pacific News*. At night the streets were half lit by the lanterns inside the saloons and filled with music and laughter from within the canvas walls. Like most seaports San Francisco looked best from the water. Bayard Taylor sketched this portrait from the bay in September:

"The houses are mostly of canvas, which is made transparent by the lamps within, and transforms them, in the darkness, to dwellings of solid light. Seated on the slopes of its three hills, the tents pitched among the chaparral to the very summits, the city gleams like an amphitheatre of fire. Here and there shine out brilliant points, from the decoy-lamps of the gaming-houses; and through the indistinct murmur of the streets comes by fits the sound of music from their hot and crowded precincts. The picture has in it something unreal and fantastic; it impresses one like the cities of the magic lantern, which a motion of the hand can build or annihilate."

Despite the crowds and the hubbub the city was still relatively small; its buildings and tents were all crowded around the little cove on the lee side of the hills. A tent-covered flat just south of town was known as Happy Valley. The northern and western slopes of the hills and the sandy, brush-dappled land between the town and the ocean were empty. John Stone, who arrived on the *Robert Bowne* at the end of August, pitched his tent in a tranquil grove at a place known as Pleasant Valley—near the present-day intersection of Jackson and Powell streets. "The spot was entirely shaded by the foliage of the trees and vines," he wrote. Rabbits dodged across a bright belt of green which began at a spring and ran west to the sandhills. Birds chirped from lilac-covered branches. A few months later the little valley was dead, buried beneath earth and sand scraped from the hilltops.

The pace of business in San Francisco left little time for amenities. "Men dart hither and thither," Taylor wrote, "as if possessed with a never-resting spirit. You speak to an acquaintance—a merchant, perhaps. He utters a few hurried words of greeting, while his eyes send keen glances on all sides of you; suddenly he catches sight of somebody in the crowd; he is off, and in the next five minutes has bought up half a cargo, sold a town lot at treble the sum he gave and taken a share in some new and imposing speculation." A woman boardinghouse keeper complained in a letter home to Connecticut that "this place is not fit for anything but business. No one spends a minute for anything else." Certainly not laundry: 250 dozen pieces of linen arrived back in the city in the late summer from China, where they had been sent to be cleaned. Or reading: about four-fifths of the *Alta* was given over to ads. Traffic in the harbor was thicker than ever: forty-two vessels from five continents dropped anchor between the sixteenth and eighteenth of September; nearly six thousand passengers landed in magic-lantern city during the month.

The most aggrieved of the seaborne arrivals were the surviving passengers of the ship *Brooklyn*, who charged in a $5,000 lawsuit that deplorable conditions aboard the overcrowded, poorly ventilated ship and the captain's cruel indifference had contributed to the deaths of six men from scurvy, and the illness of several others. Doctors tried to cure some of the sufferers by burying them up to their chins in San Francisco sand. A jury awarded $2,000 to the plaintiffs.

Overland emigrants arrived in the city with stories of the thousands still inching across the Great Basin deserts and the Sierra Nevadas. The rear guard of the great migration, including almost all the trains carrying women and children, struggled toward these crucibles of stamina and courage with their resources exhausted: they were physically depleted; their animals were either dead or drooping from fatigue and short rations; provisions were low; many had been forced to abandon their wagons and continue on foot; the Indians along the Humboldt had grown bolder in their raids on forty-niner livestock as the season advanced. The emigrants' appearance had altered drastically. "I look in vain among the ragged, grave and bronzed codgers dragging themselves wearily along," a man in an Ohio company wrote, "for those dashing, sprightly and gay young fellows, full of song and laughter, whom I saw in the valley of the Blue." They would sing about the Humboldt and its godforsaken sink but not now, not until they had put it far behind them:

> *I traveled till I struck the Sink where outlet can't be found*
> *The Lord got through late Saturday night, he'd finished all around*
> *But would not work on Sunday so he run it in the ground.*

In late August General Persifor Smith, the military commander who had issued the antiforeign declaration in Panama, set up a relief expedition for the overland stragglers. Smith financed the rescue mission with $100,000 from the military government's civil fund plus $12,000 contributed by San Franciscans. Early in September the leader of the military-civilian relief team, Major D. H. Rucker, arrived in Sacramento with orders to send two caravans into the mountains with plenty of food and animals, one to aid travelers on the Truckee River route and the other to help those on the more southerly Carson River passage. Only after talking with newly arrived emigrants in Sacramento did Rucker learn that the argonauts who had been lured onto the Lassen "cutoff," 150 miles north of the other routes, were in even worse condition than those who had crossed the sink. He immediately decided to send a third rescue party up the trail from Lassen's ranch with himself at its head.

Rucker's plan was to have well-equipped rescue trains pass completely through the migration on the three trails until they reached the wagons in the rear, dispensing help as it was needed and gathering up those unable to travel. Blizzards were a threat in the Sierras from late September on, and an early storm this year would be catastrophic. Sarah Royce, whose company had stoutly stood down a Pawnee demand for tribute way back in the Platte Valley, was in one of the last wagons to slog through the axle-deep dust of the forty-mile desert en route to the Carson River. By this time it was early October and the slow-moving Royces— Sarah, her husband, and their two-year-old daughter Mary—were alone, except for the dead animals all around them. Their four faltering oxen plodded on beneath the moon after the desert sun at last relented.

"As we advanced [the dead cattle] increased in numbers," she wrote, "and presently we saw two or three wagons. At first we thought we had overtaken a company, but coming close, no sign of life appeared. We had candles with us, so as there was not the least breeze, we lit one or two and examined. Everything indicated a complete breakdown and a hasty flight. Some animals were lying nearly in front of a wagon, apparently just as they had dropped down, while loose yokes and chains indicated that part of the teams had been driven on, laden probably with some necessities of life; for the contents of the wagons were scattered in confusion, the most essential articles alone evidently having been thought worth carrying. . . . [We] soon found that what we supposed an exceptional misfortune must have been the common fate of many companies, for at still shortening intervals scenes of ruin . . . kept recurring till we seemed to be but the last, little, feeble, struggling band at the rear of a routed army."

The Royces gave the last of their water to their oxen before dawn, then fed them the remainder of their hay. Sarah moved ahead of the wagon after the sun rose, staring fiercely at the dull horizon "to catch the first glimpse of any change." At last she saw it. "Was it a cloud? It was very low at first and I feared it might evaporate as the sun warmed it." She waited for the team to come up and asked her husband about it. "I think it must be the timber on Carson River," he said, estimating that it was about five miles away. Now Sarah could see "a little unevenness in the top of that dark line, as though it might indeed be trees." Then the lead ox raised his head and stretched his nose toward the water. By noon they were resting in the merciful shade on the riverbank, the desert conquered.

But there was no time to enjoy it. They didn't know it, but the first snow of the season fell in the mountains that night. Fortunately the storm passed quickly, but it caught one group near the pass. Several members of this band suffered frostbite and all but two of their animals froze to death.

Two days later, on October 12, the Royces were trudging up Carson Valley toward the eastern flank of the Sierras when they were startled to see two horsemen, each leading a pack mule, riding toward them. The men were from the relief expedition; a family they had aided in the mountains had reported that the Royces and a few other laggards were still coming. "Well, sir," the first man said to Royce as he rode up, "you are the man we are after." They put Sarah and the baby on a strong, well-trained mule and gave them provisions. The Royce family would survive.

At Humboldt Sink the emigrants had to choose between the tortuous desert passage to the Carson and an equally arduous crossing of roughly the same distance to the Truckee River. The Truckee route through the mountains was older and rougher. Where the Carson road swung south of the magnificent mountain lake later known as Tahoe, the Truckee trail accompanied the river through the meadows where Reno would later rise and passed north of the lake. The trail then climbed a steep canyon where wagons had to ford the foaming stream more than twenty times before it crested the range near the "cannibal camp" where the Donner party had been marooned three winters earlier. Dozens of forty-niners who took this route remarked on the macabre reminders of the Donner party's ordeal: piles of human bones still littered the ground; not far away a grove of ten-foot-high stumps stood as evidence of the depth of that winter's snow.

The men in the relief force working their way along the Truckee route in early October were surprised to find no one on the trail but a few packers who needed little help; the road's rugged reputation had apparently discouraged the others. Following Rucker's orders, the party of some thirty men and more than a hundred mules moved south to join the rescuers on the Carson trail. Here they were desperately needed. Many families were traveling on foot, some subsisting on dead animals they found along the way. An old man was discovered hiking through the mountains with his wife and daughter, packing nothing but a few blankets. Two German pedestrians found in Carson Valley had been living on the flesh of dead mules for a week.

The last train on the Carson trail was a St. Louis company led by Captain Charles Sackett. The men in this band were not altogether convinced that the crisis had come. The Californians in the relief party, knowing that snow could fall any day now, finally persuaded them to jettison some property and to let their women and children go ahead on mules. The Sackett train was safely over the summit and nearing the settlements when snow fell on October 27. The relief workers on the Truckee and Carson had done their job.

The task of Major Rucker, ex-newspaperman John Peoples, and the crew sent to relieve the Lassen route emigrants was much more formidable. The elements of a potential tragedy intersected on this road. The "cutoff," with its bogus promise of avoiding the worst of both desert and mountains, was the most popular route after mid-August. Hundreds of teamsters swung their wagons northwest at the bend in the Humboldt in the belief that they were taking a more direct road to the northern mines. The truth was just the opposite. The cracked, dun-colored expanse of the Black Rock Desert was even more forbidding than the gray wastes of the forty-mile desert. Worse, the trail beyond the Black Rock entered California near the Oregon border, leaving the emigrants with several more weeks of rugged travel. No one, not even the sturdy J. Goldsborough Bruff, was prepared for the devastating news that he had reached the mountains but was still more than two hundred miles from the trail's end at the Lassen ranch. The trek along this endless cutoff exhausted the travelers' food supplies and exposed them to the danger of paralyzing storms. Every forty-niner who chose the Lassen route regretted it soon enough, and many concluded that they were the victims of a callous scheme to divert them and their spending money to Peter Lassen's ranch. James Pratt, one of the Wolverine Rangers from Michigan, charged bitterly that the route was promoted "expressly to bring the rear [of the] emigration into the northern settlements, to their utter ruin."

The relief team led by John Peoples began to distribute food and pack animals on the Lassen route in late September. On October 6, moving slowly up the Pit River Valley north of Mount Lassen, the rescuers encountered Bruff and the blue-topped wagons of the Washington City company. Bruff, precise as ever, calculated that he had eleven days' rations on hand: he needed no relief. A day later it was Peoples who required help. Ill with fever, he returned to Bruff's caravan to be treated by the company doctor. He remained with the Washington company for a week.

Bruff was still filling voluminous notebooks with his detailed, painter's-eye descriptions of everything he saw. On October 10, the same day that the Royce family reached Carson River, Bruff gazed at Mount Lassen (he called it the "Snow Butte") from the divide between Pit River and the headwaters of the Feather. "What a scene from here!" he wrote, "the Snow Butte and his blue neighbors, deep vales, silver thread-like streams, near mountains, dense forests, bright deep valleys in every tint of one of nature's most extensive landscapes." Abruptly he scolded himself for his deviation from business: "Pshaw!—enraptured with a landscape! How ridiculous! . . . No time now for the fine arts, we must patronize the *rough* ones."

He was still maintaining the rigid discipline which rankled many of his men. A meeting was held that night to fix punishment for the latest guard duty delinquents. Several days earlier he had permitted two of the most persistent grumblers to take six days' rations and leave.

Bruff also continued to copy the inscriptions on trailside graves. By this time his journal was a compendium of forty-niner fatalities containing scores of names; it would have been an invaluable source for the relatives of men who vanished in the rush for gold. On October 12 he noted two—John Hensley, aged 73, of Washington County, Missouri, and Allen McLane, 36, Platte County, Missouri. On the thirteenth there were four more: David Myers, 53, Missouri; B. M. Prewitt, 38, Missouri; Abner Needham of Morrow County, Ohio; and Joel Lock, 33, Southport, Wisconsin.

Bruff's wagons rolled heavily over forest trails carpeted with pine needles, through emerald meadows, and along narrow, silver-tipped streams. He was now less than a hundred miles from the Sacramento Valley. On the fourteenth he met the rescue team commanded by Major Rucker, who had set out from Lassen's ranch several days behind Peoples. Rucker had already assisted hundreds of emigrants, many of whom were on foot. Mindful that the greatest need was with the companies still to come, he had begun to dole out his stock of meat and bread more sparingly.

Bruff visited Rucker's tent, where a crowd of emigrants clamored for food. Bruff thought there were some in genuine need, "some meanly bent on an increase of stores and others who would steal a dying man's shoes." He was disinclined to ask any favors for his own company, of course, despite pleas from his men. "I told them that we had enough to take us in on short allowance, and that those stores were sent expressly for starving families—*women and children*." His attempt to shame them failed; they still insisted. Rucker gave them thirty-one pounds of pork and a sack of crackers; they gobbled up the crackers before Bruff even saw them.

The relief train moved up the trail the next day, heading deeper into the mountains to bring in the fifty to a hundred wagons still coming. Bruff, meanwhile, was mulling one of the most agonizing decisions he had ever faced.

By October 21 the cumulative toll of the desert and the passage along the western slope of the Sierras had left his company with only six of their thirteen original mule teams. Three mules had given out only a day earlier. They were down to the last of their food. The company was camped at a hillside clearing amid oaks and pines. They were not far from upper Deer Creek, the same stream that watered Lassen's rancho thirty-two miles (and 2,500 feet) below. Barring snow or heavy rain, the final pull would probably take three more days.

Bruff was anxious to get the company to the settlements in a body. It was a question of pride. His observations along the trail had convinced him that many companies splintered into selfish factions at the first sign of dissension. He had held his men together with stern discipline, intelligent planning, and a dedication to their collective welfare. Having "brought them to this point together, and more prosperous than any company of men in this vast emigration," he wanted to finish that way. There was validity to the boast; no man in the company had starved or suffered scurvy, and they had come this far on the supplies they started with.

At sundown, smoking his pipe by the campfire, Bruff was ready with his decision: they would leave two wagons and their contents here and take the other four, pulled by the strongest of the mules, on the last lap to the valley. The rub was that someone would have to stay with the wagons until they could bring a fresh team out to retrieve them. Bruff volunteered.

In the morning he said good-by to the men he had lived with for more than six months, from the great hall of the White House to the rim of the Sacramento Valley. They left him with the wagons, three weak mules, plenty of guns and ammunition, and a promise to return with more mules. He had only two pounds of beef, two biscuits, a few ounces of parched coffee, and some rice. Just before the company departed a Baltimore man named Josias Willis offered to stay with him. Bruff readily accepted.

Bruff might well have felt glad to be rid of the company. He had been commander, confessor, and proctor for too long. He had earned their respect if not their affection. But if he had any deeper, more personal reasons for wishing to stay behind in the mountains he kept them to himself. "There are a few whom I never wish to see again," he wrote in his journal that night, "but there's many of that company, yes most of them, I shall ever be happy to meet with or travel with again." He cooked his beef and coffee and afterward fired up his pipe, thinking that at last he could sleep through the night.

Bruff now changed from leader to chronicler, participant to spectator. Helping when he could, talking with everyone who passed, he watched the ragged remnants of the migration labor by his tent—"scattered, broken, selfish stragglers, dusty in faces and dress, many of them thin with hunger as well as anxiety." Some stopped for a day or two, shared his fire, slept in one of his wagons, and moved on. Others gave him food. At first he had plenty of company, especially in the evenings—"busy throngs of every age and sex around their bright campfires. . . . People singing, laughing, whistling and some quarreling." One day he interviewed a six-year-old boy. "I'm a great hand for walking," the boy chirped. "I walked all day yesterday . . . and when we camped here on the hill I said I wasn't tired, and I wasn't." The snow was still holding off.

Six men from his company appeared after a week. Bruff was stunned by their indifference toward him. No one asked how he was, or how he had been faring; they didn't even invite him to share their coffee. When he inquired about his horse, which he had loaned to the company on the assurance that it would be returned, he was told that somebody had it in the valley. Bruff flared angrily. One of the men remarked sourly that he had kept his word to come after him and this was the thanks he received.

Bruff exploded. "You came for me!" he screamed. "You came to afford me the privilege of walking in beside you, eh? No, sir, you came for those wagons and their contents." They stared at him; the old man was finally boiling over. "Take the plunder and roll on," he shouted. "I'll not disgrace myself by further companionship with you. I shall go in when it suits me." In the morning the men loaded one wagon and started back to the valley.

Bruff's prickly pride had committed him: he would accept no help from the ingrates of the Washington City company. But the days were growing shorter, the mornings colder—*someone* would have to help, and soon. The cold aggravated his rheumatism, which made walking difficult. Rain and snow fell on the night of the thirty-first, and the bad weather persisted for several days. He wrote on November 3 that several emigrants had refused his request for a ride down to Lassen's—"they are generally too selfish." By now almost every wagon carried women and children. On the next night he offered the comforts of his camp to the notorious Jenkins family, who had been involved in the triangle and attempted murder back in Bear Valley. They were walking. Jenkins was suffering from scurvy. His wife and four children were "wet, cold, tired, hungry and disheartened." Bruff and Willis rigged up a cart to carry their supplies the rest of the way.

Deep in the mountains the stalwart John Peoples was rounding up the last strays on the trail, a company of thirty-two men and twenty-five women and children from St. Louis. They had lost most of their oxen to Indians before they stumbled into Peoples' Pit River camp on October 26. Peoples ordered the women, children, and sick men into wagons and fell in alongside them. The healthy men followed. He urged them to dump some of their gear, but they refused.

Snow caught up with them on the thirtieth. The next few days were a stark struggle for survival. Blizzards alternated with periods of thawing as they pushed and tugged their wagons through the drifts. It snowed all night on November 4 and into the next day. Finally the wagons could go no farther. Peoples tried to ride ahead with some of the women and children, but only a few could manage. He then set up a camp and left the bulk of the company with ten days' rations while he went ahead with six women who were able to ride. Three hours later they came down out of the snow. On the next day, November 7, they passed through Bruff's camp. Peoples took a note to the settlements for Bruff and promised to send help.

The tattered procession kept passing, now mainly on foot. Bruff's guests that night included a man and his son from the Wolverine Rangers company, two Germans, and "an old man, with a sore foot, who had served under Napoleon." The old warrior carried a rusty cavalry saber. A few days later the still ailing Bruff got a break: an unhurried pedestrian named William Poyle, whom Bruff had first met on the Platte, agreed to remain with him. Poyle proved to be a skilled hunter and a faithful companion.

On November 16 the population of Bruff's little encampment increased again: a man named Lambkin asked if he could leave his four-year-old son with him. He promised to return in a few days with supplies. Bruff, who had already sized Lambkin up as an "unfeeling wretch," agreed. The child cried constantly. On the twenty-first the relief detachment passed again, this time bringing the people who had been left behind in the storm. Their condition was desperate. "There were cripples from scurvy," Peoples wrote later, "women prostrated by weakness and children who could not move a limb. In advance of the wagons were men mounted on mules who had to be lifted on or off their animals, so entirely disabled had they become from the effect of scurvy." Bruff, complaining of his rheumatism, declined an invitation to travel with them to Lassen's. Another reason for his reluctance now emerged: he couldn't bring himself to abandon his documents, the hundreds of pages of notes and sketches he had so carefully compiled. His records were everything; he would endure much more than this before he would risk losing them. He did send another message, asking for a team "or at least a riding animal" to bring him in.

Days passed with no word from Lambkin; the boy was apparently Bruff's for the duration. Peoples sent flour and pork on the twenty-fifth along with a note that he could spare nothing more; high water had cut off communication between Lassen's ranch and the valley towns. All of the emigrants were now in with the exception of Bruff's little band and a group of seven or eight who planned to winter on the Pit River. Bruff heard that these men were already "used up with alcohol, snow, Indians, grizzly bears, starvation and wolves." There was nothing to do now but prepare for the worst: Bruff, Willis, and Poyle added another layer of canvas to their tents and laid down a board floor. They felled an oak and chopped it up for firewood.

On December 4 Willis left to try to get help from below. Bruff, fearing that he might not return, pointed to the three pounds of smoked beef that constituted their supply of meat and reminded him that they had only that until he came back. Willis smiled and promised to return in three or four days at the most.

Seven days later Bruff was still giving him the benefit of the doubt. "We . . . fear he is sick," he wrote, "but trust it is some difficulty on the road." "Unless Willis returns in a few days," he noted on the thirteenth, "we will be in a *snap*." On the fifteenth the boy appeared to be weakening from hunger. Bruff and Poyle shared some of their own meager rations with him. Bruff debated with himself: "I know that [Willis'] animal propensities are strong, but I cannot think that he could abandon us to what would appear to him, a certain fate. . . . [He] must surely entertain a spark of gratitude towards me. . . . Unless ill, he will assuredly come out soon!" Or else, or else—"We have two or three weeks before us to sustain life by our wits. . . . The chance for us is very slender."

THE ONLY WAGONS still clanking west in this season were far to the south, where several hundred emigrants were crossing the final desert passages on the Gila Trail. Others, who had set out in early October from Salt Lake City, had been seduced by the promise of yet another "cutoff," this one even more ruinous than the Lassen trail. By mid-December this scattered and leaderless procession was heading inexorably toward the salt basin later known as Death Valley.

There had been more than four hundred emigrants in this band at their rendezvous on Hobble Creek near present-day Provo. Most had arrived in the Mormon capital too late in the summer to risk the Sierra crossing. A few had lingered in the city simply because they enjoyed it; the irrepressible Joe Hamelin had refused to budge until November, and then departed only after a prolonged farewell to his good friends Lucinda and Harriet. "There is too much fun in the world for a poor man," he complained.

At Hobble Creek they organized themselves into the San Joaquin Company, under the direction of a taciturn Mormon guide named Jefferson Hunt, a Mexican War veteran who had traveled the Salt Lake–Southern California road before. The 107-wagon company was broken into seven divisions, each of which elected a captain. Hunt collected $10 per wagon as they waited for the weather to cool. In the first week of October he moved them out.

Their trail slanted southwest, merging with the Old Spanish Trail from Santa Fe to Los Angeles on the Sevier River in southwestern Utah. It passed the site of present-day Las Vegas, crossed the Mojave Desert, and climbed over Cajon Pass in the San Bernardino Mountains. The company had covered about a quarter of this distance when a pack train led by a Captain Wesley Smith overtook them. Smith showed them a map, purportedly drawn by a mountain man, which outlined a much quicker route to the gold country. He estimated that by turning west off the Los Angeles trail and following the map they could save some five hundred miles and reach the southern mines in twenty days.

Several angry emigrants demanded to know why Hunt had not told them about this route earlier. He pleaded ignorance. On November 3 the conflict came to a head. Most of the company was for trying the shortcut. The Reverend James Brier, an Iowa Methodist traveling with his wife and three young sons, declared his intention to try the cutoff "sink or swim, live or die, go it boots." Others enthusiastically agreed. Hunt, reluctant to dissuade them, finally allowed that the route was probably unsafe for families. He said that he felt obligated to stick to the Los Angeles road if anyone still wished to go that way. If they unanimously opted for the cutoff he would accompany them "even if the road leads to hell!" When they reached the junction the next morning all but seven of the wagons turned onto the shortcut. Hunt and the seven rolled on down the trail. They celebrated their parting by exploding gunpowder.

On their third day on the cutoff the emigrants reached the lip of a steep bluff several hundred feet high. Far below them, a bright ribbon strewn carelessly on the canyon floor, was Beaver Dam Wash. The only way down was a narrow mule trail. Search parties were dispatched to find a feasible wagon route, but one by one they returned with the disheartening news that there was none. At length one man turned his wagon around and headed back to the old trail. Most of the others hitched up their teams and followed. Just then scouts appeared with a report that they had found a pass to the north. Twenty-seven wagon parties—about a hundred men, women, and children—decided to stay on the new route and moved on around the canyon. The other seventy-three backtracked to the Los Angeles trail.

The voyagers now nosing foolishly into the unknown were a representative cross-section of forty-niner greenhorns. The largest group was a band of some forty men from Knox County, Illinois, who called themselves the Jayhawkers. There was a company from Mississippi with three slaves, and a Georgia aggregation known as the Bug Smashers. The family groups included the Briers, a British couple named Wade with their four children, and two Wisconsin families, the Bennetts with three children and the Arcanes with one. Traveling with the Bennetts and Arcanes was the man who would ultimately be the chronicler of this beleaguered band, twenty-nine-year-old William Manly. The unmarried, Vermont-born Manly was a capable and level-headed outdoorsman who had spent the last few years drifting around the Great Lakes states, working as a lead miner, lumberman, and trapper. His last job had been in a lead-smelting furnace in Mineral Point, Wisconsin, where he had boarded with the Bennetts.

Manly and the others on the cutoff were heading into what one of them described charitably as "damned dubious looking country." They were without a guide, a marked trail, or a reliable map. Leaderless and disorganized, they traveled in little clusters, uniting at times into larger caravans and then separating again. Range after rugged range of dry and treeless mountains crossed their path, separated by dusty sagebrush plains and the burning white playas of long-dead lakes. From a distance the flat and glistening playas looked like water. Scrawny Indians camped near the few creeks and springs.

The country became more desolate with every mile. Manly and other scouts roamed ahead of the wagons in a constant search for water. Unknown to the wagon parties, the man who had sold them on this route had soon recognized its perils and hustled back to the Los Angeles road. The wagon companies began to lighten their loads as their animals flagged. The Jayhawkers endured three days and nights without water, until their tongues were so swollen that they could neither swallow nor sleep. They were saved by a providential snowstorm. The snow melted within hours.

Manly scaled a peak in early December and surveyed their prospects through a telescope. "It seemed as if pretty near all creation was in sight," he wrote. "North and west was a level plain—fully one hundred miles it seemed—and from anything I could see it would not afford a traveler a single drink in the whole distance or give a poor ox many mouthfuls of grass. On the western edge it was bounded by a low, black and rocky range extending nearly north and south for a long distance, with no pass through it which I could see; and beyond this range was still another one apparently parallel to it." Due west was a snow-crested peak he had been looking at for several days. Manly thought it looked hopeless, but they were too far along now to turn back. All he could do was report to the Bennetts and Arcanes, for whom he felt responsible, and try to combat the despair that was beginning to grip them all.

The real terror was not hunger or even thirst, though both would come. It was the anguish of not knowing when or how this ordeal would end. Every peak overlooked another expanse of dreadful emptiness. It was as if they had passed beyond a final frontier and entered some trackless demon-land lacking twig or leaf or landmark. Nothing was familiar, nothing was even logical: logic told them that you descend to water; in this country you climbed to water; you found it in springs and pools on mountainsides. So far they had found enough to survive, but for how long? How many more ranges lay ahead of them? How many more deserts? How long would their animals last? What was beyond the snowy peak they had stared at so long? California? Manly did his best to hide his fear, but even he was weakening. Alone, away from the others, he wept.

By mid-December their weary oxen were struggling up a long canyon and drawing closer to the high peak. The rocks on the flanking ridge looked lavender in the afternoon light. This mountain, the highest point in the Panamint range, would later be named Telescope Peak. Death Valley lay at its eastern base.

"NO YOUNG MAN ever left home for the California mines and arrived at San Francisco the same person," wrote the historian Hubert Howe Bancroft. If America was a nation of men who roamed the land in quest of their dreams, then no grander vision than California ever seized our tribal soul. Here lay wealth and freedom, nestled together in the beds of mountain streams. Here was work that any man could do, the splendid fulfillment of the egalitarian creed that prevailed in Jacksonian America; here every man might be a prince.

An illusion cherished so ardently bore the elements of its own destruction: California could never live up to the dream; Eden itself would pale in the harsh light of such expectations. It was no wonder that disillusion rushed in at the forty-niners' heels. If every man would be a prince, then a prince must work like every man; democracy in the mines meant that everyone labored, everyone suffered, everyone risked, but not everyone won. It was a simple lesson and the hardest: a hundred must fail for every one who succeeds. Some men knew it instinctively. Most learned it quickly, often too quickly—they fled too soon, as precipitously as they had come. And some men never learned.

Bill Johnston, the Pittsburgh youth who had run a chariot race all the way to the Sacramento Valley, rushed home after four months. It took him only a few weeks to discover that gold mining was someone else's good fortune, not his. He worked with his hometown mates on the north fork of the American River in September and October, toting heavy bags of dirt to the river to wash, averaging $8 a day. One of his friends died. He tried the monte tables. Somehow nothing was as he had expected.

Several days of rain in the first week of November settled it. He decamped for Sacramento, there to spend a sleepless night with a platoon of loud and restless men in a hotel dormitory. A strange sign hung on the wall: "No spitten on the stoav." A man died du ing the night. Johnston went on to San Francisco and looked in on the casinos there. On December 6, he sailed for Panama.

For Henry Crandall, the lovelorn young man from upstate New York who pined for his sweet Mary Mills, the urge to mine subsided with comparable alacrity. He was so eager to hear from his fiancée that he snatched any excuse to flee the diggings for Sacramento and its post office. Dejection followed disappointment: he cleared only about $5 a day on the American River and found no letters on two visits in September. "What happened to the fortune I was supposed to amass in a week or two?" he wailed in his journal. Then he came down with yellow jaundice. Nothing awaited him, he wrote, but "darkness and despair." Worst of all, it was probably his own fault: "I chose the bubble instead of reality, the shadow for substance, the land of humbug."

But on November 6 came Mary's wonderful letter in verse ("I just have nothing else to do, But spin, and work, and think of you"), and his spirit soared; there was once again a reason to keep going. "Mary, Mary, My Own Dear Mary, I could fill this sheet on both sides with the repetition of that sweet name," he wrote. He felt a need to confess: the overland trek had not been the pleasure jaunt he had described in his earlier letters but an ordeal he barely survived—it wasn't the Indians, it was "bad water and no water at all." He was done with the mines, he told her, and contemplating a speculation in lumber. He wanted her to know that he thought of her constantly. He would be home just as soon as he succeeded.

Mary wrote him at about the same time. "Come home," she pleaded. "Forget the nuggets. I would rather see you than any other *lump* in California. . . . I do not care to have the strength of my affections tested by a much longer absence."

The pain of separation was even more acute for the men in California. The rare spectacle of a woman in the mining district was a reminder of the void in their lives. A seventeen-year-old New England boy was so anxious to see a "home-like lady" that he rode thirty-five miles to gawk at a newly arrived miner's wife. He reported back to his father at their claim: "Father, do you know, she sewed a button on for me, and told me not to gamble and not to drink. It sounded just like Mother." John Letts, hiking head down along the trail from Mormon Bar to Sacramento, was propelled into reverie by the sight of a female footprint: "There was such a witching air about it, so pert, the toes turned a little out, the heel set down with just enough decision, and something coquettish in the way she raised it up." He fancied that she might be one of his old dance partners. He remembered "having met her at a cotillion party, and then I noticed a change in the track, as if she had been thinking of the same thing, and taking some of the old steps."

But the life of a "home-like" California woman (there were more of the other kind) was no cotillion: it was drudgery. A woman who kept a mining camp boardinghouse in 1849 described the way she lived for her children back in Maine. Their lodge was a single room, fourteen feet square, with a cloth divider in the middle; the ten boarders slept on one side, she and her husband on the other; their beds were plain cots without pillows or sheets. She baked in a dutch oven. She felt isolated both physically and socially: the rainless summer had left "not a green thing to be seen except a few stunted trees"; she avoided other houses, "not that I am homesick, but it is nothing but gold, gold—no social feelings." The good news was that they were clearing $75 a week and "as soon as we are worth ten thousand I shall come home."

Almost everyone fell ill sooner or later. Hundreds of emigrants survived the cholera plague on the Platte only to die of fever or dysentery or scurvy in California. Doctors and pseudo-doctors discovered quickly that they were working the richest diggings of all. A physician from Alabama who opened a hospital tent in Sacramento in the summer was immediately deluged with patients. Charging $15 a day for a bed and $10 for a house call, he was able to go home a wealthy man in November.

The number of sick increased in the fall with the arrival of the last stragglers on the Lassen trail and the beginning of the rainy season. One doctor described Sacramento as "a perfect lazar-house of disease, suffering and death." There was no convenient place to be ill in California. Those who reached Sacramento or San Francisco might be treated somewhat better than the unfortunates marooned in the camps, but the character and velocity of life in California left little room for compassion. Charity medicine was unknown at first. An ailing miner was an encumbrance, a drag on the time and provisions and patience of his partners, provided he was lucky enough to have any. Most men were too selfish and preoccupied to aid an afflicted stranger.

Dr. Jacob Stillman saw an unconscious man lying on a muddy Sacramento street. "Someone with more humanity than the rest will have a hole dug for him," he reflected, "someone else will furnish an old blanket, he will be rolled up and buried. . . . Money, money is the all-absorbing object." Bayard Taylor noticed a lone, blanket-wrapped man shaking convulsively on a San Francisco beach, his pale face masked in "an expression of suffering so utterly hopeless and wild that I shuddered at seeing it."

Alonzo Delano, who had come to California for his health, was besieged by a succession of illnesses during his first few months there. Delano and a friend bought a load of groceries in Sacramento and erected a tent store at Bidwell's Bar on the Feather. The plan was for one of them to mine and the other to run the store, but first Delano and then his partner were felled by fever. They spent most of their time taking care of each other.

He returned to Sacramento with $600 profit and bought another stock of goods. The first of the November storms caught him near the Yuba River on the way back. He could make only twelve miles in five sodden days. A severe case of diarrhea halted him for several more days while the rain continued; by this time the road was impassable. Delano built a brush shelter and waited out the weather. Long lines of men passed daily, coming down from the mountains while they could. He noticed that they slept wherever they stopped, sometimes lying on the wet ground in the rain. Many were sick. When he finally got back to Bidwell's Bar he found that most of the miners had gone, his provisions were soaked and useless, and he was suffering from neuralgic fever.

Cal Gardiner underwent a similar buffeting in the southern mines. He first fell victim to dysentery, then was stricken by fever at his camp on Sullivan's Creek. He returned to Hawkins Bar on the Tuolumne at the onset of the rainy season. The sun-kissed summer's idyll was past: the bar was now a graveyard where men were buried daily. Many of the sick, lacking friends to care for them, were "left to die or recover as heaven might please." But Cal had friends, and one of them finally cured him. An old man they called the Squire prescribed a potion of brandy, absinthe, sugar, and peppermint to cure his malady. Cal administered several doses at the nearest grogshop. The next morning his fever was gone.

THE DELEGATES to the constitutional convention called by Governor Riley assembled at Monterey in September. The forty-eight men elected to draw up a constitution reflected a society in flux: Californio dons like

Mariano Vallejo and Pablo de la Guerra sat beside pre–gold rush settlers like John Sutter and Thomas Larkin and newcomers like ex-Congressman William Gwin and New York lawyer Elisha Crosby. Their meeting room was a spacious chamber on the second floor of Colton Hall, a balconied sandstone building which former alcalde Walter Colton had built.

Bayard Taylor, who covered the proceedings for the New York *Tribune,* was charmed by the "soft, vaporous atmosphere" of the placid little port on Monterey Bay, even if the available excitements were limited to ship arrivals, fandangos, and an occasional "horn burning," the gathering and burning of the malodorous remains of slaughtered cattle which littered the town. Larkin, who had tantalized eastern readers with his letters to the New York *Herald,* entertained the visitors at his handsome home.

The delegates approached their responsibilities soberly. The constitution was a necessary first step toward the statehood that Californians so ardently desired. Accession to the Union at this delicate moment in north-south relations, however, demanded a choice on the overriding issue of the day: the Californians voted unanimously to outlaw slavery. The balancing of northern and southern interests in Congress would delay statehood for another year.

Despite their opposition to slavery, the Monterey delegates were no more willing than most of their countrymen to grant equal rights to blacks. A clause that would have barred free blacks was first passed and later rejected. They were reasonably progressive, in the context of the time, on most issues: married women would be permitted to own property; judges, along with executive and legislative officers, were to be popularly elected. The question of the eastern boundary provoked the longest debate before a line close to the present California-Nevada border was agreed upon. The general tone of the convention was aggressively democratic. One delegate objected hotly to the clause assuring a citizen the right to a trial by a jury of his peers. "It ain't republican," he argued. "I'd like to know what we want with *peers* in this country."

The peerless Californians celebrated the end of their work with a grand ball, followed the next day by the formal signing of the constitution. As the delegates began to sign their names a signal was given and the American flag was raised. The cannons at the presidio boomed out over the bay. The emotional Sutter leaped to his feet with tears streaking his face. "This is the happiest day of my life," he cried, swinging his arm over his head. The delegates stood and cheered. The guns fired thirty-one times, once for each existing state and the last time for California.

An election to ratify the constitution and choose a governor was scheduled for November 13. Peter Burnett, the former Oregon lawyer who as Sutter's business agent had enriched himself and settled the old man's debts, became one of the first candidates for governor. Sutter, who had grown disenchanted with Burnett and fired him, was also a candidate. Most California voters had only the skimpiest acquaintance with either constitution or candidates. Taylor, watching the voting in a saloon polling place at the rain-washed Mokelumne diggings, noticed that drinking was considerably more popular than voting. One man declared proudly that he had voted as blindly as he had come to California in the first place: "I voted for the constitution," he said, "and I've never seen the constitution. I voted for all the candidates and I don't know a damned one of them." A voter who had at least heard Burnett speak was hardly any wiser: "By report Burnett stood fair," he noted in his journal, "but his address is a miserable affair. Voting for him was a leap in the dark into the mire."

Enough voters made the leap to give Burnett more than double the votes of the runner-up, a former New York legislator named Sherwood. Sutter ran third. The constitution was approved by a lopsided 12,061 to 811. Less than a quarter of the eligible voters bothered to cast ballots.

The stunning fact that California now possessed both a constitution and a governor-elect was an unmistakable sign that civilization was prowling nearby. Other evidence was beginning to appear as well, especially in the cities. The *Alta California* now published a "steamer edition" for eastern readers. The "Placer Intelligence" column of one early copy showed that the well-developed frontier tactic of gulling the greenhorns was still rewarding. Nobody in the northern mines, the column said, was gathering more than a cartload of gold dust a day.

River steamers began regular service between San Francisco and Sacramento in the fall, and culture was blooming on both ends of the run. "Rowe's Olympic Circus," featuring the equestrian talents of the richly endowed Mrs. Rowe, opened in a 1,500-seat big-top in San Francisco in October. In the same month the Eagle Theatre in Sacramento launched a brief but lively tenure with a production of *The Bandit Chief, or: The Forest Spectre*, starring a Mrs. Ray "of the Royal Theatre, New Zealand." The ubiquitous Bayard Taylor plunked down $3 for a box seat at an early performance and described the ensuing histrionics:

"The curtain rolls up and we look upon a forest scene, in the midst of which appears Hildebrand the robber." After several acts with "the usual amount of fighting and terrible speeches," the star "rushes in and throws herself into an attitude in the middle of the stage; why she does it no one can tell. This movement, which she repeats several times in the course of the first three acts, has no connection with the tragedy; it is evidently introduced for the purpose of showing the audience that there is actually a female performer. The miners . . . applaud vehemently."

The shortage of women may well have inhibited any further advance of civilization, but the tremendous volume of mail handled by the San Francisco post office proved that the ladies back home were keeping in touch. More than 45,000 letters, plus uncounted bushels of newspapers, arrived on November 1 on the steamship *Panama;* a month later the *Oregon* delivered a load of comparable size. Clerks locked themselves inside the post office for two days and nights while they sorted the mail alphabetically, ignoring the door pounding and shouting by the eager hordes outside. When the windows finally opened the line of waiting men stretched for several blocks. A few with more patience than prospects made a modest living by getting in line early and selling their places for $20 and more. Vendors peddled pastry and newspapers.

The absence of a letter from home could produce an indefinable sense of dread, a fear John Durivage described as "infinitely more depressing than the actual possession of evil tidings." The receipt of mail, on the other hand, could bring on a giddiness leading to doggerel:

They wish to know if I can cook and what I have to eat
And tell me should I take a cold be sure to soak my feet,
But when they talk of cooking I'm mighty hard to beat—
I've made ten thousand loaves of bread the devil could not eat . . .

I never changed my fancy shirt the one I wore away
Until it got so rotten that I finally had to say
Farewell old standing collar in all thy pride of starch,
I've worn thee from December to the seventeenth of March . . .

Desertion, which continued high, remained the most visible failing of both military and civil authorities, but in September a particularly shocking incident gave Commodore Thomas Jones an opportunity to set a chastening example. Five sailors on the U.S. schooner *Ewing* deserted in one of the ship's boats after knocking an officer into the choppy bay. He was rescued by a passing boat. Captured the next day, the deserters were tried, convicted, and sentenced to death by a court-martial. Commodore Jones, responding to a plea by the assaulted officer, commuted the sentences of three of the five. The other two, considered the leaders, were hanged in the harbor on October 23.

"There was heavy weight to one end of the rope," a spectator on shore wrote, "and the man noosed by the other. The rope was so fixed that the discharge of a cannon parted it and he was twitched up like a fish, flying some way above the yardarm." Jones ordered all seamen to witness the execution from the decks of their vessels.

The most persuasive evidence that the anarchic, amoral, and irreligious San Francisco of only a few months earlier was drifting toward wholesomeness was the commencement of street preaching on Portsmouth Square by the Reverend William Taylor, a fearless Methodist from Baltimore. Standing on a workbench in front of a gambling house on December 3, the reverend sailed into a hymn and soon drew a crowd of a thousand. His text was a familiar theme in a California context. Under "your favorite rule in arithmetic, the rule of loss and gain," he thundered, "what is a man profited if he shall gain the whole world and lose his own soul?" He was gratified to see that this lesson was greeted with "perfect order and profound attention."

THE HEAVY November rains ended the 1849 mining season at most camps. Many of the forty to fifty thousand miners scattered between the Trinity River on the north and the Mariposa on the south descended to the towns in the valleys or on the coast. They had produced an estimated $10.6 million in gold. With the exception of J. Goldsborough Bruff and a few hundred unfortunates on the southwest deserts, all of the overland emigrants—about forty thousand by all routes—had arrived in El Dorado. Another thirty-nine thousand had come by sea. Thousands—no one can ever know how many—had perished of cholera on the trail or other diseases in California. The great majority of the hastily chartered mutual-stock companies were gone, along with the gold-finding machines they had purchased in such an access of hope.

And still they came. The first sixty members of the La Californienne Company—farmers, merchants, artisans, even a few noblemen—assembled at Le Havre, France, in late November. Each had bought at least nine shares in the company at 100 francs ($20) each. On the twenty-fourth they held a banquet. There were toasts and fine food, and every member shook the hand of the expedition's leader. A collection was taken up for the poor of Le Havre. The next day was Sunday, and the sixty went in a body to the church of Notre Dame for a special mass. A band followed them through the streets afterward. They sailed for California on November 27.

XI

FIRE AND ICE

SACRAMENTO CITY, 1849

COLOMA, the exquisite little pocket valley where James Marshall had come to build Sutter's sawmill only two winters earlier, was now a clangorous mountain metropolis. Stores, saloons, and hotels paraded in uneven ranks along both sides of the main street. The toll of a gong announced dinner at Little's Hotel, where the Sunday meals—boiled salmon and corned beef and veal, rice pudding and green peas and peach pie—rivaled any in the first-class hostelries of New York and Boston. Sunday was the day that the miners shambled into town with their earthborn currency and hastily unloaded it. Coloma's Sunday temptations were bunched so thickly that a man might part with his poke before he had advanced a full ten yards: auctioneers hawked tools and clothes; "thimbleriggers," practicing an early precursor of the shell game, challenged the curious to choose which of three wooden thimbles covered a paper pellet; a man with a looped string would bet that he could close the loop before a finger could enter it; another held up a padlock equipped with a hidden spring and wagered that no one could open it.

Prices, though still high, had tailed off since Edward Gould Buffum and his friend invested $43 in breakfast a year earlier: two dollars now bought a good meal at Little's. Miner Charles B. Gillespie, wandering through a Coloma Sunday, noticed that mealtime dress standards were considerably more casual than they were back East: "there was not a single coat in the whole crowd," he wrote, "and certainly not over half a dozen vests, and neither neckties nor collars." Gillespie scanned the untidy, sunburned, bearded, and fiercely mustached men around the table and wondered if "a crowd of rougher or apparently lower characters" had ever been assembled anywhere. "And yet," he added, "many of these men were lawyers and physicians, and the rest principally farmers and mechanics from the States."

Gillespie, who wrote his recollections more than forty years later, told one story about his Sunday in Coloma which has passed into forty-niner mythology. The scene was the spacious first-floor casino in the elaborately colonnaded Winters Hotel. Silver dollars were stacked in piles of sixteen on monte tables covered with blue cloth. A waiter darted amid the tables with free drinks for the bettors while two fiddlers pried a tune from their instruments. The voice of the monte banker was a modulated hum: "Jack and deuce. Make your bets, gentlemen." Gillespie stopped at a table to watch. The dealer turned over two more cards. "Seven and ace. Come down, gents, come down." The dealer eyed the bearded men pressing close to the table. "All down, gents?"

Gillespie was startled to see a small hand clutching two coins shoot forward. He glanced down and saw a curly-haired boy so short that the top of his head barely crested the stack of dollars. "Two dimes on the ace," the boy cried. Everyone laughed except the banker. "We don't take dimes at this bank," he said coolly.

The boy then produced a buckskin bag and tossed it onto the table. "I guess you'll take that," he said. "Six ounces on the ace." The table fell quiet. The ace won. The boy was $96 richer.

He bet the bag again and again he won. The banker grabbed a new deck and shuffled it, permitting the boy to cut. The other players bet with him. He raised the stakes to twenty-five ounces and won again. The others nervously dropped out: now it was the kid against the house.

The dealer laid out an ace and a five. "Fifty ounces on the five," the boy said. One by one the man flipped over the cards: deuce, three, king, queen, seven—then a five. The boy doubled his bet again and once more he won. Miners crowded around the table as the word spread.

"How much have you in the bank?" the boy asked. "A hundred and fifty ounces," the dealer replied. He dealt a queen and a three. "I tap the bank upon the queen," the youth said calmly; he was betting his winnings against the bank. The crowd was silent.

Slowly the perspiring banker turned the deck over—one card, then another, then three more. No one breathed. The next card was a three—the run was over. The boy "looked about with a stern defying air," Gillespie wrote, "as if to chide us for our sympathy." Everything was gone now except his buckskin bag of dust. He bet the bag on the next layout and lost that too, then wheeled and walked out through the crowd "with all the importance of a noted hero."

Gillespie, feeling both pity and curiosity, followed the boy outside and offered him money. The boy put his index finger to his lips. "You want to know how much was in that bag?" he whispered. "Well, I'll tell you—four pounds of duckshot mixed, and nothing more." Gillespie stared openmouthed. The boy laughed. "What a swearin' and cussin' when they open it," he said.

Coloma's indoor pleasures helped to leaven the oppressive dreariness of winter in the mines. Winter dealt the camps a mixed hand: the same storms that brought snow to J. Goldsborough Bruff's lonely high-country outpost on the fringe of the northern mines saturated the foothills and valleys with heavy rain, turning trails to mush and making travel impossible. A miner could work the "wet diggings" in the north until high water washed over his claim, but the food wagon couldn't always get through. The first blast of winter forced a choice: he could stock up on flour and dried meat, build or buy a cabin and brazen it through until spring, gambling that his health and food supply would hold out and digging when he could; or he could flee to the lowlands. But in the southern mines it was reversed: a winter storm often brought deliverance, turning the dusty ravines and summer-brown washes, the "dry diggings" of the hot season, into fast-flowing streams with plenty of water for gold washing.

Winter descended on a well-traveled thirty-year-old Scotsman named William Downie only a few weeks after he had discovered one of the biggest bonanzas in the California mountains. Prospecting the bars and banks around a pine-rimmed fork in the north branch of the Yuba River, Downie found dirt so rich that he could kick the gold loose. He and a partner, an ex-slave from Virginia, plucked fourteen ounces of gold from a single pan of earth. Their most useful tools were the pan, a crowbar, and a butcher knife. In four days the two men gathered more than $1,750 in dust.

With their food supply declining, eight of the twelve men in Downie's party plodded off on mules to buy provisions. Downie stayed behind with the other three and stared bleakly at a sack of flour so depleted that they could tie an overhand knot in it. Then the rain began. Days passed with no word from their friends; the realization that they would not return finally dawned. For several days they subsisted on a soup made with the bones of a dead steer. Downie recognized the paradox: their bag of gold was so heavy that they frequently argued about who would carry it, yet they were starving. At last a supply train arrived. Downie bought nearly two thousand pounds of flour, canned meats, and vegetables at two dollars a pound, a price that lightened the gold bag enough to preclude further squabbling. In December they built a log cabin at the confluence of the two gravel-bottomed streams, the first wooden structure to rise at the site. By spring this romantic, mountain-walled camp would have fifteen hotels, five thousand residents, and a name: Downieville.

John Woodhouse Audubon greeted the winter in Stockton. He had landed in town only a few days earlier after riding up the San Joaquin Valley with the last of his cholera-shattered band of New Yorkers. He gazed incredulously at the end of his long and tortuous trail: Stockton was a ramshackle river town filled with raucous and hard-drinking men, each "on guard against his fellow man." The place smelled of whiskey and greed. Audubon's purpose had been to study the natural phenomena he encountered, to sketch them and collect specimens. But the desert had claimed his painting materials and his specimens had been lost. He felt bereft. A visit to San Francisco in December didn't help; there were no letters for him at the post office; the city was "a hellhole of crime and dissipation."

Why was he here? "Again and again I am overwhelmed by the thought that I am at these dreary mines," he wrote from the southern mines in January. He followed a desultory path from Stockton to Angel's Camp to Hawkins Bar, going through the motions for the sake of his still eager men. In February they dissolved the company; like everyone else they had learned that placer mining might be successfully pursued alone or with a few partners, but never in companies of a hundred. As always it was nature and broken men that touched Audubon most deeply: the California valleys were "roseate yellow and blue, so soft that the purest sky cannot surpass the color for delicacy." At a riverside camp he met a man lying ill with scurvy in a leaky mud hut, broke and dejected and "unable to move even a few steps." The man told Audubon he was P. T. Barnum's brother.

Cal Gardiner suffered through the first weeks of rain in his soggy tent on the Tuolumne; so much water oozed up from the spongy earth inside his shelter that the pine boughs covering the floor sank in the mud. The winter of 1849–50 would be recalled in a calmer time as one of the harshest ever in California, in part because thousands of men endured it in tents like Gardiner's, but also because the rain was both hard and unrelenting. By mid-December it was raining six out of seven days along the Tuolumne, and Gardiner wanted out. "Supplies were nearly exhausted," he wrote, "and it became necessary to get away to avoid actual starvation." Cal and his Sag Harbor friends stowed their bottle with the menu taped on the side and separated; he and another man elected to winter in San Francisco.

Just before he left he had a chance to observe the evolving gold country justice. Cal was idling near a friend's campfire when a Texan inexplicably laid claim to his friend's tin drinking cup. When the man refused to yield the cup, the Texan grabbed his gun and fired. Cal's friend shot back and killed him.

Cal promptly wrote out a statement which recounted the details of the incident and asserted that his friend fired in self-defense. Then he obtained the signatures of several witnesses and hiked off with his friend to find the nearest alcalde, a one-legged miner named Miller. The magistrate was only too pleased when they found him on a riverbank a few miles away, mainly because his wooden leg had become wedged between two stones and he couldn't move. He studied the paper they showed him after they liberated him, remarked that it was "evidently a case of justifiable homicide," and demanded to know what they expected him to do. The dead man, he explained, had "taken the chances and got wiped out, and no jury would ever correct the wiper." He advised Gardiner and his friend to forget about it.

California law in the winter of 1849–50 was in a state of careless suspension. Most camps of any size had chosen alcaldes with no more knowledge of law than the earthy Miller had. A criminal code could not be implemented until Congress voted statehood, a decision that was in turn delayed because of the complex and delicate politics of balancing free states and slave states. Justice in the mining country thus remained, for better or worse, in the hands of the miners.

The usual response to a serious crime in a camp without an elected official was a hastily called meeting, the selection of a judge, a crude trial with whatever safeguards anybody could remember, a jury verdict, and instant punishment, often either flogging or banishment. There were no jails. The only difference in the larger camps—Placerville or Sonora, for example—was that an alcalde frequently presided. This primitive justice mirrored the men who created it: it was careless, impatient, bigoted, improvised, individualistic, and original; like its masters, it was sometimes cruel and sometimes merciful.

Given a system where legal retribution was hit-or-miss at best, the absence of any significant amount of theft in the 1849 camps was astonishing. Almost everyone commented on it. "There were no thieves in the mining camps," Cal Gardiner wrote. "The difference between *meum* and *tuum* was rigidly observed, and private rights generally respected." Property was safer than life; killings arising out of drunken arguments were more common than larceny, and often ignored. "Since my arrival here three Mexicans and one white man have been killed in street-fights," William Perkins wrote from Sonora in January, "but we have not yet heard of a single cold-blooded murder."

The atmosphere changed during the winter: widespread thievery arrived. Alonzo Delano's explanation for its sudden emergence has a contemporary ring—poverty and deprivation. It was only when the miners wintering in the cities hit bottom, he believed, that "stealing became as common as before it had been unknown"; hunger and sickness drove men to rob. A few suspected that the increase in lawlessness could be directly traced to an increase in lawyers and politicians. But whatever the causes, life in the mines would never be the same after this long and discouraging winter; *meum* and *tuum* would lose their sanctity; lynchings and other spasms of mob violence, rare before 1850, would become more common. The gold rush California of fictional melodramas would finally appear.

> Oh, what was your name in the States?
> Was it Thompson, or Johnson or Bates?
> Did you flee for your life or murder your wife?
> Say, what was your name in the States?

Criminal law was obviously not the miners' long suit. Mining law, the creation of a code to regulate their obsession—there was a subject that this corps of narrow-focused, optimistic, and stoutly democratic men could embrace with enthusiasm. It was in their mining codes—there were hundreds of them; every camp or "district" had its own—that California miners best expressed both their principles and their prejudices. These codes, later adopted in substance by both the state legislature and the California supreme court, were among their most enduring monuments.

The major premises of the mining laws were simple: the first claim took priority (a discoverer was sometimes rewarded with two claims), access was equal (though foreigners were frequently excluded), and most important, labor insured possession. The regulations of the Tuolumne River camp of Jacksonville, drawn up in January 1850, set the limits of a claim at twelve feet along the river, "running back to the hill or mountain and forward to the center of the river or creek." A miner could hold his claim by leaving his tools on the ground he worked. A claim not worked for more than a week would be considered abandoned, except in cases of illness. Article XI stated that "no person coming direct from a foreign country shall be permitted to locate or work any lot within the jurisdiction of this encampment."

"CHRISTMAS, 1849—Still raining," fourteen-year-old Sallie Hester wrote in her diary. "This has been a sad Christmas for mother. She is homesick, longs for her old home and friends. It's hard for old folks to give up old ties and go so far away. . . ." Sallie and her family, overland immigrants from Indiana, were wintering in the little settlement of Fremont at the junction of the Sacramento and Feather rivers. "Was invited to a candy pull and had a nice time," her Christmas entry went on. "Rather a number of young folks camped here."

John Audubon spent a gloomy Christmas in San Francisco. "Happy Christmas, Merry Christmas!" he wrote bitterly. "Not that here, for me at any rate, in this pandemonium of a city. Not a *lady* to be seen, and the women, poor things, sad and silent—except when drunk or excited." Christmas in the city was just another day "except for a little more drunkenness and a little extra effort by the hotel keepers to take in more money."

The Scotsman William Downie, finally secure for the winter at his Yuba River bonanza camp, concocted a yuletide punch from nutmeg, hot water, and the lone bottle of brandy in camp. Downie was in a mood to celebrate Fourth-of-July style. He climbed on the roof of his newly built cabin, waved an American flag, and fired a few rounds with his pistol. William Perkins passed the day unloading a cargo of freight from a wagon mired in Stanislaus River muck—"up to the knees in mud with ten feet of stovepipe strapped to my pair of blankets."

New Yorker Joseph McCloskey, working with two partners at nearby Woods Creek diggings, was out of food on Christmas. He and his friends exchanged improvised gifts—a small nugget, a broken pocketknife—and trudged off in quest of a meal. They were resting on a wooded hillside when they heard caroling from somewhere amid the trees: four young men from Boston were singing "Adeste Fideles." McCloskey and his comrades joined them for a holiday feast of flapjacks and coffee and johnnycake baked on a shovel. They continued the impromptu concert after supper.

The animosity between American and Chilean miners flared into violence a few days after Christmas in an episode which became known as the "Chilean War." A Chilean named Dr. Concha and several dozen *peones* were working a gulch off the Calaveras River when a newly arrived group of Americans demanded that they leave within fifteen days. Concha chose to fight back. He went to a judge in Stockton and secured a writ empowering him to evict the interlopers from his claims. He and his men proceeded to attack the American camp, killing two and capturing sixteen. He then set out to deliver his prisoners to Stockton. One of the captives recalled later that the Chileans debated killing them all but decided against it.

The Chileans had reason to regret that decision almost immediately. During an overnight stop the Americans slipped their bonds, seized the Chileans' weapons, and overpowered them. Dr. Concha escaped, but he was reportedly killed in a San Francisco fandango hall a few days later. The other Chileans were swiftly convicted by a miners' court. Two were sentenced to death and several others were brutally whipped. Two of the flogged men also had their ears chopped off.

The heavy rain, which had relented for a week or two in December, became incessant again in early January. Sarah Royce watched it from the tent she shared with her family in Sacramento. "Day after day it kept on," she wrote, "with only short intervals of such lovely sunshine as we had never before seen in January." Both the American and Sacramento rivers, which flanked the city, were rising ominously. The cold, pounding rain continued on the seventh and eighth. On the next day the wind direction changed and the rain, now coming from the south, turned warm enough to melt some of the Sierra snow, filling the rivers even higher. Late on the evening of the ninth the water began to seep over the banks of the American and to spread into unprotected Sacramento.

Mrs. Royce had just put her infant daughter to bed when she overheard her husband and another man in urgent conversation outside their tent. "The water is flowing over the banks fast," the other man said. When her husband expressed doubt, the stranger led him to a slight depression where water was already several inches deep. Royce decided to move his wife and daughter to a two-story house nearby. The water rose visibly in the short time it took them to pack and dress. They hurried to the house and spent the night huddled in the upper story, listening to the water slosh and gurgle around them until it reached the first-floor windows.

In the morning they could see the extent of the deluge. All of Sacramento save a few isolated patches of high ground (Sutter's fort was on one of them) lay beneath one to ten feet of dirty water. The fields on the southern edge of the city, which had been transformed into a tent encampment by hundreds of overland emigrants, were inundated. The tops of wagons arched over the rippling water like miniature tunnels. Carcasses of dead animals floated through the streets. Hundreds of people were crowded on about two dozen ships in the now indistinguishable river, while others had taken refuge at a Methodist church. Small boats nosed through the streets picking up survivors; some boat owners would not stop unless they were paid.

Dr. Jacob Stillman, the physician who had helped to oust the tyrannical captain of the ship *Pacific* in Rio de Janeiro, had opened a hospital in Sacramento only a few weeks earlier. Now he found himself crammed into the building's second floor with some forty other people, many of them sick. "Tents, houses, boxes, barrels, horses, mules and cattle are sweeping by with the swollen torrent," he wrote. "Men continue to come, begging to be taken in. . . . We take only the sick." From the small boats outside the second-story windows came the incongruous laughter of revelers who had fished a bottle from the passing tide. On the twelfth, with the water still rising, Stillman chartered a whaleboat for $40 and took the bodies of three men to high ground for burial. There were two more deaths at the hospital the following day. The exact number of drowning victims was never determined.

The fast-rising water swamped millions of acres in the valleys of the

Sacramento, Feather, and American rivers. Delano, standing atop a high hill on the south bank of the Feather, estimated that a third of the land in sight was under water. The San Francisco *Pacific News* reported that four Chinese miners drowned at Manhattan Bar on the American. Sallie Hester's clapboard cabin escaped, but the rest of Fremont was a lake. "Wish I was back in Indiana," she wrote. "Snakes are plenty . . . under our beds and everywhere." The Royce family managed to get on a boat to San Francisco on the fifteenth.

After two weeks the flood finally receded enough for repairs and rebuilding to begin. Stillman discovered that five barrels of meat and a case of wine had fortuitously lodged in his hospital. Watching the furious pace of reconstruction, he also glimpsed something of the spirit of this hectic province: "To a true Californian," he wrote, "nothing is difficult or dangerous except grizzlies." Sharp-eyed prospectors noticed that the flood had a golden lining: flakes of the precious metal appeared on the riverbanks, showing them precisely how gold had accumulated on the rivers for eons.

John Sutter, the man who had once ruled this saturated plain, was discussing a business deal at the City Hotel in Sacramento in late January when his old friend Heinrich Lienhard caught his eye. Lienhard had bracing news for the courtly old pioneer: his wife, Anna, and three of his children were waiting for him in San Francisco. Sutter had seen none of them for sixteen years.

Lienhard had traveled to Europe via Panama to gather up the haughty, grim-mouthed Frau Sutter and the children—twenty-two-year-old Eliza, twenty-year-old Emil, and Alfons, who was seventeen. Another son had died after Sutter fled his homeland to escape creditors. The young Sutters could barely recall their father, but Anna's memory was heated by sixteen years of scrimping in Switzerland; only recently had she learned that her husband was a wealthy and important man in his adopted country. Lienhard thought that her behavior on the steamer up from Panama was both rude and conspicuous. He discreetly withdrew from the San Francisco hotel room where husband and wife were at last reunited.

Sutter brought them to his farm on the Feather River, where the children could hunt and enjoy horseback excursions around his shrunken fiefdom. The old baron immediately made plans to build a larger house and to plant more fruit trees and vegetables; he hired a Swiss piano teacher for Alfons. Eliza, charming and vivacious like her father, was his favorite. He set aside a section of land across the river for a new town he called Eliza City. This venture, like most Sutter speculations, flickered briefly and then expired. One reason was that a rival town four miles upstream had jumped off to a headstart a few weeks earlier. The town was Marysville.

Marysville, which rose at the junction of the Feather and Yuba rivers, was the head of steam navigation north of Sacramento. Town lots had gone on sale for $250 each in the midst of the January flood. Stephen Field, a thirty-three-year-old New York lawyer who had landed in California only a few weeks previously, was one of the first buyers. Field, who would later be appointed to the U.S. Supreme Court by Abraham Lincoln, caused a sensation by purchasing sixty-five lots on credit. At the time, he recalled later, his cash on hand totaled $20.

Field's boldness so impressed his fellow citizens that he was nominated to be the town's first alcalde, an office he won by nine votes. "The main objection urged against me was that I was a newcomer," he wrote. "I had been there only three days, my opponent had been there six." The name Marysville was a tribute to Mary Murphy, a survivor of the Donner expedition and the wife of town founder Charles Covillaud.

Field and Marysville both prospered. As alcalde he collected substantial fees for recording property deeds. He bought several prefabricated houses in San Francisco, shipped them to Marysville, and rented them. Property values shot up; Field sold several of his lots for a total of $25,000 and still had most of them left. By early April, when Alonzo Delano turned up in town with crayons and paper and passed himself off as a portrait painter at an ounce a head, Marysville was a settlement of 150 houses. The population was between five and six hundred. Three steamboats made the daily round trip between Sacramento and the Marysville landing. There were even a few women in town.

Placerville, still known to most miners as Hangtown, enjoyed such an abundance of women that a dance was held in late January. It was apparently a success, because there was another one three days later. Some of the guests were Sacramento gamblers driven to higher country by the flood. The Hangtown weather was so persistently bad that a seventeen-year-old Iowa boy allowed in a letter home that he might be content "never to take another campaign of this kind." Miners forced indoors by the weather could try the tenpin alleys, attend a concert featuring a black singer, or dine at the Eldorado Hotel, which offered such entrees as "Roast Beef, wild—$1.50," "Beef, tame, from Arkansas—$1.50," "Sauer Kraut—$1.00," "Jackass Rabbit (whole)—$1.00," "Hash, low

grade—$.75," and "Hash, 18 carats—$1.00." A full meal with rice pudding for dessert was $3, payable in advance.

Sonora, capital of the more cosmopolitan southern mines, was losing
its Latin flavor. The young Canadian William Perkins, who had been so
captivated by Sonora's charm in the summer, noted sorrowfully that plain,
rough-hewn log cabins had replaced the gaily colored, flag-bedecked
Mexican tents. Sonora had changed from an "Eastern encampment or
bazaar" to a "dirty American country town." The principal local menace
was the profusion of deep, water-filled pits which waited in ambush for
drunken pedestrians. Bodies were fished out regularly.

The perceptive Perkins chronicled life in Sonora from the vantage
of his adobe store. It took him no time at all to conclude that mining
"entailed an amount of labor and personal suffering I was entirely un-
willing to encounter." Women were plentiful in Sonora, "but they are
all mistresses or independent. . . . The mistress occupies here the same
position that the wife does in other countries, and most of the women are
of a class that think it no disgrace." The big excitement of the winter was
the discovery of a twenty-two-pound nugget by three Mexicans a few yards
from Perkins' house.

Early in February he enlisted in a posse pursuing a band of Indian
rustlers. Indians had all but disappeared from the mining district since
the massacre by the Coloma miners the previous spring. Perkins and his
companions found three villages tucked deep in the hills. Two were
deserted. At the other one they drove the Indians off and burned their
few possessions. Perkins lacked his comrades' gusto for Indian fighting;
his conscience troubled him. "To say the truth," he confessed, "I was not
entirely satisfied with myself. . . . We invade a land that is not our
own, we arrogate a right through pretense of superior intelligence and the
wants of civilization, and if the aborigines dispute our title we destroy
them."

J. GOLDSBOROUGH BRUFF was trapped. By late December the snow
around his mountain camp was three to six feet deep. Hunger and rheumatism had sapped his strength until the slightest exertion was an ordeal.
It was obvious that his desperate little band—his friend Poyle and the
four-year-old Lambkin boy were still with him—could not survive the
winter where they were. They had subsisted for days on the tainted and
leathery meat of long-dead oxen, bone marrow, and an occasional bird or

squirrel. The boy cried almost continuously. The inside of their tent, shored up by empty kegs and crates, looked like a wet cave. Another storm would probably doom them.

But where in God's name was Willis? He had set out on the three-day trek to the valley on December 4, promising to return with help. Bruff could not believe that he would abandon them; surely humanity if not friendship or loyalty would draw him back. They celebrated Christmas with a stew made from squirrel, antique ox meat, and deer bones—and still no word from Willis. A few days later they were reduced to eating tallow candles. Bruff could still summon a spark of grim humor. If variety was the spice of life, he wrote, "we are now getting pretty well spiced."

They had to try to move. Walking any distance was agony, but the alternative was worse. Three miles farther down the trail an emigrant named Roberts had built a crude bungalow where he was wintering with his family. Roberts had been able to get some food from the settlements. Bruff and Poyle loaded their gear onto a makeshift sled with the boy on top on the last day of 1849. They struggled down to Roberts' cabin in four hours. Bruff fainted from exhaustion at the door.

Roberts' son and a man named Warren Clough had just returned from the Lassen ranch. They had seen the missing Willis, "faring well and perfectly unconcerned about us." Bruff's journal entry about his friend's betrayal was strangely restrained. It was as if his pain and disappointment transcended anger; perhaps he was too tired. Willis, they said, had given various excuses for his failure to come back. He was working as a carpenter at Lassen's rancho.

Poyle and Clough, assuring Bruff that they would return in four days, set out just after midnight on New Year's Day to buy provisions at a store near the ranch. Bruff and the boy, bunking in a tent near the Roberts cabin, suffered violent stomach pains during the night. In the morning Bruff learned that the Roberts clan had also been stricken. Suspecting poison, he discovered that Mrs. Roberts had used caustic soda instead of baking soda in making bread the previous night.

The boy's condition worsened in the morning. He died shortly before eleven o'clock. His father had never come back for him. Bruff washed the tiny body with snow and wrapped him in a white cloth. The next day he dug a grave in front of his tent and buried him beneath a pile of stones. He found a plank and wrote an inscription: "WILLIAM, Infant son of LAMBKIN—an Unnatural Father, Died Jan. 1, 1850."

Bruff's prospects for survival, ironically, were finally improving. His stomach pains eased at about the time Poyle and Clough reappeared with a hundred pounds of food and a bill for $107. The round trip took them only four days. Clough, an older man who preferred wilderness to towns, told Bruff he would stay with him through the winter. A spell of freakish summerlike weather melted the remaining snow. On February 5 Bruff dispatched Poyle once again, this time bearing letters to several officers and other friends. In the letters he pronounced himself "much recruited" and said he hoped to reach the valley in a few weeks. He asked for aid in transporting his documents, instruments, and camp gear.

On February 16 the Roberts family took advantage of the mild weather to pack their possessions and move off for Lassen's ranch. Clough went along to assist them. With Poyle still seeking help in the valley, Bruff was now alone for the first time. He barricaded his sleeping berth against the suddenly vivid danger of an Indian attack, though he had not seen an Indian for months. Clough returned on the twentieth and began daily deer-hunting excursions. Bruff dreamed that an old army friend arrived with a mule train to rescue him, but in fact his grace period was ending. Winter was about to reappear.

The storms resumed in late February. Bruff fretted constantly that Clough might lose his way or stumble into an Indian ambush while hunting. Their meat supply was again dwindling. On March 14 the ever systematic Bruff noted that Poyle had been gone for thirty-seven days, twenty of which had been stormy. The next day they put their last chunk of meat in the pot and Clough braved the storm once more. He was out all night.

Bruff scratched tautly at his journal, flailing at the nightmare visions in his mind as the wind howled around him. Maybe Clough had been attacked by a grizzly and even now lay mangled and "writhing in the cold and wet." Maybe he had been brought down by Indians. "Oh, if I knew where he was!" He caught his breath at every night sound. Clough was his lifeline. If something happened to Clough . . . it was unthinkable.

Morning dawned clear and calm. Bruff heated the last of the meat but couldn't eat. At ten-fifteen he heard a rifle, then a pistol, then—"Great God! . . . the deer song! I answered his shots by another, now shouted at the top of my lungs and hobbled off to meet him." Clough the invincible was back, dragging a fine doe.

Clough remained in camp for three days before he sallied forth again, returning that night with another doe. They were now totally dependent on his marksmanship: the rest of their food was gone. Bruff was weakening; his head was sore and fitfully feverish; his back ached. Prideful still, he continued to sleep in his damp and tattered tent even though Roberts' cabin was empty. Howling coyotes kept him awake. By the twenty-fourth their venison supply was nearly exhausted once more. Clough hunted without success. He doggedly trudged off again on the morning of the twenty-fifth, telling Bruff that he might be gone two days.

Bruff was awakened on the second night after Clough left by the barking of his bull terrier. He peered out of the tent and saw a bear less than ten feet away. The bear eyed him for a full five minutes, then slowly turned away. Bruff wondered if "he thought me too contemptible to kill."

The morning of the twenty-seventh was maddeningly beautiful; if he were only healthy he might walk in. Where was Clough? Perhaps he chased deer close to the valley and decided to visit the ranch and buy flour. Their food was gone. On the twenty-eighth Bruff shot a woodpecker, but there was barely enough meat for one meal. He foraged for deer bones, extracted the shriveled marrow, and made broth. March 29: Should he eat the dog—"for one meal, and then die regretting it? I will not!" Clough had probably been attacked by a bear while he slept. No, no—it was Indians. They had heard his rifle and crept up on him. "Magnanimous, intrepid and kind old man—shall I ever forget thee? . . . Thou wast a MAN!" Late at night there was a sound. Was it a rooster? A child's laugh? "Am I crazy?" He clutched his rifle, looked wildly around: there was nothing. March 30: Clough must be dead. But Poyle—Poyle was alive! Surely help was coming. He sank into half-sleep, dreaming that his young son was parting his long and matted hair with his tiny hands. Dinner was another swig of gamy bone broth. April 1: he had survived the winter in these terrible mountains; could he survive the spring? He clumsily knocked over the kettle containing the last of his broth. "I must exert myself or die at once," he told himself. He remembered that he had two candles and a dozen acorns in his collection of specimens: sustenance for a day, perhaps two or three. If his legs were strong enough he could try to walk—he *would* try! But the notes, the drawings, the specimens . . . he would leave them, come back for them; carrying them was impossible. He brewed more soup from a piece of frozen deerskin. His legs were stiff and sore. How could he hike thirty-two hard miles?

Bruff carefully packed a haversack, shouldered his rifle, and set out on the morning of April 4 with the dog at his side. He fell frequently as he descended a long hill into a hollow. On the climb up the other side he had to rest after every ten feet. The dog trotted ahead and whined as if to encourage him. To his surprise he made ten miles before he dropped from exhaustion. He struggled through a light rain the next day but could cover only a few miles before camping under an abandoned wagon. He wolfed down some vegetable sprouts he found growing at a forty-niner campsite. Maybe he would make it after all; nature at last seemed to be helping.

On the sixth he met a group of men who were apparently scavenging the trail for jettisoned supplies. In his excitement Bruff stumbled and fell as he approached them. They gave him pork and flapjacks and shared their campsite with him, but the food only teased his ravenous appetite; he felt as if he could eat for days. The men moved off in the morning after telling him that he was only sixteen miles from the settlements. Bruff desperately wanted to ask them for food to carry with him, but his pride wouldn't permit it. "They saw my pale and haggard face and my weakness," he wrote in his journal, yet no one offered even a handful of flour. Nor had any of them seen the vanished Clough. The old hunter's disappearance was never explained.

Bruff camped that night in a cold and steady rain—"the most wretched night I ever knew." On April ninth he forded an icy creek, clambered up an embankment, and gazed out at the flat green expanse of the Sacramento Valley. He staggered a few miles farther and collapsed against a fallen oak beside the stream. He was so spent that he felt paralyzed. He closed his eyes.

The yapping of the dog woke him. Bruff blinked and saw a figure approaching. Could it be? He tried to get to his feet but his legs failed him. Was this a hallucination? No, by God, it was Poyle! Poyle was coming toward him, wearing a pack! His friend was heading into the hills to rescue him! Ten months and five days after crossing the Missouri River, Bruff had at last come to the end of the trail.

Poyle half carried him the final three hundred yards to a small ranch house occupied by a family named Davis. This was the same cabin that had rendered Alonzo Delano speechless seven months earlier. Bruff ate his fill and drank a toddy. His back was so sore that he couldn't sit in a chair so he sat on the floor instead, contentedly puffing his pipe. "Well," he said after a while, "I'm not dead yet."

ONE BY ONE the little caravans dropped down into the deep and narrow basin at the foot of Telescope Peak. They had dispersed into a half-dozen separate bands as they inched across the interminable desolation east of Death Valley. It was close to Christmas when the first wagons emerged from the dark canyons of the Funeral Mountains and rolled onto the powdery surface of the continent's lowest valley. Juliet Brier, the wife of the minister from Iowa City, Iowa, hobbled into the gray-white valley on Christmas Eve with her four-year-old son Kirke on her back.

"I was sick and weary and the hope of a good camping place was all that kept me up," she recalled later. Her husband had gone ahead to find water. "About midnight we came around a big rock and there was my husband at a small fire. 'Is this the camp?' I asked. 'No, it's six miles farther,' he said. I was ready to drop and Kirke was almost unconscious moaning for a drink. Mr. Brier took him on his back and hastened to camp. It was 3 o'clock Christmas morning when we reached the springs. . . . Nobody spoke very much."

The Briers and their three sons were traveling with some of the Jayhawkers. Several other bands were scattered around the 154-mile-long valley on Christmas morning: a second Jayhawker detachment was camped a few miles to the northwest; a group of Mississippians and their slaves were somewhere on the west side of the valley; the Bennett and Arcane families and their four children were still laboring through the Funeral range with the watchful William Manly scouting in front of them; not far away was a small party of Germans.

Manly reached the Brier camp at dusk on Christmas Day. He was astonished to find the Reverend Brier lecturing his sons on education. Manly regarded the reverend as a talker and not a worker. His wife was something else. "She was the one who put the packs on the oxen," he wrote, "she it was who took them off at night, built the fires, cooked the food [and] helped the children." Gritty Juliet Brier was in fact the best example of a phenomenon cited repeatedly in 1849: the women were tougher than the men. Bayard Taylor observed that forty-niner women surpassed their men in both energy and endurance. Overland traveler Ansel McCall told of a Boston woman he met on the Humboldt River who had become utterly disgusted with male nervousness about Indians. Manly was convinced that the soft-handed Reverend Brier and his boys owed their lives to Juliet.

A few days after Christmas the Jayhawkers learned from their scouts that the Panamint range, which blocked their passage west, was impassable for wagons. They burned their wagons for firewood and packed their gear on the oxen. The Briers followed the lead party up a rugged canyon to five-thousand-foot-high Towne's Pass and across the ridge to Panamint

Valley, another strip of waterless desolation. Manly and his little band meanwhile probed the Panamints in a vain search for an easier way out.

The best exit lay to the south, where the mountains eventually gave way and permitted access to the trail to Los Angeles, but there was no way for them to know that. Manly, scouting just ahead of the Bennett and Arcane wagons, hiked up a canyon near the base of Telescope Peak until he was stopped by a high rock wall. Two starving oxen gave out before the Bennetts and Arcanes got back to a small spring they had found on the western edge of the valley.

They discussed their dilemma that night. Their provisions were all but gone; the only remaining food was the oxen. Stragglers from other groups had attached themselves to Manly's band until they numbered more than twenty. Asahel Bennett proposed that two of their strongest men load their knapsacks with dried ox meat and hike west until they came to a settlement where they could obtain supplies. The others would remain at the spring. Manly and Tennessean John Rogers were chosen for the rescue mission.

It was probably mid-January when the two men set out; Manly had lost track of dates. In their ignorance they estimated that the round trip to the nearest ranch would take fifteen days, but as they stared west from the Panamint ridge they knew they had underestimated the distance: mountains cluttered the horizon as far west as they could see. Near the summit of the next range they found the body of a man who had traveled with them two weeks earlier.

They soon caught up with a party of Jayhawkers camped near a water hole. These men told them that the Briers, traveling alone, were some distance behind them. Manly and Rogers stayed the night and moved on in the morning, scanning the horizon for signs of water. They descended into a canyon where they squeezed through an aperture barely wide enough for a man, then skirted a dry lake. A line of snow-mantled mountains slanted off to the south. On their tenth day out the country finally softened: a gorgeous little brook glistened at the bottom of a broad ravine; quail rustled in the streamside brush. Two days later they crested a ridge and looked down on Paradise: "before us was a beautiful meadow of a thousand acres, green as a thick carpet of grass could make it and shaded with oaks"; thousands of cattle grazed on the lush greensward.

They tried to buy provisions from a Mexican rancher at the first house they came to, but they couldn't make themselves understood. An American directed them to the nearby Mission San Fernando, and in a few days they acquired two saddle horses, a pack horse, and a mule. The Californios helped them load their pack animals with flour, beans, wheat, and dried meat. A Mexican woman, hearing that they had left four children in the desert, tucked four oranges in their packs as they prepared to head back.

Their trip had already consumed more than the fifteen allotted days, but now they were mounted. They also knew where the water holes were, which saved the time it took to find them. They feared the Bennetts and Arcanes might have given up and started out on their own; Indians might have seen their vulnerability and attacked.

Their horses weakened rapidly as they moved across the barren terrain. One horse died in the ascent of a canyon wall. As they neared the west slope of the Panamints they found the grave of a man named Isham; the Jayhawkers they had met on their trek out had told them that he died of thirst. At least five of the forty-niners who chose this shortcut forfeited their lives for their mistake: one Jayhawker fell dead after he drank too much of the first good water he had tasted in weeks; another man was shot by his companions after he broke his leg.

At last only the Panamint range stood between Manly and the forlorn little band in Death Valley. Sharp rocks sliced through their thin moccasins and slashed their feet. The two remaining horses balked at a rocky incline on the eastern slope and they had to leave them. They divided the precious sacks of food between their own knapsacks and the back of the sure-footed little mule. At one point they built a ramp of rocks to get the mule up a precipice and then coaxed her across a four-inch-wide ledge over a chasm fifty feet deep.

They found another body on the scramble down to the valley: this was a man named Culverwell, who had been with the Bennetts and Arcanes when they left them twenty-six days earlier. He lay on his back with a small canteen by his side. Culverwell, who came from Washington, had begun the overland trip as a member of J. Goldsborough Bruff's Washington City company.

Manly wondered if this was an ominous sign: were all of them dead? Finally the wagons came in sight. It was early afternoon but strangely still. They moved closer, keeping low in case there were Indians nearby. "One hundred yards now to the wagons and still no sign of life and no positive sign of death, though we looked carefully for both," Manly wrote. He fired a shot in the air. "Still as death and not a move for a moment, and then as if by magic a man came out from under a wagon and stood up looking all around, for he did not see us. Then he threw up his arms high over his head and shouted, 'The boys have come! The boys have come!' Then other bare heads appeared, and Mr. Bennett and wife and Mr. Arcane came toward us as fast as ever they could. . . . Our hearts were first in our mouths, then the blood all went away and left us almost fainting. . . . Bennett and Arcane caught us in their arms and embraced us with all their strength and Mrs. Bennett fell down on her knees and clung to me like a maniac." Manly and Rogers described their adventures and answered their friends' excited questions until after midnight.

Only the Bennetts and Arcanes remained in Death Valley; the others had moved off soon after Manly left. Surprisingly, they had managed to save four oxen. With the women and children mounted on the oxen, Manly and Rogers guided the two families out of the valley by the same route they had taken. They paused atop the ridge for a final look at the scene of their anguish—"a corner of the earth so dreary," Manly wrote, "that it requires an exercise of strongest faith to believe that the great Creator ever smiled upon it." Nineteen days later they reached the welcome little brook and, soon afterward, the Eden-like meadow where thousands of cattle grazed.

It was now early March of 1850. The Brier family and the Jayhawkers had emerged from the desert at this same point, the Del Valle ranch near present-day Newhall, more than a month earlier. The Mississippians, traveling northwest from the Panamints to Owens Lake and the San Joaquin Valley, had turned up at Agua Fria in the southern mines late in January. Manly and Rogers, lacking money to get to the mines, pushed on to the village of Los Angeles to hunt work. They wandered into the parlor of a boardinghouse and sat down. A few moments later the well-dressed proprietor appeared. It was the Reverend James Brier.

SAN FRANCISCO in the winter of 1849–50 "was like the scene of a great battle," journalist Frank Soulé wrote. "There were victorious warriors braving and flaunting on all sides, while hope swelled the breast of every unwounded soldier. But unheeded amid the crash and confusion of the strife lay the wounded and dying, who had failed or been suddenly struck down in the melee. . . ."

Bayard Taylor was stunned by the city's transformation. In August he had found "a scattering town of tents and canvas houses with a show of frame buildings on one or two streets"; in December he beheld "an actual metropolis" with street after street of fine buildings. Then the town huddled around the wind-rippled cove in San Francisco Bay; now it marched up the hillsides and chased seagulls along the shoreline. True, the mud on Montgomery Street was as much as four feet deep in this soggy season, and the tobacco crates used for sidewalks were sometimes completely submerged. "This street is impassable, not even jackassable," said a sign at the corner of Clay and Kearny streets. True also that the debris of commerce—unwanted boxes of calico, shoes, razors, and other nonessentials—had a tendency to collect in mud-spattered neglect near the clamorous waterfront, and some of Taylor's admired buildings—"gaudy with verandas and balconies"—looked rather like lopsided shanties with doors. Perhaps the man from the New York *Evening Post* was suffering some unidentified indisposition when he described the city's rambunctious plutocrats as so many "madmen . . . looking wondrously dirty and out at elbows for men of such magnificent pretensions." Or perhaps he was a Tory snob; Taylor liked the hearty, plainspoken, if somewhat rank, society of masculine San Francisco; it was a fellowship "infinitely preferable" to the niceties and refinements of that older coast; these bravos reminded him of Vikings "who exulted in their very passions."

But now it was time for Taylor to pack his passions and go home. He was eager to get back to New York to begin work on his book. A week before Christmas he climbed aboard a minimally seaworthy Peruvian brig with the intention of sailing to Mazatlán, but on Christmas Eve the vessel was still bobbing at anchor in the bay, immobilized by a combination of storms, mutinous crewmen, and timidity. The delay gave Taylor an excellent vantage for the first of the city's disastrous fires, which broke out on Christmas Eve.

Peering through the mist at daybreak, Taylor saw a spark and then a spiral of flame. "In fifteen minutes it had risen into a broad, flickering column, making all the shore, the misty air and the water ruddy as with another sunrise. . . . Above the clang of gongs and the cries of the populace I could hear the crackling of blazing timbers and the smothered sound of falling roofs." Taylor climbed into the ship's rigging. "As the flames leaped upon a new dwelling there was a sudden whirl of their waving volumes, an embracing of the frail walls in their relentless clasp" and then "a jet of fire, steady and intense at first but surging off into spiral folds and streamers as the timbers were parted and fell." The fire burned unimpeded for some time before a number of houses were blown up to check its progress. The *Pacific News* estimated the damage at $1 million. No deaths were reported. Reconstruction began before the ashes had cooled. "One calamity more or less seems to make no difference to these Californians," wrote Ernest de Massey, a thirty-seven-year-old French nobleman who had just landed in town.

Taylor's fragile craft made a feeble pass at sailing down the coast only to hurry back to the city the next day with a leak. Taylor hastened ashore to survey the damage: the Parker House, Denison's Exchange, and most of the hotels and gambling houses on two sides of Portsmouth Square were gone. He learned that hundreds of spectators had refused to help fight the fire unless they were paid. Frames of new buildings were already going up; "all over the burnt space sounded one incessant tumult of hammers, axes, and saws."

On New Year's Eve he boarded the steamer *Oregon*, which was Panama-bound with $2 million in gold and a quorum of politicians aboard. Colonel John Frémont and William Gwin, the newly elected U.S. senators from this impatient would-be state, were on board along with the congressmen-elect and Thomas Butler King, President Taylor's special envoy to El Dorado. Major D. H. Rucker, leader of the mountain relief expedition, boarded the ship in Monterey with Lieutenant William Tecumseh Sherman. Sherman was shepherding two young Mexican boys to Washington, where they were to enroll in Georgetown College.

SAN FRANCISCANS craved any reminder of home. The arrival of a shipment of bonnets during the winter set off a stampede. Hundreds of men rushed to the wharf for a look. The Presbyterian preacher Albert Williams protested when a woman with a bawling baby got up to leave during his sermon; the infant's cry spoke to the congregation more eloquently than any sermon. When Eliza Farnham's mercy ship sailed into port in December with only three potential wives aboard, the city foundered in frustration and gloom. "I verily believe," one San Franciscan wrote, "that there was more drunkenness, more gambling, more fighting, and more of everything that was bad that night" than ever before.

Mrs. Farnham herself, the onetime matron of Sing Sing, took a disapproving look around and congratulated herself on her failure. "There is little in the condition of California society up to this date," she declared, "to engage the higher orders of female intelligence." Women here had to endure loneliness, menial labor, and an atmosphere of moral wretchedness. Male conversation was limited to mining and money. She asked one man if he had read *The Last of the Mohicans*. He replied that he had missed that one, but he had been "very much pleased with the First."

Prostitution was one of the city's leading growth industries. The first whores to arrive had come from South America and France—"outcast damsels," the historian Bancroft called them, whose beauty and virginity were "renewable at pleasure"—but in February of 1850 the *Pacific News* reported that more than two hundred new recruits had landed on a ship from Sydney. The most elegant house in town was run by a madam known as the Countess. Her invitational soirées paired the town's political and business leaders with her polite and accomplished girls for a diverting evening of supper, music, conversation, and sex; the toll was six ounces plus tips. The less affluent could visit a Chinese woman named Ah Toy at her shack in an alley off Clay Street. The "Model Artist Exhibition and Tableaux," which displayed undraped women in a variety of artful positions, opened to a somewhat tepid reception in March.

Ships from Panama and the East continued to disgorge passengers into the damp gray city through the winter. The Cape Horn voyagers now arriving had departed the East in the summer, which suggested that they were slow starters. Enos Christman, a thin, dreamy-eyed, twenty-year-old printer's apprentice from West Chester, Pennsylvania, had hesitated for reasons of love and money. The first was resolved when he convinced his fiancée, Ellen Apple, that he would bring home a stake for their wedding. The second was taken care of when his boss, the publisher of the village paper, agreed to subsidize his trip in exchange for half his earnings. He sailed into San Francisco Bay on the *Europe* on February 9.

Christman hurried to the post office and found letters from both Ellen and his friend Peebles Prizer. Romance was on their minds. Prizer sounded envious: the girls in town, he wrote, "appear to be waiting for you California boys." Ellen said she was trying to avoid social entanglements: "I do not wish a gentleman to gallant me about if I can possibly get out of it." She sincerely hoped that Enos would soon tire of his adventure.

Enos pitched his tent in Happy Valley. He hunted along the bay shore and took in a horse race at Mission Dolores. It seemed to him that about a third of the dwellings in town were either hotels or gambling houses. He saw the boxer Yankee Sullivan, who had just turned up in San Francisco. One day he found a body near his tent—"no unusual occurrence," he noted.

Early in March he set out for the southern mines. "Whatever happens," he wrote Ellen, "I can never forget the image that has been present in my mind's eye for so long." He bade her "a sad adieu, a long farewell," and told her to go ahead and have a good time.

THE NORTH AMERICAN winter was the healthy season in Panama. The weather was dry. An American who could suppress his impatience long enough could enjoy the pastel sunsets, the palms bulging out of the tropical dusk, the soft evenings that descended like a satin shawl. Americans had made a halfhearted attempt to transform the carefree Isthmian ambience with Yankee enterprise, but the prospects were not encouraging. A projected route for an American-financed railroad had been surveyed, but construction would not begin for another nine months. Chugging little river steamers now carried travelers part of the way from Chagres to the riverhead villages, but they were unable to get beyond the upstream rapids. No amount of high-pitched complaining by American females could dissuade native boatmen from shedding their loincloths and diving into the Chagres River when the impulse seized them. A "sleeping shed" for women had been built along the river, but it was more difficult than ever to get a meal. New York–bound traveler A. C. Ferris had only one dish—an egg of uncertain parentage—between Panama City and Chagres. At Chagres he joined hundreds of other hungry Yanks at a long table for a feast of mackerel, bread, and coffee.

Traffic on the Isthmus was heavy in both directions. The American-owned *Panama Echo* reported on March 9 that about a thousand Americans were awaiting the overdue steamers *Tennessee* and *Sarah Sands* for California. A dozen windjammers offered passenger service between Panama and San Francisco. The *Tennessee* dropped anchor off Panama City on March 12. The happy crowds ashore greeted her with a song: "Away down in Tennessee, a-li, e-li, o-li, u-li, eee . . ."

The gold frenzy still gripped the East. The New York *Herald* commented during the winter that there "appears to be no letup in the tide of emigration" to California. Newspapers ran every item about the gold coast they could find. Dozens of streamlined new clipper ships were being built to hasten cargo shipments to the Pacific. In an office on Wall Street a short, bull-necked young man with bright eyes and a winning smile was recruiting men for a new expedition which sounded particularly intriguing: French's Express Passenger Train.

Parker H. French was a lawyer, a politician, and a gifted snake-oil salesman. The attractive broadside advertisements he circulated in Manhattan during the winter promised a "comfortable and easy" ride across Texas and the Gila River route in a spring coach wagon for a modest $250 per passenger. The trip would take no more than sixty days, with a refund of $5 a man for each additional day. French's ad promised large tents, portable stoves, an escort of Texas Rangers, and even two howitzers to intimidate any foolishly aggressive Comanches or Apaches. "To the hardy and adventurous of whatever nation, but especially to the excitement-loving people of our own country," he wrote, "this route has charms that no other possesses." He pointed out one charm not generally known, then or ever: there was gold on the Gila River too.

French's timing was fortuitous: eastern readers were not yet aware of the suffering experienced by Audubon and other Gila Trail travelers in late 1849. His pitch proved irresistible. A smitten bookkeeping student named Michael Baldridge believed it offered "in happy combination novelty, romance, and adventure with bushels of gold lying about loose in the distance." Baldridge was among the thousands of young men who had passed up the first rush the preceding winter and had cursed themselves for their timidity ever since. He and forty-eight others signed on with French as "enlisted men" who would work their way across for a discount fare of $100; another 132 men paid $250 in advance to ride in the six-mule coaches as passengers; French had $38,000 in hand by April. The expedition would sail for New Orleans in May.

DISENCHANTED ex-Californians were meanwhile returning east at a steadily increasing tempo. Young Bill Johnston of Pittsburgh, like most of them, chose the Isthmus as the quickest route. Johnston came home in February and discovered to his surprise and delight that he was a celebrity. "For the first and only time of my life I was a lion," he wrote. "Marvelous was the fact that I had been to . . . California, among the first to go and the first to return." He could enjoy, if only for one brief season, the bittersweet taste of fame. He was playing the lion at a large party when the realization suddenly came to him that "my mane was being stroked."

XII

MUSTER OF STRANGERS

A ROAD SCENE IN CALIFORNIA

THE NOISE rose from the banks of the river and from the low, flat gravel bar that bulged into the glistening water at the bottom of a brush-covered hillside: the rhythmic rumble of gravel clattering through a hundred wood-and-metal rockers, the clink of tools against rock, the deep roar of the stream. The din of the gold camp echoed down the canyon like the muffled thunder of crashing ninepins that Rip Van Winkle heard.

High-booted men in month-old beards squatted beside their cradlelike gold washers at the river's edge and gently rocked them; tiny grains of placer gold gleamed from behind the riffle bars on the floor of the rockers. Some men worked in deep pits, hacking at the rocky soil with pick and shovel. Others carried buckets of dirt between their claims and the rockers, which were set up by the river to assure a constant water supply. A few men, felled by fever or scurvy or dysentery, squirmed restlessly on their blankets. Makeshift canvas tents and brush shelters—little lean-tos covered with leafy branches and sticks and scrap wood—were scattered amid the trees at the base of canyon walls so steep that they barred the morning and evening sun. Two larger tents—the store and the combination saloon–gambling house—sat in a clearing several hundred yards downstream. A dozen idlers relaxed on a pine log in front of the saloon.

The diggers went to work as early as the dawdling sun permitted. Campfires crackled into life at first light. Breakfast was coffee and a piece of hard bread or biscuit, perhaps a flapjack. If a man could stay dry the morning was a good time to work, especially the hours before the sun exploded over the rim of the canyon. They usually mined in groups of three or four, taking turns digging, lugging the dirt to the river and working the rocker. Gold digging was a formidable test of grit: swinging a pick or prying boulders loose with a shovel was punishing work. The muscles tightened, cramped, and finally sagged. This was a career for the young; a miner past forty was a curiosity.

In early spring it was possible to work through the day, but as the season advanced it was not; in most camps the miners halted for several hours at midday and resumed in late afternoon. In a day a band of three miners—"pards," they called themselves—might wash out eighty to a hundred pails of dirt. Depending on the richness of the area and their particular claim, their take—"wages," to them—would probably fall between $5 and $15 per man.

The sublime mountain twilight stole in and out of the canyon like a phantom. There were no lingering pastel sunsets in this country; night closed on the camp with the crisp finality of a slamming parlor door. Campfires were rekindled, the coffee brewed once more. The pan that had washed out paydirt all day became a skillet for frying pickled pork. The more fortunate might have a potato or a plate of beans with their meat. An evening breeze whined through the pine needles and stirred the woodsmoke. Pipes and rumors—"I hear tell there's *pound diggin's* on the Middle Fork"—were fired up after supper. A chorus of coyotes commenced their nightly serenade. A few men gathered up their dust and drifted off to the gambling tent to watch it evaporate. Most were too tired for anything but the dream-teased slumber of the pilgrim.

It was here, finally, here on the pine-scented banks of the Feather or Yuba or American, here in the dun-colored canyons of the Tuolumne and Stanislaus and Calaveras, that their race was done. The dreams and plans and travail, the months of ragged anxiety and boredom, the brushes with death and the awful loneliness had ended here on the damp earth of a California canyon as steep as a silo. They had deserted the ordered precincts of home for this tattered village of gold-hungry men, three thousand miles from mother and a hundred miles from law. Their reward was ten dollars a day and all the rumors they could swallow. It was a life of brandy, monte, blackjack, and whores, of the smell of fear and the taste of failure, of nettlesome memories of the family back home, of long days of toil and short nights of blessed relief.

Selfishness pervaded the mines: a man came here to grab and be gone; he was constantly surrounded, as a young Missourian wrote his father, "by strangers who care nothing for him, nor he for them." If the diggings ran dry it was easy enough to pack up and move on to the place of the moment. There was always a chance; it had happened, God knows, right next to him, right across the stream. *Why not me?*

And so he moved, and moved again: "He goes on to his new diggings," the man from Missouri explained, "hunts another tree to shield him from the sun, deposits his load and recruits his wasted store of plunder at a high price and goes to work as before, with probably the same success. He takes the diarrhea, as nearly everyone does, gets well in three or four weeks, or well enough to do half work, and takes it again. Or else he dies and is buried somewhere close by, by someone who don't know his name."

THE RIVERS in the northern mines, freighted with snowmelt from the severe winter just past, ran high through most of the spring of 1850. The lowlands along the Sacramento and American, the scene of the worst flooding in January, were swamped again in March. Several days of heavy rain in mid-April threatened the spongy valley once more. A miner writing to the *Alta California* reported that the American River was as high in May as it had been in January. High water brought frustration: the best diggings were often in the shallows near the riverbanks and the low ground on the banks themselves, most of which now lay under several feet of water.

But the sodden winter contributed radiant dividends as well. The foothills blazed with brilliantly hued flowers. "It seems as if every variety were here," wrote an enchanted John Banks, an Ohio farmer, "from the small flower just seen in the grass to the large scarlet that flaunts before the sun. All nature looked gay."

The inaugural issue of the triweekly Sacramento *Transcript* published a highly dubious report in April that pound diggings—dirt that yielded a pound of gold a day—had been discovered at Murderers Bar on the

Middle Fork of the American. Hundreds of men promptly lit out from the valley and mushed upriver. John Banks was already there. The crowd was "almost one continuous stream of men," he wrote. "Every place is snatched up in a moment." But all they could do was record their claims and pace impatiently. "All are in wild excitement," he noted in early May, "or calmly waiting for the water to fall that they may jump and catch the gold."

Diggings along the summer-dry washes and smaller streams were a safer prospect this spring. The miners at a camp called Deer Creek Dry Diggings were doing so well that they organized a town and found a family man to serve as alcalde. The new town, christened Nevada City, would soon become one of the richest and wildest in the gold country. The amorous Henry Crandall of Greenwich, New York, still pouring his heart into letters to his fiancée Mary Mills, landed in Nevada City in April, and immediately began worrying that his experiences there might render him unfit for Mary's devotion. Eschewing details, he wondered if California was changing his personality. He also arrived at the conclusion that success smiled exclusively on drunkards, idlers, and fools.

Hangtown, meanwhile, had fallen on such sorry times that it was beginning to look ghostly. The serene contentment of the days when "the happiest set of men on earth" labored there had yielded to a growing conviction that Hangtown's placer was played out. The *Transcript* stemmed any further defection with a mid-April dispatch claiming that a dry "sink" between two ravines was paying at the rate of a pound a day per man. Before long there would be even more delights in Hangtown:

> *Hangtown gals are plump and rosy*
> *Hair in ringlets mighty cozy*
> *Painted cheeks and gassy bonnets*
> *Touch them and they'll sting like hornets.*
> *Hangtown gals are lovely creatures*
> *Think they'll marry Mormon preachers*
> *Heads thrown back to show their features*
> *Ha, ha, ha, Hangtown gals!* . . .

The most popular destination at the moment, however, was the Trinity mines, north of the Sacramento Valley near the Oregon border. Ernest de Massey, an erudite French nobleman who had passed an unhappy winter in San Francisco, resolved to try the Trinity as soon as weather permitted.

"It is all the rage at the present," he noted in his journal. The ever helpful *Transcript* chimed in with the intelligence that the six hundred diggers at Big Bar on the Trinity River were making $25 to $50 worth of dust a day.

There were hints this spring, especially in the southern mines, that the halcyon days of 1848 and 1849 were finished. The decline was inevitable: more and more men were chipping away at a steadily decreasing lode; the best-known deposits were already exhausted; the rookie miners of 1850 would find skimpier pickings. The Reverend Daniel Woods of Philadelphia and the Tuolumne River averaged less than six cents a day during one particularly barren week. John Audubon, roaming through the southern diggings in April, learned that the average daily take had receded from an ounce in 1849 to a half-ounce in 1850. Audubon carried his sketch pad everywhere, but his enchantment with California scenery kept colliding with his contempt for California morality. "California will for the present lower the moral tone of all who come here," he declared. He would not risk it much longer himself.

Prices, especially in the more isolated camps, remained high. John Banks rented a crosscut saw and a broadax for $2 a day apiece. A pair of socks set him back $1.50. Cheese and raisins were $1.50 a pound on the Middle Fork, potatoes and dried apples $1. Recognizing that mail was the most precious commodity in the mines, enterprising "expressmen" now collected letters at the San Francisco and Sacramento post offices and delivered them to the camps at $2 or $2.50 per letter. Hotel keeping was even more lucrative. Even with expenses of more than $2,000 a month, the manager of the largest hotel in Marysville calculated that he could clear from $15,000 to $20,000 in six months.

The heterogeneous population in the mines was a revelation to most American miners; few had been aware of the yeasty variety that their own nation offered. Inevitably they responded by stereotyping each other and creating stock regional characters. The New England Yankee, for example, was viewed by his countrymen as shrewd, industrious, and cheap. Southerners—"the Chivalry" to the rest—were generous but quarrelsome, honorable but indolent. The men from the frontier West—Missouri and Illinois and Indiana—were thought to be adventurous and competent but crude. One story told of a Yankee and a westerner in the lively little camp of Rough and Ready. The westerner wanted to sell his claim, a piece of ground widely believed to be rich. The Yankee offered a proposition: he would work the claim; if he took out more than $200 the gold would belong to the owner; if he got less than $200 the profit would be his. The owner, certain that the claim was worth more than $200, agreed. The Yankee put it in writing.

By noon the next day the New Englander had removed $180 in dust. He set down his pick, walked over to the owner, and announced that he was quitting. The westerner fumed that he had barely begun, but the Yankee was firm. He had honored his agreement, he explained, and the owner could do as he wished with the claim. The Yankee was encouraged to leave town soon afterward.

Living in a society without a conventional pecking order, California miners invented their own informal equivalent. An obviously well-educated man was called Doctor or Professor. An individual with visible leadership ability was generally given a commission: he was identified as Captain, Major, or even Colonel. The Scotsman William Downie, discoverer of the fabulous diggings at the forks of the Yuba River, found himself a major by common consent at about the same time that the settlement he pioneered was named Downieville. Miners had little interest in each other's last names. They preferred descriptive nicknames, rather like Indian names. Frank ("Doctor Frank") Lecouvrer, a Prussian-born civil engineer, met at least six men named Johnny at Long Bar on the Yuba: Long Johnny, Little Johnny, Red Johnny and Blue Johnny (for the color of their shirts), Swedish Johnny and Johnny Snakes (who drank too much).

Judgments based on appearance were unwise. A bearded, tattered, and generally unkempt miner turned up one day in the lobby of the Tremont House in Marysville. Depositing his gold dust at the desk, he eyed a piano which the hotel had recently acquired. Oblivious to the snickers from the lobby idlers, he sat down and played a flawless rendition of a favorite melody of the day called "Sweet Home." For an encore he launched into "Katy Darling," but he stopped abruptly when he realized he had attracted a crowd. "He caught up his old, greasy hat," a witness reported, "and vamoosed."

Uneasy in the absence of some form of government, the diligent democrats in the camps called mass meetings, elected alcaldes, and established rudimentary civil and criminal codes. John Banks walked four miles along a perilous ridge to attend a gathering of the Middle Fork diggers in May. He was surprised to see that "several men of intelligent appearance were loud in praise of mob law as more expeditious and economical." Banks joined the majority in endorsing the more tedious jury system instead. Violent crimes, often precipitated by gambling arguments, were gradually becoming more commonplace. Lynchings, however, were still surprisingly rare: the first reported 1850 lynching did not occur until the fall.

THE TOWN-BOUND miners, restive after the damp and dreary winter, were poised and ready to rush in the spring of 1850. The first major discovery of the new season occurred in an oak-shaded gulch about three miles north of Sonora. The site had once been a Miwok Indian village.

Five Yankees tried the gravel in the gulch in late March and were astounded to find that it paid eight to ten ounces a day per man. They dug furiously, knowing that the news was bound to escape. Another prospector happened by after a week; he took out two and a half pounds ($640) in his first day. They named the camp Hildreth's Diggings, after a member of their group.

Word of the strike skittered through Sonora and the dozens of little camps on the nearby Tuolumne and Stanislaus rivers and along Carson and Angel creeks, then spread to Stockton, Coloma, Hangtown, and Sacramento. The ensuing boom was phenomenal, even by California standards. In another week—two weeks after the original find—there were more than three thousand men camped along the gulch. Monte bankers rolled into camp by the score, along with merchants and bartenders and boardinghouse keepers. Mexicans opened fandango houses and filled them with black-haired "percentage girls." Miners' tools and tents lined the gulch for more than a mile.

On April 29, four weeks and two days after Hildreth and his crew had first seen color, the citizens gathered to name the town. They decided on Columbia. At a second meeting a few days later they elected an alcalde and drew up rules. One regulation reflected Columbia's main liability— a shortage of water: heaps of gold-bearing earth awaiting the winter rains would be considered private property. Another rule stated that "none but Americans, or Europeans who intend to become citizens, shall be allowed to mine in this district."

In June the men in the northern mines stampeded. The spark was an electrifying rumor about a lake of gold with walnut-sized nuggets on its shore. The lake was said to be high in the mountains near the headwaters of the Feather River, at the bottom of a gorge so steep that the lake was visible only from the adjacent peak. It sounded suspiciously like the demon's dwelling place that the Yalesumni Indians had once described to

John Sutter. But the miners thought that it might be the fountainhead they had dreamed about. They had noticed that gold became coarser as they ascended the rivers, and that the ore was sometimes packed together in little pockets. The source had to be higher, near the crest of the Sierras, perhaps in this very lake.

The Gold Lake story apparently originated with a man named Stoddard in Marysville. The newspapers characterized him as "a gentleman of the first respectability." The miners reacted immediately. "In a year's experience of local excitement from the same cause," the Sacramento *Placer Times* said, "we have seen none equal to that which prevails [now]." The *Transcript* leaped aboard with a report that the Indians in the vicinity used golden fishhooks and arrowheads. A man had purportedly lassoed a gold rock on the lake bottom and spent three days trying to haul it in. Stoddard said he had been driven from the lake by hostile Indians. In a matter of hours he enlisted several dozen men in an expedition to the high country. A second party moved out from Nevada City soon afterward. Hundreds and eventually thousands of prospectors followed.

Stoddard led them past the blooming village of Downieville and onto the snow-covered west face of the high Sierras. A young miner named Luther Schaeffer was with a party tracking Stoddard's band. After about a week he met the Stoddard group coming back. They told him they had been halted by snow. The subsequent accounts by men in Stoddard's company said that he had led them to a lake but its shores were bereft of gold. He protested that he was lost. Some men in the expedition proposed lynching him on the spot, while others argued that he was deranged. While Stoddard plodded back to Marysville, hundreds of disconsolate veterans of the Gold Lake hunt fanned out to search for other likely sites. One group struck rich dirt at Nelson Creek, a tributary of the Feather's Middle Fork. Another opened the productive diggings at Rich Bar on the North Fork of the Feather.

Practically everyone in California heard about the elusive lake. Alonzo Delano watched the ragtag remnants of the Stoddard band pass his store on the Feather River above Marysville. John Banks resisted the temptation to hike across the divide from his camp on the American. William Manly, the savior of the Death Valley emigrants, hurried north from the Tuolumne to join the hunt. He learned the melancholy truth at Hangtown. Manly had ridden from Los Angeles to San Jose on horseback and then prospected in the southern mines with scant success.

The Gold Lake tale even reached J. Goldsborough Bruff. "A rumored discovery of immense deposits of gold around a lake," he noted in his journal in June. Still too "tottering weak" to travel, Bruff passed the spring at Peter Lassen's Sacramento Valley ranch. His only foray out of the valley was a trip back to the hillside clearing where he had suffered through the winter. He was disgusted to find that men searching for cached goods—"two-legged wolves"—had disturbed the grave of the little boy who had shared his tent.

Bruff occupied himself by surveying and laying out a town that Lassen was promoting on his property. He pitched his tent under an oak tree and rigged a wagon board as a table. Inevitably he and Lassen clashed; the proud, perfectionist West Pointer and the easygoing, roughhewn frontiersman were a mismatch from the beginning. "My old friend is so very perverse and interferes with the survey so much that I shall have to leave it," he grumbled. A few weeks later he took a job tending Lassen's store.

Bruff accumulated information and impressions with his habitual thoroughness. Four men just back from the Trinity told him that the diggings there were crowded, expensive, and unremunerative. A band of prospectors bound for Gold Lake passed through; Bruff had an impulse to join them, though he suspected that the rumors were spread by "catchpenny" traders and speculators. On June 30 he was amazed to see two men ride down from the mountains on exhausted mules—the vanguard of the 1850 overland migration. Bruff the old trail boss clucked at their mistakes: they had started too early, their supplies were inadequate, several had discarded their weapons. As a result they were easy prey for the Pit River Indians, who had killed several of their party and stolen their animals. The two men had ridden ahead to obtain food for their starving comrades.

Unaware that Gold Lake had already been exposed as a chimera, Lassen set out in early July to find it. Bruff, who had not yet panned his first grain of gold, decided to go along. "I do not believe the story," he wrote in his journal, "but . . . we may be so fortunate as to find a rich gold place if not a Gold Lake." Poky as ever, he moved off four days behind Lassen.

FOR A MAN like Ernest de Massey, thirty-eight-year-old scion of an aristocratic French family, the gold rush presented a chance to investigate an exotic corner of the uncivilized world while simultaneously gilding the family fortune. Massey fancied himself a gentleman-explorer in the nineteenth-century manner, but in fact he was a pampered dandy who had never learned to take care of himself. In common with many other Frenchmen, Massey was under the impression that California gold could be picked off the ground at one's leisure. This notion was so prevalent in France that one company arrived in the New World bearing rakes with which to gather the golden harvest. Their wives brought embroidered silk stools on which they might lounge while plucking the nuggets with delicate silver tongs.

Accompanied by his "inherently worthless" servant Pidaucet, Massey set sail from San Francisco in April for the Trinity mines. He was irritated almost immediately: the captain drank all night, the food was salty, Pidaucet was a clod. It was worse after they landed at the raw village of Trinidad: a fierce wind blew off the ocean, the local Indians were sly and larcenous. Massey suffered acutely from thirst on his first day of hiking through the thickly forested hills en route to the Trinity River.

The trek to the mines at Big Bar took almost a month. Massey's mood vacillated between impatience and despair. Pidaucet, "with his usual negligence," lost their ammunition. They joined a caravan bound for the mines but impetuously pushed ahead, only to wander off the trail. They lived for several days on herbs and roots and two snakes they killed. Massey thought he had reached "the most critical moment in my life" when he became separated from the others and found thirty Indians following him, but they left him alone.

Big Bar was a settlement of thirty or forty tents and shacks on a ledge above a wide bar in the Trinity River. The gold rested in crevices in the bedrock below the gravel surface. Massey ordered Pidaucet to build a rocker and a shack. On their first day they dug out $8 worth and spent $7 on food. He raged at the impudent Pidaucet for refusing his command to catch them some fish. When Pidaucet injured his wrist Massey was forced to hire himself out to an American ("boorish in the extreme") for $4 a day plus food. "I have descended all the rungs of the social ladder in a year," he lamented. He was fired after three days of "irksome" labor—toting pails of sand. Like most Frenchmen in the mines, Massey spoke no English.

He joined a group heading north to the Salmon River. He fell ill with chills and cramps, but an American revived him with a dose of brandy. By this time he had scaled down his objectives: "I shall be well satisfied if I can only save the family reputation and fortune." There were moments when even that seemed impossible; he meditated on suicide—"Why not die here as well as some other place? And why tomorrow and not today?" He earned barely enough to sustain himself; the labor was too difficult.

At last he gave up and trudged back down the trail to Trinidad to catch a ship for San Francisco, where he belonged. He had learned, among other things, that he was not the man of action he had imagined himself to be. Gold mining was immeasurably more romantic from a distance. He returned with "a large fund of philosophy, some energy, a gun, ammunition, a good blanket, some biscuits and about $60."

Shortly before he left the Trinity, Massey had been accosted by a man who identified himself as a tax collector. The man said that he was authorized to collect a $20 monthly "license fee" from all foreign miners, and empowered to arrest those who refused to pay. The new California legislature had in fact legitimized the pervasive nativist bigotry by enacting a tax on foreign miners in April. Massey fumed that the measure merely "gave certain jealous and ill-tempered Americans a pretext for picking a quarrel" with foreigners. It was his good fortune that he was working the Trinity mines, where the foreign population was relatively small and feelings were consequently less intense. The trouble came in Sonora and the southern diggings.

The official rationale for the tax, as expressed in a report by the California Senate finance committee, was that the lure of gold had filled California with "the worst population of the Mexican and South American states, New South Wales and the Southern Islands, to say nothing of the vast numbers from Europe." The tax was merely a "small bonus for the privilege of taking from our country the vast treasure to which they have no right." The unofficial rationale was the elimination of foreign competition: the $20 fee was prohibitive for thousands of miners who were barely getting by. The author of the bill was Senator Thomas Jefferson Green, a former Texas slaveowner who was otherwise celebrated for labeling this first California governing body "the legislature of a thousand drinks." Green anticipated that the tax would produce $200,000 a month in revenue. Governor Burnett signed it into law.

The appointed tax collectors reached the mining camps in May and June. Anonymous posters immediately appeared in the heavily foreign Sonora-Columbia district. "It is time to unite," one said. "Frenchmen, Chileans, Peruvians, Mexicans, there is the highest necessity for putting an end to the vexations of the Americans in California." The placard called for a meeting in Sonora "to guarantee security for us all."

The confrontation came on Sunday, May 19. Armed groups of foreigners gathered outside Sonora early in the day. By noon they numbered between three and five thousand. They sent a delegation into town, asking if the tax might be overruled by a higher authority. They said that they would be willing to pay $4 or $5, but that $20 was excessive. A scuffle broke out between the foreign contingent and some Americans, but there was no bloodshed.

The Americans sent hasty calls for help to the nearby camps of Sullivan's Creek, Jamestown, and Mormon Diggings. By evening more than five hundred armed men were in town. The Canadian-born merchant William Perkins, who agreed with the foreigners that the tax was oppressive, reported that the reinforcements "marched into town like disciplined soldiers." The foreigners quietly dispersed. "The only thing to be feared," Perkins wrote, "is the misguided zeal of the Americans, who . . . are incensed that the foreigners should presume to take the law into their own hands."

The American force was buttressed the next day by the arrival of more men from Wood's Creek, Murphy's, Carson Creek, and other camps. The Yankee vigilantes escorted the tax collector to Shaw's Diggings, where a few foreigners grudgingly paid the tax. Most had already decamped.

Perkins, who feared the economic impact of a sudden exodus on his Sonora dry-goods store, said that five hundred Mexicans left for home within the first few days. The populations of Sonora, Columbia, and other southern towns declined drastically. Merchants petitioned Governor Burnett, protesting that the tax would cost California far more than it netted. The tax was later reduced, repealed, and then revived at a lower rate, but the short-run damage was done: the majority of foreign miners quit the southern mines. One traveler saw them "scattered along the roads in every direction" like refugees before an army.

Persecution of California Indians, though lacking the formal sanction of the legislature, was even more severe. Most miners regarded the gentle and relatively backward California tribesmen as contemptible, subhuman nuisances, an opinion shared by the Taylor administration's special envoy to California, ex-Congressman Thomas Butler King. King described them in his report to the secretary of state as "degraded objects of filth and idleness" who were bound to disappear under the relentless pressure of the whites. In fact they were already well along the road to extinction. King saw the deserted remains of dozens of Indian villages in the foothills and mountain valleys.

Indians were decimated by the white man's diseases. They died from the effects of his whiskey. Hundreds were shot down by posses avenging real or imagined crimes. Many miners fired at Indians as readily as they would shoot a deer or a bear. The *Transcript* noted on May 9 that about twenty-five Indians, including several women and children, were killed in a raid on a village near the North Fork of the American. A miner wrote from the Yuba in April that seven whites and about eighty Indians had died in recent clashes. News of an even worse slaughter surfaced in the *Alta California* in late May. It was reported that a detachment of soldiers from Sonoma had systematically annihilated between two and three hundred Indians near Clear Lake.

This story, involving as it did the military, was serious enough to provoke a curious semidenial from Major General Persifor Smith, the commander in chief of the California forces. Smith wrote a letter denying that his troops had massacred an entire village. Outrages had been committed, he conceded, but by civilians and not soldiers. He clouded the issue further by stating that troops had indeed "attacked" and "punished" the defiant Clear Lake Indians.

A chain of events at the Colorado River ferry that spring showed how one unscrupulous white could precipitate an Indian war. The white man was John Glanton of San Antonio, the leader of a band of scalp hunters and desperadoes who had taken over the lucrative ferry trade by destroying the boats of the Yuma Indians. The Yuma chief offered to split the business with him, but Glanton's reaction was to beat the chief with a stick. One evening in April the Yumas waited until most of Glanton's men were drunk and then attacked, slaying Glanton and ten others. Governor Burnett, fearing further raids on emigrants traveling the Gila Trail, recruited a militia company to pursue the Yumas. The militiamen consumed a three-month supply of liquid and solid rations in a matter of days while galloping aggressively around the desert, but they failed to find a single Yuma.

Alonzo Delano, the long-nosed ex-Illinois storekeeper, was one of the few forty-niners who befriended the Indians. Delano had a store at a townsite he hoped to develop about twenty miles up the Feather River from Marysville. His closest neighbors were the Oleepa Indians, whose village began about sixty yards from his house. A tolerant man with a lively curiosity, he made it his "chief amusement" to cultivate their friendship and study their character.

He described the Oleepas as gentle, generous among themselves, and good-natured. He saw not a single quarrel in three months. When two boys entered his store together, Delano sometimes tested their generosity by giving one a cracker: "he would invariably break it in two and give half to his companion." The women gathered the acorns which were pounded into flour and baked to form their principal food. Their courtship rite was a kind of high-stakes hide-and-seek. The boy first asked the permission of the girl's parents. If it was granted, the girl would run into the woods and hide. If the boy found her two out of three times, "she is his without further ceremony." A girl who didn't want to marry could simply hide where she would not be found.

Delano came to trust the Oleepas completely. Once he told them that he was going to Sacramento and would be back in seven days, but he was delayed by illness and stayed away thirteen days. When he returned he found that all his provisions were gone. Suppressing his shock and anger, he went to the chief and explained why he had been gone longer than he anticipated. Then, after a pause, he asked about his goods. The chief "called several Indians together and gave them directions, and in 30 minutes every box, every sack of flour was piled up precisely as they had found them in my house, and even a hatchet and a dozen nails were returned to me unasked." The chief had moved Delano's stock to his own house for safekeeping.

Delano heard about a more typical example of Indian-white relations that same spring. Higher up the Feather a group of miners missed their oxen and accused the Indians of stealing them. A posse rode to the nearest *ranchería* and spied some bones, all the evidence they required. They surrounded the huts and fired on the Indians as they attempted to escape, killing fourteen. On their way back to their camp the avengers found their oxen grazing placidly in a remote gorge.

THE HANDSOME little steamer *Governor Dana* eased along the bank of the Feather River and tied up in front of a large frame-and-adobe house shaded by oaks and sycamores. The hundred revelers aboard, dressed in their summery best for this pleasure cruise in early June, cheered and waved from the railing as the band on the ship played "Hail Columbia." A cannon boomed a welcome from behind the house.

The lord of this 1,200-acre riverside manor stood on the bank and greeted the guests as they disembarked. His ruddy round face framed by silvering sidewhiskers, the host was elegantly turned out in a high-collared blue frock coat and his inevitable cane. John A. Sutter, buffeted but unbowed by the bedlam of California, was once again the baron of the Sacramento Valley.

In earlier years he had offered a roof and a welcome meal to the blistered emigrants who limped down from the mountains to his fort. Now he led his visitors to a spacious quadrangular courtyard where a long table was piled high with the spoils of his new prosperity—bread from his wheatfields, fruit and vegetables from his gardens, meat from his cattle and sheep. Sutter's gifts as a patient and innovative man of the soil, coupled with his long-delayed Sacramento real-estate profits, had restored his wealth and his confidence.

His guests could choose from a splendid selection of imported wines poured by attentive Indian servants. An American flag hung limp in the afternoon heat. Still struggling with the language, the bright-eyed Sutter delivered a gracious little speech of welcome. A toast was proposed: "Captain Sutter first, Captain Sutter last." Others followed in leisurely succession—to the shy Mrs. Sutter, to their pert daughter Eliza, to Hock Farm, to "our absent wives and mothers," to Republicanism, "to the beauties of California—wild flowers and tame ladies."

The sun was dipping below the rows of neatly aligned fruit trees when the *Dana*'s whistle signaled departure time. A wobbly but still courtly Sutter escorted his guests to the bank for the trip back to Sacramento. The river looked like a broad ribbon of dark green silk. Birds flitted through the high grass on the opposite bank. The ship's band struck up "Yankee Doodle" as the steamer glided into the current. The squire of Hock Farm beamed from the shore as the passengers gave him a parting three-times-three.

Sutter's renascent affluence permitted him to indulge in the lordly excesses of old. His generosity again became the stuff of folk tales. A doctor who had tended his family on the Panama steamer was invited to the farm. When he unfolded his napkin, the story ran, a pile of nuggets worth $700 dropped on his plate. Sutter supposedly spent $15,000 on a four-week spree in San Francisco and had to borrow to get home. There were frequent soirées like the banquet for the *Governor Dana*'s passengers.

Sutter's pride intervened to squelch a romance between his daughter Eliza and the young Swiss musician he had hired as a piano teacher for his son. Sutter declared that the youth's social standing was inadequate and banished him from the house. Eliza was so crestfallen that she tried to slash her wrists. The impoverished merchant who had fled Switzerland to elude his creditors would occasionally refer to his family's noble lineage. He spoke casually of his close friendship with Louis Napoleon, later Emperor Napoleon III of France.

The ignoble side of his character resurfaced as well. His old friend and countryman Heinrich Lienhard, who had brought the Sutter family to California, encountered him in a state of slobbering drunkenness one day in Sacramento. "Old Sutter was shaking from head to foot," Lienhard recalled. His sons had to drag him from the tent of a French prostitute. Lienhard, who was eagerly preparing to return home to Europe, was so disgusted that he snubbed Sutter the next—and last—time he saw him.

The fastidious, moralistic Lienhard had parlayed his rewards as Sutter's majordomo into $24,000 in traveling money. He had become contemptuous of the "grotesque pageant" of California, "the land of murderers, drunkards and cutthroats." In May he spent $300 for a first-class ticket on the steamer *California,* which would sail for Panama on July 1. On the day of his departure he treated himself to a shave and a warm bath—"to remove all traces of California soil."

John Woodhouse Audubon, another defector from the promised land, fled San Francisco at about the same time. Audubon left his nearly two hundred watercolors and sketches, which depicted both Mexico and California, with a friend. They were later lost in a shipwreck.

SACRAMENTO was making the transition from frontier village to valley metropolis. The tents of seasons past had given way to frame houses. A mile-long levee had been raised along the Sacramento River. Hardin Bigelow, the most vocal advocate of the levee, was the newly elected mayor. The Alpha Bath House ("Warm, cold and shower baths") was a short walk from the K Street boardinghouse that advertised "Rest for the Weary and Storage for Trunks." The famous pianist Henri Herz performed a series of concerts on the town's lone piano, a cut-down instrument with only six octaves. Herz was "a little cramped," the *Transcript* said, but still masterful. The April 25 opening of the Pacific Theater was celebrated with a grand ball to which a hundred ladies were invited. The *Transcript* reporter was dazzled by both the decorations (flowers, banners, and mirrors) and the female guests ("Miss H was all grace and elegance, Miss W all life . . ."). Storekeeper Frank Buck wrote home to his sister in Maine that he had "no doubt that by fall [women] will glut the market, as is the case with lumber."

The town appeared to be growing healthier. The persistently high incidence of sickness declined so sharply during the spring that one doctor said his colleagues were forced to try mining. Twenty fatalities were reported in May and twenty-seven in June. Diarrhea and dysentery were the leading causes of death.

San Francisco, meanwhile, seemed to be in a continuous uproar. Life in the city swept along at the furious pace of a river in flood. The spring months alone were enlivened by two major fires, two elections, a political scandal, and several shipments of Australian women. It was difficult to find time to rest.

The three men who aspired to be sheriff, all of whom answered to "Colonel," staged a series of rallies and parades in late March. Colonel J. J. Bryant, a hotel owner running on the Democratic ticket, plied the electorate with free food and drink. His chief rival was Colonel Jack Hays, a former Texas Ranger who ran as an Independent. Bryant, aided by an election-day parade, got off to an early lead when the voting began on April 1. Suddenly a bareheaded rider on a beautiful black horse appeared amid the crowds on Montgomery Street. It was Jack Hays. With an air of cool command he galloped to the plaza and greeted his cheering supporters. Hays won the election in a breeze.

The first of the season's fires, which broke out in the early morning of May 4, destroyed most of three square blocks north and east of Portsmouth Square. The fire raced through dozens of precut wooden buildings which had been shipped from the East. "What little assistance could be offered toward checking the flames was of no avail," the *Alta* reported. Soaring scraps of burning wood spread the blaze from block to block. The handsome brothels on the north side of the plaza were reduced to ashes, along with the *Alta California* office and the "Model Artists" emporium. Damage was estimated at $4 million. Shortly afterward the city council authorized fines of up to $100 for refusing to help fight a fire.

The burned-out merchants were barely back in business when a spark from a stovepipe ignited a cotton wall and kindled another major blaze on June 14. This time the count was four hundred houses leveled and $5 million in damage. Astonishingly, no deaths were reported in either fire. Frank Marryat, a young English travel writer, sailed into the bay from Panama while smoke was still rising from waterfront buildings. He was flabbergasted by the "daring confidence" of San Franciscans: new buildings were going up within forty-eight hours. Marryat reported this conversation between two undefeated businessmen:

"Burnt out?"

"Yes, and burst up."

"Flat?"

"Flat as a damned pancake."

"It's a great country."

"It's nothing shorter."

The harbor was so jammed with ships that they looked to one arriving passenger "as if they were piled up one on top of the other." He jotted down the names and home ports of a fraction of this rotting armada: the *Chateaubriand* of Le Havre, the *Thomas Bennett* of Charleston, South Carolina, the *Sarah Parker* of Nantucket, the *Carib* of Salem, the *Naumkeag* of Providence, the *John Allyn* of New Bedford. The steamship *California* cruised through the Gate in June with 114 bags of mail and the news that three thousand people were waiting for a ship on the Isthmus. Four men had died in night-long rioting following a fight between an American and a Panamanian. *California* passengers also brought word of the publication of *El Dorado*, Bayard Taylor's two-volume account of his travels in California.

But the most tumultuous excitement on the waterfront that spring was triggered by the arrival of three ships from Australia carrying about two hundred adventurous women. Many were whores—"Cyprians," the miners euphemistically called them. The randy San Franciscans were so eager to get a gander that they rowed out to the ships in lighters and scrambled over the railings. The *Transcript* commented drily that they were "trying to engage housekeepers." Housekeeping was never the forty-niners' long suit.

THE WAGONS began rolling into the Missouri River outfitting posts in March and April. The vanguard of the 1850 overland emigration quickly filled the four hotels in St. Joseph and spread through the valley at the base of the Blacksnake Hills. Bustling St. Joseph and the Mormon settlement at Kanesville—present-day Council Bluffs, Iowa—would get the bulk of the emigrants' business this year. Independence, a few days farther from the main Platte River trail, was already receding from its sunlit eminence of 1849.

The pilgrims gathering in 1850 had heard and read enough about California to know that there were weeds in this paradise. News accounts had confirmed the stories of returned forty-niners about the high rate of death and disease and the inflated prices. An increasing skepticism was evident in the New York *Herald*'s comment about the reliability of death notices in California newspapers. They "pay no sort of attention to deaths in that territory," the *Herald* said. But "about a week after the arrival of a steamer we find in the papers throughout the union quite a number of deaths, intelligence of which probably comes by letter."

The majority of people in the East and Midwest, however, still viewed California through a golden haze. The papers accentuated the positive. A report in early June noted that gold dust worth more than $1.25 million had just arrived on the East Coast. GOLD STILL ABUNDANT was a frequent headline. Most of the men who had already been to California and returned had brought at least a modest pile of the glorious dust. The busted and embittered prospector was not yet the stock character in eastern neighborhoods that he would be later, after the 1850 emigrants came straggling home.

The ambivalence of the eastern press was neatly summed up in a *Herald* headline which announced the OPENING OF NEW MINES OF WEALTH AND MISERY. The fact that the wealth was much better documented than the misery was probably one reason why the gathering thousands found it easy to ignore the negative news. Indeed the lure of California seemed even stronger in 1850 than it had been a year earlier.

The best evidence that a glittering optimism still bewitched the American public was the size of the army now massing on the Missouri: there were approximately twice as many overland emigrants as there had been in 1849. Other differences from the previous year were apparent immediately. Many more women and children were among the travelers. There was more of a western air about the 1850 trekkers; the now established Panama route attracted most of the East Coast gold seekers; these people came from Missouri, Ohio, Indiana, Iowa, and other heartland states. William Rothwell, a doctor's son from Fulton, Missouri, met enough Indianans in St. Joseph to believe he could recognize them by their personality and appearance. They were "plain, open, free and sociable, with a certain simplicity of countenance and manner peculiar to Hoosiers."

The emigrants of 1850 reckoned that they had learned from the mistakes of their predecessors. It was generally conceded, for example, that loads had been too heavy in 1849—there had been too many gold-washing machines, traveling forges, too many unnecessary tools and clothes. The letters printed in their home-town papers invariably remarked on the mounds of jettisoned cargo. The second-year crowds heard the message and traveled light. They also knew that the late starters in 1849 had suffered most. The solution to that was to set off early, even if it meant carrying a month's supply of feed for the animals, and to maximize speed: many chose horses instead of the lumbering oxen.

The tempo accelerated in mid-April. Tickets went on sale for McPike and Strother's passenger coaches, the 1850 version of the ill-fated Pioneer Line of a year before. Lighthearted messages appeared on wagon covers: "Ho for California! If you get there before me, say I'm coming"; "Pilgrim's Progress—Traveling Edition." The numerous blacksmiths and wagonmakers in St. Joe worked overtime. Merchants sold out their stocks of flour, salt meat, and other provisions at high prices. "Every little thing costs three or four times as much as it does at home," one man wrote to his family in Illinois. "The markets are filled with broken-down horses jockeyed up for the occasion, and unbroken mules which they assure you are as handy as sheep." The weather was cold and wet; the prairie would flower late this year. Expressmen from the military posts reported that the plains were still bare of grass. The most impatient among the waiting throngs—a twenty-four-man detachment from Kendall County, Illinois, and a 250-man company from Wayne County, Ohio—ferried the river and moved out anyway.

Many 1850 emigrants took to the trail in whatever was available. "Every mode of travel that ever was invented since the departure of the Israelites has been resorted to this year," a St. Louis correspondent wrote from St. Joseph in May. "Many have taken it on foot. . . . frequently I have met with the old-fashioned ox-cart, filled with [German] women and children." Some rode in drays, with one horse hitched in front of the other. A Missourian passed two men whose entire outfit consisted of one elderly white cow. A Baltimore paper reported that two New York circus impresarios were offering a complement of thirty-one camels for the overland trek, but the camel caravan never materialized.

The most conspicuous eccentric to leave St. Joseph this year was a lean Scotsman who came to be known as the Wheelbarrow Man. This strong-armed loner stowed his possessions in a wheelbarrow which he rolled over the prairie at a pace of twenty-five to thirty miles a day. He outstripped most wagons. Setting out on April 19, he took only ten days to cover the 290 miles to Fort Kearny, where a letter writer described him as about thirty-five, well armed, and not in the least fatigued. He declined an invitation to join a wagon train, "saying in his own peculiar dialect, 'Na, na, mun, I ken ye'll all break doon in the mountains an' I'll gang

along myself.' " The 315-mile jaunt to Fort Laramie took him two more
weeks. A dumbfounded admirer at Laramie reported that he was still
feeling chipper. He "pushed on to the tune of 'Yankee Doodle' toward
the setting sun—such a man must succeed."

By early May the wagons were strung along the trail in an endless
dusty chain. "Wagons block the road as far as the eye can see," William
Rothwell wrote. "It is impossible to camp within any short distance of
the road without being surrounded with trains." The men in the lead
caravans paid a price for their haste: they ran out of feed before the
late-rising grass came up; many animals starved to death as a result. As
yet, however, the toll in human lives was slight. The terrible cholera
epidemic of 1849 would not recur; this time the disease would strike relatively few companies.

A numerically minded spectator at Fort Kearny noted that 2,754
wagons, averaging four and a half men per wagon, had passed by May 21.
He had counted seventy-six women. Writing in the St. Louis *Republican*,
this statistician also ventured the opinion that the emigration had started
too soon. "It is now over a month since the first train passed," he wrote,
"and there is scarcely a sufficiency of grass for the animals." A few heed-
less travelers had compounded the dilemma by setting fire to the prairie
stubble "to see it burn." Rothwell commented in his journal that "white
Indians" were rustling horses and mules.

Most red Indians steered clear of the onrushing wagons. "Seven-
eighths of [the emigrants] have not seen an Indian," the man at Fort
Kearny wrote. One of the few confrontations took place just west of
Chimney Rock along the Platte. A band of about eighty Crows charged
to within some four hundred yards of a caravan and began circling the
wagons. The Indians acted menacing enough—they drew their bows "as
if they were going straight through us," a member of the company wrote—
but they didn't attack.

The weather brightened as the main body of the emigration passed
Fort Laramie and ferried the dangerous North Platte in late May and
June. Improvements along the trail—a road worn smooth by forty-niner
wagons, the addition of several ferries and even bridges—enabled the
wagons to move at a slightly faster clip this year. The ferry tolls were
higher: boats at the North Platte charged $4 and $5 per wagon. Many
chose to swim their animals across. Rothwell, arriving on June 17, was
told that thirteen people had drowned in the preceding week. At either
Laramie or the ferry the emigrants were apt to run into a genuine frontier

celebrity: mild-mannered, sandy-haired Kit Carson. Kit had ridden up from New Mexico with several dozen horses and mules to sell.

The trail register at Fort Laramie was the closest thing to a roster of the 1850 emigration on the Oregon-California Trail. On June 18 the register listed a total of nearly 32,000 men, women, and children. By late August the figure was 42,660. Adding an arbitrary 10 percent for those who neglected to sign the book yields a total of 47,000, more than twice the estimated figure for 1849. Midwestern newspapers claimed that Missouri alone sent more than seventeen thousand people in 1850 and Michigan another six thousand.

Some companies, like John Audubon's band the previous year, seemed to be cruelly singled out for suffering. Diarist John Wood chronicled the fortnight-long siege that beset his caravan on the Platte in June. The first cholera case was spotted by the doctor on June 6. Three men died in the next three days. By then nearly everyone was sick. Many, Wood wrote, "now feel determined to go home." Two more died on the tenth and eleventh, but Wood and several others began to improve. Then came two more deaths—the sixth and seventh victims. Wood, hearing a child sobbing beside the road, investigated and found a small boy crouched beside the unburied body of his father. "Father, Father, what will become of me?" the boy cried. By the seventeenth the plague was finally past. "Oh, God," an anguished Wood wrote in his journal, "shall I ever see such sights again!"

By the end of June the bulk of the wagons had rolled over South Pass. The packers in the lead had already tramped through the late Sierra snow and reached Sacramento. The men on the trail felt like veterans; they were acquiring the mental and physical toughness that the journey demanded. William Rothwell decided that "energy, patience and perseverance" were the qualities that would carry him through. The most severe tests, as always, were farther west, in the waterless deserts and perpendicular mountains that lay athwart the highway to gold. Their circumstances were already "growing ticklish," Rothwell wrote, due to the crowds on the trail and a shortage of grass. Harder times were coming.

THE NARROW-EYED Captain Parker H. French led his band of avid adventurers aboard the steamer *Georgia* in New York on May 13. The 189 men who had paid up to $250 each to travel in his "express train" from Texas to California had been promised speed and luxury—sixty days from coast to coast and first-class fixings. French had a flair for the grand gesture. On the first night out he treated his dazzled company to 150 bottles of champagne. When the groggy survivors of the departure party finally staggered to the hold in search of their berths, they found that six hundred tickets had been distributed for 250 sleeping places. Many could hardly find a place to sit, much less sleep. Their meals were equally catch-as-catch-can: passenger William Miles held out his tin plate and watched in mounting dismay as it was filled with a lumpy casserole of rice, molasses, soup, crackers, and beans.

Ashore in New Orleans, French again played the flamboyant host. He quartered his men at the comfortable St. Charles Hotel and spoiled them nightly with expensive meals. After a week they moved on to Port Lavaca, the jumping-off point for their projected carriage ride across Texas and the southwest deserts. The brightly painted carriages were waiting for them, but not the five hundred wagon-trained mules that French had promised. He purchased wild Mexican mules and hired vaqueros to break them, which occupied another twelve days.

Pulled by the reluctant mules, the caravan moved out of Port Lavaca on June 16. Their sixty days were already half gone, and the 150-mile trip to San Antonio consumed another twenty. The vision of a joyride to the gold fields was finally beginning to fade. They ran out of food, only to be saved by the fortuitous appearance of a Mexican wagon train. In San Antonio, where they paused for another two weeks, French found trained mules and cattle. But here also the company found out more about the character of their leader.

A messenger from New Orleans caught up with them and told French that the drafts he had used to buy supplies in New Orleans had bounced. Unfazed, French produced a letter of credit from the steamship owners Howland and Aspinwall. The letter directed army posts, including the San Antonio camp, to give French whatever supplies he needed on Howland and Aspinwall's account. Persuaded by his imperious manner and the impressive-looking document, the agent from New Orleans apologized and accepted French's drafts for his debts. French's performance was so convincing that army officers competed with each other to entertain him while he carefully selected the wagons, animals, and goods he wanted.

In mid-July the newly crisp and trail-ready expedition set out on the eight-hundred-mile journey to El Paso. It would prove to be the last stop for Parker French's bluff-powered express.

XIII

TWILIGHT IN EDEN

MINING A RIVERBED

THE EXHIBITION that opened in Peoria in the summer of 1850—an "Immense Moving Mirror of the Land Route to California," the advertisement called it—drew turn-away crowds for a week. The "moving mirror" was actually a watercolor painting on a belt of canvas ten feet high and several hundred feet long. It was unrolled between two large cylinders on either side of the stage while the painter, who had sketched his way along the South Pass route a year earlier, commented on the wonders thus depicted: Scott's Bluff ("picturesque and grotesque-shaped rocks of enormous size"), Devil's Gate on the Sweetwater ("a terrific chasm"), the Sandy Desert ("strewn with the skeletons of stock and property of every description"), and finally the awesome summit of the Sierra Nevadas ("the backbone of the elephant") and the golden land itself. Peoria spectators were so enthralled, a writer in the local paper commented, that the panorama could have played to full-house audiences for a second week; "we have never seen a more universal satisfaction expressed." But painter James Wilkins preferred not to be held over; he was already booked to appear in his hometown of St. Louis, where still bigger crowds and bigger proceeds (admission was 50 cents) were waiting.

The painter's vivid, almost photographic tableau of life on the trail generated powerful reactions in greenhorns and trailwise veterans alike. "We see all the dangers to which the emigrant is exposed," a Peoria spectator wrote, "we can almost feel his fatigue, we can almost hear his deep breathing after a day of perilous toils." A self-described "Californian" from St. Louis said the panorama "seemed like a dream of former sufferings, yet filled with many bright visions of beauty."

The American public was still buying California in whatever form it was offered. Bayard Taylor's *El Dorado* and T. T. Johnson's *Sights in the Gold Region and Scenes by the Way* were doing well in the bookstores. Dozens of other returned forty-niners were refining their dog-eared journals for publication. The gold rush, still less than three years old, was already perceived as an American epic. In time it would come to be seen as a kind of allegory for greed and its deserts, but in 1850 a properly grizzled ex-miner might still enjoy a modest veneration. "Wear your whiskers home and you'll be entitled to a great deal of consideration," a former argonaut advised a friend in the mines. "People will say, 'There goes a forty-niner,' and will believe all you say. But if you shave 'em off it's ten to one that nothing you say will be believed." A second canvas panorama, which transported the chairbound viewer to Sutter's mill by way of Panama and Acapulco, was seen by more than 150,000 people in New York, Albany, Troy, Buffalo, and Cincinnati.

The gold mania still gripped France as well. France had already sent thirty-five vessels and more than two thousand citizens to California. Some French gold companies offered credit for the price of the passage. Investors were promised enormous profits at minimal risk. "All commercial transactions presenting uncertain odds," one company brochure avowed, "are prohibited by the statutes."

The gold rush infiltrated French culture. At least three plays with California settings were presented in Paris, while the bookshops offered Hippolyte Ferry's *Description de la nouvelle Californie* and *California Unveiled* by Trény. A single issue of a Paris newspaper in August contained advertisements for five different California enterprises: two were mining companies seeking investors, a third proposed to ship prefabricated houses to San Francisco, another was interested in making miners' clothes, and the last announced the departure of a California-bound association. Sidewalk posters calling for Frenchwomen to emigrate to the gold coast reportedly excited "certain classes of the female population."

The French exodus was propelled in part by politics. The fragile republican government led by Louis Napoleon, which ruled during the interlude between the 1848 revolution and Louis Napoleon's designation as Emperor Napoleon III in 1852, viewed the California mines as a dumping ground for political troublemakers. The officers and men of the Gardes Mobiles, a military unit with antigovernment leanings, were shipped off to California, where their snappy military air made them even less popular than they were at home. "They are all well-armed and live and travel in military style, having their officers, music, flags, etc. with them," Lucius Fairchild of Wisconsin wrote from the southern mines. He added ominously that "the Americans do not like it."

The French devised the single most spectacular and successful scheme for transporting gold seekers to California: the Lottery of the Golden Ingots. The lottery's organizers, with the government's blessing, began selling tickets at one franc (20 cents) each in mid-1850. Their objective was to raise seven million francs. More than four million would be set aside to pay passage to California for up to five thousand poor emigrants. The rest of the money would go for lottery prizes (the winner would collect 400,000 francs), operating expenses, and profit. Potential miners were to register with the police, who would choose the lucky emigrants from among the applicants.

From Louis Napoleon's perspective the lottery was a masterstroke. Here was a way to rid the country of thousands of prospective enemies— discontented, out-of-work proletarians who might be attracted to socialism —while simultaneously appealing to their greed. *La Société des Lingots d'Or* opened a handsome office on the Boulevard Montmartre and exhibited ingots worth 400,000 francs in the window. Alexandre Dumas *fils*, the twenty-five-year-old son of the famous novelist, wrote a promotional pamphlet. Tickets were sold in England, Italy, and Spain as well as France. Ultimately the lottery came close to achieving its purpose: 3,885 Frenchmen traveled to El Dorado on the proceeds. But most arrived too late to do well in the mines; hundreds were stranded and needed help from the French consulate to get home. They apparently didn't read the consistently bleak reports that Parisian journalist Etienne Derbec filed from California in 1850 and 1851. "The life one leads here," Derbec wrote, "is not worth the most modest existence under the skies of his homeland."

In Washington the long stalemate over California statehood finally ended in the summer of 1850. Resolution of the bitter impasse between proslavery and antislavery senators was credited to the Senate's most artful compromiser, Henry Clay of Kentucky. Clay came up with strong inducements for both sides: California's admission as a free state was balanced by the establishment of a territorial government in New Mexico with no antislavery provision. The chances for the compromise improved after President Zachary Taylor died of typhoid in July. His successor, Millard Fillmore, backed Clay's plan. The Senate approved California statehood on August 13. Fillmore signed the admission bill on September 9. It would take almost six weeks for the news to reach the new state.

THE MEN rambling restlessly through the foothills in 1850 were gradually refining the crude techniques of California gold mining. The pan and rocker were still the primary tools, but tinkerers had improved upon the wood-and-metal rocker, creating an elongated version known as a long Tom. The Tom, unlike the rocker, was stationary. An inclined wooden trough between eight and fourteen feet long carried a stream of water—the precise volume was later accorded legal definition as a "tomhead"—down to an uptilted sheet-iron sieve at the lower end. The dirt and gravel which the miners shoveled into the trough dropped through the sieve to another trough cleated with riffle bars, behind which quicksilver amalgamated with the gold-bearing particles.

The flow of water through the Tom did the work that cradle-rocking did with the rocker, but it had to be constant. This required a connection by either pipe, hose, or "flume"—an elevated sloping wooden aqueduct—to a water source. The Tom had long been a fixture in the Appalachian mines, but it did not appear in the California diggings until the winter of 1849–50. By the following summer it was in general use. Normally operated by three to six men, the Tom dramatically increased the quantity of paydirt that could be washed in a day.

Another new technique was the excavation of narrow hillside tunnels, known as coyote holes, to get at the gold in the underground beds of ancient river channels. The tunnels took the most direct route to the gold by burrowing horizontally into a hill rather than digging vertically. Windlasses were sometimes rigged to haul paydirt to the surface. Hundreds of precarious tunnels, only a few shored up with timbers, were punched into a hillside near Nevada City in 1850; one thirty-by-thirty-foot claim reportedly yielded $40,000 in a month.

The real revolution in California gold mining would come later, in 1851 and 1852, with the playing-out of most placer deposits and the switch to quartz or hardrock mining, which demanded heavy machinery and a formidable investment. The shift to quartz mining would ultimately transform gold mining into a corporate enterprise with little room for the lone pick-and-shovel prospector, but only a few quartz veins had been detected by 1850. The most popular innovation this summer was riverbed mining.

Damming and draining a riverbed was a high-risk gamble even by California standards, and it was as arduous as it was risky. The members of a company formed for the purpose first dug a canal or built a flume to channel the diverted river. Then they waited for the river to subside to its midsummer low so they could hastily construct an earth and stone dam above their claim and drain the river bottom, which they would then attack with pick and pan. A successful riverbed claim could be a genuine bonanza, but it was a two-stage gamble: first, they gambled that there was gold in the bed, and second, that the rain would hold off long enough to let them get it.

Lucius Fairchild, the eighteen-year-old son of a prominent merchant in Madison, Wisconsin, joined one of the dozens of riverbed companies at work on the American River in early summer. Lean and angular, with a thin tuft of chin whiskers fringing his narrow face, young Fairchild had matured rapidly since he left home. The overland trail had taught him about human behavior ("every feeling, every passion is brought into action") and the mines had taught him self-sufficiency and caution. Still the prospects of his riverbed company were so glorious that he couldn't help crowing. "I am just as certain of a fortune this summer as though I had it in my pocket now," he wrote home in July. His twenty-man company had finished its canal on the South Fork of the American, four miles below Sutter's mill, and was waiting to start the dam. "It will take two weeks to complete it which will make three or four weeks before we can know what our show is for the 'pile' about which there is so much talk. . . . I may have got my pile before you receive this and I may be farther from it than I am now, only there is no chance for the latter assertion to be true."

A month later his confidence was beginning to ebb. The river was still too high to dam. "It will be late, but I think there is no danger but that we will get a month's work in the stream." He had taken the precaution of adding "other strings to my bow"—a partnership in a tavern in the southern mines, a chance for part-interest in a store. He was definitely not coming home broke; pride would not permit it.

By September it was obvious that they could not build the dam: the river had remained high. His prospective store fell through as well. Scrambling to salvage something from the mining season, Fairchild bought an interest in another riverbed claim, helped dig a second canal, and joined in building a small "wing dam" partway across the river. Then came the final insult: "We should have been at work in three hours more when the river rose and come over our dam a stream three feet deep which tore our dam and race all to ————" well, they knew where.

Three months of toilsome labor had left him without a single flake to show for it. "I have not made anything and in fact am behind considerable," he wrote to his parents. But he was not yet ready to quit: "You can bet your life I will never come home until I have something more than when I started."

The Reverend Daniel Woods of Philadelphia, the Mexican trail veteran who had cleared a dime on his first day in the diggings, endured a similarly frustrating season of riverbed mining on the Tuolumne. Woods and the two dozen other members of the Harts Bar Company worked all summer to build a hundred-foot-long, twelve-foot-wide wooden aqueduct and a dam. They swarmed eagerly over the dry channel when they finished. The profit on the first day was an encouraging $176; on the second, $415. On the third day the water rose dangerously. It lapped at the top of the dam just above theirs as Woods and his partners watched helplessly from a hill. "The black line of the wall was suddenly broken, and the torrent poured through a small opening . . . in a few seconds the river ran foaming over the entire length of the wall, which bowed and sank." With a kind of grim fascination they shifted their gaze downstream to their aqueduct. For a few moments the structure withstood the thundering water. Then "it yielded, swayed forward and moved away with the ease and rapidity of a thing of life."

Makeshift dams rose and fell on every gold country river during this year of high water. Woods nosed around the Tuolumne and found fourteen separate dam companies. He inquired about their profits and came up with an average of $3.16 per man per day; five didn't pay a penny. Alonzo Delano was involved in two dams on the Feather River. One had to be abandoned before it was finished. The other drained its claim (at a cost of $16,000) but produced no gold. The South Fork of the Feather was blocked wherever feasible for forty miles, Delano wrote, with dams costing up to $80,000, "and not one paid a moiety of its cost."

And when the miners suffered, so did everyone else—merchants who had given them credit, tavern keepers, expressmen, town speculators, even doctors and lawyers. Delano found "disappointed and disheartened men" everywhere. He also found another way to fail: he packed into the mountains and opened a store at a camp on the Middle Fork of the Feather. A few weeks later the first storm of September precipitated a mass flight to lower ground by his customers. He lost $1,000.

Hosts of men spent the summer in the fitful pursuit of rumors and new diggings. They drifted along the shining rivers and over the timbered divides singly and in small groups, pushing ever deeper into the high country as the foothill placers played out. Every settlement with two shacks and a saloon gave itself a name: Helltown, Fair Play, Grizzly Flats, Piety Hill, Whiskey Flat, You Bet, Nary Red, Lousy Ravine, Petticoat Slide. Prospectors trudged into a camp or a clearing, unpacked their mules, tested the dirt for color, and moved on.

The major new discovery of the summer was Rich Bar, an outcrop of gravel at the base of a steep, heavily timbered hill on the North Fork of the Feather. Defectors from the Gold Lake chase gingerly picked their way down the hill to the bar in July. Two of them washed out a pound of gold from their first pan of gravel and the rush was on. Claims were marked off. Five hundred men showed up in a week. The two who made the original find harvested $6,000 each in the ensuing fortnight. The Sacramento *Transcript* reported in August that two other prospectors gathered fifty-six pounds ($14,336) in two days. Two similar bars less than a mile away proved to be almost as productive.

The most improbable rover puffing through the northern Sierras this summer was the still ailing J. Goldsborough Bruff. Bruff was part of a large prospecting party led by Peter Lassen. As always he was noting every novelty, every change of weather, and every physical infirmity— chills, headaches, sleeplessness, hemorrhoids—in his commodious journal. Bruff spent most of his time at various base camps while Lassen and others prospected. He was in no hurry to dig gold.

Bruff was outraged by the barbarities of his companions. Three of them caught an Indian squaw alone and raped her. "It is such enormities," he accurately observed, "which often bring about collisions between whites and Indians." He judged two "Oregonian Frenchmen"—half-breed offspring of French trappers and Indian squaws—as particularly degraded: all they asked of life was whiskey, a horse, a squaw, a slab of raw meat, and a place to sleep. Bruff saw himself as the lonely bearer of civilization's flickering torch.

It was September before he got his first glimpse of gold. They were camped on a tributary of the Feather's North Fork above Rich Bar. His description of his find was characteristically restrained and precise: "I noticed a vein of white quartz," he wrote. "It was eight or ten feet wide. . . . In a lump of the rock the size of a small biscuit I found on one side needle crystals and on the other, two pear-shaped nodules of gold as large as robin shot." He neglected to say whether he tried to extract them.

SONORA, the gaudy fiesta town of the southern mines, was transformed in early summer into a community of frightened strangers. Americans and Mexicans who had formerly been friends now exchanged baleful stares. The foreign miners' tax, which had forced hundreds of Mexicans to leave the mines, had poisoned the atmosphere. A rash of murders broke out in late June: two Massachusetts men were hacked to death in their tent; a Chilean was shot down on a Columbia street; a barkeep was stabbed with a sword; two Chinese were murdered at their camp near Jacksonville. "Scarcely a day passes but some murderous atrocity is committed," the merchant William Perkins wrote on July 3. Travel was increasingly perilous.

Perkins and most other whites blamed the killings on marauding bands of Mexicans. The townspeople voted at a public meeting to form a twenty-five-man posse to pursue the slayers and "use all lawful means to bring them to justice." A request for a company of cavalrymen was dispatched to the military command.

Enos Christman, the youthful Pennsylvania printer who had advised his fiancée to enjoy herself at home, happened into town at precisely this ticklish moment. Christman, who had accumulated nothing but debts since landing in the mines a few months earlier, had leaped at a job offer on the new Sonora *Herald*, the first newspaper to be published in a California mining town. He wrote his fiancée, Ellen Apple, that murders had been committed at the rate of one a day for a fortnight, but that he personally was contented and finally prospering, "having found employment at my trade at a good salary"—$50 a week. His friend Peebles Prizer advised him by letter that Ellen remained devoted, "almost too devoted. The Apple," he assured him, "is sound to the core." As to his own romantic entanglements, Prizer wrote that he sometimes went out with "Sallie Cope, an old friend, whom I hug occasionally when I feel like it, but she is rather old and tough."

The tension in Sonora boiled over within a week of Christman's arrival. A group of Americans came upon four Mexicans burning a tent in the nearby camp of Green Flat Diggings. Two bodies were found in the ashes. The Americans brought the Mexicans into Sonora, where a mob quickly gathered. An uncomfortable Perkins found himself part of it. "I could not help joining," he wrote. "The murders daily committed . . . leave no room for a feeling of mercy." Justice of the Peace Richard Barry tried to question the prisoners amid a bedlam of shouts and threats. The Mexicans claimed that they were cremating bodies which had been in the tent for several days. "The demeanor of the prisoners was calm and becoming to an extreme," the report in the *Alta California* said, "exciting, in some minds, a sympathy which was most marked."

But the sympathetic were an ineffectual minority. When court adjourned the mob seized the prisoners, looped ropes around their necks, and marched them to a large oak on the edge of town. They were given a cursory trial and sentenced to hang. Perkins noticed that two of the Mexicans lit cigarettes as their executioners readied the ropes. The first man was jerked into the air. Then, astonishingly, Judge Anson Tuttle, Sheriff George Work, and several deputies galloped up. The judge begged them to return the prisoners. At the same time the sheriff's men grabbed the ropes and spurred their horses. The prisoners, still bound by the neck, clutched the ropes and sprinted behind them. All four—at least one with a very sore neck—made it safely to the lockup as the startled mob howled in disappointment.

Hundreds of miners from neighboring camps descended on Sonora for the formal trial five days later. A rumor that a guerrilla band was nearby led the sheriff and a posse to round up 110 Mexicans; they were penned in a corral and held overnight. The trial threatened to erupt into a riot when a guard dropped his pistol and the weapon fired during the reading of the indictment. Christman saw several men burst out of the courtroom with guns drawn, scanning the street for invisible enemies. The four prisoners again testified that they were merely burning long-dead corpses. This time a doctor who had examined the bodies confirmed their testimony; he estimated that death had occurred more than eight days before the bodies were found. With no evidence against them, the defendants were acquitted.

"We are happy to state that the excitement in Sonora and vicinity, although still great, is on the decline," the Stockton *Times* commented on July 20. Before it subsided further, however, there were reports of new outrages. The consensus at an urgently called Sonora mass meeting was that all foreigners except those of proven "respectable character" should be expelled from Tuolumne County within fifteen days. Foreigners were ordered to surrender their weapons to committees elected by the Americans in each camp. The same committees could grant permits of good conduct to the respectable. The vivid, easygoing Latin ambience of Sonora, the sense of an exotic bazaar which so appealed to the well-traveled William Perkins and others—"I had never seen a more beautiful, wilder or more romantic spot"—would now, finally, be gone forever. Enos Christman watched some two hundred dispirited Mexicans depart for the friendlier Sonora below the border.

Even though the Sonora resolution banished "all foreigners," it was in practice aimed at Latin Americans and especially Mexicans. The Mexican miners were the principal targets of the foreign miners' tax as well. As usual, officially sanctioned bigotry encouraged private efforts: some Americans demanded gold from Mexicans on the pretext that they were tax collectors. In August Governor Burnett finally modified the tax, reducing it from $20 monthly to the same amount for four months, but the migration south was already underway. "We infer, with tolerable certainty," the San Francisco *Evening Picayune* said on August 14, "that from fifteen to twenty thousand Mexicans, and perhaps an equal number of *chileños*, are now leaving or preparing to leave California for their own country."

The atmosphere throughout the mines was becoming uglier in this summer of 1850; life was cheaper now; evicting the Latin Americans would have no effect on the rising tide of murder. Two men were waylaid and killed on the Yuba in early August. A few weeks later two partners from Vermont were slain with axes as they slept in their tent near Nelson Creek. One young man in Sonora killed another when their careless roughhousing exploded into a fight. Something toxic—desperation, perhaps, or the squalid death of hope—had drifted into the California air. It remained for the original gold discoverer, quirky old James Marshall, to find the most grisly example yet.

Marshall and a companion were prospecting near the headwaters of the American River, searching for a mysterious deposit the miners called the Ohio diggings. The diggings were named for four men from Delaware County, Ohio, who had turned up a few weeks earlier with seventy-five pounds of gold but wouldn't say where they got it. Camped on an oak-shaded plateau between two creeks, Marshall and his friend found the skeletons of four men and the remains of their horses in a thicket. A nearby *mochila*—a light leather haversack—and scattered bits of clothing suggested that the dead men were Latins. Marshall recalled that four Spanish-speaking miners, carrying a large quantity of gold dust, had disappeared from the same area about three months before. The condition of the bodies indicated that these men had died at about that time. Marshall recognized what it meant: "the Ohio diggings," he said.

CALIFORNIANS celebrated the Fourth of July with oratory and band music and barbecues and balls. San Franciscans rallied around a new 110-foot-high "liberty pole" of Oregon pine, a present from the city of Portland. The festivities at Downieville commenced hilariously enough but turned ugly after one drunken reveler wounded another with a knife. The assailant was tried by a suddenly sober jury, sentenced to thirty-nine lashes, and flogged on the spot by a sinewy ex-sailor.

In Sacramento there were separate fetes for wets and drys. The newly organized Sons of Temperance listened to an abstinent orator and toasted the flag with river water. Everyone else enjoyed the more traditional refreshment at a civic banquet at which Governor Burnett, John Sutter, and a clutch of visiting Hungarian officers were special guests. The only spirit dampener occurred when the duty cannoneer suffered a broken arm and facial burns as his weapon misfired. The residents of the old pueblo of San Jose roasted three steers, three hogs, and ten sheep in a grove outside town.

San Jose, the seat of the state government, was one of the few places in California where there were enough women and children to support the amenities of a small-town social life—dances and taffy pulls, piano lessons and church socials. Sallie Hester, a penny-bright fifteen-year-old from Indiana, lived with her family in a small house in San Jose; the front room was her father's law office. Sallie studied Spanish and music, sang in a choir, gobbled fruit from the bountiful Santa Clara Valley orchards, and complained that her father wouldn't let her dance. "Last Friday evening I went to my first ball," she wrote in her diary in August. "[My father] let me go with the promise that I would not dance. Of course everybody was there, but I had a rather dull time looking on."

A few days later she attended a bullfight: "The fight was horrible. There were several men wounded and a number of bulls killed. We left perfectly disgusted. After the fight we all went over to [an] orchard and ate all the pears we wanted."

Boys and young men—"good-looking and bright fellows, lawyers and state officers"—were always nearby. Sallie's summer was a season of tentative flirtations on long, flower-scented evenings. Her father finally capitulated—"I have gained my point about dancing." One day she visited the sun-baked village at Mission San Jose and met Mrs. Juliet Brier, the heroine of Death Valley. When her father was elected district attorney the family at last had a parlor. "We live like all the newcomers—" Sallie wrote, "haphazard, anyway and everyway."

San Francisco remained the hub of gold country comings and goings. Cal Gardiner, describing himself as "a loose fish ready to snap at any bait," came down to the city from the southern mines in July. He worked at a succession of odd jobs and felt lucky that he could always cadge a meal on credit at a restaurant owned by a fellow Long Islander. Unwanted cargoes piled up along the wind-raked waterfront. Arriving Frenchwomen took ornamental jobs at hotels and gambling houses. They charged $16 to sit with a man at a bar or card table; for $200 and up they would go home with him. The city's journalistic eminences threw a farewell dinner in September for Edward Kemble, the *Alta* editor who had once pronounced the gold discovery "as superb a take-in as was ever got up to guzzle the gullible." The twenty-one-year-old Kemble was sailing for Panama and home on the *California*. The major cultural event of the summer was the opening of the enormously popular *Seeing the Elephant*, a burlesque of mining life performed by a local showman named Yankee Robinson. Californians roared at their own follies in numbers such as Robinson's woeful ballad "The Used-Up Miner":

Oh, I ain't got no home, nor nothing else I s'pose,
Misfortune seems to follow me wherever I goes,
I come to California with a heart both stout and bold
And I've been up to the diggins there to get some lumps of gold.
Oh, I'm a used-up man, a perfect used-up man,
And if I ever get home again, I'll stay there if I can.

San Franciscans saluted the late President Taylor with an elaborate funeral procession in August. The various delegations marching behind a symbolic hearse illustrated the city's emerging diversity: besides the predictable politicians and clergymen there were ranks of foreign consulate officials, a mounted unit of Britons, and several hook-and-ladder companies. The wholesome Sons of Temperance were followed by the more convivial members of the Odd Fellows and Davy Crockett lodges. The most distinctive band was a hundred-strong aggregation of blue-coated, pigtailed Chinese marching beneath a banner identifying them as "China Boys."

Chinese were just beginning to make their presence felt in California. Less than a thousand of the quiet, deferential men the miners called Celestials had crossed the Pacific during the first year of the rush, but by mid-1850 they probably numbered between two and three thousand. A reporter watched a shipload of Chinese miners debark, all "bearing long bamboo poles across their shoulders" and wearing "new cotton blouses and baggy breeches . . . slippers or shoes with heavy wooden soles [and] broad-brimmed hats of split bamboo." The Americans' first reaction was benign; the miners regarded them as somewhat comical but otherwise harmless and even admirable. "The Celestials are very useful, quiet, good citizens and are deserving the respect of all," the *Alta* declared. The Sacramento *Placer Times* pronounced them honest, efficient, and orderly. San Francisco Mayor John Geary celebrated East-West harmony with a special ceremony in honor of the Chinese at Portsmouth Square in August. Norman As-sing, an 1849 arrival who had become a prosperous merchant and restaurateur, formally thanked the mayor and later hosted a banquet at his home.

Most Chinese emigrants were peasant farmers from the populous Pearl River Delta region near Canton in southeastern China, an area that had suffered repeated crop failures and high unemployment during the 1840s. Shipping agents in Hong Kong and Canton lured them with flyers describing California as *Gum San*, "Gold Mountains," and offered passage for as little as $40. The onset of the Taiping Rebellion in 1850 led to more economic troubles and a surge of emigration. Brokers in the China ports advanced passage money to emigrants on the understanding that it would be repaid out of their profits in *Gum San*. Forty-five ships left Hong Kong for the gold coast during the year.

The Chinese emigration reached its zenith two years later when the San Francisco customhouse reported 20,026 arrivals from the Celestial Empire; more than two thousand came ashore in a single forty-eight-hour period. San Francisco's Chinese merchants organized companies which provided the newcomers with supplies, transportation to the diggings, and whatever else they needed. Working in self-contained bands of fifty or more, Chinese miners dug placer from dozens of sites the Americans had deserted as played out. They furnished their own food—mostly rice and tea and dried fish—and their own pleasures, principally opium and gambling. Most eventually returned to their families in China.

The initial American cordiality began to curdle as the Chinese population increased. The quiet efficiency of the Chinese miners seemed to rankle the more wasteful Californians. The criticism most often expressed was that the Chinese miner left nothing in return for the gold he took; unlike his often profligate American counterpart, he spent little and escaped with his profit intact. Americans also derided them as slave laborers, though they were not. In time the peaceable Chinese became everybody's favorite target: Americans forcibly expelled them from several camps, harassed them with the foreign miners' tax and passed ordinances excluding them; Mexican bandits preyed on them. Even the Indians, who were at the bottom of the California pecking order, took advantage of them. The story was told of a band of Indians on the Merced River who couldn't decide whether the Chinese were whites or Indians. They devised a test: if they were Indians, they reasoned, they could swim; if they were white they would sink. They waylaid two Chinese and threw them in the river. They were white.

THE MOST volatile issue of this ragged summer in Sacramento was neither crime nor race; it was land. Conflict had been simmering for months over the ownership of town lots that had been sold the previous year by John Sutter's agents. Many of these lots were now claimed by squatters who regarded Sutter's original Mexican grant as irrelevant and foreign to boot. They had put up their shacks on vacant ground, as frontiersmen had always done, and they would damn well live in them. Arrayed against them was the Sacramento Establishment—Sutter, the unintimidated Sam Brannan and other landowners, the mayor and town council and courts. Their position was that vacant or not, the lots had been bought and sold. In August the argument moved into the streets.

The squatters, having tried the courts and lost, concluded petulantly that the courts had no jurisdiction anyway. They would "protect their sacred rights," they announced, in their own way. For several days squatters and police took turns seizing disputed pieces of property, but they avoided a direct confrontation. A public meeting on the levee on August 11 deteriorated into a shouting match between Brannan and squatter leader Charles Robinson, a fiery orator who would later become governor of Kansas. Two squatters were taken to the prison brig on riot charges. Rumors flitted through the saloons: the squatters planned to set the town ablaze; they would attack the prison ship.

Robinson and about forty well-armed followers mustered on the morning of August 14. Their first move was to recapture one of the houses in dispute. Then they marched off in the direction of the prison ship. Mayor Hardin Bigelow rode through the streets and rounded up a posse of self-styled "law and order" men to oppose them. The two sides faced each other a few minutes later at the corner of 4th and J streets. The squatters formed a single line from one side of the street to the other. Bigelow, at the head of the posse, ordered them to lay down their weapons. The squatters opened fire.

Bigelow tumbled from his horse as four bullets tore into his flesh. The posse returned fire, then charged into the wavering picket line of squatters. Four men—three squatters and city assessor J. M. Woodland—died in the exchange of fire. Bigelow, Robinson, and three others were wounded. The rest of the squatters fled with the law-and-order men in pursuit.

The atmosphere remained taut through the afternoon and evening. Rumors circulated that hundreds of miners were en route to Sacramento to support the squatters. Hastily organized squads of militia patrolled the streets. Robinson and several other squatters were locked up on the prison brig amid muttered threats of lynchings. Lieutenant Governor John McDougal left for Benicia and San Francisco to seek military help.

There was more bloodshed the next day when Sheriff Joseph McKinney led a raid on a roadhouse known to be a squatter rendezvous. The men in the tavern greeted the sheriff and his deputies with a blast of gunfire. McKinney reeled, staggered a few steps, and fell dead. His men killed two squatters and galloped off with four prisoners. Reinforcements were added to the night patrols when the news reached the city. Dr. Jacob Stillman, assigned to the south end of town, spent a nervous night prowling the streets "with fixed bayonet, stopping every man for the countersign." Those who didn't know it were escorted home.

McDougal returned from San Francisco on the morning of the sixteenth with Brannan, Mayor Geary, and about 130 militiamen—the eighty-man "California Guard" and fifty volunteeer firemen. Stillman encountered the San Franciscans on the street; "all were eager for the fray and I thought if they fought as well as they swore, the country would be safe." But the fighting was over. Many of the squatters had escaped to the mountains; others were in jail on charges that eventually collapsed. The Establishment was back in control. The militiamen joined hundreds of Sacramento citizens at Sutter's fort for McKinney's Masonic funeral that afternoon. A few mourners threw sprigs of evergreen in his grave.

LABORING across Texas in the sullen August heat, the men in the Parker French train were uneasy. Most now realized that their leader, who had barely eluded his creditors in San Antonio, was something other than the ingratiating bon vivant he had pretended to be, something at once more interesting and more menacing: French was a gritty, tenacious, and utterly amoral frontiersman. French could get them there, but it would be on his terms. When two men fell asleep on night guard he peremptorily sentenced them to six lashes each. When a soft-spoken Texas Ranger refused his order to move, French challenged him to a duel. The men in the company disliked him, but they also knew that he was their best hope. "He had our money, we were a thousand miles from anywhere and must look to him to put us through," one wrote.

The company straggled into El Paso on September 18. Their mules were emaciated; three men had died on the trek across Texas; twenty had defected and headed for Mexico on their own. French found the army post, pulled out his ever-serviceable letter of credit, and secured $8,000 worth of livestock. The next morning a government expressman from San Antonio rode in with a warrant for his arrest. The letter of credit had been repudiated by Howland and Aspinwall, the firm that had purportedly issued it. An officer of the firm denied any connection with French. In effect he had been writing checks on a nonexistent account all the way from New Orleans.

French went into hiding while the shocked and outraged men he had duped debated their next move. Fearing that their newly acquired stock would be seized against French's debts, they moved across the Rio Grande to Mexico. On the next day French brazenly appeared at their camp. He demanded the company property, insisting that they either proceed as planned or turn the supplies over to him. But the men had finally had enough: they refused. French warned that they would never reach California without him—they didn't realize at the time that this was also a threat—and rode off.

But if French had paid for everything with forgeries, where was the $38,000 they had given him? Suddenly they remembered the safe he kept in his wagon. A posse rode to El Paso, found the safe, and opened it: empty. The safe had been a decoy all along. French had stashed the money back in New Orleans. The dispirited men voted to sell all company property except the mules. They distributed the profits among themselves at the rate of 20 cents on each dollar they had paid French. Then they outfitted themselves, split into small parties, and set out once again.

Charles Cardinell, a young Canadian, joined thirteen men headed across the dry wastes of northern Chihuahua in early October. The group was camped beside an arroyo near the village of Corralitos when Cardinell heard what sounded like an Indian war whoop. He turned and saw a dozen to fifteen men riding down on him. At their head was French, waving a pistol. Gunfire erupted on both sides. Two of Cardinell's companions were killed along with several of French's gunmen. French took a bullet in the hand which shattered his wrist bone before he roared off with the Cardinell party's horses. From where Cardinell watched, it looked like French's hand was hanging from his wrist by skin alone.

French reportedly next appeared at the home of the owner of a nearby silver mine and asked for a doctor. There was none. The story is that he then downed several quarts of mescal and called for someone to amputate his arm above the elbow. A schoolteacher agreed to try. "He couldn't be stupefied," the teacher wrote later. "I tried him with spirits of nitre, after which I administered about an inch of chloroform." Still the beady eyes stayed open. The surgery was performed. The teacher then packed the stump in hot charcoal powder. French was back in action within ten days. The beleaguered men of his company would hear from him again.

THE EMIGRANTS who traveled the overland trail in 1850 were closing a chapter in the story of the American West. Never again would the suffering on the trail be as terrible as it was in the gold rush years of 1849 and 1850. Before 1849 there had been so few wagon trains in any one season that grass and water remained plentiful. After 1850 trading posts and primitive settlements would spring up to help them past the most difficult places. But in 1850, with the trail twice as crowded as ever before, the pitifully underequipped emigrants faced the worst of it on their own.

The young bravos in some companies were trail-toughened and confident as they rattled past the landmarks between the Green and the Humboldt—bubbling Soda Springs, the imposing granite pinnacles of the City of Rocks. "When we commenced this journey," wrote Eleazer Ingalls of Illinois, "trifling hills were considered great obstacles. But now we lock our hind wheels and slide down a thousand feet over rocks and through gullies with as much sangfroid as a schoolboy would slide down a snow-bank."

The Fourth of July caught most emigrants along the high-country rivers on either side of South Pass. William Rothwell's company of Missourians hurried down the snow-bordered trail west of the Green River ferry without pausing for the usual patriotic rites. Eleazer Ingalls halted briefly at Soda Springs to toast Old Glory from a pail of snow-cooled punch and emit three dutiful cheers. A company called the Wisconsin Blues, fittingly camped at Independence Rock on the Sweetwater, demonstrated more of the customary gusto. They built a bonfire of sagebrush, discharged a fusillade of gunfire at the stars, and shouted into the lonely night. The answering cheers of companies camped nearby echoed back across the darkened plain.

A few of the 1850 travelers had already glimpsed the cloud that shadowed them. John Steele of Wisconsin bowed his head at the burial of a cholera-stricken infant beside Bear River and heard the parents' brave prayer: "By Thy hands the boon was given, Thou hast taken but Thine own; Lord of Earth and God of Heaven, Evermore Thy will be done." A few companies came upon solitary emigrants who had been left to die by the trail.

The true dimensions of the ordeal they faced did not become apparent until they rolled through the sage-cluttered Goose Creek Valley and emerged at the headwaters of the mysterious Humboldt. The grassy meadows of 1849 were under water. The combination of heavy winter snows and a hot spring had baked the grass and flooded the valley, turning it into a fetid quagmire. They would have to blaze new and more difficult trails through the barren bordering uplands. Livestock would have to wade or swim for the isolated islands of waving grass.

The muddy and malodorous water of the Humboldt was barely adequate to sustain life. One popular way to make it fit to drink was to soak a blanket in the river and then wring it into a pan; even then it was difficult to keep down. "It is fairly black and thick with mud and filth," one emigrant wrote, "but there is one advantage one has in using it—it helps to thicken the soup." The soup needed additional thickening now that their skimpy supplies were running low. "We are no longer troubled with preparing dinner," John Steele wrote self-mockingly. "Our rations are dealt out so sparingly that we seldom eat anything at noon." So many horses and oxen died of starvation and alkali poisoning that Ingalls described the river as "a horse broth seasoned with alkali and salt."

The daily struggle for survival drained their strength. "The only way we could get grass," a Missourian wrote, "was to swim the river (or wade the sloughs) and cut it from among the willow brush." The constant grass cutting, combined with nocturnal sentry duty to protect the horses from Indians, left them "so tired and brokendown that we didn't care for anything." But there was no time to rest. "If we did, thousands of stock were passing every day and destroying everything before them." Alonzo Delano heard that five emigrants—three women and two men—were driven to such despair that they drowned themselves in the putrid Humboldt.

"The destruction has reached its height now," Ingalls wrote near the end of July. "Hundreds are entirely out of provisions, and there are none who have any to spare, and but very few who have enough to carry them into the mines." Mrs. Margaret Frink of Indiana, one of the few women who kept a journal, benefited from the generosity of an anonymous samaritan. She found a cow tied to a willow bush beside the trail. A card fastened to her horns said, "This cow is only footsore. Use for food."

The 1850 emigrants had heard enough about the long *jornadas* and hostile Indians on the Lassen route to spurn the cutoff in favor of the main trail across Humboldt Sink and the forty-mile desert. The sink was boggier than ever this year. "Imagine a vast plain of sand and clay," Ingalls scribbled in his journal, "stunted sage, salt lakes . . . burning wagons, horses lapping empty water casks." One novelty was a trading post at the point where the travelers set out across the sink. The enterprising grocer offered bacon, flour, and other necessities at $1 and $2 a pound. Other entrepreneurs peddled water on the desert at a dollar a gallon.

Margaret Frink reached the shaded sanctuary of the Carson River on August 20 and found "a woebegone, sorry-looking crowd—the men with long hair and matted beards, in soiled and ragged clothes covered with alkali dust, have a half-savage appearance. There are but few women." Proud caravans of twenty and thirty wagons had shrunk to "three, four, or at most a half dozen, with three-fourths of their animals missing. Their former owners now trudge along on foot packing on their backs the scant provisions left." The majority of the emigrants were now pedestrians.

The frequent reports on the emigration in California newspapers were eagerly read by men who vividly remembered the hardships of their own journeys. The Sacramento *Transcript*'s readers were told in July that the overland suffering would be "unexampled" by late summer. Cholera was once again stalking the emigration, this time on the Humboldt instead of the Platte. Committees were appointed to raise funds for another relief expedition: San Franciscans contributed $6,000 in a single day; Sacramento residents kicked in $2,800 more; the proprietor of the famous "Model Artists" exhibition in San Francisco, newly reopened after its destruction in the May 4 fire, donated one night's profits.

Captain William Waldo led a relief force across the mountains in late August. He reported in mid-September that many emigrants were living on the carcasses of dead animals. Disease was "mowing them down by the hundreds." John Steele's company encountered the relief party in the Sierras on the seventeenth. It convinced him that not all Californians were "soulless, avaricious Shylocks."

Stragglers filed down from the mountains through October. There was no way to estimate the number that lay buried along the trail; one emigrant counted 963 graves and guessed that five thousand had perished altogether. The *Transcript* found three young children among the survivors. Their parents had died en route, and they were brought the rest of the way by a doctor whose wife had also died; they were adopted by three different Sacramento families. A ninety-year-old Revolutionary War veteran had made it overland from Illinois. The man with the wheelbarrow was also on the scene. He told a *Transcript* reporter that he had rolled his one-wheeler to Salt Lake City before he abandoned it and joined a company. "That man will make his pile," the reporter predicted.

CALIFORNIA and its restless inhabitants were changing each other in large and small ways by 1850. They were "a percussion people," Alonzo Delano said, "living in a percussion country." The tempo of their life was so accelerated, so nerve-jangling and explosive, that it could render them temperamentally unfit for the sluggish pace back home. How could a drowsy village in Kentucky or Massachusetts satisfy a Tuolumne River gold digger or a Sacramento monte banker? Often enough it could not. Hundreds of men hurried home with their gold and rushed back a few months later. Dr. Berryman Bryant of Alabama, a successful profiteer of 1849, discovered that he "could not be contented in the States"; he hustled back to St. Joseph in time to join an 1850 overland company. Where else but California could a vagrant recoup so fast? "If a person lost his all he was perfectly indifferent," Bayard Taylor wrote. "Two weeks of hard work gave him enough to start on; and two months, with the usual luck, quite reinstated him."

A Californian prided himself on his generosity in a bountiful land. "There is more intelligence and generous good feeling than in any country I ever saw," Jacob Stillman observed. "Men are valued for what they are." The ideal in this masculine society was "the opposite of what is commonly called meanness," the historian Hubert Howe Bancroft wrote. Openhanded liberality, bigheartedness—"if it ran its possessor upon the shoals of bankruptcy or into a drunkard's grave it was lamentable, but no such black and accursed evil as parsimoniousness, stinginess, niggardliness, or in a word, meanness. There was nothing in the world so mean as meanness." Californians were soft touches. The miners at one American River camp raised $200 in twenty-four hours for a newcomer who broke his leg in a fall.

Another badge of the Californian was his breezy self-possession. "A man that lives here two years," the Sacramento *Transcript* declared, "will contract a free and easy habit, a habit of independence to a greater or lesser degree that will mark him, wherever he goes, as a Californian." These were men who had bet their health and wealth on the race for gold; it was no surprise that they possessed the gambler's bravado.

The changes that the argonauts wrought in California reached a climax in 1850. The euphoric flush of 1848 and the headlong rush of 1849 were past, and in their place were milling throngs of dangerously disgruntled men. The mines were jammed by midsummer. "I thought the country full to overflowing some time ago," a Baltimore man wrote in early August, "but still they come. There are a thousand a day arriving by the overland route. They come into the country strapped and have no place to strike a lick, for all the diggings are claimed that can be worked." More than 35,000 additional emigrants arrived by sea during the year. A guidebook author wrote that "every gulch and ravine in the whole country were completely filled by the first of October."

Mining profits dropped sharply. Where in 1849 the miner's take had worked out to about $16 a day, in 1850 it was roughly half that. Cal Gardiner estimated that two-fifths of the diggers averaged between $5 and $10 a day and another two-fifths earned from $3 to $5; the rest barely paid expenses. The easily accessible gold was all but gone, along with the good claims. The persistent high water further eroded profits as it washed out dams. "Dissatisfaction is almost universal," the Missourian William Rothwell wrote soon after he arrived. "On the first part of the trip all was California. Now all is home." Mining failures led to bankruptcies in Sacramento and a late summer run on San Francisco banks.

The darkest stain on this grim summer was the increase in crime, riot, and racial violence, a trend that would continue with the coming of statehood. The explanation probably lay amid several phenomena—the pressure of numbers, the decline in mining profits, and the foreign miners' tax, among others. Or perhaps the Chilean Vicente Perez Rosales, who tried California for two years and left in 1850, perceived the cause: "Everything went well at first in California," he wrote. "It was only when things reached the middle that they collapsed."

THE MORNING AFTER

SAN FRANCISCO

Fortune, tis written, smiles on fools wherever they may labor
And surely I've been fool enough to win her choicest favor;
But ever she eludes my grasp despite the proofs I gave her
That I'm an ass; she turns from me to wanton with my neighbor . . .

Oh for one hour where early life flowed passing merrily,
Where youth still hung on low-toned words and not upon—a tree,
Where friends could wrangle and debate about each passing trifle
And meet a flash of wit instead of bowie knife or rifle.

—John Stone, "An Oft-Told Tale"

T HE TIME of miracles is past," the French correspondent Etienne Derbec wrote from the southern mines in September 1850. "The sweetest illusions are lost. . . . The awakening is all the more terrible as the dreams had been so glittering." Nothing was colder than yesterday's dead fantasy.

"From a distance California appears all golden," Derbec went on. "From close at hand, the gold disappears." Daily he watched the lonely legions plodding from one exhausted camp to another. "Homesickness grips these poor people," he wrote. "They take it with them from placer to placer and they detest the gold, the mines, and their own destiny. Half of the miners are at that point today."

Acknowledging the inevitable—that the California cornucopia had to run short eventually—did not make it any easier when it happened. "I do most solemnly assure you," an 1850 emigrant wrote to his brother in Missouri, "that the stories you hear so frequently in the States are the most extravagant lies imaginable—the mines are a humbug." The newcomers could peer through the bleak light of the morning after and see the mining camps for what they were—tatterdemalion refuges for an increasingly desperate and disgusted horde.

The mines were overcrowded, overpriced, and overadvertised. "The fact is that nothing but the bright side of things here has been seen at home," Missourian A. M. Williams wrote to his father, "and that much exaggerated." Merchants had gilded the reality of California for their own purposes. "Many have written home that they were making fortunes when they were scarcely paying expenses. . . . The thousand dollar piles are about dug out. He who mines after this winter will, I think, do so with very gloomy prospects of making anything. The rivers are dug over again and again, and the dry diggings will be pretty much gone over this winter."

Alonzo Delano, strolling past the site of an abandoned riverbed claim on Nelson Creek, was startled to see a dummy dressed in the ragged outfit of a hard-luck miner. A note pinned to the effigy showed that its creator had at least retained his sense of humor: "Californians—Oh Californians, look at me! Once fat and saucy as a privateersman but now—look ye— a miserable skeleton. In a word, I am a used-up man."

Delano, who was tending store, watched a remarkable transformation come over the miners at Nelson Creek after a monte banker arrived in camp. Normally hard-working men began drinking heavily. They neglected everything—work, meals, sleep—in their mania for gambling. The members of two companies, each of which had been earning up to $150 a day, dissipated their dust "as if the gold blistered their fingers." The dealer sheared $3,000 from Nelson Creek in two nights, then moved on to Onion Valley and lost $4,000. The moral tone was similar in Coloma, where gambling was merely one amusement among many; one transient found "preaching one hour, auction the next, a horse race or shooting match and always on the Sabbath, and each person boldly endeavoring to fleece his neighbor."

It seemed as though some final barrier in the miners' code had collapsed this fall, had buckled and splintered like a wooden flume before a foaming stream. The last vestiges of the conventional constraints were vanishing. Debauchery was all too common. A black dancer was gang-raped by several members of the audience after a performance in Mariposa. Three men were killed when a gunman sprayed bullets around a Nevada City saloon. Murders, bloody accidents, and thievery were becoming so routine in Sonora that William Perkins no longer recorded them in his journal. An accidental shooting death in a gambling house stirred hardly a ripple. "Some of the players got up to have a look at the dead body," Perkins noted, "and returned to their game quite unconcernedly."

Perkins' neighbor Enos Christman, the new owner of a half-interest in the Sonora *Herald,* was still gambling that his steamy love letters would keep his fiancée Ellen Apple "sound to the core." A letter he received in the fall—it took two months for mail to travel between the coasts via the Isthmus—made him wonder if Ellen was wavering: she wanted to know if his feelings about her had changed. Enos gallantly confessed that they had—"to more ardent love"—and promised that he would be home in a year with a stake for their life together. Ellen's reply was all he could wish for: "I would love you as devotedly without a dollar as if you had thousands." His friend Peebles Prizer, who had been studying the now discouraging reports from the mines, reported his sober conclusion that "a trip to California is but an adventure, and not of much benefit in a pecuniary sense."

At this moment it seemed of dubious benefit in any sense. Delano felt that "an evil had taken root" in California soil. One reason for the galloping lawlessness, he thought, was poverty; mines and cities both were jammed with broke and desperate men. Another reason was the continuing absence of effective government—"a grand stimulant to the perpetration of crime." Even impending statehood made no difference—California still lacked both a published criminal code and the lawmen to enforce it.

It was also at this time that a cadre of professional criminals began to arrive in force. These were the men the Californians called Sydney Ducks, British convicts who had been exiled to Australia and later made their way to California. By late 1850 scores of these outlaws were clustered in the sordid Sydney Town district of San Francisco or adrift in the mines. Their presence made it necessary, Delano said, "to guard property with as much care as in towns of the older states."

An incident in Rough and Ready in 1850 illustrated the brutal methods of the Sydney men. One of them had deposited a nugget worth several hundred dollars with a young storekeeper from Missouri. When he and his friends returned for the gold that evening it was gone. The storekeeper protested his innocence and offered to pay them the value of the nugget, but a crowd of Sydney men bustled him to a hilltop and tied him to a tree. "The poor fellow begged and pleaded," a witness wrote, "avowing his innocence and at the same time offering them the contents of his little store and all he had in the world," but it was futile. They lashed him until a doctor forced them to stop, then looted his store. He died that night.

The first of several lynchings during this fall and winter took place in Georgetown, a popular dry-diggings camp just north of Coloma, on a pretext of misguided chivalry. The story was told by William Manly, the hero of Death Valley, who was then working a nearby canyon. The victim was an Englishman named Devine, who lived in Georgetown with his wife. The hard-working Mrs. Devine had accumulated a modest pile of dust by laundering miners' shirts for $1 apiece. One day in early October her husband drunkenly demanded some of her money for a redundant visit to the saloon. He shot her dead when she refused him.

A mob quickly gathered—"a pack of reckless backwoods Missourians who seemed to smell something bloody," Manly called them. He saw them return to the saloon "in unusual good humor." A group of accommodating ex-sailors had assisted them with the hanging rope. "They watched the suspended body till the last spark of life went out," Manly wrote in disgust, then "whooped and yelled at the top of their voices as they came down along the mountain trail. . . . They said justice must be done if there was no law, and that no man could kill a woman and live in California."

The careful and industrious Manly was earning "fair wages"—more than $2,000 since midsummer—from his claim on Canyon Creek. He and his partner Asahel Bennett, who had waited with his family for Manly to lead them out of Death Valley, had improvised a wooden pump to drain underground water from their claim. But despite his success Manly was growing restive. The raw lawlessness sickened him. Eventually he hoped to farm, but the prospects did not look promising in a land "where there were only two seasons, one wet and the other long and dry." He made up his mind to return to Wisconsin where his pouch of dust would buy "a good farm in healthy country."

Another lynching occurred in Placerville before the end of October. A young monte dealer known as Irish Dick plunged his bowie knife into the breast of a man who had accused him of cheating. The mob waited impatiently while a justice of the peace examined him and then dragged him away. One contemporary account says that Dick jumped as high as he could when his executioners drew on the rope.

One way to avoid the cheerless atmosphere in the mines was to tramp the high-mountain wilderness, as J. Goldsborough Bruff continued to do until mid-October. Bruff was still wandering the ridges with a band from Peter Lassen's ranch, ostensibly searching for the already discredited Gold Lake but in fact doing what he did best—observing and describing the countryside. A few desultory attempts at prospecting left him empty-handed but undiscouraged; the country was the thing. From an eminence northeast of Mount Shasta he beheld "the hills rising from the level plain [of Pit River Valley] as if from the bosom of the calm sea, growing darker, bolder and loftier, in all the tints of green, gray and blue, till they reached the majestic snow-crowned Tschastes [Shasta]." A dream he recounted suggested that gold might have meant more to him than he cared to admit: "dreamt that I was abandoned by my family, my friends and the whole world because I had not found a gold mine." He returned to Lassen's ranch on October 19. Soon afterward he decided that it was time—"as soon as I recover from fatigue and indisposition"—to have a look at the California cities.

BY OCTOBER the original passengers in Parker H. French's sixty-day express to California were straggling miserably across Mexico and the southwest deserts in scattered and leaderless platoons. French himself, having sacrificed an arm in his vengeful attack on one such band, returned to the pursuit of quick cash. He recruited a gang of highwaymen and robbed a silver-laden mail coach in the mountains between Durango and Mazatlán. This was crude work for a man of French's dimensions, and he had no knack for it. He was captured by Mexican troops and jailed in Durango, where he was presently sentenced to death.

It was only a matter of days before French separated himself from the more common felons, his own hired guns included, and found a more suitable niche. A New York *Herald* correspondent reported that French had secured "most excellent and comfortable quarters in a private house opposite the jail." He was, the *Herald* man concluded, a "remarkable scoundrel." What happened next isn't clear; the accounts disagree. Somehow French talked his way out of both jail and his death sentence and emerged at the head of a company of Indian fighters, charged with ridding Durango of the dreaded Comanche raiders. One version attributes his release to the timely intervention of a wealthy *señorita;* another alleges that he charmed the priest who came to administer last rites.

French led what he claimed was a successful assault on the Comanches and collected bounty money for the scalps he offered as evidence. For a giddy day or two he was a gringo hero. Then, still aiming for California, he slipped over to Mazatlán on the Pacific, where he found several dozen men from his original company. The express train's ex-passengers had not fared as well as their agile leader. Some had been so tortured by thirst on the desert west of El Paso that they drank the blood and urine of their mules. Many lacked money for passage to San Francisco. Their situation, Michael Baldridge wrote, was "bilious in the extreme."

Incredibly, French gulled them one final time. One of his victims later identified French's gift as "a combination of rascality and generosity I have never seen equaled." With money in his pocket again, he offered to pay the passage for anyone who lacked the fare. He doled out a quarter a day to the neediest. For men with cash he had a different proposition: he would take whatever they could spare, or their notes, and arrange passage on the next steamer. A number of men agreed.

The steamer arrived, the men trooped aboard, and the officers asked for their tickets. No tickets, but Mr. French had taken care of it. Mr. French had not taken care of it. They filed back ashore and looked for French. He had disappeared.

The first detachment of survivors of the French expedition finally landed in San Francisco in December, seven months after they had left New York amid champagne corks and promises. The rest, including

French, trickled in during the next few months. There is no record that any passenger ever brought legal action against French. Passenger William Miles wrote what could stand as their benediction: "Here at San Francisco we meet each other in the streets and feel as though we had arisen from the dead. . . . We were sadly deceived, but why complain? It is all past as a dream. It cannot be recalled."

PHYSICALLY, commercially, culturally—every way, in fact, but socially—San Francisco was evolving into a metropolis. Socially it would take a while yet. The population of 25,000 to 30,000 in the fall of 1850 included only about 2,000 women, and a generous proportion of them were "of base character and loose practices," as a journalist commented. For ladies of nobler character and stricter practices the preservation of virtue and dignity was a struggle as dispiriting as a San Francisco hill. "The moral life of California is to the character," the former prison matron Eliza Farnham intoned, "what the seventimes heated furnace is to the ore of the metallurgist—only purity itself can come unwasted through it."

The appearance of the city was changing radically. Sand and dirt were being scraped from the hills, carted to the waterfront, and dumped into the bay, filling in the little crescent-shaped cove which the first visitors to Yerba Buena had found so enchanting. A dozen wharves now jutted into the bay from the advancing shoreline; the longest extended two thousand feet across the low-tide mud flats to a dependable deep-water anchorage. Construction was under way on a 2¼-mile plank road between the plaza and Mission Dolores. Factories were rising on the old tenting grounds at Happy Valley. Brick buildings were beginning to appear.

San Francisco still looked to the sea for sustenance, but the sea was an unpredictable provider. Prices depended on the cargoes that were delivered by the fast-growing clipper fleet and other merchant ships arriving daily. An oversupply drove prices down, while a shortage emboldened would-be monopolists. Business was a high-stakes adventure. "No land ever lay beneath the sun which so favored the natural speculator," Mrs. Farnham wrote. Enterprising merchants sometimes rowed out to meet ships outside the Gate in an attempt to corner a particular market. The cunning Collis Huntington, who had turned a $4,000 profit while stalled in Panama, enjoyed monopolies on shovels and blasting powder at various times. Sam Brannan once tried to buy up all the tea in town. A bid for a monopoly could also prove ruinous, as it did for the prosperous British-born merchant Joshua Norton. Norton lost both his fortune and his sanity in an attempt to corner the rice market in 1853. Several years later he became a tolerant city's favorite eccentric as the self-proclaimed "Emperor of the United States and Protector of Mexico."

Most of the city's wealthy men acquired their fortunes not in mining but in trade and real estate. A little book published in 1851 called *A Pile, or a Glance at the Wealth of the Moneyed Men of San Francisco and Sacramento*, presented a list of the richest Californians and estimates of their worth. The irascible James Lick, the onetime Peruvian piano maker, was credited with an estate worth $750,000. Ex-army officer James Folsom was reportedly worth $400,000. Sam Brannan's wealth was put at a relatively modest $275,000, less than a half-dozen others. *A Pile* suggested that politics was also profitable: Governor Burnett had accumulated $100,000 and San Francisco Mayor John Geary $125,000. Domingo Ghirardelli, the candymaker who had been Lick's neighbor in Peru, was listed at $25,000. The largest fortunes were amassed by men who had been in California before the gold discovery.

Wealth was leaving San Francisco, of course, on every outbound vessel. Much of it was unreported. When an officer on the steamer *Antelope* inquired about the contents of an iron safe being loaded on board, the safe's owners assured him that it contained "only clothing." Questioned further, the men admitted to having $3,000 in gold dust, then $5,000. At this point the shipping agent ordered the safe opened. Inside was $67,000 in dust, which called for freight and insurance charges of $670.

The cultural sensation of the season was the opening of the two-thousand-seat Jenny Lind Theater in October. The man behind the Jenny Lind (named for the famous Swedish soprano, who never visited California) was Tom Maguire, a former New York hack driver who yearned to be an impresario. Maguire had shipped a theater around Cape Horn in sections in 1849, then worked as a bartender and gambler while awaiting his moment. The bill at the Jenny Lind changed almost nightly. Melodramas with titles like *The Widow's Victim*, *The Spectre Bridegroom*, *The Iron Chest*, and *Money and the Family Jars* alternated with California's first taste of Shakespeare—*Hamlet*, *Macbeth*, and *The Merchant of Venice*.

A theater was the setting of one of the early San Franciscans' favorite

stories. A chart had been published showing the various signals used by
the semaphore atop Telegraph Hill to report the arrival of different
ships. One night a black-clad actor raced on stage and overdramatically
extended his arms at right angles to his body while declaiming, "What
means this, my lord?" "Sidewheel steamer," shouted a voice from the
audience. The theater exploded in laughter. Another often told story is
attributed to Lieutenant George Derby, one of the city's first-generation
wits. Derby, a Mexican War veteran who arrived in California in mid-
1849, wrote sketches for the *Alta* over the pen name "Squibob." He was
cruising a San Francisco street when he spied a carriage with the legend
EAGLE BAKERY on its side. He immediately demanded a baked eagle.
"I pakes pread," the startled German baker replied. "You're an im-
postor," Derby declared. "Here I have been for six weeks trying to get a
baked eagle, which my medical adviser prescribes for my health, and
you have raised my hopes only to deceive me. Away!"

Another major fire—the fourth in ten months—destroyed property
worth half a million dollars in the four blocks between Washington,
Pacific, Montgomery, and Dupont streets on September 17. Cal Gardiner
was sleeping a few blocks away on Battery Street when he was awakened
before dawn by Spanish-speaking men crying *"fuego, fuego,"* but the
blaze stopped short of his building. Gardiner was scrambling for whatever work he could find in a city "full of impecunious specimens of
humanity ready to jump at any means of subsistence." He flopped as a
fruit tree salesman, then found work loading kegs of nails on a storeship.

The public response to emergencies was still, lamentably, less than
wholehearted. The *Evening Picayune* clucked that several "loungers" had
declined an opportunity to help fight the fire. A day later three affluent
merchants—Brannan, William Howard, and Talbot H. Green—donated
$600 apiece to the city for the establishment of a municipal fire depart-
ment.

Green, a Californian since 1841, was soon to become the central character in a stunning scandal. Genial and well liked, the stocky, forty-year-
old Green was one of the city's leading businessmen-politicians. Twice
elected to the city council, he was frequently mentioned as a candidate for
mayor. His friends—Brannan, Howard, Geary, Thomas Larkin—were
among San Francisco's most important men. *A Pile* placed his worth at
$150,000, and his judgment was so esteemed that he often served as the
sole arbiter in business disputes. "He was decidedly the most popular
man of all the old Californians that we found here before us," one forty-

niner wrote. He married an attractive widow and became the father of a son they named Talbot Jr.

But in the winter of 1850–51 the buzz around San Francisco was that Talbot Green was not who he said he was. An old acquaintance recognized him as Paul Geddes of Lewisburg, Pennsylvania, a father of three who had absconded with $8,000 belonging to a Philadelphia bank. Green claimed that it was a case of mistaken identity, but said that he would go east to clear his name. His still loyal friends escorted him to the steamer after toasting him with champagne at a tearful bon-voyage party.

In time it became clear that Green-Geddes had no intention of either returning or clearing his name. Eventually he confessed, resumed his real identity, and became a land speculator in Texas. Sam Brannan settled his debt with the Philadelphia bank. His first wife agreed to take him back after his California wife divorced him. He made one final visit to California many years later, but most of his old colleagues were too busy to see him.

DR. JACOB STILLMAN was ready to go home. He had survived a tyrannical ship captain, flood and riot in Sacramento, poverty and prosperity and a lifetime of sobering adventures in just over fourteen months. "It is man here that passes into sere and yellow leaf," he wrote as he prepared to depart, "and not trees." Stillman was aboard his anchored ship in San Francisco Bay on the morning of October 18 when he heard cannon fire across the whitecaps. He peered over the railing and saw the steamer *Oregon* chugging around the point between the city and Alcatraz Island. Dozens of flags streamed from the ship's rigging. Cannons boomed from her deck in rapid succession. Then he spotted a large banner amid the bunting. Printed on the banner were the words that everyone was waiting for: CALIFORNIA A STATE.

The officers on Stillman's ship grabbed their guns to answer the *Oregon*'s salute. More gunfire roared from the shore. Seamen on the idle ships shouted the news from deck to deck. Cheering crowds gathered on the wharves.

The city immediately declared a holiday. Stores closed. Courts were adjourned. Newspapers ran off special statehood editions and hawked them at up to $5 each. The ships in the harbor were festooned with bunting. Bonfires flared. Flags blossomed everywhere.

At sundown the milling crowds began to drift toward the plaza, where the first meetings to discuss statehood had been held more than a year earlier; everything important happened at the plaza. Guns blazed in the lamplit dusk. Speakers came forward to extol the Union and her thirty-first member. Then the revelers moved indoors, toasting themselves with champagne and brandy at Delmonico's, the rebuilt Parker House, and a dozen other hotels and taverns.

The steamer *New World* churned upriver to Sacramento overnight and awakened the town with a volley of cannon fire and a burst of fireworks the next morning. The excited throng at the levee represented not only all sections of the United States, a newspaper reported, but "every part of the *habitual* globe." Governor Burnett climbed up beside the driver of a stage in San Francisco and set off in a wild race with another stage for the capital at San Jose. He shouted the news to the people they passed. Expressmen and teamsters carried the word to the mountain-walled mining camps and the ramshackle towns in the foothills. At Coloma there were free drinks and a torchlight procession led by a Texan waving a Lone Star flag.

A more formal celebration, with a grandeur befitting such a spectacular addition to the Union, was clearly called for. It was set for Tuesday, October 29. Of course there would be a splendid parade. The grand marshal would be Colonel Jonathan Stevenson, who had come to California at the head of a regiment of New Yorkers during the Mexican War. Lest anyone forget the new state's principal resource, Stevenson would wear a white scarf trimmed in gold, the mayor and councilmen would wear gold-bordered blue, and the parade marshals would be in red fringed with—gold. An ode would be composed for the occasion by Mrs. Elizabeth Wills, the headmistress of a girls' school. The oration would be delivered by Judge Nathaniel Bennett, a veteran of New York politics who had done handsomely on the Tuolumne River. In the evening there would be a banquet and a grand ball. Fireworks would soar into the night from Telegraph Hill and Yerba Buena Island. The only sour note came when a surly troupe of musicians refused to perform unless they were paid $25 per man in advance.

The great day began with a cannon salute as the flag was run up the plaza flagpole at sunrise. A signal gun announced the start of the parade at ten. Crowds pressed against the storefronts as Colonel Stevenson and a squad of buglers led the marchers up the Washington Street hill to Stockton and swung left to Clay. A platoon of native Californians astride beautiful horses bore a blue satin banner ornamented with thirty-one stars and the inscription "California—E Pluribus Unum." Another banner depicted an arriving Yankee being greeted by a serape-clad Californio.

Uniformed militiamen swaggered by. Judge Bennett waved from a shiny barouche. Down Clay Street to Kearny they came—Mexican War veterans, judges, Governor Burnett and the state legislators, Talbot Green and the city councilmen, soldiers, sailors, foreign diplomats. A rooftop spectator thought the parade looked like "a moving flower garden." The plaza's guns fired continuously. At Kearny the marchers turned south and walked a block to Sacramento, then down to Montgomery.

The salty harbormen ambled by in front of their float, a boat on wheels. Horse-drawn fire engines were ornamented with pastel flowers and gaudy streamers. The richly dressed Chinese tossed firecrackers and pinwheels into the street as they marched beneath their blue silk banner. The lodges filed by—Masons, Odd Fellows, the New England Society, and the two-month-old Society of California Pioneers. The first California printing press trundled by on a float while marshals passed out copies of Mrs. Wills's ode, to be sung at the plaza later. Mayor Geary, who had taken the precaution of appointing himself chairman of the arrangements committee, beamed at the cheering spectators. The procession moved up Montgomery, turned back onto Clay, and headed into the plaza.

The loudest cheers greeted an immense open chariot drawn by six white horses. Thirty boys, each dressed in identical white shirts and dark pants, surrounded a pretty little girl in a white dress and gold and silver lace. Each of the boys bore a breastplate containing the name of a state. The girl carried a plate reading, "California and the Union—It Must and Shall Be Preserved."

The celebrants swarmed into the plaza behind the parade. By now the midday wind was snatching an occasional hat. Sunlight glanced off the bay and the flag-bedecked ships at anchor. The band played "Hail Columbia," after which the crowd of some five to ten thousand fell silent for a prayer in honor of the newest state. The handbills containing the words of the ode fluttered in the breeze as the orator spoke. Thousands of voices joined a choir in singing the ode:

> *Tho afar on the verge of the ocean we lie*
> *Our hearts are as true as the sun that shines o'er us*
> *Our treasures we bring of earth, ocean and sky*
> *Our souls that exult to join freedom's full chorus . . .*

The program closed with "The Star-Spangled Banner" and selective cheering: the composer of the ode was given six cheers; the grand marshal and the mayor received three each; California got nine.

Ernest de Massey, the French aristocrat who had mulled suicide in the Trinity mines, was a somewhat detached spectator at the plaza festivities. "By nature Americans are very impressionable," he noted. "Anything that strikes their imaginations and makes their hearts flutter is translated into noisy manifestation." Massey eschewed the banquet and ball that night in favor of his customary routine: "I went my way as usual and dined as I always do, then returned quietly to my palace of fleas."

Some eight hundred more convivial—and prosperous—San Franciscans made their way through an enveloping fog to the cotillion. The mist turned lamplit windows into glowing little cones in the raw darkness. The guests danced to a twelve-piece orchestra and admired the patriotic decorations contributed by the popular Lieutenant George Derby. The next day's papers complimented the ladies on their grace and skill on the dance floor.

The newspapers also carried news of a catastrophe that had gone unnoticed by most celebrants. Late in the afternoon of the festive day a boiler on a Stockton-bound steamer had exploded as the ship pulled away from Central Wharf. The blast sent passengers flying through the air like canvas dolls. Between thirty and forty were killed. As many more were taken to City Hospital with serious injuries, but their travail was not quite over: early in the morning a fire broke out at the hospital, forcing their evacuation.

THE CALIFORNIA gold rush was over. The stories reaching the East no longer told of pound diggings and nuggets for the plucking. The messengers of late 1850 were bitter men who felt betrayed. There wasn't enough gold on California's rivers to justify their effort. Maybe there once was—there must have been—but not now. Too many hands had already clawed at this vaunted earth. Too many shingle men had fleeced the lucky and lied about the yield. The volume of outward-bound traffic in San Francisco harbor was beginning to rival the numbers arriving. The message the defectors brought home was a revelation.

"We, the undersigned, passengers in the steamship *Alabama*, direct from California," a letter in the New Orleans *Delta* began in November, "deem it necessary to give some facts." Their sole motivation, the passengers wrote, was a "desire to serve those who may be induced to leave comfortable homes for the desperate chance of making a fortune by gold digging."

Their manifesto deplored misleading tales in eastern newspapers, many of which derived from California entrepreneurs. Washington bore part of the blame as well, especially the "exaggerated report by the government agent [Thomas Butler King]" and congressional rhetoric on the abundance of gold-bearing quartz.

The bleak truth they wished to convey was that gold mining was a disaster for almost everyone. Thousands of riverbed miners had been forced to borrow to live. In the dry diggings "not more than one in 20 has realized a dollar clear of expenses during the season. . . . All hopes of making a fortune in California are lost sight of in 99 cases out of a hundred," they concluded, and the "almost universal feeling is to get home."

El Dorado had lost its sheen, even if the prospects were not quite as dark as the angry men of the *Alabama* contended. Indeed there were placer camps such as Rich Bar that were still paying well, and others yet to be discovered. The total amount of gold produced in the California mines had risen steadily, from an estimated $3.7 million in 1848 to $10.6 million in 1849 and $45.3 million in 1850, and it would continue to increase until it peaked at $63.8 million in 1853.

But the mines were different now, and everyone recognized it. California gold had not been exhausted—it never would be—but the odds against a lone prospector had become prohibitive. The easily accessible placers were gone. What remained were deep-lying riverbed deposits and quartz veins, and both demanded major investments of time and equipment. The day of the laboring man had passed. Now it was capital's turn.

"There is gold still in those banks," the *Alta* declared in February of 1851, "but they will never yield as they have yielded. The cream of the gulches, wherever water could be got, has also been taken off. We have now the river bottoms and the quartz veins, but to get the gold from them we must employ gold. The man who lives upon his labor from day to day must hereafter be employed by the man who has in his possession accumulated labor, or money."

The techniques of mass production were finally beginning to appear in the mines. The natural progression from the two- or three-man rocker to the five- or six-man long Tom advanced in the winter of 1850–51 to the sluice, an almost indefinite extension of the Tom which could occupy as many as two dozen men. A sluice was simply a succession of cleat-lined wooden troughs which stretched as far as lumber and terrain permitted—some were more than a thousand feet long. At the lower end it sloped down to a sieve and riffle box as did the rocker and Tom. Long rickety flumes kept a steady stream of water flowing from the rivers to the sluices. The owners of the larger sluices would sometimes let the gold-bearing paydirt accumulate behind the riffle bars for days at a time before cleaning it out, which meant that guards were necessary to prevent thievery. A variation on the wooden sluice was the ground sluice, a long, narrow trench with holes in the bottom where the gold settled—not unlike the tailrace in which James Marshall found the first glittering flakes.

Riverbed mining, which had yielded so little in the summer of 1850, developed in the ensuing years into a large-scale and often successful industry involving thousands of men and dozens of seasonal dams. Quartz mining in California had begun with the primitive and rarely used arrastra, a contrivance in which a mule hitched to a short spar dragged heavy stones over gold-bearing quartz until it was crushed. The expensive stamp mills which appeared in the early 1850s used steam power to pulverize the quartz with iron-shoed wooden shafts. Hydraulic mining, the Californians' most original contribution to mining science, emerged at about the same time. In this method high-pressure hoses directed tremendous volumes of water at cliffs and hills until the soil overlying gravel deposits was washed away, often silting up the nearest stream in the process.

But the most conclusive evidence that the rush was over was the drastic decline in the number of emigrants on the California trail in 1851: barely more than a thousand, down from 47,000 in 1850. Panama remained busy—more than fifteen thousand reached California by way of the Isthmus in 1851—but California-bound travelers practically vanished from the sea route via Cape Horn and the dry trails across Mexico and the Southwest. The number of emigrants on the Platte River road surged again in 1852, but by then the character of the emigration was changing. The westering men of 1852 were settlers. They sought not instant riches but land, a home, and steady work at good wages. Many brought their families.

Late in 1850 the federal census takers fanned into the hills and along the coast. An accurate population count was impossible, if only because miners were restless by nature and almost reflexively elusive. The census ignored Indians. Nor did it help when the figures for three counties—San Francisco, Santa Clara, and Contra Costa—were lost. The Census Bureau total was 92,597, which may have been within fifty thousand of the true total.

The census data portray a youthful, heterogeneous, literate, and masculine society. More than half the population were men in their twenties. Californians came from all thirty-one states and more than twenty-five countries (the main exceptions were Japan and Russia, both of which barred emigration). Almost a quarter were foreign-born. New York contributed more natives than any other state, followed by Missouri, Ohio, Massachusetts, and Kentucky. The thirteen thousand who were born in either Mexico or California showed that the Latin influence was still strong. There were 962 blacks.

The survey found that only 2.86 percent of California residents were illiterate as compared with 10.35 of the national population. This supported the widespread belief that California had assembled a talented and well-trained work force; "as the wants of a large community began to be felt," a British traveler observed, "the men [to fill them] were already at hand." About two-thirds of those interviewed ignored their previous training or occupation and identified themselves as miners. Californian and miner had become synonymous, much as Californian and horseman or vaquero had been a decade before.

The most important statistic was that women were still only 8 percent of the population: California was a male preserve. The effects of this lopsided social order were visible everywhere. A society with a minimal female influence was among other things a society with a minimal social life. Only on rare occasions like the statehood ball would a quorum of "the fair" be assembled. The few homespun women in the mining towns were treated with an exaggerated deference that was more than gratifying; it was embarrassing. One lady wrote home that men had traveled forty miles just to gaze at her, and "I was never called a handsome woman, even in my best days and even by my most ardent admirers."

The bond between "pards" acquired a correspondingly exaggerated importance. Men drew together in their remoteness from home and in their shared willingness to gamble. In the absence of a social life they devoted themselves to their work and their partners.

> I'd comrades then who loved me well,
> A jovial, saucy crew;
> A few hard cases I'll admit
> Though they were brave and true.
> Whate'er the pinch they'd never flinch,
> Would never fret or whine—
> Like good old bricks they stood the kicks
> In the days of '49.

The crudity of the available diversions was another consequence of a male society. "Gambling, drinking and houses of ill fame are the chief amusements of the country," the youthful Lucius Fairchild reported to his parents. Profanity strained toward new frontiers. "It seemed truly wonderful," Mrs. Farnham clucked, "how many oaths could be crowded into the commonest conversation." The Presbyterian clergyman James Woods of Stockton calculated that "all the imprecations and oaths uttered in California in one month," joined together in one great blast, would "cause a peal of thunder whose reverberations would make Perdition tremble to its lowest depths."

The well-lit frankness of California vice demolished the satisfactions of furtiveness. At home, a Unitarian minister declared, "sin is stealthy and cunning and still, and goes in the dark. Here it is open, unmasked, makes no apologies and asks none. It unfurls its flag in the most public and conspicuous places." Peering past the flags, the more optimistic moralists detected some evidence by the autumn of 1850 that the devil's wave had crested. Most preachers and a few guidebook writers so assured their respective flocks. They could point to such phenomena as the nascent theaters and their more elevated entertainments, the opening of several private schools, and—most astonishing of all—the passage of an ordinance in San Francisco forbidding Sunday gambling.

The rude society fashioned by these womanless men was nonetheless both dangerous and reckless. Life was cheap in California. Governor Burnett believed that 30 percent of the forty-niners died as a result of disease, accidents, or violence. Hundreds simply disappeared as men did in war, leaving their families with nothing save year-old letters and stubborn hope. Advertisements sought the missing: "INFORMATION WANTED: Any person having information of Dr. Ormsby, who left St. Louis for California last season in 'Water's Train,' will confer a favor on his family by addressing N. M. Guild in San Francisco."*

The cruel combination of racism and a weak legal framework resulted in dozens of lynchings and other wanton killings. Miners developed a preference for the ad hoc justice that they had originally administered out of necessity; too often they reverted to mob action even after a formal legal structure had been erected. This disintegration of social and legal order was a direct result of attitudes they had borne with them on the westward trek. They had come in quest of wealth, not homes or land or

---

* Might this have been Dr. Caleb Ormsby of Ann Arbor? (See page 167.) Other evidence shows him to have been on the Merced River, in the Southern Mines, at about the time (July, 1850) that this advertisement ran.

community but gold—gold and adventure. Stability, order, and the obligations of citizenship were abstractions they associated with the homes
and families they had left, not the uncluttered land they found. They
lacked the commitment and the patience for the tedious business of civilization building—attending political meetings, paying taxes, serving on
committees, establishing colleges and hospitals. Californians "would
freely give their money," Reverend William Taylor wrote—indeed, their
munificence was legendary—"but not so often their time." Time, in both
the cities and the mines, was reserved for making money. The new state
would be buffeted by alternate waves of corruption and vigilantism until
that attitude changed.

Indians, Californios, and frontiersmen—the three groups that had
coexisted in pastoral California prior to the discovery of gold—were
among the casualties. Ravaged by disease and driven from their foothill
villages, the Indians had retreated by late 1850 to starvation camps in
the high Sierras. Many Californios, hounded out of the mines along with
Mexicans and other Latins, had withdrawn to ranchos in southern California. The little corps of whites who were in the state before Marshall's
discovery—the forty-eighters—had been decimated by a variety of natural and unnatural calamities.

George McKinstry, who had once been Sutter's manager, tallied up
the toll in an 1851 letter to another old Californian: "The old fort is
rapidly going to decay; the last time I was there I rode through and there
was not a living thing to be seen within the walls. Ah, what a fall is there,
my fellow! The old Sacramento crowd are much scattered by death and
disaster since you left. William Daylor by cholera; Jared Sheldon, shot
in a row with miners; Perry McCoon by a fall from his horse; Sebastian
Keyser drowned; Little Bill Johnson, who knows? Captain 'Luce' missing
in the mountains; Olimpio, Sutter's Indian messenger, shot by miners;
old Thomas Hardy, *rum;* John Sinclair, cholera; William E. Shannon,
cholera; Old William Knight, *rum* as expected. . . .

"Our good friend Captain John Sutter seems to be smashed to flinders;
Daylor and Sheldon estates said to be insolvent. . . . Old Kitnor made
a fortune and went bust; William A. Leidesdorff, dead; old Eliab Grimes,
dead; Jack Fuller, ditto—also Allen Montgomery. Montgomery's widow
married the man who called himself Talbot H. Green. . . . Pierson B.
Reading is on his farm raising wheat and pumpkins in abundance. He
was the Whig candidate for governor but could not make it. It was said
his friendship with Captain Sutter cost him the squatter votes. . . . I

could fill a foolscap sheet with busted old guard, including your humble servant."

The most striking fact about California may be that its myth survived everything—delirium and devastation, not just the gold rush but the morning after as well. The myth of a land of perpetual plenty, of a heaven-blessed province where food grew wild and disease was unknown, had begun before the rush and it lingered when the stampede was past. The argonauts had peopled this bountiful land, created a state, and hurried its metamorphosis from an isolated island of tranquillity to a raucous emporium of business and bedlam. But the forty-niners had not changed the California dream; they had merely brushed it with gold. And the dream would outlast the dross.

California was never like home. It distorted the reality of the America of 1849—life was faster here and richer, more beautiful and more violent, meaner and freer. Myths clung to California naturally, like wild flowers to a stream bank. The forty-niners might have scraped out the gold and trampled the flowers but they had left gifts of character which were equally precious—openness, a careless good humor, a taste for change, and a gambling spirit, qualities that would endure as long as the California dream persisted.

THE JUBILANT revelers celebrating California's admission to the union paid little attention to the death notice in the Sacramento newspaper on October 21, but doctors saw the implications immediately. The victim had been a passenger on the steamer which brought the news of statehood to Sacramento. The cause of death was cholera. The terrible disease that had pursued them across the plains and the Isthmus had finally caught up with them in the new state.

The contagion had arrived from Panama on the steamer *Carolina* two weeks earlier, but San Francisco port officials had decided against a quarantine despite the fourteen deaths on the ship. The cholera did not surface again until it appeared in Sacramento on the twentieth, but after that it spread with stunning speed. Several outbreaks were reported on the twenty-first. Twenty deaths occurred in the twenty-four hours prior to 8 p.m. on October 25. The Odd Fellows lodge set up a temporary hospital and donated coffins. There would be no statehood gala in Sacramento: twenty-eight more deaths were reported on October 31, two days after the San Francisco fete.

"To be sick in California is one of the hard things of this world," wrote a thirty-one-year-old Ohioan named George Evans. Evans had left a wife and infant son at home and traveled across Mexico. In late 1850 he was working as an auctioneer in a Sacramento commission house. He had recently calculated his profit for a year in California at $749.76, most of which he had sent home.

The epidemic reached a climax in the first week of November. One hundred and fifty cases were recorded in a single day. Special squads were dispatched to burn all refuse. Thousands fled to San Francisco and the foothills, but the disease pursued them; deaths in San Francisco increased to a dozen a day. Sixteen doctors perished in Sacramento. "Our cemeteries look like newly plowed fields," the *Transcript* commented.

Evans felt the first flush of fever on November 3, a few days after he took a job that looked like it would carry him through the winter. On the fifth he wrote in his journal that he felt pain throughout his body. The next day brought a trace of hope: "fever abating but dysentery threatens."

By November 16 the plague had moved from Sacramento to Placerville and the camps. The only business during the preceding few weeks, a Sacramento paper said, had been transacted by "physicians, the clergy, coffinmakers, and gravediggers." The best estimate is that some 850 to 900 Californians died of cholera between October and December. George Evans, who lay ill for a month before he succumbed, was one of the last.

Through the dry November afternoons the dispirited men in the mines waited for rain. They had finally learned not to bolt for the lowlands at the first drizzle but to exploit the perverse California seasons; the rain might pry a few more flakes loose from the quartz-locked lodes in the high country and send them tumbling along the river bottoms; rain would fill the narrow washes in the dusty ravines the miners called dry diggings; most important, it provided the water they needed for their rockers and Toms.

But the rain held off. The golden haze of the summer-bright fields turned a lifeless brown. Leaves on the hillside chaparral disintegrated at the touch. Brittle ferns snapped beneath their boots. The land itself seemed dead. The rivers crept timidly past naked stone sentinels and great gravel islands. The capricious torrents of the spring just past had savaged the miners' hopes; now drought paralyzed them.

Like the cholera, the floods, and the suddenly active Indian raiders who attacked a few isolated camps in November, drought was a short-term natural hazard. In time it would end, though deliverance might not necessarily follow; "a rainy week but the ravines are not running," John Banks noted when the spell finally broke in late November. "The prospect seems worse as the season advances."

It seemed that way all over California, and for thousands it was time to leave, not because of drought or cholera or any single diabolical visitation but because of all the natural and manmade afflictions of this demanding land—dugout placers and the drift to anarchy, overcrowded camps and long womanless evenings, the hell of the cities and of illness far from home. The Reverend Daniel Woods, who had watched the raging Tuolumne destroy his dam and his hopes, climbed to a hilltop in the fall to print a final California vision in his mind: the river, now low and feeble, wound sinuously past the debris of a half-dozen attempts to block it; little knots of men clustered around glowing campfires. "There is the scene of my labors for long months," he wrote. "There is my own arbor, and its last fire still smoking, and there our place of worship; lower down is where our company meetings were held. And there the graves. . . ." He made his way to San Francisco and boarded a Panama-bound ship on November 26.

William Manly was also packing up. He savored a long farewell to the Bennetts, whose lives he had saved in Death Valley. "I don't suppose you will ever come back," Mrs. Bennett told him, "but we may come back to Wisconsin sometime and we will try to find a better road than the one we came over." Manly walked to Sacramento, took a steamer to San Francisco, and declined a chance to part with some of his $2,000 savings for a chunk of urban real estate. "It seemed very doubtful to me that this place would ever be much larger or amount to much," he explained. The mines "would be worked out in a short time and the country and town both would be deserted." He sailed out the Gate on the twenty-ninth.

There were other men, however, who felt bound to California. Some stayed because they differed with Manly about its prospects; others had simply found a home. James Marshall, whose luck had soured since his original discovery at the mill race, would play out his string in California. Marshall remained intrigued by the possibility of a golden fountainhead high in the Sierras. Late in the fall he asked Sutter to outfit him with food and pack animals for another venture in search of what he called "the big lumps." The ever generous Sutter furnished the supplies and a few Indians but the trip failed, as did several subsequent expeditions.

Sutter's erratic fortunes had plummeted once again by the end of

1850. The dapper little Swiss would never starve—he was too good a farmer for that—but self-indulgent sprees and disastrous investments had left him as George McKinstry described him—"smashed to flinders." Greedy business advisers had taken advantage of his careless inattention to detail to pick him clean. "If he had more of the Yankee in him he would today be one of the richest capitalists in the world," Ernest de Massey wrote. "His followers have tricked, deceived and plundered him; taking advantage of his weakness for drink, they have cajoled him into making transactions involving land concessions which contain clauses so cunningly worded that they brought ruinous and endless litigation."

Having trusted too readily in the past, the old pioneer now trusted no one. His son August, who had protected Sutter from himself for a while, fled to Mexico in frustration. His other two sons worked in the fields at Hock Farm, his only remaining property, while his daughter Eliza helped with the housework. Sutter's manner would never sag: to the end he remained the gracious if somewhat imperious California squire. What had faded, finally, was the innocence of a man who had dreamed of empire.

THE WAGON carrying J. Goldsborough Bruff, his trunk, his weapons, his instruments, and his encyclopedia-sized journal rattled placidly down the Sacramento Valley in late November. Bruff gazed at the riverside oak groves, flocks of geese, prowling bands of coyotes, and several deserted Indian villages. Nearing the city he passed through a tule-choked bog. The weather was cold and drizzly.

On the afternoon of the twenty-ninth his wagon rolled up to the ferry landing across the river from Sacramento. "What a sight for me—a city!" he exulted. "Steamers, ships, brigs, schooners, and all the bustle and appearance of our old Atlantic home!" He dined on roast elk and immediately ran into several old friends. In a few days he was at work— "somewhat professionally"—lettering signs. He watched a parade of squatters, looked in on the gambling houses, and visited the cemetery with its "long parallel lines of graves of cholera victims . . . the resting places of upwards of 1,700 persons who had fallen in 15 months." He listened to a candidate for a municipal office summarize his platform: "I am an advocate of an extensive importation of females and reduction in the price of leather." On Christmas he feasted on grizzly steak, venison, and mince pie and reflected on the contrast with his Christmas a year earlier. If he saw any irony in the fact that his arrival in mining country coincided with a widespread exodus, he kept it to himself.

The city's attractions soon palled on Bruff. He spent a day investigating the decaying adobe fort, now a hospital. He sampled the ale produced by a neighboring brewery. The entries in his journal became shorter, only a fraction of their length when he was leading his company along the trail or marooned in the mountains. Bruff would spend a few more months in California, but his gold rush was already over. More than most he knew that California was an anticlimax. The journey, the adventure—the quest—was everything.

EPILOGUE

NINETEEN-YEAR-OLD Hubert Howe Bancroft, hurrying across the Isthmus of Panama on his way to California in March of 1852, stood on a sandy bank beside the sluggish Chagres River and contemplated an extraordinary sight: two large groups of Americans were simultaneously descending on the little riverhead village of Gorgona—from different directions. Bancroft's fellow passengers from New York were still climbing out of the bungos they had ridden upriver. The others were homeward-bound ex-Californians, plodding into the village from Panama City.

It was an unforgettable moment for a youth who would ultimately become California's leading historian. "Narrowly they eyed one another, the going and the returning," he wrote, the California-bound "with the confident swagger of greenness yet upon them, rude and unaccommodating in their grumbling selfishness, stupid in their perverse independence and surly in their unreasonable opposition to order and regulations; the others, men of like origin and caste but licked into some degree of form and congruity by their rough experiences, rude and ragged . . . but quieter, more subdued, more ready to yield some fancied right for the common good."

It seemed paradoxical that these veterans of frenzied California would be the more tranquil travelers, but there was something almost mellow about these rough-looking young-old men. They walked with the weary discipline of soldiers returning from an inconclusive but costly battle. California had shredded their illusions and exposed them as the vainglorious follies that they were. They had learned that survival depended on adaptability. They had seen the elephant.

The velocity of California life was as furious in 1852 as it had been in 1849. "The everyday jog-trot of ordinary human existence was not a fast enough pace for Californians," the Scotsman J. D. Borthwick noticed. "The longest period of time ever thought of was a month. Money was loaned and houses were rented by the month. All engagements were made by the month. . . . In the space of a month the whole city might be swept off by fire and a totally new one might be flourishing in its place."

Speed alone was not enough for the California metabolism; there had to be regular transfusions of excitement. The precipitating sensation could be almost anything—an election, a lynching, a fire, even a good dogfight. Hinton Helper, a languid young North Carolinian who arrived in 1852, was repelled by this craving for action: "If a terrier catches a rat or if a big turnip is brought to the market the people cluster together and scramble for a sight," he wrote. If a man steps on the toe of another "it only requires one minute for the injured party to shoot the offender, two minutes for somebody else to stab the shooter, and three minutes for the whole crowd to hang the stabber." The enemy was boredom. "Yesterday was frightfully dull," the *Alta* noted wryly in late 1851. "Nobody was killed, no coroner's inquests were held, no robberies, no legs broken, [there was] only an old horse running away down Washington Street."

Gold, as always, generated the greatest excitements. The years after 1850 were enlivened by a series of rushes to the sites of new discoveries. The place of the moment in early 1851 was Gold Bluffs, a line of steep, fog-shrouded cliffs on the Pacific between Humboldt Bay and the mouth of the Klamath River. A report that the beach beneath the bluffs contained a mixture of gold and black sand lured at least eight shiploads of prospectors from San Francisco, among them the ever mobile J. Goldsborough Bruff. The miners found that the tiny particles of gold on the beach were too fine to be separated from the sand.

The discovery of gold on a creek in New South Wales, Australia, precipitated a transoceanic rush by several thousand Californians in late 1851 and 1852; the Australian who found the first flakes had served his prospecting apprenticeship in California. The Kern River, on the rim of the San Joaquin Valley, attracted five thousand rapidly disenchanted gold seekers in 1854. Four years later the new Golcondas were the Fraser River country in British Columbia and Cherry Creek ("Pikes Peak or Bust") in Colorado. The most spectacular find was the fabulous silver deposit in the Comstock Lode, which was only a few miles from the trail the emigrants had traveled across Carson Valley in 1849. The stampede to the Comstock in 1859 and 1860 almost emptied the California mines.

The sordid "justice" preferred by what one forty-niner called "their majesties the mob" boiled to a peak in the two years after 1850. The frequently ineffectual mining camp justices of the peace were routinely ignored when a murder occurred; it was easier to seize a suspect, elect a judge and jury from the crowd, and mete out instant retribution. Lynchings took place in Rich Bar, Jackson, Weaverville, Murphys, Mokelumne Hill, Shasta, Rough and Ready, and several other camps in 1851 and 1852. Lashings were even more common. Occasionally a man was lashed for a crime of which he was later cleared; similar mistakes probably occurred with lynch victims. The most barbaric spasm of mob violence was the lynching of a young Mexican woman in Downieville on July 5, 1851. Her name was Juanita.

She was seen arguing with a miner named Cannon that morning at the door of the small cabin she shared with a Mexican gambler. Suddenly she grabbed a long knife and drove it into his chest; Cannon died a few minutes later. A mob of sore-headed Fourth of July celebrants quickly gathered, seized her, and hustled her to the town plaza for what passed for a trial. A man who spoke in her defense was knocked to the ground and beaten. A physician who argued that she was pregnant was shouted down and threatened; three other doctors, ordered to examine her, disputed his testimony. The mob of some two thousand was baying for blood by the time she was sentenced to be hanged and marched to a bridge over the boulder-strewn Yuba.

A reporter sketched this word picture of her last moments: "She extended her hand to each of the bystanders immediately around her, and bidding each an 'adios, senor,' voluntarily ascended the scaffold, took the rope and adjusted it around her neck with her own hand, releasing her luxuriant hair from beneath it so that it should flow free. Her arms were then pinioned, to which she strongly objected, her clothes tied down, the cap adjusted over her face, and in a moment more the cords which supported the scaffolding had been cut and she hung suspended between the heavens and the earth."

In San Francisco the response to a tide of unsolved crimes and police corruption in the summer of 1851 was the organization of an extralegal "committee of vigilance." The urban vigilantes, who conducted trials and passed sentences in secret, were more refined than their mountain counterparts; their roster included many of the city's most sophisticated businessmen. Supported by a majority of both press and pulpit ("When a government does not protect," a Congregational minister explained, "there is no government"), the committee systematically hanged four men (one for a minor robbery), lashed another, and banished twenty-eight. Groups modeled on the San Francisco committee sprang up in

Sonora (where Enos Christman served as secretary), Sacramento, and elsewhere. A renewed siege of crime and fear led to the formation of another San Francisco vigilance committee in 1856.

The continuing sway of nativist bigotry was evident in the fact that a disproportionate number of lynch victims in both the city and the camps were foreign. Three of the four men hanged in San Francisco in 1851 were immigrants from Australia; the fourth had come from England. It was no accident that the only woman ever lynched in the mines was a Mexican. There were at least two lynchings of American blacks, but Latins remained the principal targets of Californian discrimination until they were gradually replaced by Chinese. The foreign miners' tax, resurrected at $3 per month in 1852, was raised to $4 the following year, and to $6 in 1855; the legislators thoughtfully appropriated funds to translate the statute into Chinese.

To the rest of the country California was and would remain a rowdy delinquent, but for the wrong reasons. The outrages that aggravated the Victorian sensibilities of mid-nineteenth-century America were invariably breaches of personal morality—profanity, the heroic scale of intemperance, prostitution. "I have seen purer liquors, better segars, finer tobacco, truer guns and pistols, larger dirks and bowie knives, and prettier courtesans here," the chivalrous Hinton Helper wrote, "than in any other place I have ever visited, and it is my unbiased opinion that California can and does furnish the best bad things that are obtainable in America." But the real evils in California were the national curse of bigotry, the hot-blooded impatience that found law too time-consuming, and what one historian aptly called "social laziness," an immature aversion to the drudgery of building a stable society.

HARBINGERS of change were visible by 1852. Buried in the special census of that year was the astonishing statistic that an estimated twelve thousand Californians were farming—this in a state where men had died of scurvy for lack of fresh food only a few years earlier. Farmers were nesters; they came to stay and to grow with the state. They also recognized the remarkable potential of the California valleys: by 1855 the state was producing almost all the food it consumed and exporting wheat, potatoes, oats, and barley.

The census put the 1852 population at 264,435. More than half were miners. A quarter, including about ten thousand Chinese, were foreign-born. Women still comprised less than 15 percent of the total, but this was changing also, and too fast for the fact-gatherers. By 1853 the irrepressible Alonzo Delano could write that "live women are now so plenty that a miner wouldn't take the trouble to drop his pick to look at one." J. D. Borthwick observed that the birth and marriage columns in the newspapers were becoming as lengthy as they were in many larger cities. The most gratifying evidence of change in the character of the population was displayed in a May Day parade in San Francisco in 1853: more than a thousand schoolchildren marched.

The dramatic increase in the parasol and petticoat population had an immediate impact on San Francisco: gambling houses closed for lack of patronage; churches enjoyed a corresponding boom (there were eighteen by 1853); men began to dress with more care. The city evolved in other ways as well. A catastrophic fire in May of 1851, which leveled eighteen square blocks, killed a dozen people, and left the city smoldering "like a great bed of lava," had prompted the long-overdue development of efficient and well-equipped fire companies. Industries—sawmills, brickyards, shipyards, foundries, flour mills—were now operating.

It was easier to get to California by 1853, and easier to travel inside the state. Cornelius Vanderbilt developed a route across Nicaragua which competed successfully with the Panama passage until the completion of the Panama railroad in 1855; the train slashed the travel time between New York and San Francisco to twenty-five days. Daily stagecoaches linked Stockton and Sonora with the blooming village of Oakland on the eastern shore of San Francisco Bay, while others ran between Sacramento and the towns in the northern mines.

At length the tempo of life in the gold country itself subsided into a rhythm only a few beats quicker than the pace of existence elsewhere. "Weaverville has had much the appearance of a quiet country village lately," a merchant in that Trinity River camp wrote in early 1853. Lynchings, with isolated exceptions, finally stopped. Men toiled for wages at the quartz-crushing mills along the Mother Lode. Companies of industrious Chinese built wing dams and took their chances on twice-tried placers. Lone prospectors, forever in quest of the fountainhead, drifted like phantoms through the high Sierras. A few of the roaring camps of 1848 and 1849 already lay deserted and still. At times it was possible to stand amid them and see the incomparable colors this land had worn before and would wear again—silver and emerald and deep blue and gold, always gold.

The enchantment of California could captivate anyone, even a cultured and initially hostile New England doctor's wife named Louise Amelia Clappe, who spent a year and two months at Rich Bar in 1851 and 1852. Mrs. Clappe, who wrote a series of brilliantly evocative letters to her sister and signed them "Dame Shirley," railed at first at the deprivations of her rugged life: "no newspapers, no churches, lectures, concerts or theaters; no fresh books, no shopping, calling nor gossiping little tea-drinkings; no parties, no balls, no picnics . . . no promenades, no rides nor drives, no vegetables but potatoes and onions, no milk, no eggs, no *nothing.*"

But eventually even Dame Shirley felt at home in the mines: everyone should go, she said, "just to see how little it takes to make people comfortable." She left in November of 1852 with a hard-won respect for "divine nature, into whose benign eyes I [had] never looked," and with genuine regret. She escaped just in time. A few days later a blizzard blocked every trail out of Rich Bar.

HUNDREDS of gold rush veterans went home to write about it: they chronicled their experiences in articles and books while they tried to readjust to the dawdling pace of town and village life. Many couldn't do it: they gathered up the family and returned to California. Others lingered in the promised land, pinned by pride to their dreams until they were fulfilled or forsaken. For most of them, the gold rush was the epic adventure of their lives.

Sam Brannan, the onetime Mormon elder who electrified San Francisco with his quinine bottle of gold dust in 1848, was widely regarded as the wealthiest man in California by 1854. He owned substantial chunks of both San Francisco and Sacramento, issued his own currency at the bank he founded, and generously supported local charities. But Brannan eventually skidded and lost everything: he never recovered from a costly divorce settlement which drained away most of his capital. When he died in San Diego in 1889, his body lay in a vault for a year awaiting funds for burial.

Edward Kemble, the young editor who suspected that the gold story was a hoax, worked on California newspapers for several years, served as a Union officer in the Civil War, and later became an inspector in the Bureau of Indian Affairs. He was fifty-seven when he died in New York in 1886.

Edward Gould Buffum, the ex-army officer who narrowly escaped dying of scurvy on the American River, became an editor and later a California assemblyman. In 1857 he moved to Paris as a correspondent for the New York *Herald*. He committed suicide there a decade later. "The sea of trouble," the obituary in a San Francisco paper commented, "swamps many a worthy craft."

Navy Chaplain Walter Colton, the author of the first tales of California gold to appear in eastern newspapers, was reassigned to the Philadelphia navy yard in 1849. He died two years later.

Dr. Jacob D. B. Stillman was one of several forty-niners who later tried to track down the men he had sailed with. He learned that a fifth of his ninety-five shipmates were still in California a generation later; another fifth had died; most of the rest had returned east. Stillman himself resumed his Baltimore practice in 1851 but later settled in California, where he had cherished "the hopes that made radiant the morning of our lives."

Mark Hopkins, Stillman's fellow sufferer on the woeful *Pacific*, owned a half-interest in a Sacramento hardware store in 1853. His partner was Collis Huntington, the canny trader who had shown such a talent for accumulation during his interlude in Panama. In 1859 Huntington and Hopkins joined two other Sacramento merchants, Charles Crocker and Leland Stanford, in financing the phenomenally lucrative Central Pacific railroad.

Cal Gardiner, the well-bred Long Islander who measured his success by a list of meals taped on a glass gold container, persevered in the mines until 1857, when he departed with "a few thousands." Later a lumberman in Green Bay, Wisconsin, Gardiner looked back on his California years as his happiest. The "memory of that wild life" was still green when he wrote his reminiscences forty years later—"its risks, its sense of animal health, its constant series of adventures, the exciting gallop over hill and plain, the thrilling explorations amid mountain gorges. . . ." He was ninety when he died.

New York *Tribune* writer Bayard Taylor remained a connoisseur of the exotic throughout a peripatetic life. The publication of his two-volume *El Dorado* in 1850 was followed by popular travel books on Africa, India, the Orient, Russia, Egypt, and Iceland, in addition to novels and collections of poetry. He was the United States minister to Germany when he died, aged fifty-three, in 1878.

Bill Johnston, the impetuous young man from Pittsburgh who hurtled across the plains in the vanguard of the 1849 emigration and then dashed home, was again living in Pittsburgh when he published his recollections of "the one eventful adventure of my life" in 1892.

Alonzo Delano stayed in California as a quartz mill superintendent and later a banker in Grass Valley, and as a writer who helped develop a distinctively western style of humor. "His prospects were fine," he wrote of a miner in one sketch, "they have continued so, and probably always will." A collection of his pieces (*Chips off the Old Block*) appeared in 1853, and a play (*A Live Woman in the Mines*) in 1857. He appeared to appreciate the rumors linking him romantically with Lola Montez, the internationally famous actress and courtesan who passed a few tumultuous months in Grass Valley in 1854.

John Woodhouse Audubon, who rallied his cholera-ravaged company in Texas and led his men across the southwestern deserts, returned to New York in 1850. He and his brother published their father's final nature books after the great naturalist's death in 1851. John Woodhouse died— "overworked and careworn," his daughter wrote—only eleven years later. He was forty-nine.

William Manly, the Death Valley pathfinder, grew restless after his return to Wisconsin in 1851. The enforced idleness of winter unnerved him, and spring wasn't much better—"every day was like Sunday." He hurried back to the mines by way of the Isthmus after only a few months. Later he was a storekeeper in Nevada County and a rancher in the Santa Clara Valley. His book, one of the finest personal narratives of the gold rush, was published in 1894.

The man the 1850 emigrants knew as the Wheelbarrow Man was revealed in an 1852 newspaper story to be a Mr. Brookmire of Warren, Pennsylvania. The story reported that the hard-handed Brookmire, as predicted, had earned his pile: he went home with $15,000.

The Canadian-born merchant William Perkins continued to record the pleasures and pains of life in Sonora through the spring of 1852. The arrival of a Yankee woman inspired a protest that the competition between "virtue in the shape of tall, gawky, sallow, ill-dressed down-Easters" and "elegantly adorned, beautiful and graceful vice" was clearly uneven. By March 1852 he was complaining about Sonora's torpid dullness—"no fights, no murders, no rapes, no robberies to amuse us." Perkins' years in Sonora gave him an affinity for Latins; he later settled in Argentina, where he became a businessman and newspaper editor. He died in 1893.

The French aristocrat Ernest de Massey, having recovered from his painful foray to the Trinity mines, found surcease in San Francisco as a furniture dealer, a columnist (for French readers), and eventually as the proprietor of a European bookstore.

Enos Christman, who had left his fiancée Ellen Apple back in Pennsylvania, succumbed to her plaintive pleas ("Please, do not put it off longer") and returned home in the summer of 1852. The hundred ounces of gold he had amassed was enough to repay the man who had staked him and to marry the loyal Ellen, the treasure he had been seeking all along; "my hopes have been gratified," he concluded, "and I have realized a fortune." His stay-at-home comrade Peebles Prizer had already married the "old and tough" Sallie Cope.

Lucius Fairchild, the Wisconsin teenager who had vowed not to return without "something more than when I started," worked in the mines until 1855, when he went home with a modest stack of dust. He later lost an arm as a Union colonel at Gettysburg and became one of his state's most prominent politicians: he was elected to three terms as governor of Wisconsin and afterwards served as U.S. minister to Spain.

The nimble swindler Parker H. French surfaced in 1854 as a California state legislator and a uniquely qualified member of the ways and means committee. The lust for adventure seized him again shortly afterwards: he joined a filibuster expedition to Nicaragua and even served briefly as Nicaraguan minister to the United States. In 1861 he was jailed in Connecticut as a Confederate spy. French was last sighted on a Washington, D.C., sidewalk in 1876. He looked like an old drunk, an acquaintance said, but he was still talking big money: he said he was suing the Mexican government for $106,000 for breach of contract in his Durango escapade.

J. Goldsborough Bruff tolerated unruly California for only five months after his arrival in San Francisco in January 1851. He worked as a draftsman between trips to Gold Bluffs and Sonoma. Bruff gave no reason for his decision to leave, but it might have been related to two entries in his journal just before he sailed: one described the first hanging by the San Francisco vigilantes; the other said simply, "I received a letter from my daughter—8 years of age."

Bruff resumed his career as a draftsman and architect for the government in Washington. He was still doing his daily stint when he died at eighty-four in 1889. The obituary notice in the Washington *Weekly Star* reduced the great adventure of his life to two sentences: "For the past

63 years Mr. Bruff [had] been in government employ, and there was only one interregnum, when, in 1849, with other young men, he was stricken with the gold fever and started for California to amass a fortune. He was unsuccessful, and in 1851 he returned to Washington and resumed his work in the Treasury Department."

THE YEARS after the gold rush were cruelest to the two men who had shared the thrill of discovery on that January day in 1848. John Sutter, shorn ultimately of everything but his dignity, was transformed by the new Californians into a beribboned and powerless presence at ceremonial events. The costs of a long court battle to establish the legality of his original land grants drained the last of his fortune. Squatters pillaged his property. He lost his beloved Hock Farm to his creditors, regained it, and lost it again to fire in 1865.

In 1870 he finally abandoned the state he had adorned for so long and moved with his wife to the little German hamlet of Lititz, Pennsylvania. His repeated requests for federal aid—on grounds that he had contributed materially to the settlement and development of California—went unheeded. Bancroft found him at Lititz in 1876—kind and courteous as ever, still soldierly in bearing, and tearful as he recalled the vivid past. He died in Washington on June 18, 1880.

The reclusive James Marshall, who had glimpsed the first golden flake in the tailrace of Sutter's mill, grew increasingly bitter and mistrustful of anyone but pre–gold rush Californians. "Those men I mostly found to be true to honor," he wrote to a friend, "but the grabbers, no." Marshall prospected and worked at a succession of jobs in Coloma and the nearby village of Kelsey. The state legislature voted him a pension of $200 a month in 1872, but later let it lapse amid reports that he spent most of it on liquor. The legislators rejected a new request for help for the impoverished Marshall shortly before his death in 1885. Five years later they spent $9,000 on a monument to him at Coloma.

SOURCE NOTES

THE FOLLOWING is neither a compilation of the sources for every fact in this book nor a comprehensive catalog of the books, manuscripts, and periodicals that I consulted. It is rather an acknowledgment of the primary and secondary sources that I found most significant and helpful. If a source is mentioned in the body of the text I do not repeat it in the notes after the initial citation. I have also tried to streamline the notes by eschewing the notation of sources used solely for corroboration. The date and place of publication are those of the edition I read.

CHAPTER I: SUNRISE IN A BOTTLE

The most pertinent contemporary and reminiscent accounts of the discovery at Sutter's mill have been conveniently assembled by Rodman W. Paul in *The California Gold Discovery*, published by Robert Greenwood's Talisman Press in the old mining town of Georgetown, Calif. (1966). The most reliable on-the-scene observer at the mill was the earnest Mormon workman Henry W. Bigler, whose diaries were edited by Erwin G. Gudde and published as *Bigler's Chronicle of the West* (Berkeley, 1962). James Peter Zollinger's *Sutter, the Man and His Empire* (New York, 1939) is the finest of several Sutter biographies and considerably more trustworthy than Sutter's recollections. Sutter's friend Heinrich Lienhard gives a lively and valuable account of the early days at the fort in *A Pioneer at Sutter's Fort* (Los Angeles, 1941), translated and edited by Marguerite Wilbur. The luckless career of the discoverer himself is superbly narrated by Theressa Gay in *James W. Marshall, A Biography* (Georgetown, Calif., 1967), one of the half-dozen best gold rush books. Sutter's attempt to lease mining rights from the Indians is documented in *Letters of the Gold Discovery* (edited by George Hammond, San Francisco, 1948); the military response is described by William T. Sherman in his *Memoirs* (New York, 1886).

San Francisco and the rest of California on the brink of the golden era are described by Richard Henry Dana, Jr., in *Two Years Before the Mast* (New York, 1964), Charles Howard Shinn in *Mining Camps* (New York, 1948), Frank Soulé et al. in *Annals of San Francisco* (New York, 1855), and William Heath Davis in *Sixty Years in California* (San Francisco, 1889). Bigler, Lienhard, and Ralph

P. Bieber in "California Gold Mania" (*Mississippi Valley Historical Review*, June 1948) recount the adventures of the earliest prospectors. The material on Sam Brannan comes from *The First Forty-Niner*, by James Scherer (New York, 1925), and various biographical references, including the *Latter Day Saint Biographical Encyclopaedia* (Salt Lake City, 1920); James Lick's career is discussed in the *Society of California Pioneers* (hereafter *SCP*) *Quarterly* of March 1924. My description of Kit Carson's gold rush role was drawn from his *Autobiography* (edited by Milo Milton Quaife, Chicago, 1935) and "Kit Carson at Cajon," an article by John Adam Hussey in the *California Historical Society (CHS) Quarterly*, March 1950. The story of the first news reports dispatched eastward is in Victor Fourgeaud's *Prospects of California* (San Francisco, 1942) and in "Sam Brannan, Herald of the Gold Rush," by Douglas S. Watson (*CHS Quarterly*, September 1931).

CHAPTER II: THE GILDED SUMMER

The true "feel" of the gold rush, the texture of the event, emerges most vividly in the contemporary writings of the men who participated in it. These accounts—journals, diaries, letters, and narratives written on the fly or shortly after the incidents they describe—are also the most dependable sources; they were set down before time and the miners' taste for veneration had gilded their memories. I have based my narrative as much as possible on these primary sources, the descriptions and experiences of men who were there. There are hundreds of them.

Even in the summer of 1848, during the last extended interlude before the deluge from east and south, the journal keepers were roaming the foothills. The best writer among the 1848 rovers was the Reverend Walter Colton, whose *Three Years in California* (New York, 1850) was published soon after he was transferred from Monterey to the East Coast. James Carson's *Recollections of the California Mines* (Stockton, Calif., 1852) is another good 1848 account. Chester Lyman's diary and letters appeared in the *CHS Quarterly* of June 1934. The longer, reminiscent view is provided by John Swan, who wrote *A Trip to the Gold Mines of California in 1848* (San Francisco, 1960) about a generation after the fact, and by Antonio Coronel, as quoted by Dale L. Morgan and James R. Scobie in their introduction to *William Perkins' Journal* (Berkeley, 1964). Morgan and Scobie are also among the best sources on the forty-eighters; others include the preeminent California historian Hubert Howe Bancroft (*Works*, Vol. 6, San Francisco, 1888) and William Grimshaw (*Grimshaw's Narrative*, edited by J. R. K. Kantor, Sacramento, 1964).

The technique of gold mining is well described by Rodman W. Paul in *California Gold* (Lincoln, Neb., 1965) and limned further in John W. Caughey's fine *Gold Is the Cornerstone* (Berkeley, 1948). Colonel Richard Mason's report on his 1848 visit to the mines, which convinced the East that the gold was real, is reprinted by Paul in *The California Gold Discovery*. The Frenchman Jacques Moerenhout narrates his less hurried trek in his *Inside Story of the Gold Rush* (San Francisco, 1935), edited by G. Ezra Dane. Ralph P. Bieber's *Southern*

Trails to California in 1849 (Glendale, Calif., 1937) and Ferol Egan's *The El Dorado Trail* (New York, 1970) recount Ned Beale's remarkable ride across Mexico. The eastern reaction to his arrival is shown by Bieber, Theressa Gay, and contemporary reports in the New York *Herald.* Heinrich Lienhard and James Peter Zollinger describe the troubles that beset the family Sutter.

CHAPTER III: HO FOR CALIFORNIA!

The gold-shadowed maiden voyage of the steamship *California* is sketched by Victor Berthold in *The Pioneer Steamer California* (Boston, 1932), John E. Pomfret in *California Gold Rush Voyages* (San Marino, Calif., 1954), and John Haskell Kemble in *The Panama Route* (Berkeley, 1943). Theressa Gay and the San Francisco *Californian* offer details on the murder at Sutter's mill. The ebullient E. Gould Buffum hastily recounted his 1848 ramblings in *Six Months in the Gold Mines* (Philadelphia, 1850); Governor-to-be Peter Burnett published his reminiscences as *Recollections and Opinions of an Old Pioneer* (New York, 1880). Information on the unimposing overland emigration of 1848 was drawn from George R. Stewart's excellent *The California Trail* (New York, 1971) and Walker D. Wyman's invaluable anthology of gold rush letters, *California Emigrant Letters* (New York, 1952). James J. Rawls describes California Indians in "Gold Diggers: Indian Miners in the California Gold Rush," in the *CHS Quarterly,* Spring 1976. The statistics for gold production in 1848 are taken from Thomas Senior Berry's "Gold, but How Much?" in the *CHS Quarterly* for Fall 1976.

The wild excitement generated by the arrival of Colonel Mason's gold-bearing emissary, Lieutenant Lucien Loeser, is described by Gay, Bieber, and such contemporary sources as the New York *Herald* and New Orleans *Picayune.* The steamship sailings that immediately followed are discussed in Kemble and in *First Steamship Pioneers* (San Francisco, 1874), an artless collection of forty-niner narratives issued in celebration of the twenty-fifth anniversary of the gold rush.

CHAPTER IV: OH! SUSANNA

My description of the gold hysteria in the eastern states derives primarily from newspapers. The experiences of individual forty-niners were drawn from their diaries, letters, and narratives, including Elisha Oscar Crosby's *Reminiscences of California and Guatemala* (San Marino, Calif., 1945), *Seeking the Golden Fleece* by Jacob Stillman (New York, 1877), *California As I Saw It* by William M'Collum (Buffalo, 1850), and T. T. Johnson's speedily composed *Sights in the Gold Region and Scenes by the Way* (Philadelphia, 1849). The impromptu rendition of a forty-niner version of "Oh! Susanna" was reported in the New York *Herald* and detailed further in an article by Edward E. Chever ("The History of 'Oh, California, That's the Land for Me'") in the *SCP Quarterly* (January 1930). The poignant letters of Dr. Horace Pond are preserved in manuscript at the Beinecke Rare Book and Manuscript Library at Yale University.

S. Laird Swagert analyzed British reaction to the gold discovery in the *CHS Quarterly* of January 1953 ("British Comment 1849–51"). Gilbert Chinard (*When the French Came to California*, San Francisco, 1944) is the best of several sources for the French role. The story of the exquisitely well-prepared Boston and California Company is told by company member Willard Farwell in "Cape Horn and Cooperative Mining in 1849" (*Century Illustrated Monthly*, August 1891) and reconstructed by Octavius T. Howe in *Argonauts of '49* (Cambridge, Mass., 1923). Mexican gold miners are discussed by Morgan and Scobie in their introduction to *William Perkins' Journal*, by Doris Wright in "The Making of Cosmopolitan California" (*CHS Quarterly*, December 1940), and by Carl Meyer in *Bound for Sacramento* (Claremont, Calif., 1938).

The frenzied scramble by the first gold seekers to cross the Isthmus of Panama was recorded in the New York *Herald*, the New York *Tribune*, *First Steamship Pioneers*, and Kemble's *The Panama Route*. Eliza Farnham discussed her scheme for furnishing wives for the lonely miners in *California Indoors and Out* (New York, 1856). The detective work on the Vizetelly hoax was performed by Douglas S. Watson in "Spurious Californiana" (*CHS Quarterly*, March 1932). The details of Rufus Porter's improbable career come from his own writings in *Scientific American* and elsewhere, from biographical references, and from Jean Lipman's excellent *Rufus Porter, Yankee Pioneer* (New York, 1968). The P. T. Barnum anecdote was told by J. F. B. Marshall in "Three Gold Dust Stories" (*Century Illustrated Monthly*, March 1891).

CHAPTER V: THE ARGOSY

A few veterans of the long, miserable voyage around Cape Horn tried to enliven their narratives with invented dialogue and dramatic if implausible incident. My first criterion for a contemporary source was reliability, primarily established by checking parallel accounts against each other and by the accumulation of verifiable detail. But the validity of a given narrative may also be supported in less scientific, more subjective ways—by a certain solidity, for example, a sense of overall authority which becomes recognizable after one has read dozens of such books. My second criterion was the quality and quantity of the writer's descriptions, and his skill in evoking the sensory character of the experience.

The Cape Horn narratives which best met my criteria were *Around the Horn in '49* by Linville Hall (Wethersfield, Conn., 1898), *Notes of a Voyage to California via Cape Horn* by Samuel Upham (Philadelphia, 1878), *Journal of a Voyage to California and Life in the Gold Diggings* by Albert Lyman (Hartford, Conn., 1852), *Gold Rush Diary* by Moses Pearson Cogswell (New Hampshire Historical Society, 1949), Jacob Stillman's *Seeking the Golden Fleece* (noted earlier), and the previously cited Farwell and Howe accounts of the odyssey of the Boston and California Company. I also found excellent material in manuscript form: the letters of John Cowden and Dr. Horace Pond and the journal of William Beecher at the Beinecke Library, Yale; and the *Petrel*, the handwritten newspaper produced by the passengers on the ship *Duxbury*, at the Bancroft Library in Berkeley, Calif. *Sea Routes to the Gold Fields* (New York, 1949), by Oscar Lewis, is a good overall account of the golden argosy.

CHAPTER VI: THE EASY WAY

My portrait of the brotherhood of the impatient in Panama City relies most heavily on the previously mentioned contemporary narratives by T. T. Johnson and William M'Collum and on those by James Delavan (*Notes on California and the Placers*, New York, 1850) and Julius Pratt ("To California by Panama in 1849," *Century Illustrated Monthly*, April 1891). Forty-niners John Letts (*California Illustrated*, New York, 1852) and James Ayers (*Gold and Sunshine*, Boston, 1922) contribute information on the more desperate attempts to sail from Panama to San Francisco. The material on the financially adroit Collis Huntington and the similarly endowed Darius Ogden Mills comes from biographical sketches at the Bancroft Library in Berkeley. The eruption of outrage at the practices of Panama steamship agents is discussed in "The American Meeting" (*SCP Quarterly*, October 1929).

Cal Gardiner describes his wide-eyed transit of the Isthmus in his remarkable narrative, *In Pursuit of the Golden Dream* (Stoughton, Mass., 1970), written more than forty years after the rush and masterfully edited by Dale L. Morgan. Bayard Taylor set down his experiences in the two-volume *El Dorado* (New York, 1850), the finest of all contemporary gold rush books. The misadventures of Roger Baldwin and the other members of Gordon's California Association were related by Baldwin in "Tarrying in Nicaragua" (*Century Illustrated Monthly*, October 1891) and in his letters, preserved in manuscript form at Yale's Sterling Library. The tortuous voyage of the *Alexander Von Humboldt* was described by Julius Pratt, Collis Huntington, and Charles Clar ("Pioneer among the Argonauts," Bancroft Library manuscript). The even more trying ordeal of the men who were obliged to hike up Baja California was recounted by Jacob Stillman and Louis Bonestell ("Autobiography," *SCP Quarterly*, September 1927).

CHAPTER VII: REVEILLE ON THE RIVERS

Ralph P. Bieber's *Southern Trails to California in 1849* (previously cited) is an excellent summary of the various southern routes to California. The best source on the Arkansas way west is *Marcy and the Gold Seekers* by Grant Foreman (Norman, Okla., 1939). John Woodhouse Audubon tells the story of his expedition's travail in *A Western Journal, 1849–50* (Cleveland, 1906); additions to the Audubon record appear in "Audubon's Ill-Fated Western Journey" by Jeanne Van Nostrand (*CHS Quarterly*, December 1942) and in *William Perkins' Journal*. The bulk of the material on the Canadian River migration is drawn from Foreman. He and Bieber are the principal sources for my references to Cherokee forty-niners.

The depiction of San Francisco in the spring of 1849 derives from contemporary descriptions by William Redmond Ryan (*Personal Adventures in Upper and Lower California* (London, 1850), Vicente Perez Rosales ("We Were 49ers," *American West*, May 1976), the French writer known as Trény (*California Unveiled*, San Francisco, 1944), and Wyman's *California Emigrant Letters*. Theressa Gay and James J. Rawls, both noted before, describe the slaughter of the Coloma Indians. The experiences of Chilean and Mexican forty-niners are dealt with by Abraham P. Nasatir ("Chileans in California during the Gold Rush Period," *CHS Quarterly*, Spring 1974), Leonard Pitt (*The Decline of the Californios*, Berkeley, 1971), and by William Perkins in his journal.

J. Goldsborough Bruff's massive journals were brilliantly edited by Georgia Willis Read and Ruth Gaines and published as *Gold Rush: The Journals, Drawings and Other Papers of J. Goldsborough Bruff* (New York, 1949). Bill Johnston brought forth his recollections as *Experiences of a Forty-Niner* (Pittsburgh, 1892). Other descriptions of the emigrants as they gathered at the jumping-off points appear in Roland D. Crandall's *Love and Nuggets* (Old Greenwich, Conn., 1967), *The California Letters of Lucius Fairchild*, edited by Joseph Schafer (Madison, Wis., 1931), *Trail to California: The Overland Journal of Vincent Geiger and Wakeman Bryarly* (edited by David M. Potter, New Haven, 1945), the previously cited works by Walker Wyman and George R. Stewart, and the manuscript of Joseph Hamelin at Yale's Beinecke Library. Wyman portrays St. Joseph and Independence ("The Outfitting Posts") in the *Pacific Historical Review* (1949). Alonzo Delano (*Life on the Plains and Among the Diggings*, New York, 1973) and Reuben Cole Shaw (*Across the Plains in '49*, New York, 1966) describe the arrival of cholera in the river towns.

CHAPTER VIII: THE COURSE OF EMPIRE

As I researched the great emigration of 1849 I began to suspect that every third wagon contained a diarist. Journals proliferated: many forty-niners had at least a dim awareness that they were part of a great event in American history, and they wished to record their role in it; others wanted to describe the supreme adventure of their lives. In reading the archives they left behind, I tried to extract the common themes, sensations, and attitudes, and then to concentrate on a few whose experiences might stand for them all. As with the Cape Horn narratives, I based my selections on both the reliability of the journalist and the energy and skill with which he set down his observations. Focusing on J. Goldsborough Bruff, Alonzo Delano, and Bill Johnston permitted me to deal with three widely varying personalities of different backgrounds and temperaments. It also happened that each traveled at a different pace—Johnston in the lead, Delano in the middle, and Bruff in the rear—and thus saw a different aspect of the migration.

My narrative of their journey is interspersed with more general passages in which the material is drawn from both contemporary and secondary accounts. These include *The Buckeye Rovers in the Gold Rush* by Howard Scamehorn (Athens, Ohio, 1965), *Diary of a Pioneer* by Niles Searls (San Francisco, 1940), and previously noted works by Wyman, Potter, Crandall, and Hamelin (who here makes his debut, as far as I can reckon, in the literature of the gold rush). Irene Paden's *Wake of the Prairie Schooner* (New York, 1943), part history and part inspired travelogue, is in a class by itself as a latter-day evocation of the trail.

Of the various ills that forty-niner flesh was heir to, I found Isaac Wistar (*Autobiography*, Philadelphia, 1914) and Sarah Royce (*A Frontier Lady*, New

Haven, 1932) most useful for Indian episodes; Russell Bidlack (*Letters Home: The Story of Ann Arbor's 49ers*, Ann Arbor, Mich., 1960) and Niles Searls were illuminating on the subject of cholera; David M. Potter enumerated the accidents that befell the emigrants.

William Perkins' Journal is my most reliable source for events in Sonora and the southern mines; John Morse's *First History of Sacramento* (Sacramento, 1853) is replete with information about that board-and-canvas metropolis; and the previously cited accounts by Burnett, Buffum, and Soulé provide a portrait of California politics. Ernest A. Wiltsee writes of the mania for speculative cities in "The City of New York on the Pacific" (*CHS Quarterly*, January 1933).

CHAPTER IX: THE UNYIELDING LAND

The narrative of the overland journey across Mexico and the Southwest relies primarily on Audubon's *Western Journal* and Foreman's *Marcy and the Gold Seekers*. Other useful forty-niner accounts include *The Santa Fe Trail to California 1849–52* by H. M. T. Powell (edited by Douglas S. Watson, San Francisco, 1931), *Records of a California Family* by Lewis C. Gunn (San Diego, 1928), *Mexican Gold Trail* by George W. B. Evans (edited by Glenn S. Dumke, San Marino, Calif., 1945), *Sixteen Months at the Gold Diggings* by Daniel B. Woods (New York, 1851), and the journal of John Durivage, which appears in Bieber's *Southern Trails to California in 1849*. Robert Eccleston (*Overland to California on the Southwestern Trail in 1849*, Berkeley, 1950) contributes to the record on the Gila River trial and execution. William Brandon (*The American Heritage Book of Indians*, New York, 1961) and Alvin J. Josephy, Jr. (*The Indian Heritage of America*, New York, 1968) are valuable sources on the southwestern Indians.

My main companions on the trek along the Platte, of course, are Johnston, Delano, and Bruff. Other emigrants added details on specific places and incidents: Ansel McCall (*The Great California Trail in 1849*, Bath, N.Y., 1882) described the anniversary party in Salt Lake City; John Banks (in Scamehorn's previously cited *Buckeye Rovers*) and the Michigan men in Bidlack's *Letters Home* (also noted before) recount the romantic triangle involving the Jenkins family; Niles Searls narrates the travail of the "Pioneer Line"; and Palmer C. Tiffany (manuscript at Beinecke Library, Yale) gives us John Grantham's verses on the painfully disappointing Humboldt.

The best sources for the "Hounds" riot are the San Francisco *Alta California*, the *Argonaut*, Bancroft's *Popular Tribunals* (San Francisco, 1887) and Nasatir's article on Chileans in the gold rush. Farwell records the melancholy dissolution of the superbly organized Boston and California company.

CHAPTER X: MAGIC LANTERN COUNTRY

The descriptions of mining life by John Cowden, Cal Gardiner, John Letts, and William M'Collum are all from accounts cited earlier. E. G. Waite reports his prospecting experiences in "Pioneer Mining in California" (*Century Illustrated Monthly*, May 1891); the letter from the Missourians who made $16,000 in eight

days appears in Wyman's *California Emigrant Letters*. My sketch of San Francisco in mid-1849 draws on the recollections of Jacob Stillman, the *Alta California*, and the letters of Mrs. Jerusha Merrill (manuscript at Beinecke Library, Yale).

The best account of the rescue of the overland stragglers is in Stewart's *The California Trail*. Contemporary references appear in Bruff, Sarah Royce, James Pritchard (*Overland Diary*, Denver, 1959), and the *Letters 1849–51* of the Wolverine Ranger Company (Mt. Pleasant, Mich., 1974). The song about Humboldt Sink was in John A. Stone's *Put's Golden Songster* (San Francisco, 1868).

William Manly's *Death Valley in '49* (New York, 1929), which belongs on the short shelf of the finest gold rush books, is the definitive account of the Death Valley wanderers. Other sources for this unlucky band are John Ellenbecker (*The Jayhawkers of Death Valley*, Marysville, Kans., 1938), Louis Nusbaumer (*Valley of Salt, Memories of Wine*, edited by George Koenig, Berkeley, 1967), and "Trailing the 49ers through Death Valley" (*Sierra Club Bulletin*, 1939) by gold rush scholar Carl Wheat. Leroy and Ann Hafen (*Journals of Forty Niners*, Glendale, Calif., 1954) trace the travels of the other companies that set out from Utah for Los Angeles.

The letter from the unhappy female boardinghouse keeper appeared in Wyman's *California Emigrant Letters;* Charles Howard Shinn (*Mining Camps*, cited previously) related the anecdote about the boy who rode thirty-five miles to view a woman "just like mother." Bayard Taylor, Hubert Howe Bancroft (*Works*), and Elisha Oscar Crosby provide a savory description of the constitutional convention at Monterey; Taylor and Charles V. Hume ("First of the Gold Rush Theatres," *CHS Quarterly*, December 1967) discuss the fare at Sacramento's Eagle Theatre. The song about letters from home was published in *Put's Golden Songster*.

Hiram Pierce (*A Forty Niner Speaks*, Oakland, 1930) and gold rush historian Erwin G. Gudde ("Mutiny on the Ewing," *CHS Quarterly*, March 1951 and December 1957) describe the execution of the *Ewing* mutineers; William Taylor recalls his street-preaching days in *California Life Illustrated* (New York, 1858). The departure of the La Californienne Company from Le Havre was chronicled by Gilbert Chinard (*When the French Came to California*, cited previously).

CHAPTER XI: FIRE AND ICE

Charles B. Gillespie tells the story of the pint-sized gambler in "A Miner's Sunday in Coloma" (*Century Illustrated Monthly*, June 1891). The Scotsman William Downie wrote his gold rush recollections in *Hunting for Gold* (San Francisco, 1893). The mining rules at the Tuolumne River camp of Jacksonville appear in Woods's *Sixteen Months at the Gold Diggings*. Sallie Hester's diary was reprinted by the *Argonaut*, a San Francisco weekly, in September of 1925. Joseph McCloskey published his Christmas story as *Christmas in the Gold Fields, 1849* (San Francisco, 1959).

My sources for the "Chilean War" were Nasatir's article in the *CHS Quarterly* and James Ayers' *Gold and Sunshine*, both cited earlier, and *Chile, Peru and the California Gold Rush* by Jay Monaghan (Berkeley, 1973). The Sacramento flood was best described by Sarah Royce, Jacob Stillman, and the newspapers, particularly the San Francisco *Pacific News*. Stephen J. Field (*Personal Reminiscences*, Washington, 1893) and Earl Ramey ("Beginnings of Marysville," *CHS Quarterly*, September 1935) recount the early days in Marysville. William Perkins remains my favorite journal keeper in Sonora.

The account of the Death Valley emigrants relies on sources cited in the preceding chapter notes plus *Goodbye, Death Valley* by L. Burr Belden (San Bernardino, Calif., 1956). Enos Christman narrated his adventures in *One Man's Gold* (New York, 1930). The story of the Parker French expedition was patched together from the narratives of survivors Michael Baldridge (*Reminiscence of the Parker French Expedition*, Los Angeles, 1959), William Miles (*Journal of the Sufferings and Hardships of Capt. Parker H. French's Expedition to California in 1850*, Fairfield, Wash.; 1970), and Charles Lockwood (*My Trip to California in 1850*, Daytona, Fla., 1910); additional material came from *The Strange Eventful History of Parker H. French* by Edward McGowan (edited by Kenneth Johnson, Los Angeles, 1958).

CHAPTER XII: MUSTER OF STRANGERS

Walker Wyman included the young Missourian's lament about the lonely restlessness of mining life in *California Emigrant Letters*. The lyrics of the song "Hangtown Gals" were published in John Stone's *Put's Golden Songster*. Bancroft's *California Inter Pocula* (Vol. 35 of his *Works*, San Francisco, 1888) contains the anecdote about the Yankee and the westerner in Rough and Ready; Frank Lecouvrer (*From East Prussia to the Golden Gate*, Leipzig, 1906) notes the excess of Johnnys at Long Bar; and Mrs. D. B. Bates (*Incidents on Land and Water*, Boston, 1858) tells the story of the unkempt pianist at Marysville.

The rise of Columbia was documented by Hero Eugene Rensch in *Columbia, a Gold Camp of Old Tuolumne* (Berkeley, 1936) and by Charles Howard Shinn in *Mining Camps*. The search for the elusive Gold Lake was described by J. M. Guinn ("The Myth of Gold Lake," *Historical Society of Southern California*, 1903), Luther M. Schaeffer (*Sketches of Travels*, New York, 1860), and William Downie. Ernest de Massey chronicles his anguish on the Trinity in *A Frenchman in the Gold Rush* (San Francisco, 1927). *William Perkins' Journal*, together with the introduction by Morgan and Scobie, contains valuable material on the uprising in Sonora triggered by the foreign miners' tax. Grant Foreman (*Marcy and the Gold Seekers*) and J. M. Guinn ("Yuma Indian Depredations and the Glanton War," *Historical Society of Southern California*, 1903) report on the Yumas and the Colorado River ferry.

Descriptions of the soirée at Sutter's Hock Farm appear in Samuel Upham's *Notes of a Voyage to California via Cape Horn*, mentioned earlier, and the Sacramento *Transcript*; Zollinger's biography and Lienhard's narrative flesh out the Sutter story. The tumultuous campaign for sheriff of San Francisco was recounted by George W. B. Evans (cited earlier) and the *SCP Quarterly* ("San Francisco in 1850," December 1925). Frank Marryat's anecdote about the resilient burned-out businessmen is in his *Mountains and Molehills* (San Francisco, 1855).

My account of the first stage of the 1850 overland emigration draws on the contemporary narratives of William R. Rothwell (manuscript at Beinecke Library, Yale), Eleazer Ingalls (*Journal of a Trip to California*, Waukegan, Ill., 1852), and John Steele (*Across the Plains in 1850*, Chicago, 1930), supplemented by the previously cited works of George R. Stewart, Walker Wyman, and Irene Paden; *Saleratus and Sagebrush*, by Robert L. Munkres (Wyoming State Archives and Historical Department, 1974) was also helpful. My sources for the Parker French company are given in the notes for the preceding chapter.

CHAPTER XIII: TWILIGHT IN EDEN

The popular gold rush panoramas are described by John F. McDermott in "Gold Rush Movies" (*CHS Quarterly*, March 1954). Gilbert Chinard and Etienne Derbec (*A French Journalist in the California Gold Rush*, Georgetown, Calif., 1964) record the gold mania in France; the great French lottery is discussed by Abraham P. Nasatir in "Alexandre Dumas fils and the Lottery of the Golden Ingots" (*CHS Quarterly*, June 1954). The perils of riverbed mining are well illustrated by forty-niners Lucius Fairchild, Daniel Woods, and Alonzo Delano; the gifted Louise Clappe (*The Shirley Letters from the California Mines*, New York, 1961) details the first remarkable discoveries at Rich Bar. William Perkins, Enos Christman, and Charles Howard Shinn are my principal sources for the grim transformation of Sonora. Theressa Gay narrates James Marshall's discovery of the "Ohio diggings."

The ballad of the "Used-Up Miner" appears in *Taming the Forty-Niner* by Elizabeth Margo (New York, 1955). Chinese gold diggers are analyzed by David Lindsey ("Cathay Comes to El Dorado," *American History Illustrated*, July 1975), Stephen Williams (*The Chinese in the California Mines 1848–60*, San Francisco, 1930), and Doris Wright ("The Making of Cosmopolitan California," cited previously); the story of the Chinese and the Indians is passed on by Joseph Henry Jackson in *Anybody's Gold* (New York, 1941). My account of the Sacramento squatter riot draws on the contemporary narratives of Samuel Upham, Jacob Stillman, and John Morse. My sources for the final weeks of the 1850 overland trek include Lorenzo Sawyer (*Way Sketches*, New York, 1926) and Margaret Frink (*Journal*, Oakland, 1897) in addition to those mentioned earlier; the California newspapers, notably the Sacramento *Transcript*, were most useful in depicting the 1850 relief effort.

CHAPTER XIV: THE MORNING AFTER

Dozens of contemporary sources record the trend to violence and brutality in the California of late 1850: the sordid incident involving the "Sydney Ducks" at Rough and Ready was recounted in a San Francisco newspaper and included in *The Mining Frontier* (Norman, Okla., 1967), an anthology edited by Marvin Lewis; the lynching of Irish Dick was described by Palmer C. Tiffany (previously cited) and John Carr (*Pioneer Days in California*, Eureka, Calif., 1891).

My final portrait of San Francisco rests in part on Frank Soulé's *Annals of San Francisco*. Thomas Senior Berry tells the story of the trunk full of gold in

"Gold, but How Much?" noted earlier; the material on showman Tom Maguire comes from "Tom Maguire, Showbiz Impresario," by Lois Foster Rodecape, in the *CHS Quarterly* of December 1941; Bancroft's *California Inter Pocula* is the source for the "sidewheel steamer" anecdote; the episode of Lieutenant Derby and the baked eagle is from *Men and Memories of San Francisco in the Spring of 1850* (San Francisco, 1873) by T. A. Barry and B. A. Patten. John Adam Hussey ("New Light on Talbot Green," *CHS Quarterly*, March 1939) is the best authority on Talbot Green's charade. The account of the statehood parade and fete relies principally on Bancroft, Ernest de Massey's *A Frenchman in the Gold Rush*, the *SCP Quarterly*'s "San Francisco in 1850," and the contemporary papers.

The bitter manifesto issued by passengers on the steamer *Alabama* appears in Wyman's *California Emigrant Letters*. Berry is the most reliable source for statistics on gold production. Alan Bowman compiled California census data in *Index of the California Census of 1850*, Berkeley, 1972; Ernest Siracusa provided additional information in *Black Forty-Niners* (Berkeley, 1969). The verse from "Days of '49" appeared in *The Mining Frontier* by Lewis. The Sacramento cholera epidemic was chronicled by John Morse, George W. B. Evans, and the newspapers.

EPILOGUE

Bancroft describes the 1852 meeting of once and future Californians in Panama in his *California Inter Pocula*. The best of the other writers who observed California in 1852 and 1853 are J. D. Borthwick (*The Gold Hunters*, Edinburgh, 1857), Hinton Helper (*Dreadful California*, edited by Lucius Beebe and Charles Clegg, Indianapolis, 1948), Elisha Capron (*History of California*, Boston, 1854) and the previously noted Frank Marryat.

George R. Stewart (*Committee of Vigilance*, Boston, 1964) and William Secrest (*Juanita*, Fresno, Calif., 1967) recount the lynching of the Mexican girl Juanita in Downieville; Stewart's book is also the leading source for the San Francisco Vigilance Committee of 1851. *The Shirley Letters* (cited earlier) assembles the Rich Bar correspondence of the witty and observant Louise Clappe.

ACKNOWLEDGMENTS

I DID MOST of the research for this book at the Beinecke Rare Book and Manuscript Library at Yale University in New Haven. I am grateful for the cooperation of Archibald Hanna, curator of the magnificent Western Americana collection, and the courtesy and knowledgeable assistance of Joan Hofmann and the rest of the library staff. I also want to thank Mary Brown and the staff of the American Antiquarian Society library in Worcester, Massachusetts, and Estelle Rebec and her fellow librarians at the Bancroft Library in Berkeley. Robert Hawley of the Holmes Book Store in Oakland and Robert Greenwood of Talisman Press in Georgetown, California, were particularly helpful in finding books I needed to buy. Alvin McLane of Reno was generous with his private library. I am indebted to my friends Terry Crowley of San Jose, Don Thackrey of San Francisco, and Meade Treadwell of Newtown, Connecticut, for assistance in my constant quest for books.

My literary agent John Hawkins, Professor James Sheehan of Stanford University, and Wayne Woodlief of Boston all read the manuscript and offered valuable suggestions. Charles Elliott of Alfred A. Knopf, an editor of unfailing grace and discernment, was a durable provider of material, ideas, and consistently good advice.

INDEX

Note: Wherever appropriate, subdivisions of topics in the index are arranged *chronologically*.

ILLUSTRATION CREDITS

A NOTE ABOUT THE AUTHOR

Donald Dale Jackson was born in San Francisco and educated at Stanford University. He has worked as a reporter for UPI and as a writer and reporter for *Life* magazine. In 1968 he won the National Headliners Award for magazine writing. His previous books include *Judges*, a study of the American legal system. He lives in Connecticut with his wife and two teenage children.

A NOTE ON THE TYPE

This book was set on the Linotype in Bodoni Book, so called after Giambattista Bodoni (1740–1813), son of a printer of Piedmont. After gaining experience and fame as superintendent of the Press of the Propaganda in Rome, Bodoni became in 1766 the head of the ducal printing house at Parma, which he soon made the foremost of its kind in Europe. In type designing he was an innovator, making his new faces rounder, wider, and lighter, with greater openness and delicacy. His types were rather too rigidly perfect in detail, the thick lines contrasting sharply with the thin wiry lines. It was doubtless this feature that caused William Morris to condemn the Bodoni types as "swelteringly hideous." Bodoni Book, as reproduced by the Linotype Company, is a modern version based not upon any one of Bodoni's fonts, but upon a composite conception of the Bodoni manner, designed to avoid the details stigmatized as bad by typographical experts and to secure the pleasing and effective results of which the Bodoni types are capable.

Composed by Maryland Linotype Composition
Company, Inc., Baltimore, Maryland
Printed and bound by American Book-Stratford Press,
Saddle Brook, New Jersey
Typography and binding design by Virginia Tan